GOLD RUSH CAPITALISTS

Greed and Growth in Sacramento

MARK A. EIFLER

UNIVERSITY OF NEW MEXICO PRESS
ALBUQUERQUE

LIBRARY OF CONGRESS CATALOGING-IN-PUBLICATION DATA

Eifler, Mark A., 1956–
    Gold rush capitalists : greed and growth in Sacramento / Mark A. Eifler. — 1st ed.
        p.   cm.
    Includes bibliographical references and index.
    ISBN 0-8263-2821-0 (cloth : alk. paper) — ISBN 0-8263-2822-9 (pbk. : alk. paper)
    1. Cities and towns—Growth—Case studies.
    2. Sacramento (Calif.)—History—19th century.
        I. Title.   HT371.E37 2002
    307.76′09794′54—dc21

                                                                        2002007833

DESIGN: Mina Yamashita

Contents

Introduction

Capitalism and urbanization are linked in the United States. Americans are proud that most of their major cities are commercial cities. When one looks across the landscape, there is something almost predestined about the growth of New York City or San Francisco. Beneficiaries of the natural resources of their vast hinterlands, these cities and others like them seemed to grow rapidly and powerfully due to the implacable combination of environment and entrepreneurship.

Yet the rise of these cities was hardly so simple. New York City's growth was due as much to the man-made Erie Canal as to the natural wonders of its waterfront. And although a city at the mouth of the Hudson might indeed have been a natural development, its location on Manhattan Island was not. That location left early New York cut off from easy access to the continent's mainland and would eventually fragment city development until modern technology could bridge these divisions, allowing for the consolidation of Greater New York nearly 350 years after its founding. Likewise, San Francisco's "natural" site might better have been on the great bay's northeast coast, near present-day Benecia, which would more easily allow the commercial city to be connected with the California mainland and allow much easier growth than the wet and dismal tip of the peninsula where the city actually grew.

In both cases, military considerations outweighed commercial concerns at the city's founding. The Dutch built Fort Amsterdam at the tip of Manhattan Island with an eye to controlling New York Harbor, whereas the Spanish built their presidio on the northern tip of the peninsula to control San Francisco Bay. Early merchants realized that the immediate protection offered by these strategically located bases outweighed possible future commercial disadvantages. As time passed and these cities developed, military considerations withered in importance, leaving later city merchants to cope with difficult geographic obstacles to their commercial growth.

Given the frontier conditions that attended the founding of most American cities, such difficulties were hardly unique. But they do raise questions about the nature of commercial capitalism and urban origins. When a new city was founded in America, who and what set the agenda for its commercial development? Certainly the placement of natural resources and transportation routes played roles, but these roles were hardly decisive. To what extent did commercial interests dictate the establishment of urban settlements? And who were these commercial interests? Were they individual founding fathers? In a fiercely democratic nation, and especially on its more lawless frontier—where most of these new cities would be founded—who established the patterns of urban life? How did urban order emerge from the chaos of conflicting interests?

In this book I will try to answer some of these questions by examining a case study: Sacramento, California. Unlike its more famous neighbor on the bay, Sacramento is not as easily recognized as a major American city. Though one of the largest cities in the West in the latter half of the nineteenth century and capital of one of the most powerful states in the nation, Sacramento has received little attention from urban historians. Yet Sacramento's less than prominent position in the landscape of American urban history belies its initial potential as a commercial city. Sacramento's founders and early residents imagined great commercial success when they looked at the rising city and at times entertained notions that their city might one day surpass San Francisco. Situated between the bay's abundant warehouses and the golden resources of the Sierra foothills, Sacramento seemed to fit the pattern of natural urban growth capitalized on natural resources and transportation routes.

Sacramento offers the historian a nearly unprecedented opportunity to examine its founding years in detail. As a supply center for gold rush miners, Sacramento was visited daily by thousands of wide-eyed adventurers, who wrote detailed letters and lengthy journals of their travels in the West. Sacramento's early life was played out under the watchful eye of hundreds of amateur reporters, who compiled a rich record of the early years of city development. Rarely have the almost daily events of a newly established city been so open to historical inquiry.

Furthermore, Sacramento during these years was battered by a series of natural and man-made disasters and torn apart by one of the most violent land riots in California's history. Through this turmoil, Sacramento's many observers—residents and visitors alike—commented in great detail on what they perceived as the strengths and weaknesses of its urban leaders. Such commentary opens to the historian the almost daily struggle for leadership and authority in a boom city when patterns of tradition are first being debated and established. Certainly such struggles occurred in newly established cities and communities across the nation; few were written about, however, in such detail.

This book is divided into three parts. Part one examines the earliest founding of the city by speculators looking to cash in on the gold rush trade. Long before the gold rush itself, the Sacramento region was transformed into an area that attracted frontier traders, who were thus on-site when the first nuggets were discovered at Sutter's Mill. The initial development of Sacramento is in part the story of the personal competition of a handful of men to create a city that would dominate the mining trade. Part two discusses the arrival of thousands of miners in the region, who had their own ideas about the role that a city on an isolated mining frontier should play. Determined to create a city that would support their efforts rather than exploit them, gold rush miners obstructed the city founders' designs at nearly every turn. Hardening into organized parties, city speculators and gold rush miners grew more militant in their opposition, erupting in open warfare barely twenty months after the city's founding.

Part three examines the aftermath of the riot, which discredited both the city's speculative founders and its reckless miner/settlers. As more and more would-be miners came to see commercial activity as a substitute for the labors of mining and California as a home rather than an exotic sojourn, a new urban class began to form in the city. Attempting to maintain the chaotic elements of the gold rush that provided for opportunities while at the same time harnessing the more destructive extremes of this chaos, this new class of city residents best defined the urban commercialism of the American city in the mid-nineteenth century. Far from creating an all-encompassing urban order on the land, Sacramento's residents sought to create stable urban institutions that could safely ride the wild waters of unrestricted commercialism. Rather than imposing civilization, cities could be tools of exploitation. Cities would not end the chaos of commercialism, but could render such confusion admirable.

>--<

This book began as my doctoral thesis ten years ago and suffered in the intervening years from a kind of schizophrenia. My initial interest in the topic was related to the 1850 Squatters' Riot. As I tried to root out the causes and consequences of the riot, I came more and more to see how much the riot was tied up in the growth of the city. But I only hesitantly shifted my primary focus from the riot to urban development. The riot was a more pronounced event, with a generally clear beginning and ending. The development of the city was more diffuse—where to begin, where to end? Certainly the development of Sacramento continued after my own end date, though I believe the major themes I have tried to trace were all in essence laid down by the spring of 1852. But as is often the case in life, the project I finished was not the project I started.

Over these past ten years I have benefited greatly from friends and colleagues who have read my shifting manuscripts, prodded me with questions about urban and community development and structure, and rallied my flagging spirits when the questions I was grappling with seemed too diffuse to ever find clear resolution. I am especially indebted to Gunther Barth, who chaired my dissertation committee and helped guide much of my early thinking about the instant growth of Sacramento. A number of people read either chapters or entire drafts of this book and offered insights into the gold rush and urban community development, especially James Kettner, Terry Wilson, Malcolm Rohrbough, Elliot West, John Findley, and Timothy Mahoney. I also owe a great debt to my former colleagues and graduate students at the University of Nebraska at Kearney, who generously offered their time, expertise, and encouragement as this project threatened to grow more and more unwieldy; I want to thank especially James German, Carol Lilly, Thomas Clark, Vernon Volpe, Roger Davis, Michael Schuyler, Kenneth Nichols, Thomas Frasier, and David Stevenson. Support for this project was provided by grants from the Andrew Mellon Foundation and from the Research Services Council at the University of Nebraska at Kearney. I also wish to express my deep appreciation to the helpful and professional staffs of the Bancroft Library, the Beinecke Library, the Huntington Library, the California State Library, and the Sacramento City and County Archives. Any factual or interpretive mistakes in this book are my own fault but are certainly far fewer than would be the case without the generous assistance of these special people.

As this project took longer and longer to complete than I originally thought, I was encouraged to continue by the kind words and acts of people who believed in me and the work when my own mood was dark. My stepfather, Earl Livingston, guided me through the early land title records of California with a professionalism and deep understanding of California land claims that is uniquely his own. He and my mother, Virginia Livingston, offered encouragement and at times a quiet place in the Santa Cruz mountains to work. Jeff Ravel offered his friendship, support, and a spirited optimism that would cheer anyone. Larry Durwood Ball and David Holtby of the University of New Mexico Press patiently guided me through most of the revisions of this book; their support has been crucial. My son, Conor, originally offered unsolicited but trenchant editing marks in crayon and now helps me download pertinent files from the Internet; he has never known a time when "the book" was not hanging over his father's head, but he found ways to take me on his adventures. And to my wife, Karen, I owe more than can ever be written in so short an introduction. She has been a passionate and compassionate editor, partner, and lover in every sense of those words; to her I dedicate this work.

GOLD RUSH CAPITALISTS

Greed and Growth in Sacramento

✦ ⸺ ❖ ⸺ ❖ ⸺ ❖ ⸺ ❖ ⸺ ❖ ⸺ ❖ ⸺ ❖ ⸺ ❖ ⸺ ❖ ⸺ ✦

Sacramento *City* is no misnomer indeed.

Already the "outward tokens" are visible,

the business hum and bustle of our

landing and market places . . . presents

a scene of admirable city-like confusion.

—Edward Kemble,
editor of the Sacramento
Placer Times, May 5, 1849

✦ ⸺ ❖ ⸺ ❖ ⸺ ❖ ⸺ ❖ ⸺ ❖ ⸺ ❖ ⸺ ❖ ⸺ ❖ ⸺ ❖ ⸺ ✦

Prologue

Questions in the Dark

On the hot and humid evening of Saturday, August 12, 1850, Charles Robinson sat alone in his tent in Sacramento City, California, and tried to compose a letter to his fiancée, Sara T. D. Lawrence. The thirty-two-year-old doctor had journeyed to California the previous year as the physician to the Congress and California Mutual Protective Association, a stock company formed by a group of over fifty Massachusetts men, primarily Bostonians, who hoped to secure their fortunes in the great 1849 gold rush. Though Robinson certainly entertained notions of finding his own wealth in the West, his reasons for journeying to California were more complex. In 1843, Robinson had married Sarah Adams. The couple had two children, but both died in infancy and Sarah herself had died in 1846, shortly after the death of their second child. During the next two years, Robinson suffered a physical breakdown. The doctor welcomed a new start when the news of the California gold rush swept the nation. So, despite his growing relationship with Sara Lawrence, Robinson set out overland for California with the Boston company.[1]

Now, nearly one and a half years after leaving New England, Robinson wrote by lantern light in the gathering darkness of a late summer evening in Sacramento. The bustling activity of the overwhelmingly male boomtown on a Saturday night surrounded Robinson as miners and residents cavorted through the saloons, eating houses, and gambling halls that constituted some of the city's most impressive buildings. Murmurs may also have reached Robinson's ears from the small gatherings of men around nearby campfires. The first overland migrants of the year were beginning to trickle in, telling of their hardships traveling the dusty, crowded trails and seeking to make connections with relatives or friends who had preceded them. And throughout the city conversations touched on the most vital issues of the day: which mining camps were producing the biggest nuggets, what new strikes had been discovered, who had made a fortune, and who was giving up and going home.

In the midst of this frenetic activity, it is natural that Robinson's thoughts when writing to his beloved Sara would turn to discussing the conditions of the mining camps and booming cities, his luck so far in procuring a fortune, and his projected date for leaving California to return home for an already much delayed wedding. But such were not the concerns uppermost in Robinson's mind. "We have seen much and experienced much of a serious and important character, as well as much excitement," he began.

> The county judge, before whom our cases were brought, decided against us, and on Saturday morning declared that from his decision there should be no appeal. The squatters immediately collected on the ground in dispute, and posted, on large bills, the following: "OUT-RAGE!!! Shall Judge Willis be dictator? Squatters, and other republicans, are invited to meet on the Levee this evening, to hear the details."

And as the night grew darker around Robinson, so did the message he penned.

> This morning I was early on my feet, silently and quietly visiting my friends, collecting arms, etc. Our manifesto appeared in the papers and bills early, and the whole town is aroused. Nothing is thought or talked of but war. About two hundred men assembled on the disputed territory, and most of them sympathized with us. A few, however, were spies. We chose our commander, and enrolled such as were willing and ready to lay down their lives, if need be, in the cause. About fifty names could be obtained.[2]

Two days later, Robinson helped lead an army of squatters against the mayor and a hastily assembled city militia. The battle, later called the Sacramento Squatters' Riot, would last two days and was the most violent of the squatter confrontations that would plague California for over a decade. The struggle virtually plunged Sacramento into a civil war and cost the lives of several prominent city leaders, including its new and respected mayor, Hardin Bigelow. Dr. Robinson himself would be one of the first to fall in the fighting. Severely wounded and expected to die, city officials threw him into prison unattended.[3]

Robinson's letter, which was found not mailed in his tent by city officials the day after the battle, raises a number of questions. What had led Robinson, a respected member of the Boston company, to turn against Sacramento's city government? Why did he lead the city's squatters into violent rebellion against the city's recently elected and popular mayor, a man who earlier that same year had literally saved the city from a devastating natural disaster? Indeed, Robinson had also proven himself to be as heroic as Mayor Bigelow. During the long journey to California, the Boston doctor had struggled tirelessly to save a number of his companions from cholera and had continued to provide medical care for many of Sacramento's more destitute residents, often for little or no compensation. Nor did his outstanding public service end with the riot. After recovering from his near-fatal wounds in Sacramento's prison brig, Dr. Robinson was elected to the California legislature. Returning to Massachusetts later, he joined the Emigrant Aid Company of New England, which sent colonists to Kansas in the 1850s to prevent pro-slavery forces from taking control of the state, and he eventually served as the state's first governor.

Even Josiah Royce, California's early philosopher and historian, who in 1885 attempted to determine the causes of the Squatters' Riot and who viewed the squatters with open contempt, found it difficult to criticize Robinson's character. Royce declared Robinson to be "a high-minded and conscientious man, who chanced just then to be in the devil's service, but who served the devil honestly, thoughtfully, and, so far as he could, dutifully, believing him to be an angel of light."[4]

The letter Robinson wrote to his fiancée reinforces Royce's characterization of Robinson. Far from being the radical revolutionary, Robinson can be seen asking the same difficult questions Royce and later observers of the riot would ponder. "What will be the result," he wrote to Sara as he sat alone in the darkness on the eve of the rebellion. "Shall I be borne out in my position? On whom can I depend? How many of those who are Squatters will come out if there is the prospect of a fight? . . . Have I defined our position in the bill? Will the *world,* the *universe,* and *God* say it is *just?*"[5]

Robinson's soul-searching questions in the dark trouble our interpretation of the riot. In a classic case of "the victors write the histories," the Squatters' Riot, when it is examined at all, is portrayed as a case of selfish squatters recklessly threatening social order "in the devil's service." Yet we need to consider how such a thoughtful, dutiful, and honest man as Robinson could become so thoroughly misled into leading such a mob.

And more important, we must consider the mob that followed him. Were all these people misled by a few devils in the dark, or was something more fundamental happening in Sacramento? The answer to this question, however, has been shrouded in darkness. For though the California gold rush has been researched and written about for decades, the researcher has often overlooked the early history of Sacramento and its community. Past writers have tended to focus in detail on two aspects of the California gold rush: the experience of the thousands of miners in the gold fields and the awesome rise of the city of San Francisco. These studies have told us much about the development of California and the West. Yet although Sacramento is often portrayed as a smaller version of San Francisco, the differences between Sacramento and the great city by the bay—its unique character and history—remain hidden. What led Robinson and others to fight over land titles in Sacramento is unanswered.

These unanswered questions, however, suggest that our interpretations of the gold rush may be incomplete. For why were men willing to fight to the death over land titles *in Sacramento* in 1850? Certainly we could understand battles over land titles in the mineral-rich foothills of the Sierra Nevada or the cramped and limited building areas adjacent to the wharves of San Francisco. Yet the most violent squatter rebellion took place not in the rich gold fields or on the lucrative, crowded waterfront, but in the middle of a vast, undifferentiated, and unremarkable inland plain. That the riot took place at all challenges our traditional understanding of the nature of Sacramento and the logic of the California gold rush itself.

Studies of the gold rush have examined those places where power, influence, and human activity have been most focused. The obvious centers were the gold fields and the rising city by the bay, where fortunes in mining and speculation were frantically pursued. Sacramento had neither direct control over a mine nor over commodities. Since these twin activities defined the gold rush experience, Sacramento seems to have played only a supporting role in the drama, not a main part. But it is precisely here that one of the most violent conflicts of the gold rush took place. That it was premeditated—that Robinson could sign men up to lay down their lives in a cause that involved neither gold nor speculation days before the riot—suggests that, at least to the participants, something of importance was happening in Sacramento.

A closer look at Sacramento, however, does not easily resolve the questions raised by the riot. Situated roughly halfway between the Sierra Nevada foothills and San Francisco, Sacramento acted as a middleman between San Francisco speculators and Sierra miners.[6] Though over one hundred miles inland, Sacramento benefited from the deep channel of the Sacramento River, which allowed oceangoing vessels smooth sailing right up to the city's embarcadero. Both square-rigged sailing ships and steamboats were operating on the Sacramento River by December 1849, and they quickly became a familiar sight along the city's waterfront. Ships arrived daily at the waterfront, sailing or steaming their way up the Sacramento River from San Francisco and occasionally from ports farther away.[7] Sacramento City also benefited from its proximity to Sutter's Fort, the traditional terminus of the California Trail. Most overland migrants came to the city for at least a short visit, to buy provisions for the mines or to post a letter to family back east. As the natural terminus of both oceangoing shipping and the California Trail, Sacramento City could be sure to draw heavy numbers of people to its streets.

San Francisco, however, trumped Sacramento's advantages. When the U.S. Army at the end of the Mexican War in 1848 situated its headquarters and supply depot on the tip of the peninsula to guard the entrance to the bay, early merchants established their businesses on the tip of the peninsula as well. San Francisco in effect became a warehouse city.[8] Goods from the city needed to be distributed to the mines and were shipped inland to convenient sites. Sacramento, Stockton, and Marysville quickly became the distribution nodes for the central, southern, and northern mining camps, respectively. Though some early residents hoped that Sacramento would one day surpass San Francisco as the preeminent California city, the flows of goods going in and out of San Francisco Bay dictated otherwise. Sacramento's role in the hierarchy of gold rush cities quickly relegated the city to a subservient position in the economy and, it would seem, in history, too.

This quick synopsis of Sacramento's role in the gold rush, however, glosses over too many issues that are not clearly understood. How exactly did Sacramento become the agreed-on distribution node? Other sites in the area not only would have served the same purpose, but would in fact have served it better. Sutterville, for example, was already in existence when the gold rush began and was situated on higher ground, above the seasonal flooding of the American River that several times inundated Sacramento. Why create a new town in a poor location when one already existed in a superior location?

And what of the residents of Sacramento? If, as is assumed, the big profits were to be made in either the gold fields or in the great game of speculation centered in San Francisco, why would men who had gambled all on the long and difficult journey to California satisfy themselves by working in a city that did not seem to offer the most lucrative rewards? As middlemen between San Francisco and the mining camps, Sacramento residents were theoretically in a perfect place to capitalize on the latest information of either site. At the least they would certainly have been aware of the profits to be made in both the mining camps and San Francisco. What drew them to and held them in this city of the crossroads?

Cities, of course, offer amenities other than opportunities for profit. And perhaps by interpreting Sacramento through a merely economic lens one misses other, more important social or political opportunities the city might have offered. But here, too, Sacramento seems not to have offered attractive rewards. Founded during the gold rush, the city still lacked a political infrastructure as well as many social or cultural amenities. During its early years, the city even lacked a coherent street grid or permanent buildings. Though a small core of buildings sought to define the city grid, the majority of buildings were made of canvas and the city was quickly overwhelmed by overland migrants, who pitched their camps within city limits in almost total disregard of the proposed urban grid.

As a newly founded, undeveloped city, Sacramento not only still needed to develop the infrastructure to support the distribution of goods of an urban hierarchy, it needed to develop a variety of city services. And given the frenetic pace of the gold rush, it needed to do so quickly just to survive. The confrontations that led to the Squatters' Riot suggest the challenges of building an instant city were not easily met. Sacramento residents came from all over the United States and the world and met in the city for a variety of purposes. They were divided about the direction the city should take. And they were divided about how to even decide on a direction. Due to the lack of congressional action over extending slavery into the western territories, California lacked a legitimate state or territorial government until the fall of 1850. And since only the state government could provide the city with a charter, Sacramento's city council was itself illegitimate during the city's early years. Though a city council was formed, opponents could rightly call into question the authority of any governing body in the city.

Sacramento's internal divisions were real and heightened the struggles that took place in the new city. But these problems were not unique compared to those of other frontier towns in America. Rather they were one of degree, not kind. In many ways, Sacramento's struggles were shared not only by other California towns during the gold rush, but by other American towns as well. Most towns in the United States were relatively new, many founded only a generation or two ahead of Sacramento. Aside from a handful of cities that came to dominate their regions' economies, most also were cities within an urban economic distribution system. Most needed to accommodate the needs of all their citizens, economic as well as social and political. And most had to do so during a frontier period, when outside support was weak and internal structures were undeveloped.

In the great majority of these towns the evolution of the early town is obscured. The processes were slow and often unremarked on. But in Sacramento, the process was both fast paced and documented in detail by hundreds of visitors and residents alike. Letters, journals, diaries, and memoirs recorded what to many participants was clearly a historic event. These sources have provided rich detail on the evolution of the mining region and San Francisco, but also careful and considered observations of the development of Sacramento.

The history of Sacramento as a unique place, not merely a supporting player in the drama of the gold rush, can be compiled from these records.

And the history that emerges from these records provides new and interesting insights into both the gold rush and the evolution of American urbanity. Sacramento's role in the gold rush was not that of a mining camp writ large or of San Francisco scaled down. Its role was instead that of a meeting ground between two different streams of gold rush experience: those of miners and speculators. And although the goals of each were similar, the ways that they defined those goals and the methods that they felt were acceptable for achieving them were quite different. In other words, in Sacramento we see the collision of two different cultural systems, one based on rural resource extraction and the other based on the urban buying and selling of commodities. In the development of Sacramento we can trace the ebb and flow of these two different attitudes, not in the separate worlds of San Francisco and the gold fields, but in direct confrontation in the streets of Sacramento.

Furthermore, the evolution of Sacramento suggests how many cities and towns in the United States evolved. The twin strands of mining and speculation may be different, but other towns had similar discontinuities between a rural and an urban population. The stereotype of the country bumpkin lost and in awe of the metropolis is a comic cliché of the transformation of Americans from a rural people to an urban people. Such characterizations draw their humor from the stark contrast in lifestyles and experiences of country folk and city people. Yet these figures were more imaginary than real. Few rural folk left the farm for New York City, Chicago, or San Francisco; most moved first to smaller towns, lower down the urban hierarchy.

In these towns the great differences in urban and rural life were less clear. Rural Americans reacted against what they perceived as the irresponsible ways of urban elites; civic society was still rooted in and responsive to rural ways. Urban experiences transformed newly arrived rural residents, but these new residents also fought to shape the urban environment to their own tastes.

Sacramento, in its own fast-paced and dramatic way, thus reflected the struggles throughout the United States in the nineteenth century of a rural people transforming themselves. In this process the gold rush was not an entirely isolated or exceptional event. California gold and California cities did not so much create a new type of American society as simply allow Americans in California to develop along already chosen paths at a quicker rate. In Sacramento, though, perhaps more so than in either the mining camps or San Francisco, these paths were hotly debated, more fluid and flexible. Trying to create stability out of chaos, Sacramento residents were not so much trying to curtail the opportunities of the frontier as to balance opportunity with traditional cultural values. Confusion might be inescapable, but it could at least be rendered compatible, even admirable, within an emerging structure of society.

PART ONE

> --- < > --- < > --- < > --- < > --- < > --- < > --- < > --- < > --- < > --- <

THE GRAND BAZAAR

> --- < > --- < > --- < > --- < > --- < > --- < > --- < > --- < > --- < > --- <

Many traders deposited their goods

in my store, which was in charge of a

trustworthy Indian. Soon, however,

every little shanty in or around the Fort

became a store, a warehouse, or a hotel;

the whole settlement was a veritable bazaar.

—John Sutter, commenting on the effects
of the gold rush on his settlement in 1848

CHAPTER ONE

The Empire Builder

It was the best of times, it was the worst of times. Or at least, that was the story the aging John Sutter wanted the American public to believe. Living in poverty near the end of his life and seeking a pension from the government, Sutter told of his efforts in California to create his New Helvetia colony, paving the way for the successful Americanization of what had been Mexican California. Then, just as the United States was concluding negotiations with the Mexican government over the acquisition of California, workers at his new lumber mill had discovered gold. The resulting rush had produced wealth for the nation but had ruined the region's founding father, who lost both his land and his livelihood. Ruined by the effects of the rush that had made so many others wealthy, a rush he himself had been responsible for starting, Sutter's life during the early days of the gold rush was a mix of triumph and tragedy.

It makes for a good story, as Sutter himself realized. And in many ways, it fit the accepted vision of frontier development. A great man with a vision had single-handedly ventured forth into the wilderness and created an outpost of civilization. Ultimately one of the misunderstandings to emerge from Sutter's version of events, and subsequent histories based on it, relates to the founding of Sacramento. The credit Sutter is given in founding Sacramento, directly or indirectly, is fairly widespread. One author calls Sutter the "number one pioneer of Sacramento," while another begins by commemorating "the 150th birthday of Sacramento, born with the epic landing on August 12, 1839, of Capt. John Sutter." Recently the city celebrated its sesquicentennial in 1989, or 150 years after Sutter's arrival, though the city was actually established in 1849.[1]

But Sutter's penchant for exaggerating the events of his life, or even making them up entirely, was well known.[2] That Sutter would be seen as the founder of Sacramento, however, is ironic, for Sutter not only did not found the city, but bitterly opposed its development. Not that Sutter was opposed to cities; he had founded a city for New Helvetia, a city that would unmistakably proclaim its heritage throughout the ages: Sutterville.

It is easy to discredit Sutter because he exaggerated or fabricated so many of his personal achievements. Sorting out the myth from the reality, it becomes apparent that much of what Sutter claimed as personal accomplishment might be better attributed to being in the right spot at the right time. Sutter did not so much create an empire as focus existing energies for a brief and spectacular moment. That he lost control of his empire is not surprising; his hold was never more than marginal at best. But the existing forces converging at the mouth of the American River in the 1840s were quite real. That even a bumbling empire builder such as John Sutter could fashion a profitable enterprise in that location testifies to the power of those forces. In a very real sense, Sutter did not create Sacramento so much as the Sacramento region created John Sutter.

> — <

On July 4, 1839, John Sutter introduced himself to Juan Bautista de Alvarado, governor of the Mexican province of Alta California. Sutter had arrived in Monterey the day before on the brig *Clementine* and had quickly wrangled an invitation to U.S. consul Thomas O. Larkin's Fourth of July party, to which the governor was also invited. At the party, Sutter asked Alvarado for a land grant, to be situated away from the coast somewhere in the great valley behind the coastal mountain ranges. Here Sutter proposed to establish a new settlement, much like the one Moses Austin had proposed in Texas nearly twenty years before. In case Sutter's vision sounded unrealistically ambitious, the Swiss adventurer had come armed with letters of reference from James Douglas, commander of the Hudson Bay Company's Pacific coast headquarters at Fort Vancouver; from Captain Ivan Kuprianov, governor of the Russian-American Company at New Archangel, Alaska; and from John C. Jones, U.S. consul at Honolulu.[3]

Alvarado was impressed by Sutter's references and intrigued by the story Sutter spun of his experiences before reaching Monterey. And Alvarado was willing to give Sutter the chance to prove himself. He advised Sutter to venture into the central valley, to pick a site and begin settling himself on it, then to return to Monterey one year later and apply for Mexican citizenship. If all went well, Sutter could then apply for the land grant he desired.[4]

Despite Sutter's boastful story and glowing letters, Alvarado may have been skeptical that Sutter would indeed succeed in establishing his new settlement. If Sutter set off into the wilderness of the central valley and disappeared, it would likely cause Alvarado no problems. Yet if he succeeded in his scheme, Sutter's settlement would suit the governor's designs for his beleaguered province, especially in providing badly needed revenue and pacifying the Indians who used the inland area to stage raids on the coastal ranches.[5] That

Sutter and Alvarado's visions were not identical in all details seemed unimportant at the time. But the discrepancy hints at a larger problem underlying the establishment of Sacramento.

At their most basic level, Sutter and Alvarado's visions involved ordering the physical and human landscape of California's central valley. When Sutter later retold his story of the early days of his new settlement, he claimed that Alvarado "was very glad that some one had come to start a colony in the wilderness where the Indians were very wild and very bad."[6] Both Sutter and Alvarado seem to have acted on the premise that there was no order inland from the Mexican coast and that one man—a "civilized" man—had the capacity or the potential to bring useful order to such an empty land. From this premise comes the belief in Sutter's greatness as an empire builder.

The premise, however, is seriously flawed. The region in which Sutter proposed to establish his empire already had a great deal of order and connections with other places—including connections to several outposts of Euro-American capitalism and civilization. Had Sutter truly built his empire from scratch, his accomplishment would have been phenomenal. But such a task was not required. Instead Sutter was able to tap into and reorganize a commercial center already in existence. The strength of these preexisting connections has more to do with Sutter's success than his personal efforts at empire building.

Though Sutter referred to the central valley as a "wilderness," Native Americans had lived in the region for thousands of years and had actively shaped and ordered both the physical and human landscape for centuries. The Miwok Indians used fire to aid in hunting, to promote the growth of grasses, tobacco, and oak trees, whose products they gathered.[7] They lived in developed communities defined by kinship and family associations, governed by strict rules.[8] The Native American inhabitants lived not in a wilderness, but in an intimately known and culturally ordered landscape.

Yet the region could truly be said to have a growing aura of wildness about it, even from a Native American perspective. For decades before Sutter arrived in California, European, Mexican, and American explorers and agents had ventured into the region with increasing frequency and in increasing numbers, and the effects of these inroads had substantially expanded the level of violence and disorder in the region. When Spain had established a chain of mission settlements in California in the latter third of the eighteenth century, its explorers and missionaries stayed close to the coast; seaborne lines of communications and supplies, though risky, were more reliable than the long and dangerous overland routes from central New Spain. However, San Francisco Bay, first settled by the Spanish in 1776, offered a frustrating possibility to Spanish expansionists. Although access to the interior from other mission sites was in essence blocked by the mountain ranges that define most of the California coast, the northeastern corner of San Francisco Bay opened into the Sacramento Delta and led to the San Joaquin and Sacramento rivers. Despite being dependent on oceangoing shipping for supplies, Spanish ships could have sailed up the delta to the interior of California and established a Spanish beachhead at the strategic meeting point of California's two great central valleys: the Sacramento and the San Joaquin.

Yet several factors worked against such a settlement. The delta was a confusing maze of channels, veiled in an abundance of tall tule reeds. Explorers frequently lost their way, while the tall tule reeds provided excellent cover from which Native Americans could launch ambushes on threatening invaders. In addition, the Spanish government in the late eighteenth and early nineteenth centuries was hardly able to hold on to the settlements it already had in the Americas, much less launch new ones. Thus, though missionaries had reached the lower reaches of the Sacramento River as early as 1811 and had proposed building a mission near what would become the future site of the city, the Spanish built no settlements in the central valley. And though Mexico successfully rebelled against Spain in 1821, the turmoil and financial straits of the new Mexican government also precluded any drive to start a new settlement in the central valleys.[9]

But if the Spanish and later Mexican settlements beside the bay could not expand into the central valley, it did not mean that their presence was not felt there. Native Americans from the coastal regions quickly found that Spanish and later Mexican settlers intended to alter their way of life profoundly or, in the intruders' words, to "civilize" them. Civilization brought with it new ways of ordering their lives—new lifestyles, foods, languages, rituals. Indians who converted to Christianity in the missions were known as *neophytes;* those who did not were still considered savages. Beginning shortly after the Spanish arrived and continuing up to Sutter's time, coastal Indians and neophytes both periodically fled from the missions and ranches of the coast into the delta and the central valleys. Here they usually joined with the Miwok, encouraging these interior tribes to actively resist Spanish and Mexican designs on the interior. These runaways brought with them knowledge of Spanish and Mexican ways and equipment.

Perhaps most important, the runaways also brought with them stolen horses and cattle. Though initially the interior tribes saw the horses as a new food, neophytes quickly taught them horsemanship, and the interior tribes were soon hunting antelope and elk from horseback. The advantages of the horse were such that the Miwok were soon using them to raid coastal ranches and to steal livestock. Horses and livestock carried seeds on their coats and in their excrement from the European settlements on the coast to the interior as well. Within a few years, wild horses roamed the central valleys, and new plants such as wild oats and ryes were also growing in the valleys. Thus, though the Spanish and Mexican governments failed to establish a settlement in the central valley, interaction between the coastal settlements and the interior tribes began a dramatic change in the ordered native landscape.[10]

The changes introduced by the coastal settlements, however, were only part of the story. In 1826, Jedediah Smith led an expedition of American fur trappers into California. Over the next decade, American trappers came to the interior valleys annually, hunting beaver and trading for horses from the Miwok. The incursion of the Americans also provoked the interest of the Hudson Bay Company in Oregon. Eager to acquire the valuable furs of California's central valley for itself, the company began sending out its own brigades annually into the region and even established a temporary trading post on the Feather River, not far from where Sutter would eventually establish his own settlement.[11]

For the Miwok of the delta region, the American and British traders were a mixed blessing. Their presence gave the Miwok access to European and American trade goods. In exchange the Miwok offered horses, which the British and Americans sought almost as eagerly as they did beaver furs. This trade only spurred the Miwok into increased raids on Mexican settlements along the coast, thereby increasing the level of violence in the region. The Indians of the central valleys suffered most, however, from a virulent malaria epidemic, inadvertently introduced by company traders in 1833. The disease found a perfect breeding ground in the swampy lowlands of the central valley, and mosquitoes spread the disease rapidly. Before the year was over, an estimated twenty thousand Indians had died.[12]

By the mid-1830s, therefore, the ordered landscape of the lower Sacramento Valley had become a fragmented world, altered by Mexican, British, and American as well as Native American influences. It was a world still controlled by the Miwok, but that control had been weakened by the invasions of foreign animals, plants, trade goods, diseases, and peoples. Hardly a pristine or unknown wilderness, the region was well known and the growing subject of various plans for a new order. Miwok leaders, Mexican governors, and American and British traders all had different perspectives and saw different potential futures for the region. Yet few imagined the vision that John Sutter brought to the region in 1839.

><--<

By sheer luck, the long and winding road that brought Sutter to California in

1839 had also given him a unique and valuable insight into a way to unlock the potential wealth of the North American frontier.

Sutter first arrived in the United States in 1834 and, at the age of thirty-one, hardly seemed to exhibit any entrepreneurial ability. He had left behind in Switzerland a wife, five children, a domineering mother-in-law, a failed dry goods firm, and a substantial unpaid debt. Although he later claimed to have been a captain during the Spanish campaign of 1823–24, his military experience was limited to three years in the Swiss reserve corps, where he had advanced only to the rank of first underlieutenant. Though a failure at business, the young Sutter was resourceful and an eloquent speaker when he set out to create a new life for himself in America.[13]

Sutter's informal education in empire building began almost at once. After arriving in the bustling commercial seaport of New York in midsummer, Sutter set out for St. Louis. Though he later claimed he had intended to become a farmer, Sutter quickly abandoned that plan. Instead in 1835 he joined a caravan of traders headed for Santa Fe. Impressed with the apparent easy profits of the trip, Sutter set out for Santa Fe again the following year, though this time with less financial success. Sutter next tried trading with the Shawnee and Delaware Indians near Westport, Missouri. Although his stock of trade goods included alcohol, a usually lucrative item, Sutter was still unable to avoid accumulating a debt, and in 1838 he fled his debts again, this time heading for California with a caravan of American Fur Company agents headed for the central Rocky Mountains.

At the 1838 fur traders' rendezvous, however, Sutter learned that the route to California was long and dangerous, and on advice from William Drummond Stewart, a Scotsman in the employ of American Fur Company, Sutter decided to head for the Oregon Country instead and from there catch a ship to California.[14] Sutter reached Fort Vancouver, the Hudson Bay Company post in Oregon, in the fall, and from there took passage on a ship bound for Hawaii, where he still hoped to get a ship bound for California. After waiting in vain for six months, Sutter hit on the idea of purchasing a ship (on credit) and loading it with provisions in demand in the Russian fur colony of New Archangel in Alaska, where he hoped the sale of provisions would pay for the ship. Finally, in June 1839, after disposing of his cargo in Alaska, Sutter managed to catch a ship headed for California.[15] There, shortly after his arrival, Sutter met Governor Alvarado and presented to him his grand scheme for an inland settlement.

Sutter by this time had a proven record of failure in entrepreneurial ventures (which he kept well hidden from Alvarado), as well as what must be close to a record for following one of the most convoluted paths to California in the 1830s. Yet along that path Sutter had seen several of the greatest and most successful entrepreneurial ventures of the Far West. He had observed or participated in the Indian liquor trade, the Santa Fe trade, an American Fur Company trade rendezvous, the Hudson Bay Company's Pacific Coast headquarters, and the Russian-American Fur Company's American headquarters.

From each of these experiences Sutter had witnessed both the tremendous profits possible in these enterprises and perhaps had also learned something of the nature of the risks and difficulties to be overcome in them. Sutter, a loquacious and engaging traveler who easily won the confidences of American mountain men, British factors, Hawaiian kings, Russian agents, and Mexican governors, certainly had access to the sage advice of some of the most successful frontier entrepreneurs of the period. Perhaps Sutter also learned of the potential of a trade outpost in California's central valley, which could command a strategic nexus between Mexican, American, British, and even Russian traders. Sutter may have envisioned a post that would trade furs and horses to the British and Americans and agricultural produce to the Russians and Mexicans. If so, he may also have realized something he would not dare admit years later, perhaps not even to himself: that his fortune was based not solely on his ability to *build* an empire, but on his ability to co-opt a loosely defined but *preexisting* trading center.[16]

Historians have noted Sutter's amazing achievements in the Sacramento Valley between 1839 and 1846 but often seem unable to account for Sutter's success, given the rest of his personal history. Not only did Sutter lack successful entrepreneurial experience, but he set out to build his colony without capital or government backing. And although Sutter may have learned enough of the informal trade network of the West to be able to select a suitable site for his own trade empire, it would take more than a strategic site to build a successful settlement. It would require the hard work of a disciplined pool of laborers. Yet it was in this area that Sutter learned his most important lessons on the long road to California. For Sutter had not only learned the outlines of trade systems in the West, but also how to coerce Native American labor through them.[17]

Native American labor was used widely on the Euro-American frontier. Spanish conquistadors forced Indians into mining, ranching, and agriculture through both the *encomienda* and the mission system. Mexican ranchers retained much of these systems of forced labor after Mexico's independence. French, Russian, and American fur traders all depended on Native American labor to trap and prepare animal hides for the world market and used coercion of various kinds to compel Indians to continue to bring in marketable pelts.[18]

In his long tour of the West before arriving in California, Sutter had seen a number of different coercive techniques designed to ensure that Indians would work for Euro-American entrepreneurs. In Santa Fe, and later in California, Sutter had seen the labor relations between Hispanic rulers and Native American subjects. In Missouri, the Rockies, and Oregon, he had seen the effects of a labor system based on trade dependencies. In Hawaii and Alaska, he had seen Natives physically forced to do the bidding of a ruling elite. Sutter came to California not only as an able student of such systems, but as a new practitioner. Along the trail to the Rockies in 1838, he purchased an Indian boy who had once belonged to Kit Carson; in Hawaii, he acquired ten indentured servants from King Kamahameha, who set out with him into the Sacramento Valley in 1839 and helped him establish his new colony.[19]

Ultimately, Sutter's empire rested almost entirely on his ability to coerce the native population to do his bidding. It was the natives of the central valley who would build, defend, and populate his empire. It was the natives who had already begun to channel an international trading system to focus on this area. As long as Sutter could dominate the local population, his empire grew. And, as he would discover to his surprise, when that control withered, so would his empire.

>---<

Sutter's later account of his expedition up the Sacramento Delta suggests that he was indeed moving into an area where Indians were "very wild and very bad."[20] Clearly the Miwok of the delta were hostile to Mexican expeditions into the interior that sought to recapture stolen cattle and horses or return Indian laborers to ranchos nearer the coast. But at the same time the Miwok welcomed British and American traders to the region. To secure his colony, Sutter approached the Miwok as a trader. On first encountering the Indians, only twelve miles below what would later become the site of Sacramento, Sutter told his men not to attack them and instead waded quickly ashore, telling the Miwok in Spanish that he had come as a friend and offering them presents.[21] It was on such trade that Sutter would build his fortune.

After several days of wandering through the area, Sutter finally selected a site on the American River, only a few miles upstream from its confluence with the Sacramento. The site was a level plain, with a slight rise about a quarter of a mile from the river. Sutter decided to build on this rise to keep his new establishment above the floodplain of the two rivers. However, his days of wandering before he selected this site may have been more about seeking a socially suitable site than a geographically suitable one. Whether by luck or planning, the site Sutter selected was in Nisenan territory, near the villages of

Pusune and Momol and north of Miwok territory. Perhaps the Miwok were simply too suspicious of any expedition coming from the coast and speaking Spanish. The Nisenan, however, though they had suffered from the malaria epidemic and had had contact with British and American fur traders, lived to the north of the Miwok and had not had extensive contact with the Spanish and Mexican settlements of the coast. By settling between these two groups, Sutter was also able to play off the Miwok and the Nisenan against each other.[22]

Sutter's use of Indian labor in establishing his "New Helvetia" was quite effective. On arriving in the area, Sutter handed out gifts to the Miwok and Nisenan liberally but also demonstrated the use of his cannon. Over the following years Sutter combined the use of both incentives and punishments—both the carrot and the stick—in building his ambitious empire. He gave gifts to Nisenan and Miwok leaders and in return for alliances with these tribes required that they send laborers to work for him. When the laborers proved balky or deserted, Sutter attacked the villages but then told them that if they would again send laborers, all would be forgiven. Once these laborers returned, Sutter then developed a form of currency through which he could pay Indians for services rendered. Sutter's blacksmith forged a tin coin with a star in the middle, which was punched. Each hole represented a day's work; with these punched coins native laborers could buy shirts, blankets, or other items from his store.[23]

Throughout the 1840s, Sutter's New Helvetia grew in power and influence, based both on its strategic position and Sutter's skillful manipulation of Indian labor. Sutter's Indians not only built the adobe fortress and buildings that soon became known throughout the West as "Sutter's Fort," but also raised wheat, barley, and vegetables; trapped beaver; caught salmon; killed deer; raised cattle; washed and sewed; operated a tannery; ran blacksmith, tailor, and shoemaker shops; produced handicrafts, blankets, and felt hats; and even manned the fort's army and cavalry, wearing green-and-blue uniforms with red trim that Sutter had acquired from the Russians.[24]

Starting with almost nothing, Sutter by 1845 had in essence reordered the physical and social world of the lower Sacramento Valley. His efforts to impose his vision of society on the landscape succeeded not because of his entrepreneurial acumen, but through a combination of factors. The area was already a strategic site in western trade routes before Sutter arrived. Disease and the inroads of Euro-American trading practices weakened the region's native inhabitants. Sutter's ability to manipulate Indian weaknesses through a system of rewards and punishments allowed him to capitalize on preexisting trade patterns. Looked at this way, Sutter did not so much create a trading post as give more solid shape to the trade already existent in the area.

Such a view not only helps explain Sutter's rapid rise to prominence, but also his equally rapid demise. For Sutter's hold on the area was based on the lack of competition. Sutter succeeded because he provided a permanent source of trade goods in the region. Furthermore, Sutter was the only permanent authority in the region. Backed by both his growing store of goods and his Indian army, Sutter alone could shape the economic development of the lower Sacramento Valley on a permanent basis. Although the Indians of the valley had been dominant when Sutter first arrived, their power was declining with the rise in deaths from diseases and intertribal fighting and their dependency on Sutter for both material goods and protection.

Sutter would later claim that the gold rush had ruined his powerful little empire. But Sutter's world did not need thousands of miners to overturn his power. The seeds of his downfall began long before gold was discovered.

⇥ ⸺ ⸡

Beginning in the early 1840s, American immigrants increasingly began journeying across plains and mountains to California, drawn by reports of the region's fertile soil. The long wagon journey, however, took a great toll on the migrants, who often arrived at their destination late in the year, exhausted, and nearly bankrupt. To California's overland immigrants, Sutter's Fort became widely known as a friendly shelter. Here migrants from the overland trail would rest and recuperate, regaining their health and strength during the wet California winter.[25]

Sutter's generosity was not based solely on humanitarian principles, however. Though he controlled a large workforce, his Indian laborers needed to learn skills such as blacksmithing, masonry, and carpentry. Runaway neophytes often brought with them some experience at these and other trades, but Sutter's grand vision of empire required as many skilled workers as were available. He welcomed anyone capable of boosting his frontier enterprise, no matter his background. From the beginning Sutter had sheltered runaway neophytes, as well as runaway white workers—Mexican, Russian, or American—who were willing to work in exchange for shelter and supplies. Thus Sutter provided supplies to overland immigrants simply as part of his larger scheme for enriching "New Helvetia."[26]

Yet few of these immigrants wished to stay dependent on Sutter's generosity. Having come to California for land, they usually began selecting suitable sites for farms and ranches only a few months after they arrived. To maintain his control of the valley, Sutter wanted to incorporate these individualistic immigrants into his plans and so hit on a politically expedient scheme. To obtain the necessary authority to found a new colony, the Swiss adventurer sought a military title along with his Mexican citizenship and land grant from the Mexican government.

Though Alvarado refused to grant him a military title, he did appoint Sutter a representative of the government, and Sutter understood this to mean that he had "power of life and death both over Indians and white people in my district."[27] Seeing himself as a Mexican official, Sutter issued passports and other documents and sold land to unnaturalized Americans in California, all in clear violation of Mexican orders.[28] He ignored Mexican land policies, but his actions were in line with his plans for New Helvetia. His original intention was to settle the region with Swiss families, but Sutter quickly recognized that his new settlers would primarily be Americans.[29] By 1845, his settlement had become "the gateway of communication between the United States and this country," according to Mexican general Mariano Vallejo.[30]

Still seeking to control the trade of the Sacramento Valley, Sutter next set out to channel the trade between these newly arrived farmers and the Mexican coastal ranchos and settlements. A number of merchants did establish themselves in the fort, much as they did at strategic spots along the Oregon and California trails, strengthening the fort's link between the coastal traders and the interior farmers. Sutter's Fort, however, was only a temporary crossroad stop: of the hundreds of overlanders who wintered there in the 1840s, none attempted to settle in its vicinity.

Sutter continued to hope that the site could be strategically important to the development of the central valley. Situated at the head of navigation for oceangoing vessels on the Sacramento River, Sutter's Fort commanded transportation and communication between the California coastal settlements, with their access to shipping and world markets, and the interior valley of agrarian families. Yet although Sutter's choice of the site for his fortress made some sense from an administrative point of view, the site did not have any particular natural advantage for an urban setting. Even Sutter does not seem to have thought very highly of the site. Nor is there much evidence in Sutter's choice of land parcels that the adventurer expected the fortress site to become the key urban site of the region.

Of the two parcels Sutter obtained in 1841, the larger parcel, consisting of about forty-one thousand acres, was north of Sutter's settlement, along both sides of the Feather River, a tributary to the Sacramento River. The smaller parcel, consisting of about nine thousand acres, covered the land surrounding Sutter's settlement at the junction of the Sacramento and American rivers.[31] That this original land grant covered so little of the land around his fort indicates that Sutter saw his colony developing to the north along the Feather River rather than at the mouth of the American River. However, the potential usefulness of a nearby city did occur to him, and in 1844 he founded a town to serve the growing

Sacramento Valley settlements, naming it Sutterville. In order to command nearly all the commerce of the Sacramento Valley, Sutter chose a site on the Sacramento River below the river's newly settled tributaries. Sutterville could then act as a mediator between the Mexican settlement of Yerba Buena and the American settlements of the northern central valley. Significantly Sutter placed his new city three miles downstream from the mouth of the American River rather than centering it on his fort. Here the banks of the river rose high enough to keep it above the seasonal flooding of the Sacramento River, which sometimes inundated the area around the fort.[32]

Had Sutter been able to maintain his economic hold on the Sacramento Valley, Sutterville might today be the dominant city of the central valley. But Sutter was unable to make his imperial vision a reality, partly due to the circumstances of the mid-1840s, partly due to his own shortcomings. And the story of Sutter's fall suggests just how tenuous his control over the region had ever been.

Sutter's first difficulties arose as a result of California's unstable political environment. From the moment Sutter first unveiled his plans to Alvarado, the provincial governor had used Sutter to block the growing power of his uncle and political rival, Mariano Guadalupe Vallejo. Ten years before Sutter arrived, Vallejo had led a military expedition into the central valley to end the raiding of Miwoks under the leadership of an ex-neophyte named Estanisloa. Vallejo had been unsuccessful in capturing Estanisloa, but his expedition had significantly reduced the raiding for a while. Vallejo had then settled near the mouth of the Sacramento Delta as a guard of the coastal settlements, but also to conduct occasional raids of his own into the interior to procure captive Indian labor. Alvarado had blocked Vallejo's growing power by allowing Sutter to establish New Helvetia. Over the subsequent years, Vallejo and Alvarado had a falling-out, while southern Californios sought to promote their own leadership.[33]

In 1842, Mexico appointed a new governor, Manuel Micheltorena, hoping to end the bickering between California's leaders. But while Micheltorena himself sought to reform many problems in the province, his ex-convict troops created such havoc that Alvarado and other Californio leaders soon rose against the new governor. In 1845 Sutter, in exchange for an additional land grant, marched his Indian army south to defend Micheltorena. At the battle of Cahuenga Pass, Sutter and his army were captured and Micheltorena was forcibly deported. Despite Sutter's alliance with the losing side, Alvarado allowed Sutter and his army to return home after they promised loyalty to the new government. Alvarado had little choice: Sutter's ability to control the central valley and to block Vallejo's ambitions was still critical.[34]

Sutter's attempt to play politics, however, came at a cost. When he returned home in 1845, most of his native laborers had fled and, through the instigation of José Castro, a Mexican rival, and under the leadership of a Miwok named Raphero, the Miwoks rebelled against Sutter. Sutter captured Raphero, and though he was the son of an important Miwok leader, Maximo, who had been loyal to Sutter, Sutter had Raphero executed and his head displayed on a pike outside the gate of Sutter's Fort. Rather than end the rebellion, this horrific action embittered Maximo, and although some Miwok sought peace with Sutter, many continued to raid and harass Sutter's settlement.[35]

Hardly had Sutter begun to get New Helvetia's labor pool back to work when American settlers in the region, backed by Colonel John C. Frémont, launched the Bear Flag Revolt, declaring California an independent nation and then petitioning the United States for admission as a state. The revolt coincided with the start of the Mexican War and thus gave the Americans the quick backing of U.S. forces. Frémont quickly took command of Fort Sutter, renaming it Fort Sacramento, and then commandeered Sutter's Indian army. Sutter cooperated with the Americans and was appointed a U.S. Federal Indian Subagent in 1847.[36]

By this time, however, New Helvetia was in ruins. Between 1845 and 1847 Sutter's management was interrupted by the Micheltorena affair, then the Bear Flag Revolt and the Mexican War. The Miwok continued raiding, and Sutter found it increasingly difficult to acquire a steady supply of workers, especially to plant and harvest the all-important wheat crop. Even when Sutter abused his office as Indian agent in 1847 to force the Indians to harvest his wheat, he could not escape a new problem: the crushing debts acquired over nearly a decade of colony building, which were now coming due. Launching a frontier settlement anywhere entailed great expense, especially during the first few years, before the colony began producing enough income to be self-sufficient. Sutter compounded his economic problems through poor management and an extravagant lifestyle. His vanity and generosity were legendary and far outweighed his business sense. By the time of the gold rush, Sutter was deeply in debt to many of the local merchants, including the newly arrived Mormon entrepreneur Samuel Brannan.[37]

Most pressing of all was a debt owed to the Russian government. In 1841 Sutter had purchased the Russian fur trade outpost of Fort Ross on the California coast, about seventy miles north of the entrance to San Francisco Bay. Included in the sale were all of the outpost's landholdings, cattle, farm implements, a schooner, a number of cannon, and ammunition. This equipment had been sorely needed during the early years of the settlement. Sutter considered the

$32,000 price for the outpost a bargain, since the Russians required only a $2,000 down payment, with the balance to be paid over the next four years in a combination of cash and wheat and other products. Now years overdue in paying off this debt, the Russian-American Fur Company threatened to levy an attachment on all of Sutter's property unless the entire debt was paid promptly.[38]

Sutter's empire crumbled due to his inability to maintain control of his Indian laborers. This loss was in part related to Sutter's involvement in California's political turmoil, which weakened his hold on those laborers. Yet with the shifting political conditions in California and the growing American population in his vicinity, it is hard to envision Sutter's continued control of Indian labor even if he had managed to stay out of the political turmoil. Bowing to the obvious, in 1847 Sutter advertised for two wheat-threshing machines and began discharging his Indian troops. Sutter's domination of the valley's labor pool was ending, and with it his economic power.[39]

→ — ←

Still, Sutter's regional planning might have succeeded had he been able to understand the nature of the political and demographic changes that had occurred, and he may indeed have had an inkling of how to do this. Though his hold on Indian labor was gone, the logic that had suggested that Sutterville would become an important commercial center remained. American farmers in the Sacramento Valley, bringing their goods into Sutterville, could make that city a commercial hub of the vast and rich agricultural lands of the interior. If Sutter could induce businessmen to settle there and establish a flour mill and other processing facilities on the site, Sutterville's future—and Sutter's own future—looked promising.

Whether Sutter realized the importance of Sutterville to his economic schemes is difficult to determine. However, Sutter clearly understood that his future lay in catering to the demands of newly arriving American settlers. These settlers would need housing. So Sutter acquired his own treaty to secure a lease to the territory from the Koloma Indians so that he could establish a lumber mill on the American River, in the forests of the Sierra Nevada foothills.[40] The move is interesting in that it shows that Sutter was now thinking of tying his fortune to the expected rush of American settlers in newly acquired American California. But it also shows that Sutter was not focusing on the development of Sutterville itself.

The conquest of California by the United States had already quickened the economy of the former Mexican province, and its population had begun to increase during the war, mainly as result of troops stationed in the territory. Undoubtedly California would in any case have experienced a dramatic growth in population in the following years. The discovery of gold by Sutter's workers at the end of January 1848, however, made even the most dramatic expectations pale against the reality of the ensuing rush. Before the discovery California might have expected a net in-migration of perhaps several thousand; the gold rush brought one hundred thousand newcomers to the state in the following two years. Wild and fantastic reports of the ease and amount of gold obtained spurred on the rush. Typical was a report from Monterey dated August 29, 1848, published in a New York newspaper:

> People are running over the country and picking it [gold] out of the earth here and there, just as 1,000 hogs, let loose in a forest, would root up groundnuts. Some get 8 or 10 ounces a day, and the least active one or two. . . . I know seven men who worked seven weeks and two days . . . on Feather River; they employed . . . 50 Indians, and got out 275 pounds of pure gold. I know the men, and have seen the gold. . . . I know 10 other men who worked 10 days in company, employed no Indians, and averaged . . . $1,500 each. . . . I know another man who got out of a basin in a rock, not larger than a washbowl, 2 1/2 pounds of gold in 15 minutes.[41]

Horace Greeley, the influential editor of the *New York Tribune,* caught the feverish excitement of the early expectations of easy riches. "We are on the verge of the Age of Gold!" he wrote. "Fortune lies upon the earth as plentiful as the mud in our streets. . . . The only machinery necessary in the new gold mines of California is a stout pair of arms, a shovel and a tin pan. Indeed many, unable to obtain these utensils, are fain to put up with a shingle or a bit of board, and dig away quietly in peace of mind, pocketing their fifty or sixty dollars a day, and having plenty of leisure."[42] Nor did Greeley ignore the secondary gold rush that would inspire as many speculators as miners to try their luck in California. "Bakers keep their ovens hot," he wrote, "night and day, turning out immense quantities of shipbread without supplying the demand; the provision stores of all kinds are besieged by orders. Manufacturers of rubber goods, rifles, pistols, bowie knives, etc., can scarcely supply the demand."[43]

It was this subsidiary gold rush—the rush of bakers, storekeepers, and manufacturers—that spelled the end for Sutter's settlement. Though not in the gold fields, the fort's location suited merchants eager to supply hopeful miners. Sutter himself was the first to feel the ruinous effects of the "Gold Fever." He later recalled, "The whole country seemed to have gone mad."[44] Toward the end of May 1848, San Francisco became a ghost town as nearly the entire population set out for the gold fields. Only four months after the original gold discovery, Sutter could look around his carefully built fort with both awe and dismay. For nearly a decade he had succeeded in holding off both threatening Indians and suspicious Mexican officials. Yet his fort provided little protection from the determined army of hopeful miners that overran its stout adobe walls practically overnight.

Wherever Sutter looked, he saw the intruders' equipment and baggage: picks, shovels and pans, hard bread, dried meat and beans, boots, jackets, and blankets. Most of the men themselves rarely stayed longer than a night or two, but they came pouring into the fort in such numbers that several hundred were always on hand, cramping the fort's limited facilities, designed to house no more than a few dozen people. When the fort became too crowded, the gold seekers spilled over its walls. As "every little shanty in or around the Fort became a store, a warehouse, or a hotel," Sutter recalled years later, "the whole settlement was a veritable bazaar."[45] J. A. Moerenhout, the French consul at Monterey, echoed Sutter's description when he visited the fort, writing to his superiors that "one would have thought himself either in a Turkish bazaar or in one of the most frequented market places of Europe. . . . All around the courtyard inside it is divided into chambers and rooms, eighteen by thirty feet in width. . . . Now all is occupied and rented for gold."[46]

By winter, the fort had begun to take on the appearance of a wide-open frontier city, as described by William R. Grimshaw, a twenty-three-year-old New Yorker who began working for one of the Sutter's Fort merchants in October 1848. "In the middle of the fort," he wrote,

> was a two story adobe building . . . , the lower portion of which was used as a bar room and with a monte table or two in it. The bar was crowded with customers night and day and never closed from one month's end to the other. The upper story was rented by Rufus Hitchcock & wife as a boarding house. Board was $40 per week; meals $2 each. The fare was plain and simple. We had plenty of fresh beef, beans, bread, tea & coffee, no milk. . . . The few potatoes & onions that came into the market were sent to the mines as a cure & preventive of scurvy and brought such enormous prices ($1 each) as placed them entirely out of reach.[47]

Sutter's problems were further complicated by the unexpected and unwelcome arrival of his family from Switzerland. Relations between Sutter and his eldest son were especially poor. Sutter had abandoned his family years before, and the senior Sutter's debt problems, the gold rush, and his growing alcoholism further strained the reunion of father and son. For his part, Sutter resented his son, whose conception had forced him into an unwanted marriage.[48]

In establishing a sawmill, Sutter had attempted to recoup his standing; instead, the mill ensured his ruin. The discovery of gold had flooded the country with would-be miners who disregarded property rights in their quest for gold; workers for his various enterprises, already difficult to obtain, now became impossible to retain. With his creditors threatening and the intrusion of his unwanted family, Sutter abandoned his vision of empire and decided to transfer all of his property to his son, John Sutter, Jr., only twenty-two years old, who had arrived in California just two months before.

It was an act of desperation that would likely have been illegal had it not been for what one Sutter biographer has called the "hopelessly muddled legal status of California's interregnum."[49] Since the United States had not yet extended its laws over California, the administration of the law was given over to Americans but was supposed to follow Mexican precedents. Since few Americans understood these, nearly anything was legally possible. Then, only a few weeks after transferring his property to his son, Sutter went to Coloma to try his hand at mining and became trapped by winter snows (or simply decided to stay sequestered) in the small mining camp.[50]

Perhaps the crush of events overwhelmed Sutter. It was this departure, however, that would be ruinous for the ambitious colonizer. For although the events of 1848 can be viewed as the ultimate collapse of New Helvetia, one can also see in them the seeds of Sacramento's greatness. True, the disorder at Sutter's Fort would soon reduce the very walls of the adobe fortress to rubble. Yet the activity at the fort, the buying and selling, emphasized again the underlying strategic significance of Sutter's location. As it had been the informal center of the fur trade in the 1830s, before Sutter had even arrived, the same site now was becoming the informal center of a new trade in mining equipment. This new trade would not require fortress walls, but ample warehouses; not soldiers, but merchants. In short, the new trade would best be served by a city.

And Sutter had within his reach exactly that city: Sutterville. What Sutter needed to do was to abandon his crumbling fortress and relocate the assembled merchants in Sutterville. Had he done so, Sutter's fortune and fame might still have been retrieved. Yet instead of opportunity, Sutter saw only problems. Instead of shifting his focus, he hid in the gold fields.

>--<

In hindsight, it is still difficult to determine how much of Sutter's empire was the result of shrewd insight and how much of it was simply sheer luck. Sutter's actions both before and after the heyday of Fort Sutter, 1839–45, do not suggest he had great insights into the forces at work in the region. When one looks back, it is apparent that the region near the mouth of the American River had become a focal point for trade between Indians and neophytes, American and British fur traders, and potentially Mexican and Russian settlements. The native population had dominated the region but was severely weakened. Thus the site was ideal for the establishment of a commercial outpost. The site, in other words, was perfectly suited to host a commercial city.

The location of that city was determined only in small part by physical geography. Its location near the head of navigation on the Sacramento River facilitated its ties to San Francisco Bay and the outside world. But Sutter's empire was also tied to American and British traders despite intervening mountains, forests, and deserts. Its situation in the heart of an agricultural district was helpful, but agriculture in the central valley had not yet developed to any meaningful extent.

The more important bases of Sutterville were not the natural geography, but the human and economic geography of the region. Sutterville's future rested on the location of human communities and the expected flows of goods between central valley farmers and an international as well as a growing local manufacturing base. Sutter seems to have been aware of these bases when he established his sawmill to cater to the development of his former empire. But when gold was discovered, he seems to have completely misunderstood the new human and economic world emerging in northern California.

Most important, Sutter's control of the region had completely slipped. When he was the only merchant in the area, he could dominate the native population with relative ease. But that native population had dwindled rapidly, and a new local population of independent-minded American farmers had begun to replace it. This new population appeared on first arrival to be dependent on Sutter but very quickly left the orbit of New Helvetia and established an essentially American rural countryside. With them came merchants, some with better connections to capital and trade goods than Sutter could hope to have. Sutter's Mill, though providing an important service, was already something of an anachronism as it was being built. Focusing on local development, Sutter had few external connections to sustain him when the gold rush flood overwhelmed his old empire.

It had indeed been the best of times and the worst of times for John Sutter. For a few years the Swiss adventurer had been able to play the role of imperial colonizer. In the early 1840s, Sutter had briefly managed to channel and focus the flows of economic trade on his nascent settlement. He had dreamed big, farsighted dreams and planned an agrarian colony that, on paper at least, looks impressive and well designed. He had helped increase the regional population of American farmers, had begun changing the physical order of the central valley, and had established a market-city that could connect the central valley to the outside world. Yet within a decade, his plans were in shambles.

So why didn't it work? Sutter's enterprise failed not only because the gold rush overwhelmed his ambitious vision, but also because Sutter never really controlled the region in the ways that he believed he did. Powerful economic flows did concentrate in the region of Sutter's Fort, but they predated Sutter's arrival. Between 1839 and 1845, Sutter did manage to command Indian laborers to build his fort, but the availability of their labor was based as much on their recent decline after the malaria epidemic and the growing chaotic conditions of international competition in the region as on his managerial skills. Timing was everything. Had Sutter arrived ten years earlier, he would likely have received less cooperation from the Indians. As it was, Sutter's control of his Indian workers lasted less than a decade.

Nor did the newly arriving American farmers prove easy to command. Though many spent their first winter with Sutter, contributing work and teaching their skills to the Indian workers, few were willing to stay in the immediate vicinity for long. Nor were they willing to accept Sutter's authority in the region. Sutter could make all the plans for his settlement he wished, but few were willing to follow his design.

Sutter's contribution to Sacramento's history thus remains mixed. The success of his settlement pointed out the tremendous potential for trade inherent in both the physical and the demographic landscape of the region near the mouth of the Sacramento Valley. The city that rose on that site would eventually enshrine Sutter as a somewhat bumbling but generous founding father. But in reality Sutter had not created an empire in California's central valley; the empire builder was the site itself. Sutter's fame would rest not so much on what he had done for the region, but on what the region had done for him.

Brannan's Mill

Samuel Brannan was frustrated. Late in the fall of 1848, Brannan was desperately trying to find an ideal location to unload his goods. The frontier merchant had already gathered an impressive stock of miners' supplies and needed a place both to store and sell them over the coming winter. Brannan had a small mercantile in crowded and crumbling Fort Sutter, but it was not large enough to warehouse his goods. Brannan knew that miners from the scattered mining camps in the Sierra foothills would soon be coming down to the central valley to winter and acquire needed supplies—the very supplies Brannan had collected. The only question was where to put his new store and warehouse.

Logic, of course, suggested Sutterville, and indeed, Brannan had tried to locate there. Brannan had approached the city's land agent, Lansford Hastings, with a lucrative proposition: in exchange for several free town lots in Sutterville, Brannan would locate his warehouse and store in Sutter's namesake city. Brannan explained that the rush of miners to his store would soon bring other merchants and would increase the land values of the other town lots. Shortly after he opened for business, Brannan assured Hastings, Sutterville would boom.

Hastings, however, would have none of it. Brannan's logic was fine, of course, but Hastings believed that any merchant in Sutterville would boost the profitability of the site—why should he give special favoritism to Brannan? And as the city's largest landowner, Hastings saw no reason to give free town lots to anyone. Besides, Brannan and Hastings had known each other for years, and Hastings had good reasons to distrust Samuel Brannan's word. Brannan, Hastings was well aware, was given to double dealings.

Unwilling to buy lots in Sutterville (perhaps even unable to do so—Brannan had stretched his credit significantly to amass his stock of goods), Brannan was desperate to unload his supplies in a secure place in the vicinity. Sailing on up the Sacramento River a few miles, Brannan came to the mouth of the American River. Farther up that river gold had first been discovered less than a year earlier. Near the mouth of the river, shaded by immense trees, lay a small clearing, carved out of the forest some years earlier by Sutter's workers. The clearing was known locally as "Sutter's Embarcadero"; like nearly everything in New Helvetia, the name was far more prominent than the actual site. A trail from the clearing led back several miles away from the river to Sutter's Fort. Near the embarcadero George McDougal operated a ferry, bringing would-be miners across the broad Sacramento River. McDougal also sold some goods from his ferry, which operated as a kind of floating store. Business had been good.

Samuel Brannan had a keen eye for business opportunities. Landing at the embarcadero, he began erecting tents for his goods and opened a new store. McDougal grumbled about the competition, Hastings sneered at the merchant in the middle of nowhere, and Brannan himself may have wondered about the site when he saw bits of driftwood far up in the trees surrounding his new store, indicating that the site was subject to flooding. Surely this was a site chosen in desperation, to be moved to a better site after the winter—assuming it survived the spring flooding!

Yet in fewer than nine months, Sacramento would rise from that isolated, low-lying clearing, while Sutterville—despite its superior site and its established presence—would be all but forgotten.

In the emergence of Sacramento is a cautionary tale about the establishment of new towns on the American frontier. Geography was relevant but not the only factor. Economic flows—what we might term the geography of trade—were more important. But that geography was more fluid and shifting before cities were established than the turbulent Sacramento River, on whose banks a city seemed destined to rise. As a river can be roiled by hidden rocks and rise and fall with seasonal rains, so the geography of trade could shift suddenly. A city, by bringing together a number of merchants in a fixed spot, could become a landmark in the geography of trade, a site that grows more permanent and impressive as more merchants and services gather. But before a city is established— or even while it is in the process of being established—these flows can shift rapidly between various sites and even various people, between sites that had adequate goods, or ran out of provisions, or had the one or two truly necessary items, or offered easy credit. Individuals with greater access to goods and capital can exert a greater influence on the emerging city, perhaps, but the actual location and prominence of one site over another has as much to do with the competition between merchants as the farsighted plans of a single city father. In the rise of Sacramento, Sutter and his Sutterville agent, Lansford Hastings, had several important advantages on their side. But they met with a formidable opponent in Samuel Brannan, whose economic power could create financial landmarks that surpassed the geographic advantages of Sutterville. In the end, Sacramento arose more from shortsighted, daily business competition than from careful, considered planning. Though the consequences of situating the city on a floodplain would have lasting and costly impacts on the city, the decision to locate there was based on the immediate needs and frustrations of a few early merchants.

And in the fall of 1848, even after unloading his stock of goods at Sutter's Embarcadero, Samuel Brannan's frustrations and ambitions would continue to be powerful forces in the evolving story of Sacramento's foundation.

→ ⸺ ←

Like Sutter, Samuel Brannan's life before arriving in California reads like a primer for a frontier entrepreneur. And also like Sutter, Brannan's private life appears to have been tumultuous.[1] Brannan was born in 1819, in Saco, Maine, a seaport bustling with commercial and industrial opportunities. When Brannan was fourteen, he moved to Painesville, Ohio, with his twenty-seven-year-old sister Mary Ann. Brannan, who described himself as "endowed with a spirit of adventure," began his entrepreneurial career during the speculative mania that seized the nation in the 1830s. Though only seventeen years old, Brannan spent two years gambling as a land speculator and town builder. The experience left him broke. To pay off his debts, Brannan became a journeyman printer and began traveling the country. Over the next few years Brannan became a publisher in New Orleans, Indianapolis, and New York. Brannan eventually boasted that he had worked in every state in the Union, though he usually spent only one to six months in each place.[2]

As with Sutter, this period of travel provided Brannan with a great deal of practical experience that would later be useful in California. As a publisher and editor, Brannan dealt in local and regional news, giving him sharp insights into the business practices of his day. Brannan also likely watched for news on town building and real estate speculation—activities in which he had already shown an interest. Brannan was in a perfect position to learn by reporting and publishing the experiences of others who, like himself, sought fortune on the developing frontier. He noted as much himself later in life, claiming that the printing business "proved a great lever to [my] advancement" and had enabled the young businessman "to travel as an independent man only can."[3]

By 1844, after seven years of journeying, Brannan emerged in New York as both a publisher and an elder in the Church of Latter-day Saints. The reasons for Brannan's involvement with the Mormons are unknown. Brannan later broke bitterly with the church and would comment little on his early association. However, his connection to the church began in the early 1830s, and much of his apprenticeship as a printer was under the auspices of the Mormon church.[4] Though some of Brannan's early writings and activities suggest that Brannan was a true believer in the faith, other, more pragmatic reasons may also have been compelling. Brannan was persuaded to join the church by the Mormon preachers Orson Hyde, who visited Saco in 1832, and Heber C. Kimball, who was especially skilled at winning converts because he taught Mormonism with an entrepreneurial slant, promoting the church as a means of climbing the business and social ladder.[5] This may have been particularly enticing to Brannan, who noted years later that his establishment of the Mormon newspaper the *New York Messenger* "realized far more *prophet* [*sic*] than he ever anticipated."[6]

Brannan's rise within the ranks of the Latter-day Saints was swift. He quickly became one of the Mormons' preachers and elders. Very likely Brannan's wide experience as a traveling publisher had already given him the shrewd business sense that he would later show in Sacramento. But Brannan's business interests were also one of several sources of contention between Brannan and the Saints. Though appointed as the presiding elder of the New York branch of the church and noted by visitors to be a powerful preacher, Brannan and several of his colleagues were also suspected of being more interested in self-promotion than in building up the church. Then in April 1845, Brannan was "disfellowshiped and cut off from the Church."[7]

The cause of the rebuke would echo in some form throughout Brannan's life: a sexual escapade. Brannan had married Ann Eliza Corwin, the daughter of a wealthy Mormon widow, in 1844 but only a few months later was married in the church to Sarah E. Wallace, the sister of G. B. Wallace, another church leader. At the time, polygamy in the church was still hidden and controversial, and Brannan was accused of "corrupting the Saints, introducing among them false doctrines and immoral practices by which many of them had stumbled and been seduced from virtue and truth . . . while many had been turned to various dissenting parties."[8] However, Wallace claimed that Brannan had in fact seduced his sister and was simply using the obscure practice of polygamy to hide his infidelity. After an exchange of letters among the leadership, many of whom were themselves polygamists at this point, Brannan was reinstated in the church. Throughout the remainder of Brannan's life, however, his continuing sexual adventures would be legendary.[9]

Brannan's lusty affairs were not the only complication in his relationship with the church. His religious paper increasingly included political observations, and Brannan was openly proud of his ties to the Democratic Party; he met often with members of the Democratic Party leadership and attended President James K. Polk's inauguration in 1845. Late in 1845 and into 1846, Brannan became involved in a somewhat shadowy plan hatched by several businessmen, politicians, and possibly Polk himself to have the Mormons settle in California as an opening advance of American interests to seize the province from Mexico. Although many of the details of the plan remain unknown and the idea was ultimately rejected by Brigham Young, who feared that this was an attempt to prevent the Mormons from leaving the States at all, Brannan not only helped concoct the scheme but also apparently hoped to keep it alive. Part of the plot involved having a large settlement of Mormons claim lands in California and then turn half of them over to the American agents involved in the scheme. Brannan, it seems clear, would also have profited handsomely in the covert filibuster.[10]

Though this plan fell through, the Mormon leadership did propose that Brannan lead an expedition from New York by ship to California, to sail at the same time that Brigham Young was leading church followers westward over land. Church leaders planned to create a Mormon state in the far northern territories of Mexico. Brannan chartered the *Brooklyn,* a 450-ton ship equipped with staterooms, for $6,000. To pay for the charter, Brannan demanded that prospective passengers paid at least $50 each for passage. Brannan also borrowed church funds and invested his own moneys to provision the ship with the supplies needed to establish a Mormon empire on the Pacific coast.[11]

Again Brannan's political contacts intervened behind the scenes, apparently threatening to prevent Brannan from sailing unless he turned over half the western lands claimed by the church to their agents. Rather than oppose these moves, Brannan endorsed them and tried again to get the church to submit. Ultimately Brannan may even have made some separate deal with the plotters on his own.[12]

The whole affair raises a number of important issues, especially in regard to Samuel Brannan. That the U.S. and Democratic Party leadership would be party to such a deal is not surprising. Filibustering had worked in Texas and was being attempted on several levels in the mid-1840s in California. If the Mormons joined in this effort, it would simply be one more of Polk's strategies leading up to the Mexican War. Polk's followers may also have believed that even if the Mormons did not follow through, their movements would simply be one more complication to distract the Mexican government or might be built into an excuse for U.S. intervention later. Still more interesting is Brannan's willingness to participate. Brigham Young believed both at the time and later that the entire matter had been designed to harass and restrict the Mormons, but Brannan clearly favored and promoted the plan. Very likely, Brannan was both intrigued by the political implications of the plan and, perhaps even more important, stood to profit greatly from its execution.

Brannan's followers on board the *Brooklyn* left New York on February 4, 1846. According to newspaper reports at the time, the ship carried 230 passengers as well as agricultural and mechanical tools for 800 men, including but not limited to plows, hoes, pitchforks, shovels, spades, nails, sickles, glass, a printing press, books, dry goods, milch cows, pigs, and chickens.[13] The cost of all these goods estimated at over $30,000.[14] Brannan was responsible for raising the money to cover this cost and had to gamble on the expedition's success in order to get his investment back. However, he apparently thought of more than simply having his investment returned. During the journey, Brannan organized his Mormon followers into "S. Brannan & Co." and wrote up a "covenant" that would not only guarantee the continued fellowship of the Saints, but also a handsome return on Brannan's investment in the expedition. The covenant bound its members to pay the debt owed Brannan and to work communally for three years, placing the profits from the colony's early efforts in Brannan's hands. Should anyone leave the covenant, his goods would be turned over to the elders, of which Brannan himself was the leader in California. Under this covenant, Brannan simply had to make his followers productive and wealth would in time accumulate in his hands.[15]

> ---

When Brannan's party arrived in California on July 31, 1846, they were stunned to see that the United States had recently conquered the Mexican province. One of the major objectives of the expedition had been to get beyond the jurisdiction of the United States and establish a Mormon state on the Pacific coast. Still, Brannan believed the region was so undeveloped and his followers so organized that the Saints could make a home for themselves here, perhaps even eventually dominating the region completely. He thus set out with great energy to lay the foundations of a new Mormon state in California.

Brannan's experience as an erstwhile land speculator and town builder in the past gave him good insights into what would be required in California. His vision of regional development in many ways matched Sutter's, though on a somewhat larger scale. Brannan believed that the agricultural potential of the central valley, with an outlet in San Francisco, would be the key to regional growth. Within a few months the settlement at Yerba Buena Cove that would ultimately become San Francisco became, in the words of Hubert Howe Bancroft, "very largely a Mormon town." Brannan's followers rapidly built homes, commercial buildings, and a gristmill. Brannan also set up the city's only printing press. The printing office was not only profitable, but also very informative, as Brannan and his assistant, Edward Kemble, soon found themselves busy printing up notices, deeds, and papers for the alcalde, legal documents, and official proclamations for the naval authorities. In addition, Brannan began publishing a newspaper, the *California Star*.[16]

The settlement at San Francisco Bay, however, was to be the regional headquarters. Brannan deemed the establishment of an agricultural settlement in the interior valleys to be of critical importance in raising the food and market crops necessary to support the Mormon empire. Instead of settling in the northern Sacramento Valley near Sutter's Fort, however, Brannan directed his followers south to the San Joaquin Valley. The site the Mormons chose for their agrarian village was on the north bank of the Stanislaus River, one and a half miles from the mouth of the San Joaquin (in the vicinity of present-day Manteca), and was named New Hope. Brannan also provided the commune with the necessary oxen, seed wheat, implements, and a wagon and schooner and erected two flour mills, the first in the state.[17]

By April 1847, Brannan's San Francisco operations were booming, though New Hope's progress proved more difficult. Settlers complained of the weather, mosquitoes, and isolation, and a flood in January 1847 further dampened enthusiasm for the New Hope commune.[18] William Stout, Brannan's handpicked manager of the settlement, offered to help the settlers build their own cabins and homesteads but then claimed the original communal farm as his own. Brannan came from San Francisco to settle the problem, and in an open forum the settlers decided to dedicate the original farm to the Mormons' ruling council, the Twelve Apostles, who were expected to arrive shortly. Stout and a few others left the place the next day. Others soon followed, in part because the potato crop turned out to be poor, but also because the settlers felt isolated living so far inland from other settlements.[19]

Despite these difficulties, Brannan was pleased with the progress he had made in establishing a Mormon settlement in California. But he was troubled that he had received no communication from the overland Mormon expedition since he had left New York. Thus in early April 1847, Brannan began an audacious journey: traveling with only two companions, he set out to cross the Sierra Nevada mountain range, search for the overland expedition under Brigham Young, and after finding them guide them to the California paradise Brannan had already established. Since he had no idea where to find the main Mormon party, it was an extraordinary trek.

Asking directions from fur traders he met along the way, Brannan succeeded in joining Young's party near the Green River at the end of June. If Brannan saw himself as a kind of latter-day Moses who would lead the church to a promised land in California, he was in for a rude surprise. Young was unimpressed with Brannan's achievements in California and at the end of July made it clear that the church would be setting up its headquarters at Salt Lake, not in California. Young believed the church simply didn't have the resources to go any farther west, and in any case he preferred the isolation of the Rocky Mountains, telling Brannan, "We have no business at San Francisco; the Gentiles will be there pretty soon."[20]

Brannan continued to argue in favor of settling in California, believing that the Mormons would not survive in the desert near Salt Lake, but Young was adamant. Brannan was sent back to California with two letters from the church leadership for the California Mormons, telling them of the trials of Young's expedition and of the decision to settle in Salt Lake. The letters stated that anyone who wished to stay in California should be allowed to stay, but that anyone wishing to join the main body of the church in Salt Lake City should not be hindered. Brannan was left in charge of the California congregation, but Young's endorsement of his efforts there was weak. Though it provisionally accepted Brannan's communal arrangements at New Hope, the letters made clear the leadership's disapproval of the scheme. Finally, when Brannan and his small party were sent back to California, command of the party was given to James Brown, which Brannan took as a direct snub of his own leadership. During the return trip, in fact, Brannan and Brown quarreled incessantly and eventually came to blows.

Brannan tried to convince his followers in California that the Salt Lake venture was bound to fail and that within the year Young would see the folly of his action and bring the church to California. And he saw future greatness in store for California. San Francisco, he believed, would become "the great Emporium of the Pacific and eventually of the union," and Brannan proclaimed that he would make his headquarters on the Pacific coast.[21] When Brown released Young's letters, however, the majority of the Mormons decided to leave for Salt Lake. As it was already late in the year, Brown advised the faithful to remain in California and work through the winter so that they would have some earnings to take with them in the spring. About half of the Mormon colonizers did this, finding work at Sutter's New Helvetia. Sutter sent a number of them into the Sierra foothills. There, under the direction of James Marshall, they were to construct a sawmill for Sutter on the American River.[22]

Brannan, however, refused to give up on California. He remained convinced that Brigham Young's settlement would fail, that once he "has fairly tried it, he will find that I was right and he was wrong, and will come to California."[23] But his loyalty was certainly weak, if in fact it still existed. Sutter noted that Brannan had told him that the Mormons "might go to hell." And a newspaper account of the Mormons in San Francisco reported that Elder Brannan had put forth many "visions and prophecies," including the pronouncement that "he is to be the Treasurer and Banker of all the Mormons," but that in reality "this Brannan deludes the ignorant at every turn, until he gets his ends accomplished, after which he will be 'among the missing.'"[24] With the majority of his followers abandoning him for Salt Lake, Brannan dissolved the firm of "S. Brannan & Co.," which in effect also dissolved the New Hope commune. Company perty was sold to cover debts, with surplus funds to be divided among the partners. However, Brannan kept most of this money for himself, apparently because he considered himself the company's chief creditor. As one follower noted, "Samuel Brannan got the land, oxen, crops, house, tools, and launch from New Hope, and the company, who did the work, got nothing."[25]

During the fall of 1847, as Brannan & Co. was dissolving, Brannan formed a partnership with one of the men who had traveled with him to Salt Lake, and, under the name of C. C. Smith & Company, the partners established their store, the first in the Sacramento Valley, at Sutter's Fort. The store sold dry goods and groceries in exchange for "wheat, corn, rye, barley, oats; horses, mules, beaver and other skins; pork, butter, cheese, tallow hides, etc."[26] C. C. Smith & Company, though Sutter referred to it as only a "shirt-tail store," did a good business.[27] Brannan continued to see the potential of California and continued into the spring of 1848 to try to get Young to relocate the church, arguing that it would flourish easily. "Could two or three hundred families of our people be thrown into this town," Brannan wrote to Young, "within a few years the wealth and influence of this place could be entirely to our interest."[28] But by this point, Brannan was clearly thinking more of his own fortune.

In January 1848, San Francisco's business had slumped due to the end of the Mexican War. Like Sutter, Brannan pinned his hopes for future profits on the expected migration of farmers into the now American territory of California. But the news from the States suggested few overland migrants were gathering to head out for California. To encourage migration, Brannan published a special edition of the *Star* at the end of March 1848 to expound on the promise and potential of California and outfitted an express of ten men to distribute the paper to "every section of the Union" and to any emigrants they encountered on their way east.[29] Other events, however, would soon make this propaganda unnecessary.

At the end of January, James Marshall and the other Mormons erecting Sutter's sawmill discovered gold in the mill's tailrace. Over the next few days the workers found that the banks along the river were littered with nuggets and could be easily dug up with simple kitchen utensils. Sutter, called to the site to authenticate the gold, pleaded with the workers to finish the mill and to keep the discovery to themselves until he could be certain that the nuggets were indeed gold. The workers kept the secret for a few weeks and continued working on the mill, but several of the men also spent some of their off time gathering nuggets.

After several weeks, one of the workers turned up at Smith and Brannan's store, trying to make a purchase with his gold. Smith confronted Sutter, who admitted that the gold was real but again pleaded that Smith keep the discovery quiet until the mill was completed. After Smith informed his partner, Brannan rode to the American River to make his own investigations. News of the discovery leaked out slowly. Throughout March and April, the *Star,* now under the charge of Brannan's former assistant, Edward Kemble, reported the discovery, but few people paid much attention, and Kemble even published his opinion that the "mines were a sham."[30]

Then late in May, Brannan filled a glass bottle with about $500 worth of gold nuggets and dust and raced around San Francisco's Portsmouth Square, holding the bottle aloft and shouting, "Gold! Gold! Gold, from the American River!"[31] Brannan's dramatic gesture set off the local rush he had intended, and those who planned to head for the foothills soon discovered that Brannan was making his gold off their excitement. Brannan and Smith had quietly been buying up as many shovels, picks, and blankets as they could find, which they now sold at greatly inflated prices. The "shirt-tail store" at the fort made immense profits. "Receipts from May 1 to July 10, amounted to $36,000; $5000 a day, $150,000 a month was normal business for more than eighteen months, and three-fourths of this was profit!"[32]

The discovery of gold led to Brannan's final break with the Mormon church. Shortly after its discovery, Brannan called a meeting of the Mormons in California, advising them to work in a mine found by one of his followers. Brannan collected a tax or rent from the Mormons who worked the mine for a time but never met with them again. During the spring of 1849, Brannan wrote a bitter letter to his sister, denouncing the Mormons for refusing to credit his work in California. Indeed, Brannan even suggested that the church had never intended to follow him to California but had expected him to be killed there by Mexicans.[33] Young then demanded that Brannan forward the tithings the Mormons had paid him in California, especially those from the miners. Brannan reported that he told Young he would forward the money when he received a receipt signed by the Lord, a story Brannan may have made up. The church disfellowshiped Brannan in 1851 due to his personal sins, general apostasy, and leadership of vigilante movements in Sacramento and San Francisco.[34]

When Brannan touched off the local rush of May 1848, the true extent of the gold fields was not yet known. Brannan, however, believed that the rush would be major, telling one friend that "there was more gold than all the people of California could take out in fifty years."[35] In the fall of 1848, the scale of the gold deposits in the Sierra foothills began to be realized. Far from being an isolated discovery, gold was discovered throughout the region during 1848. As poor weather began to push the earliest miners down from the mountains in the later months of the year, reports of widely separated discoveries floated among the population. By the end of the year the magnitude and extent of the mining region suggested that California would be yielding up tons of gold for years to come. That realization prompted Brannan and the other merchants at Sutter's Fort to think in larger and more permanent terms.

By the fall of 1848 Sutter's Fort had already become too crowded for the fort's merchants. Already commanding most of the fort's trade, Brannan desperately needed adequate storage facilities to protect his large stock of commodities from the coming winter. In August 1848, Brannan and his fellow merchant P. B. Cornwall realized the potential of a town on the Sacramento River, where people and goods debarked to head for the gold fields, rather than inland at the fort. Brannan and Cornwall at first tried to negotiate favorable terms for town sites within Sutterville. In exchange for free town lots, Brannan and Cornwall offered to establish stores that would attract more businesses and people to Sutterville. Unable to work out an arrangement with Lansford Hastings, Brannan and Cornwall unloaded their winter supplies at Sutter's Embarcadero, the clearing on the eastern bank of the Sacramento River beside the mouth of the American River. Here Brannan and Cornwall began selling their goods under canvas tents.[36]

> — <

Secure for the moment, Brannan still needed to find a more permanent location from which to sell his goods. But very quickly he began to consider the temporary site as the ideal place for his future activities. The site had several advantages. The Sacramento River that fronted the embarcadero was deep enough for oceangoing ships to reach relatively easily. It was closer to Sutter's Fort than Sutterville, and in 1848 Sutter's Fort was still the more recognized local landmark. The ground was generally level and, though forested, should prove easy to mark out with a city grid. And though the site gave some indications of past flooding, the winter of 1848–49 proved rather dry, suggesting fears of flooding might be groundless. To the former land speculator and erstwhile town builder, the site hinted at grand possibilities.

The biggest drawback to the site, however, was not physical but economic: John Sutter already owned it. Yet ultimately this would turn out to be an even greater advantage to Brannan than all the other physical attractions combined. Attempting to get his declining empire up and running after the Mexican War, Sutter had incurred a number of debts, including several to Brannan. Brannan may have considered having these debts canceled in exchange for title to some of the land around the embarcadero. With these lands Brannan could play the land game again, but with the added advantage of controlling a large stock of goods. With luck, his new city would become more successful than Hastings's Sutterville.

But before Brannan could convince Sutter to surrender the land, Sutter pulled a stunt of his own. Rather than face his many creditors, Sutter transferred all his possessions to his newly arrived son, John Sutter, Jr., and then left for the gold fields, where he quickly became stranded by the winter snows—or perhaps simply used this as an excuse to hide.

Brannan was sensible enough to realize that he had been outmaneuvered legally, but he also hoped that he could still make the tangled mess turn out in his favor. Brannan saw that the younger Sutter could be easily manipulated. Sutter, Jr., was a frail young man, unaccustomed to California, frontier life, or the English language. The young man could not have been more dissimilar to his father. The elder Sutter was burly and effusive and often swaggered through his fort in affected martial pomp; the youth appeared lean, quiet, and completely lost in his father's world. Abandoned in a strange and rough country, Sutter's son was left to find some way to manage his father's vast, tangled accounts.[37]

Brannan struck quickly. Together with fellow merchant Samuel Hensley, he suggested to young Sutter the idea of hiring an engineer to survey and plat a new city adjacent to the crumbling fort, at the junction of the Sacramento and American rivers. The city design need not be elaborate, merely the standard grid familiar from many American cities. But it would be designed on a huge scale, large enough both to dominate the gold region trade and to provide ample profits to its founders.[38]

Brannan's arguments for a new city were powerful: Sutter needed ready money to pay off his father's debts, eager traders were seeking a place to erect stores, the fort was already overcrowded, and the land around the fort belonged to Sutter. As for the rival Sutterville—Brannan pointed out that it lay three miles off the well-established trade route. The younger Sutter, despite his father's dreams for Sutterville, agreed with the merchants. As if to complete the city's break from the elder Sutter's authority, the new town took the name "Sacramento City" from the river that Brannan hoped would make the site the key port of entry to the gold fields.[39]

Late in December, Hensley and Sutter, Jr., approached a lawyer, Peter H. Burnett, to interest him in the position of land agent for the new city. Burnett already had several years of legal experience in frontier communities. Five years earlier, in 1843, he had set out with his family from Missouri for the Oregon Territory, where he had taken up farming in the Willamette Valley. The following year he was chosen for the legislative committee of Oregon, the next year he became judge of the supreme court, and with the preliminary formation of Oregon's territorial government in 1848, he was elected to the territorial legislature. In September 1848, though, he had joined other Oregon settlers who rushed south to California to try their hand at prospecting for gold. Arriving late in the year, Burnett had tired of mining after only six weeks.

His arrival at Sutter's Fort near the end of December 1848 placed him in a fortuitous position just when other men were in need of a lawyer's services in order to launch a new city.[40]

As Burnett listened to the two men who sat in his chilly office at Sutter's Fort describe the boldness of their plan, its incredible risks and potential rewards, the ex-miner realized that he had made the right decision in returning to the legal practice. For what these men offered the lawyer was in essence a share in a different mother lode: one-quarter of the gross proceeds arising from the sale of lots in a proposed new city, one that might soon dominate the entire mining region.

The size of the proposed city would be its most impressive feature. From Front Street on the bank of the Sacramento to Thirty-first Street, the city would stretch nearly three miles from the river, ensnaring the crumbling Sutter's Fort in its wide-ranging scheme. The entire white population of the territory at that time would not have filled the new city. Yet Burnett knew that such calculations were meaningless in the short, wintry December days of 1848. Already Californians knew that the golden nuggets that James Marshall had discovered in the tailrace at Sutter's Mill the previous January were not an isolated find. Gold seekers had begun arriving from the Pacific Rim, from Oregon and Mexico, Hawaii and Chile. Even as Burnett and Sutter discussed their proposed city, rumors of the discovery raced throughout the United States. Rumors were elevated to reality after President Polk's confirmation of the discovery in his December 1848 State of the Union message to Congress. Both the extent of the gold fields and the growing rush of people to the region promised to create a huge and dynamic new city adjacent to the mining region. Sacramento City could be that city. Thus Sacramento was designed with an eye to the future, on a grand scale that would match the monumental scale of the gold fields and the gathering rush itself.[41]

Burnett's role was to act as the young man's lawyer and land agent and to handle all town lot sales. For his services Burnett would receive 25 percent of the gross proceeds from the sale of the city lots.[42] Burnett weighed his decision carefully. "There was a heavy amount of old business to settle up," he recalled later, "and, while the labor was certain, the compensation was speculative."[43] Burnett's concern, as well as that of Sutter, Jr., and the fort's merchants, was over the viability of the proposed new city. All realized that the gold rush would promote city growth in the region. But only three miles below the proposed site of Sacramento, Sutterville was already poised to reap the profits of the gold rush. Thus the fate of Sacramento hung like a question mark on Burnett's mind. The ex-miner had learned the harsh lesson of working hard over a likely looking claim with little or no reward. Now he was being asked to work on a likely looking urban claim. If Sacramento City failed, Burnett would have lost more time and would likely be deeper in debt than he already was. However, Burnett's fortune, as well as Sutter's, could be made quickly if Sacramento City did indeed boom the way that its planners envisioned.

Burnett accepted the offer. Early in January 1849, Burnett began selling the first lots in the new city.[44] Under Sutter, Jr.'s, direction, land was to be sold in the city for a uniform $250 per lot. To prevent runaway speculation, no one was allowed to purchase more than four city lots. The limited price and the prohibition against large-block sales show Sutter, Jr.'s concern with making the city a fair and egalitarian community.[45]

With the sale of the first lot, the city of Sacramento was founded. Committed to the future of Sacramento, Burnett, Sutter, Jr., Brannan, and their merchant partners began a furious struggle to establish their city against almost over-whelming odds. The remoteness of the site might hinder the development of a steady supply of needed goods, the turmoil of the gold rush could play havoc with even the best-laid plans, and competition from the rival city of Sutterville could make a ghost town of their city before it was built. Sacramento's founders, however, were caught up in the great gamble of the gold rush. Like miners staking claims in a rugged mountain valley or gamblers drawing cards in one of the many saloons found throughout the mother lode region, Sacramento's founders took the chance, invested their time, money, and talents, and gambled on the future.

→--←

Happy to get a town lot for only $250, Brannan quickly built a storehouse in Sacramento and was soon followed by several other merchants. Though the sale of city lots was brisk in the first few weeks, lot sales quickly dwindled. Sacramento's problems began before the first parcels were sold. Since Sutter, Sr., had picked Sutterville as a site for development, he had earlier given George McDougal a lease to operate a ferry at his embarcadero. McDougal had also used his ferry as an informal store on the riverbank and was running a very lucrative business at the embarcadero. The plan for the new town of Sacramento City would profit him greatly. However, McDougal's store lay on prime riverfront land that Sutter, Jr., hoped to sell. McDougal claimed he did not have to buy that land, as his lease from Sutter, Sr., granted him exclusive use of the riverbank from Sutter's Slough for four hundred yards south. In effect, McDougal's claim covered the whole riverfront of the proposed new city. Sutter, Jr., argued that McDougal's lease did not convey that right, and after a bitter legal battle, McDougal was defeated in court.[46]

Determined to wreak his revenge, McDougal initiated an economic war between Sacramento and Sutterville. The struggle lasted for several months, with the two cities fighting desperately over the future development of the area. McDougal began by moving all his goods to Sutterville. Though George McDougal left the state at this point, John McDougal, George's brother, then printed up and distributed "immense placards," declaring that his firm "had determined to take the lead in competition" and would thus sell his goods at "cost and freight." McDougal also announced verbally that if his firm "could not obtain patronage at that rate, they would sell at the primary cost of the merchandise."[47]

The placard and announcement disturbed the merchants at the fort and at Sacramento City. The McDougals would make no profit, and might even suffer a loss, just to destroy the merchants of Sacramento. Brannan and his fellow merchants in Sacramento realized that what was at stake was the future viability of their new town. If Sutterville attracted the flow of miners seeking supplies away from Sacramento City, Brannan and his partners would have to follow. Once they took up land in Sutterville, Sacramento City would all but collapse.

Brannan and the Sacramento merchants turned to violence. To secure their interests, they destroyed McDougal's stock of goods. Although the merchants' actions were not detailed, John Morse, writing four years later, noted vaguely that the area's merchants "insidiously relieved the firm of McDougal and Company of the means of sustaining an attractive opposition." Given the uncertainty of future supplies in the region at this time, the destruction was a serious setback for the McDougals. As Morse noted, "Goods once broken into at that date could not be restored."[48]

The biggest blow to Sutterville, however, came from a coup d'état administered by Samuel Brannan. After the destruction of the McDougals' stores, Sutterville's future prospects looked somewhat dim. Sutter's Fort and Sacramento combined were attracting most of the area's business. Sutterville's land agent, Lansford Hastings, now began to realize that his own hopes of making a fortune from the development of Sutterville were fading. At this point Brannan and other area merchants again contacted Hastings, claiming to prefer the Sutterville site for their operations. Given the now obvious power and ruthlessness of the Sacramento merchants as well as the dismal future that appeared imminent for his town, Hastings was in a mood to bargain. He offered Brannan and his friends eighty free town lots in Sutterville if the merchants would establish themselves in Sutterville instead of in Sacramento.[49]

Most likely Brannan never intended to move to Sutterville, since he already had constructed storehouses in Sacramento. Instead the merchants seemed more interested in manipulating the young ward of the collapsing New Helvetia into giving them more power within the emerging city. Sacramento's merchants approached Sutter, Jr., and suggested that he top Hastings's offer or they would leave the new city. Because the plan of Sacramento City was much larger than Sutterville, Sutter, Jr., could afford to be more generous. And because he needed the money for debts already owed, he had little choice. That young Sutter had no experience in such matters and was being used by his own partners in the Sacramento venture also played against him. In the end he surrendered five hundred choice town lots to the entrepreneurs—roughly 80 percent of all the town lots.[50]

This maneuver sealed the doom of Sutterville, giving Sacramento the commercial edge needed to rise above Sutterville. With the commitment of the town's merchants to their five hundred city lots and the quick profits to be realized from their rising value, Sacramento secured the interests of powerful men who were determined to make the city profitable, if not ultimately viable.

The maneuver not only gave the merchants most of the city's land, but also in essence ended power by either Sutter over the affairs of the new city. When George McDougal lost his claim to Sacramento's waterfront, he had rushed to Coloma and rousted the elder Sutter from his winter camp, alerting the errant colonizer to the city-building activities of his son. The elder Sutter finally returned from the mines, rushing to the military authorities in San Francisco to try to overturn the decision against the McDougals, and then forced his son to return the ownership and control of his previous empire. These actions, however, were taken too late. Sacramento City was an established fact, and the land on which it stood was now largely owned by the city's merchants. Sutter, Sr., could gain some slight satisfaction by firing Peter Burnett as the city's land agent, but because Sutter could not afford to pay the lawyer his fee, he ended up giving Burnett a significant amount of the remaining land in the city.[51]

+--+

Sacramento city's victory over Sutterville illustrates the influence of entrepreneurship in the establishment of new towns on the American frontier. Though the general area was an ideal spot to build a city due to the expected flows of gold and trade goods, the exact site was decided more by where the men with capital and goods situated themselves. Local physical considerations—such as the high ground at Sutterville—did not ultimately play a decisive role in the creation of the city. What mattered more was where Samuel Brannan and his partners situated their storehouses and acquired land for speculation.

The consequences of the merchants' decision to stay at the embarcadero had a profound impact on the rising city. The city was inundated in 1850, 1852, and 1861–62. Each time the city flooded, observers expected it to fail. Following the 1862 flood, despite over ten years of Sacramento's existence, the *San Francisco Morning Call* noted, "It is simply an act of folly for the people of the town of Sacramento to endeavor to maintain their city on its present location."[52] The *Nevada Transcript* was more succinct: "Sacramento is a doomed city."[53]

To the defeated land speculator, Lansford Hastings, sitting high and dry on Sutterville's higher ground, each flood brought dark humor. In a sarcastic letter to John Bidwell after Sacramento's 1852 flood, Hastings told of an "unfortunate gentleman who sat down at the corner of 7th and J streets in the *Subterranian City!* [Sacramento] . . . He arrived, or rather came up, feet foremost, in China." Hastings noted that city residents were busily filling in the muddy holes in their streets but predicted that "if they succeed with their present work, there will be no holes for the water to get out at." The streets would then form a basin, which would "monopolize the entire offal, rubbish and filth of the valley; and they will likewise produce a far greater abundance of ague and fever, cholera, and the like *tropical productions,* than any other part of the known world. . . . If fortune, fate, and the Elements favor us slightly, we [Sutterville] shall soon have much the largest town. Let Old Richardson's or Noah's flood come once, and if we don't get them then, I will leave."[54]

Yet after every flood, Sacramento residents rebuilt rather than relocated. In part, such dedication was also a consequence of Brannan's land grab in the city. Once the city's founding merchants owned the greater part of the land in the city, they were free to ignore Sutter, Jr.'s, earlier prohibitions against speculation. City lot prices, originally offered for $250, quickly rose to $3,000 and by the end of 1849 were even going as high as $8,000.[55] These economic foundations of the city put down deeper roots than Hastings could possibly cultivate in Sutterville, for two reasons. First, residents who purchased lots at such high prices were less likely to abandon them, even in the face of a flood. And much more important, many Sacramento residents considered their landholdings to be a measure of their assets. Merchants borrowed against the inflated value of their holdings to acquire the goods they intended to sell. The higher the value of the lot and the more a resident borrowed against its value, the more firmly tied the merchant was to the land—and by extension, Sacramento City itself.

As the city acquired more merchants and as land values increased, Sacramento City began to take form. Miners looking for supplies quickly found the new city to be a dependable source of goods. Late in June 1849, at the height of the merchants' power in the city, the *Placer Times* proclaimed Sacramento a business miracle. "Sacramento City," its editor wrote, "wherein six months ago was not in existence, has now about one hundred houses, and is doing more business than was San Francisco eight months since. . . . We predict that within a year the only rival in wealth and population that this city will have is San Francisco."[56]

As if in mute testimony to the rise of Sacramento City, observers needed only to look at the crumbling remains of Sutter's Fort. Just one year after French consul Moerenhout described the fort's bustling activity to his superiors, he reported, "Sutter's Fort or New Helvetia has lost all importance since the founding of the establishments on the Sacramento River. In the fort itself there is still a hotel and a few stores, but its business is languishing and there is no longer any such stir and activity as prevailed there at the time of my visit in 1848."[57]

Sacramento City's booming growth, however, still rested almost imperceptibly on a foundation of sand. As Thomas Van Dorn, who arrived in Sacramento in 1849 after making the cross-country trek, confided in his diary, "The town is active in business and busy in every department of pursuit. . . . [However,] the permanency of trade for this point will depend much on the mines." Van Dorn acknowledged Sacramento's good location but suggested that a potential new city to the north could channel much business away from the city. "Capital and competition," he concluded, "will only give Sacramento the least preference for the diggings."[58] Sacramento's founders sought only to make a quick profit. They saw the people passing through Sacramento's streets not as potential settlers, but as temporary, transitory customers. Established by merchants who viewed the site as an arena in which to speculate, Sacramento City was designed as an investment, a project intended to provide its investors with a sizable profit. If early merchants paid scant attention to or had little concern for the physical construction of the city, they likewise felt largely indifferent to the people who passed through their city.

Symbolic of their attitude toward the miners was the city's first elaborate hotel, Samuel Brannan's City Hotel. When it opened its doors for business in the summer of 1849, the City Hotel was one of Sacramento's few wooden structures and stood out even more prominently as a two-story building. Nestled on the city's waterfront, at the corner of Front and I streets, the City Hotel dominated the waterfront and was the first choice of most of the town's transitory population. Very expensive, a night in the City Hotel cost $5. Capable of accommodating 150 people per night, the City Hotel prospered. Not that it was elegant by eastern standards. Only months before, it had been a flour mill. Bought and moved to the new city by Samuel Brannan and John Fowler, the city's new transportation mogul, the two men simply changed the old mill from processing flour to processing would-be miners. To Brannan and Fowler, the thousands of hopeful young men passing through Sacramento on their way to the gold fields were human grist for their economic mill.[59]

CHAPTER THREE

The Speculators' City

Sacramento City in 1849 was the ideal of nineteenth-century urban speculators. It lay directly on the pulse of major trade routes between San Francisco Bay and the mining region. Samuel Brannan and his fellow merchants had successfully anchored the regional trade in their new city, limiting the likelihood of effective competition from other sites. California's distance from sources of manufactured goods meant that prices would be high, but nearby gold deposits guaranteed that miners would be able to pay for those supplies with a stable, valued resource. The gold rush had speeded up the operation of frontier urban speculation and heightened potential payoffs. According to the expectations of frontier urban speculators, Sacramento City should have been a classic case of the rewards to be reaped in city building.

In thousands of towns across the United States are stories of founding town fathers, men with foresight and economic good luck, who managed to first envision and then call forth quintessential American towns from the wilderness. Often the names of these founders are also the names of the town's elite families. In the face of these local histories and the strong economic functions of many of these towns in larger urban hierarchies, it is easy to make a connection between American town building and the development of nineteenth-century America's capitalistic economy. These men were the bold visionaries who created and then guided their towns toward stability, permanence, and significance in the American landscape.

Exactly how these founders shaped and guided their towns is often lost to history. Though each town sought to create an aura of permanence with self-promoting stories, details of this transition, especially accounts by those not included in this elite group, were rarely written. Sacramento's rise, however, was richly documented in letters, journals, and memoirs by hundreds of miners who visited the city. As many of these men turned their backs on mining to come to work in Sacramento, they continued to describe the town to relatives back home, many writing detailed accounts as an explanation to distant relatives for their delay in returning home after facing disappointments in the mines.

The activities of Sacramento's speculative founders provide an opportunity to see just how much control lay in the hands of the city's early businessmen.

Certainly these men had nearly every advantage they would have liked by the spring of 1849. And given the city's transient population, who were more prone to head for the gold fields during the city's first year than settle more or less permanently in an urban occupation, the city's founders had even more influence over their city.

Yet what might surprise one are the limitations to that influence, even under the optimal circumstances Sacramento's founders faced in 1849. Business was Sacramento City's raison d'être. Businessmen founded it for business pursuits. And in that lay the ultimate irony. For although the city could not have emerged without the vision, efforts, and commitments of its speculative founders, a question still remained as to whether the speculators' city was truly a city at all.

→—←

When it came to showing the potential of Sacramento as a moneymaking site, Samuel Brannan, of course, led the way. During the first few months of 1849, Brannan erected several buildings, some for his private use but more often to lease out to others. Brannan's interests in the new city were breathtaking and were larger and more diversified than those of anyone else in the city in that year. In the first issue of the *Placer Times,* Brannan advertised his re-formed company, "S. Brannan & Co.," as "Wholesale and Retail, Forwarding, Storage and Commission Merchants" and announced that he was selling a large and extensive assortment of dry goods, groceries, wines, liquors, ready-made clothing, fancy goods, and twenty horses and mares; that he was going to be auctioning off dry goods, groceries, liquors, clothing horses, and cattle; that he would also receive goods for storage and commission; that he would receive gold on deposit for safekeeping; that he had just established a new ferry at Mormon Island, a mining community a few miles outside of Sacramento; and that he wanted to hire ten men to chop wood.[1]

One week later Brannan added "Auctioneer" to his list of business enterprises and published the items that he would be auctioning off two days later. The long list of items is remarkably diverse, including sacks of cherries, saddles, tin plates, mirrors, a great variety of clothing and shoes, sickles, shovels, crowbars, hammocks, cotton and flannel sheets, bread, beans, beef, salmon, brandy, rum, gin, crockery, lace curtains, and shotguns. The eclectic list included items useful for mining as well as many whose use can only be guessed at, such as "7 large Chinese paintings" and "18 boxes of insects."[2]

This remarkable collection represented merely one auction, which itself was only one of several enterprises in which Samuel Brannan was engaged. On the same day that this list appeared in the newspaper, Brannan & Co. also advertised that they would now pay coins for placer gold. The exchange of placer gold for coin was a lucrative trade since the exact value of gold was not fixed, but fluctuated between $8 and $16 an ounce. Sacramento merchants usually paid only half of the gold's real value in coin.[3]

But Brannan's disparate list of goods also reflects the chaos of doing business in the early city. Situated far from the sources of goods and with limited communications to both suppliers and buyers, Sacramento merchants often found their world a jumble of mismatched opportunities. Dr. John Morse, after trying his hand at a number of business enterprises before returning to his profession as a physician, noted that "everything in and about the city indicated an overwhelming business, conducted without a particle of method and in such utter confusion and recklessness of manner as to make it impossible for a man to construct calculations that embraced more than the contingencies of a single day."[4] Morse's statement might contain a degree of bitterness due to several business failures, but his observation was not entirely inaccurate.

To begin with, would-be merchants faced the problem of finding a reliable source for goods. With little or no manufacturing in the city, nearly everything sold in Sacramento had to come from a great distance. Goods went to the highest bidder, often to the one who rowed out to and reached an incoming ship first. Men sometimes bid furiously against one another over newly arrived crates, the contents of which were unknown.

Even the relatively simple process of delivering supplies to the city was chaotic. Sacramento's waterfront became a maze of confusion. Ships coming up the Sacramento River from San Francisco tied up wherever they could find room. Shipping activity was concentrated in the area between I and J streets in 1849 but soon sprawled southward to I, J, K, L, and M streets. Not all ships tied up temporarily—frequently crews abandoned their ships to join the crowds of enthusiastic miners. Since city construction lagged so far behind population growth in the city, merchants put many of these ships to use as stores, warehouses, and hotels.[5] Bayard Taylor, a correspondent for the *New York Tribune,* caught the chaotic feeling of the waterfront best: "The forest of masts along the embarcadero more than rivaled the splendid growth of the soil. Boughs and spars were mingled together in striking contrast; the cables were fastened to the trunks and sinewy roots of the trees."[6] At times ships were lined two deep along the bank; by July 1849, at least twenty-four such vessels were tied up at Sacramento.[7]

The lack of adequate storage facilities and storefronts meant that supplies were often left in the open on the levee or in the streets, sometimes loosely covered with canvas, but just as often not. Again Taylor noted that the levee was a scene of intense business activity: "Signboards and figure heads were set up on shore, facing the levee, and galleys and deck cabins were turned out 'to grass,' leased as shops or occupied as dwellings. The aspect of the place, on landing, was decidedly more novel and picturesque than that of any other town in the country."[8] Due to the needs of the city, "city structures" extended out over the water, and permanent businesses lay between transitory ships—that is, until the shipowner decided to move his ship/business to another spot along the bank. To add further complications to the city's commerce, merchants in the early city moved their businesses from place to place, looking for a better site or simply trying to stay ahead of the property owners. Many merchants changed their locations weekly.[9]

In addition to the problems of securing goods and a place from which to sell them, Sacramento entrepreneurs also faced the problem of acquiring the capital needed to operate their large-scale businesses on the frontier's most distant edge. Ironically, despite the abundance of gold mined from the Sierra foothills and brought to Sacramento, California had no banks. As a response to the chaos of wildcat banking in the 1830s and 1840s, the provisional state constitution adopted in 1849 prohibited both the chartering of state banks and the development of corporation-backed commercial banks. This left banking in the hands of private individuals, who were not bound by law or governed by any regulating body.[10] Under these conditions, a few wealthy individuals gained tremendous influence over the city's economic development. Generally these men were merchants like Brannan who arrived in California early, often before the gold rush. They had amassed enough capital to be able to make investments in the new city. With their resources, they were also in an excellent position to change gold into currency, thus further entrenching their powerful position in the city's financial life. Few of these private bankers invested in the city economy unless they were also personally involved in the project. Throughout Sacramento's first two years, the city's largest speculators, in their capacity as merchant bankers, practically ruled the city.

Despite these obstacles, Sacramento's early merchants found ways to cope with the chaos. But rather than being able to impose their own practices on their city, successful businessmen were those who were flexible enough to change to meet the emerging demands of trade on the frontier.

Two companies that tended to dominate Sacramento City's economy early in 1849 were Hensley, Reading & Company and Priest, Lee & Company. Both operated mercantiles at Sutter's Fort in 1848, before Sacramento was founded. A comparison of their efforts shows the way these early merchants adapted to the changes brought about by the gold rush.

Hensley, Reading & Company had the most limited range of involvement in the city and also the shortest life. Advertising themselves as "Wholesale and Retail Dealers," they gave up their store in Sutter's Fort in the spring of 1849 and operated solely out of a storefront on Front Street, facing the Sacramento River.[11] Though engaged in some wholesaling and some land speculation, the company's advertised stock of goods was directed mainly toward individual miners. For example, in May 1849, they advertised the sale of "Oregon flour, salmon, biscuit, table salt, boots & shoes (a good article for the mines), woolen socks, powder, powder flakes, and percussion caps."[12] Selling supplies in quantities suited to individuals, Hensley, Reading & Company planned to make their fortune more as a retailer than as a wholesaler, catering to the thousands of anxious young men out to try their luck in the mines.

Hensley, Reading & Company, however, seems to have been in difficult straits from the beginning. The company soon discovered that "mining the miners" was not as lucrative as they had expected. Many would-be miners had brought much of their equipment from home and had provisioned themselves adequately in San Francisco. Even in Sacramento, Hensley, Reading & Company found they had to compete with other, smaller merchants. Once miners made it to the mining area, merchants in local mining camps met many of their needs, and in a pinch miners could live off the land, supplementing their provisions with game. Meanwhile the problems of uncertain sources of supplies and the financial turmoil of the new city played havoc with the company. On May 7, 1849, silent partner John A. Sutter, Jr., resigned from the company, a sign that the merchants had lost access to additional city lots for speculative purposes.[13] Two weeks later the company advertised that they were "compelled reluctantly to decline receiving any funds on deposit"[14] and two weeks later turned their company over to "Mssrs. Jones and Brown [who] will settle all accounts and hereafter conduct the business."[15] By the end of the year the company had ceased to exist.

Priest, Lee & Company had a somewhat more powerful and lasting impact on the city than Hensley, Reading & Company. Priest, Lee & Company advertised themselves in broader terms than their competitor. As "Wholesale and Retail Dealers in Dry Goods, Groceries, Liquors, and Provisions,"[16] Priest, Lee & Company seems to have aimed at a larger market than the hopeful miners passing through the city. Late in May 1849, the company offered for sale the following commodities:[17]

2,700 bbls flour
50 baskets of champagne
50 cases of champagne cider
70 cases of brandy
20 cases of port wine
50 bls of brandy and wine
45 bbls "Tennants" ale
69 boxes of superior raisins
& a large stock of general medicines.

Selling in such bulk, Priest, Lee & Company did not aim to equip individual miners, but to supply the growing number of saloons and bars in the city and the scattered mining camps. The company also opened a store in San Francisco and invested in banking and real estate speculation. Albert Priest withdrew from the firm in February 1850, but the firm continued doing business under the name of B. Lee and Cornwall.[18] By the summer of 1850, Barton Lee had become Sacramento's leading landholder, largest banker, and city treasurer. P. B. Cornwall, who came to California $8,000 in debt, managed in just eighteen months not only to pay off the debt, but to acquire a fortune of $640,000 through shipping, wholesaling, and real estate investment.[19]

Priest, Lee & Company more effectively capitalized on the gold rush, engaging in wholesaling rather than Hensley, Reading & Company's retailing. They also diversified their interests to include real estate speculation and banking and a larger area than just Sacramento. A comparison of these two early companies proves that simply being in the right place at the right time did not automatically ensure success in the frantic marketplace of the new city.

One merchant who was not in Sutter's Fort in 1848 but still succeeded was Roland Gelston. Captain of the bark *Whiton,* Gelston brought the first shipload of merchandise directly to Sacramento from the Atlantic coast, arriving in Sacramento from New York on May 1, 1849.[20] Immediately on arrival he threw open his ship's hold to sell his merchandise to expectant miners. The *Whiton*'s cargo directly anticipated the needs of the miners, containing "mining utensils, such as long-handled, round-pointed, steel-edged shovels, and steel-edged, square shovels, spades, &c; washing pans, for six to ten quarts each; cooking stoves, boots and shoes, ready made clothing, tin and hollow ware of every description, groceries, medicines, and a great lot of American garden seeds."[21]

While still in New York, Gelston had originally decided that he could grow rich mining the miners, as his cargo shows. And like Hensley, Reading & Company, Gelston directed his original sales directly toward individual miners passing through Sacramento. However, success in the city resulted more and more from wholesaling merchandise to city-based businesses and mining camp entre-preneurs rather than from the sale of items to be used exclusively in the mines. Two months later Gelston reinvested the profits from the sale of his mining equipment into the purchase of the entire cargo of another newly arrived ship, the schooner *Angelona.* Gelston now found himself in the business of selling foodstuffs to restaurants, boardinghouses, and saloons. His advertisement in the *Placer Times* listed the sale of "champagne in cases and baskets; canvass houses of prime quality; pilot bread; assorted pickles—half gallon, quarts, and pints; Sickel's bitters; Swain's panacea; Bailey's tonic mixture for fever and ague;

lemon and ginger syrup; lard; cheese; gold and platform scales; bandanas; tea in small packages; also a great variety of preserved meats, soups, carrots, lobster, clams, and mutton in six, two and one pound cans; rice; fruits; Worcestershire sauce; and a large assortment of mining tools, large blankets, &c."[22]

Although much of the merchandise would still be useful to miners, Gelston now considered the needs of city vendors over the miners'. The mention of mining equipment, almost as an afterthought and without the great detail provided for the earlier shipment, indicates how far he had come in two months from dealing directly with miners to dealing instead with the region's smaller businessmen. The following month Gelston's transformation was complete. In another advertisement, Gelston listed another great assortment of goods, all applicable for city use rather than for use in mining. Coffee, looking glasses, crockery, lumber and nails, and playing cards have completely preempted Gelston's mining equipment, which is not mentioned at all. And in a separate ad, Gelston announced his sale of drugs and medicines, "together with scales and weights, making a complete assortment for a drug store."[23] Gelston the retailer had become Gelston the wholesaler. His goods no longer supported miners in the gold fields, but businessmen—restaurateurs, saloon keepers, and physicians. In the process of mining the miners, Gelston found constructing a city much more profitable.

Supporting the city in other ways could also make fortunes. Transporting people between Sacramento and San Francisco proved lucrative to some Sacramento investors. Several of Sacramento's early merchants, including Hensley and Reading, bought ships, which could be easily acquired among the abandoned ships in San Francisco Bay, primarily to transport people to Sacramento. Passage by riverboat or schooner between the two cities ranged from $16 to $25. Even more profit could be made hauling goods to the new city. Schooners capable of carrying 50 to 150 tons from San Francisco to Sacramento charged anywhere from 200 to 3,000 percent of the cost of transportation. The king of Sacramento's teamsters was John S. Fowler. Using ox teams and paying his teamsters $200 to $250 per month, Fowler set up a virtual monopoly in freighting between Sacramento and the mines. Fowler's prices were exorbitant. Typical was the cost of shipment from Sacramento to Coloma, the site of Marshall's discovery of gold, about forty-five miles east of Sacramento: $1 per pound, $2,000 per ton.[24]

In this way Sacramento began to grow. Looking for a place to sell merchandise to the miners, a handful of merchants laid out Sacramento merely to have a place to operate their businesses profitably. Quickly surrounded by other businessmen with the same idea, the original merchants had by that time accumulated the necessary capital and trade connections to deal in great quantities of merchandise

and thus began wholesaling their goods to the newer local merchants. T
sales came to depend on local retailers and businessmen, the more th(
of the city's founding merchants grew tied to the development of Sacramen…

The power of these great speculators over the city was immense. Not only did
they support mining operations in the field, but they controlled the flow and
cost of goods into the city, holding the city's economic lifeline in their hands.
As the town's material suppliers, bankers, and landholders, their interest—or
lack of it—could drastically affect the city's fortunes for good or ill. The decision
of a speculator such as Barton Lee or Roland Gelston to extend credit to a
newcomer could mean the difference between a local business succeeding or
failing. During the first half of 1849, the city founders' entrepreneurial growth
defined the new city. In the struggle to establish Sacramento, the power of the
founding merchants was unchallengeable. Sacramento's speculative founding
fathers made up the city's earliest, smallest, and most powerful class.

→--←

Identifying a group of merchants as an elite class in a mercantile town might
appear questionable. Frontier merchants competed among themselves and seem
to have risen and fallen so rapidly as to preclude the formation of a stable class. In
Sacramento, as in other instant cities of the mining frontier, everyone speculated.
Speculating involved practically every city resident, from a powerful merchant
seeking to corner the market in a particular commodity, to a barkeeper laying
in a supply of whiskey for his thirsty customers, to the transient miner, staking
all his remaining funds on the purchase of a pick and a pan before heading for
the gold fields. Speculating, buying goods in the hopes that they would produce
a profitable return in the future, underlay practically every transaction in
Sacramento. In essence, *speculating* was only another word for *gambling*, and
everyone in Sacramento gambled.

However, the city's speculative founders were different from the rest of the
population. They speculated on a grander scale. Unlike the typical resident, who
gambled his often meager savings on a limited investment, these great speculators invested tens, even hundreds of thousands of dollars. The scale of such
investments had dramatic repercussions in the city. If the city's speculative
establishment succeeded, Sacramento would grow, despite the obstacles of its
location; if they failed, Sacramento itself could fail.

The scale of investment set these great speculators off from the rest of the
population in many ways. Generally they viewed the city not as a home but as an
investment. Because of their diversified investments and the usually tremendous
profits that they reaped, the great speculators had a margin of safety in their
enterprises that ordinary city residents lacked. Unlike the smaller merchants,

barkeepers, and miners, who generally depended on the success of only one or two enterprises for their survival, the city's founding speculators could shift profits and losses over a wide variety of investments. They could more easily withstand investments that went sour than the average city resident.

These differences made the city's speculative founders a separate class from the rest of the city population. For convenience, we can refer to this group as the "great speculators." Defining their number is an exercise in rough approximations. Real estate investments can be used as one guide. According to the 1850 U.S. census, roughly one-fourth of the city's residents owned at least some real estate.[25] However, the majority of these men owned only a single town lot or shared in the ownership of a single lot with partners. To refine this figure further, we can consider as a speculator anyone who owned more than two city lots. The value of town lots changed dramatically during 1849, with some lots selling as high as $8,000.[26]

With this as a rough gauge, we can identify speculators as those with real estate totaling more than $8,000. The census listed exactly one hundred such men. Only forty-two held real estate valued at least $20,000, and their names also appear prominently in the city as government officials, merchants, and lawyers. If figures are calculated for speculators who invested at least $50,000, only twenty-one men appear on the list of the 1850 federal census.[27]

Other indicators can help determine who belonged to the class of Sacramento's great speculators. The city and county's first tax rolls, from 1850, suggest who engaged in large-scale speculating. As expected, the data provided by the census and the tax rolls correlate fairly well. Another source also points toward the city's great speculators. In the winter of 1849–50, a number of Sacramento residents began to protest the rampant speculation in city lots that had put land ownership in the city far beyond the means of most residents. Organizing as the Settlers' Association, these residents soon voiced their opposition to the great speculators. In the summer of 1850, the Settlers' Association published a list of twenty-five individuals and organizations, "men of remarkable principles," it sarcastically called them, whom they accused of unfair and illegal land speculation.[28]

The Settlers' Association list also bears a sharp correlation to the census and tax roll lists. The Settlers' Association list, furthermore, underlines that Sacramento residents identified the great speculators as a separate class who displayed an attitude toward property and business principles different from attitudes held by the majority of city residents. Though the list of Sacramento's great speculators shifted over time, their numbers were small, they were seen as distinct by the rest of the population, and they held tremendous power in the creation and development of the city.

We can also begin to grasp some of the characteristics of the class that made it so remarkable to the rest of Sacramento's residents. As might be expected, the city's landholders were largely merchants, traders, or speculators. Government officials' extensive real estate holdings underscore the close relationship between the great speculators and the city's most powerful leaders. And if the occupation by which Sacramento residents classified themselves is any indication, Sacramento's great speculators, by listing their occupations as real estate broker, speculator, general land agent, or merchant or by imperiously declaring their occupation as "none," recognized themselves as a class different from the rest of the city's working population.[29]

Census data further indicate personal characteristics of the great speculators. Among the great speculators, New Englanders and East Coast migrants predominate. Perhaps not surprisingly, these real estate speculators tended to be older than the general population, with an average age of thirty-seven, as opposed to the citywide average of thirty-one. Though these figures are not conclusive, they do suggest that Sacramento's great speculators were predominantly Yankee merchants, probably with some prior experience as speculators.[30]

For the great speculators, success was measured in a ledger book. Individual success, measured by money and property, translated into social ranking. By their standards, the power of Sacramento's great speculators concentrated in their hands because they had built up the physical site, constructed its buildings, and laid out its streets. By risking their capital on Sacramento, rather than Sutterville or some other site, they had caused the town to grow. The fabulous profits reaped from commodity trading and land speculation were their just rewards.

As in any society, Sacramento's self-conscious elite found ways to make others aware of their exalted status. The sense of distinction that the great speculators felt women conveyed in the predominantly male city can be seen in their attempts to invite as many women as possible to their balls and parties, while keeping these parties exclusively for their own set as opposed to open to the general public. The first wedding in Sacramento, for example, shows how far such distinction was extended. At the wedding between Colonel E. J. C. Kewen, one of the great speculators, and the daughter of Dr. T. J. White, also a great speculator, "there was quite a party of invited guests," recalled Dr. W. B. H. Dodson. "There were present about a dozen ladies. . . . The ladies were dressed elegantly. Miss White, the bride, was one of the handsomest and finest looking ladies I ever saw." To prove their own distinction, the males invited to the wedding were also required to dress appropriately. "The gentlemen were sorely troubled for proper dress suits, as such things had not found their way to the New Eldorado," Dodson continued. "I was possessed of several suits I had

worn while attending college and medical lectures. I hauled out old trunks and
fitted a vest to one, a coat to another, pants here and boots there until we finally
succeeded by exchanging around, so as to make a pretty respectable appearance
for those days, in which all callings and professions wore flannel."[31] Respectability
thus translated into clothing and marriage.

In April 1850, when noted pianist and composer Henri Herz gave a series of
concerts in the city, the great speculators made sure the event would differentiate
between the city's elite and the common population. Though admission to the
concert was only $4, roughly the same as admission to the city's theater, no one
was admitted without a "biled shirt," and as *Sacramento Transcript* editor Samuel
Upham noted, "The audience was not large but very select."[32] To further celebrate
their distinction from the rest of the population, Herz was then invited to give a
private concert to the city's finest. As Upham observed, "At the conclusion of the
concert, Mr. Herz and several of the audience repaired, by invitation, to the cottage
of Mr. P. B. Cornwall, where they 'tripped the light fantastic toe' until a late hour.
. . . During the evening, Mr. Cornwall presented to Mr. Herz a magnificent
gold watch-chain, composed entirely of specimens artistically linked together."[33]

The great speculators' grandest attempt at distinction came with completion
of the new Pacific Theatre near the end of April 1850. The city's great speculators
staged a "Grand Soiree" to celebrate the occasion. According to Upham, the
ball was "the grandest affair of its kind that had ever taken place in California.
In order to make the event more attractive, invitations were extended to ladies
residing in San Francisco and Stockton, several of whom were present."[34]
Through this and similar affairs the great speculators drew up a consensus as to
who belonged among the city's elites and who did not. Storekeeper Franklin
Buck wrote home to his sister that "white vests have gone up and kids [gloves]
are in great demand. One of the committee told me that they had issued invitations to *one hundred ladies*."[35] "Sacramento City put on her best bib and tucker
in honor of this affair," Upham recalled. "Mr. E. C. Kemble, one of the editors
of the *Alta California,* came up from San Francisco to attend the soiree, but on
examining his apparel, found that his pantaloons were a little too seedy to pass
regulation muster. His 'biled shirt' and swallow-tail coat were unexceptionable,
and to complete his *tout ensemble,* I loaned him my best black cassimeres,
which had been laid away in lavender since leaving Philadelphia."[36]

Having attained economic dominance and social distinction within the city,
Sacramento's founders also sought to control it politically. The task of creating
a truly effective city government, however, was formidable. The city lacked
both clear political leaders and a legitimate framework for government. In this

instance, the problem lay not with the city's founders, but in the U.S. Congress. With the end of the Mexican War in February 1848, both Mexican law and military rule ended in California. Congress then got to the work of organizing California as a territory and providing for a territorial government. However, Congress quickly became deadlocked in a fight over whether or not to extend slavery into the vast regions newly acquired from Mexico.

The congressional delay in granting California a legal government would last until September 1850. City governments are based on charters granted to them by state or territorial governments. Without a territorial government, no government in the city would be legally official. In the fall of 1848, when the congressional deadlock over the extension of slavery into the newly acquired territories of the Far West showed no signs of a quick solution, Missouri senator Thomas Hart Benton published an open letter to "the People of California" suggesting how to resolve the legal conundrum. "Having no lawful government, nor lawful officers, you can have none that can have authority over you except by your own consent. Its sanctions must be in the will of the majority. I recommend you to meet in convention—provide for a cheap and simple government—and take care of yourselves, until Congress can provide for you."[37]

Benton's advice seemed both practical and simple to follow. He had given similar advice to American settlers in Oregon, and at the time there seemed little reason why the same advice would not work in California. After all, California in 1848 was on the far western rim of the continent, settlers going to California had been relatively few in number, and nearly all who went to California sought farmsteads. A small, relatively homogeneous population, spread across a large area, should be able to make do with a "cheap and simple government" until the congressional crisis ended. Benton, however, had not anticipated the gold rush. One year after his letter appeared, California had attracted a vast and diverse population, engaged in the frantic pursuit for gold, an activity for which the invaders had little practical, legal, or moral experience. Still, California's gold rush residents quickly took Benton's advice to heart. Peter Burnett summed up the feelings of most Americans in California during the fall of 1848, writing years afterward that "we were satisfied that the military government, existing during and in consequence of the war, had ceased. We knew nothing of the laws of Mexico, and had no means of learning. . . . We were of the opinion that we had the right to establish a de facto government, to continue until superseded by some legitimate organization."[38] However, given the dramatic conditions of the gold rush, California's de facto government could be neither cheap nor simple.

Most Californians were more concerned with gold mining than government building in 1848, 1849, and 1850. And the transience of most Californians in these years would have made effective organizing extremely difficult for any government. California politicians who set out to create a state government in these years realized that their tenure would be temporary and subject to review. Their only real authority derived from following established American legal and political practices as closely as their anomalous situation allowed. However, such a stance carried with it a crucial flaw. It assumed that all citizens would agree on what constituted established American legal and political practices, during a dramatic event for which there was no precedent. If Californians disagreed over their government's interpretation of legal and political practices, California's political leaders would find themselves on very thin ice.

Shortly after acquiring their land from Sutter, Jr., in the spring of 1849, Sacramento's largest merchants outlined a rough government for Sacramento County, creating the office of sheriff and providing for one alcalde, whose jurisdiction would be from the coast range to the Sierra, encompassing all of the Sacramento Valley. Though Sacramento's two officers would have been hard-pressed to cover the entire area they claimed, city founders undoubtedly hoped that by claiming to police such a great area, their city would become its political focus.[39] Sacramento City's first government came from essentially self-appointed officials, whose jurisdiction at first reached far beyond the city limits. Accounts of the offices and officeholders for this period are incomplete and contradictory. J. Horace Culver, in compiling the *1851 Sacramento City Directory*, noted that Sacramento had no organized government until August 1849.[40] Other accounts describe local elections but often disagree in detail. John Morse, in compiling the city's first history, noted that elections were held at Sutter's Fort in the fall of 1848 to choose two alcaldes for the district.[41] Burnett recalled a "public meeting" held in Sacramento in early January 1849 that elected a first magistrate and a district recorder.[42] Morse also described a meeting of Sacramento residents "under a broad spreading oak at the foot of I Street" in the spring of 1849 that either drafted or approved a few simple laws and offices for the district, including a sheriff and an alcalde whose jurisdiction would cover the entire Sacramento Valley.[43]

Whatever laws and offices were created in these early days, certain names were continually associated with each report. According to Burnett, who was named president of the Provisional Government of the Territory of California on January 6, 1849, a five-man committee was appointed to draw up a territorial government, made up of Samuel Brannan, John S. Fowler, John Sinclair, P. B. Reading, and Barton Lee.[44] Morse noted that John S. Fowler was also one of the two alcaldes elected in the fall of 1848 for the area. When the district laws were drafted in the spring of 1849, the board of commissioners was made up of Samuel Brannan, Peter Slater, James King of William, Henry Cheever, M. M.

McCarver, John McDougal, Barton Lee, William Petit, William Carpenter, Charles Southard, and John S. Fowler.[45] The Sacramento *Placer Times* also included the names of Jacob Rink Snyder and Samuel Hensley.[46] Though the exact composition of these various committees is uncertain, the prominence of the city's great speculators in the early government of the region is unmistakable.

The presence of these men occupying political positions in early Sacramento should not be surprising. Sacramento City was their investment, and they certainly sought to protect it. However, other factors most likely propelled these men into these positions. In most cases, Sacramento City was not their only concern; some of these men, such as Samuel Brannan, had wide-ranging investments and thus were interested in helping to shape the political and economic climate of the territory at a broad level. Others, like Peter Burnett, had political ambitions that were equal to or more important than their economic investments and saw the formation of California government as a chance to fulfill these dreams. Furthermore, at the time of these "elections" and "public meetings," as Morse and Burnett termed them, the population of Sacramento was quite small. As of April 1, 1849, the population of Sacramento and the surrounding area was no larger than 150.[47] In these early months the great speculators may have been the only people on the scene with either the time or the resources to serve in any governmental body.

During the first half of 1849, the city itself received little attention. With a small population and the commerce of the gold rush to be looked after, the city needed only a minimum of policing or regulation. The surveyed city plan provided a guideline for physical development, and the lone sheriff and alcalde managed disputes effectively enough that no serious problems from this period were recorded in either newspaper reports or travelers' accounts. Transients made the city streets hectic, but most cheerfully expected to be wealthy after a short visit to the mines and so remained largely peaceful.[48] If the city had little direct government in its early months, it needed very little.

By the middle of the summer, however, Sacramento City had grown large enough to have serious problems that needed more close attention. Business enterprises were growing increasingly destructive of the overall city economy. Disillusioned miners and early overland trail parties were beginning to arrive in the city, hinting at the human flood likely to be channeled into the city in the fall and the sickness and poverty that would accompany them. The time was ripe for the creation of a city government. When a territory-wide election was called on August 1, 1849, to elect delegates to attend a constitutional convention, Sacramento took advantage of the event to elect a formal city council.[49]

The election results reflected the advance organization of the city's great speculators. As the men most responsible for drafting the state and district's laws and as the most prominent men of the city at the time, their election to the as yet undefined city government met with little opposition. The nine council members came almost exclusively from the city's leading speculators.

⤙⸺⤚

The confidence with which the newly elected council set about its business suggests that the councilmen did not yet understand the limited authority that their government held. Perhaps the smooth successes of government building on the state and district levels suggested that the same authority could be wielded at the municipal level. Perhaps they did not foresee the problems that approaching overland parties and wintering miners would bring with them to the city. In any event, an energy and single-minded vision that would not be repeated in city government for over a year marked their first fifty days in office.

The councilmen moved swiftly to enact a series of policies that revealed their vision of society and Sacramento City. Though these policies apparently had no master plan or stated, comprehensive direction, both the actions that they took and those that they ignored perfectly illustrate the great speculators' vision of their world. Meeting on the night of the election itself, the councilmen quickly adopted a resolution, put forth by P. B. Cornwall, that named four council committees: (1) on wharves and streets, (2) on finances, (3) to procure a permanent meeting room, and (4) to draft ordinances for police, trash, health, and general city regulations.[50] These committees, and the priority and attention given to each, in large part spelled out the council's, and the great speculators', plan for city development.

The committee on wharves and streets dealt with the council's greatest concern: the business interests of the city's largest businessmen. Two issues were treated directly by the committee: the exclusive rights of the great speculators to the city's waterfront and the unfair business competition that ship merchants offered to these same speculators. No other issues absorbed the council's energies over the next few months as these two. After establishing a committee to draft the council's bylaws, this was the first committee the council named, the first to report in each of the following meetings, and most often the source of the only business that the council took up at its meetings.

The problems of the waterfront largely comprised a series of nuisances of varying degree, which taken together probably appeared more troublesome than they were in reality. Since the embarcadero was a natural gathering place for city residents, auctioneers, street merchants, and transients and a busy spot for unloading and temporary storage of ships' cargoes, Front Street displayed a cluttered, chaotic appearance that disturbed the great speculators. Early in the city's history, as the first lots were being sold or distributed to the city's founders, the city's early merchants had convinced Sutter, Jr., to deed to them not just the title to the surveyed city lots, but also to the exclusive rights to Front Street where their lots adjoined that street. Control of the city's waterfront obviously gave the great speculators a tremendous advantage in controlling wholesale goods in the city. According to the terms of these deeds, although the city retained ownership of Front Street itself, city residents would have access to the waterfront only at the cross streets. Owners of lots facing Front Street, therefore, could virtually control the unloading of ships in the city and could more easily bargain for shipments than other city residents.

In practice, however, the great speculators seemed unable to control the waterfront. Competing city merchants who tried to buy and sell ships' cargoes from the waterfront ignored the great speculators' protests with impunity. Furthermore, the great throngs of people who gathered on Front Street daily impeded the orderly unloading of ships and, the great speculators undoubtedly suspected, pilfered from their own goods temporarily waiting on the levee. The degree to which these problems really hurt the great speculators is unknown, and it is possible that the clearance of the waterfront began for the great speculators as merely a first step toward gaining some sense of control over their wide-ranging city investments.

Yet to the council's surprise and growing consternation, Front Street remained a cluttered, chaotic mess. On August 21, the council passed a resolution to have the sheriff clear the waterfront of all obstructions if citizens did not remove their own materials within ten days.[51] Four days later the committee on wharves and streets reported its findings, declaring that the obstructions on Front Street constituted a public hazard.[52] Five days later the council hired James C. Zabriskie as legal counsel and devised a series of stiff fines for failure to remove items from the waterfront. Anyone leaving goods on the levee would be fined $100 for the first offense, $250 for the second, and $500 and confinement for the third.[53] Four days later the sheriff reported to the council that he had had no serious problems in clearing the levee, though he had granted some property owners extensions on the deadline.[54] But within two and a half weeks the waterfront was as cluttered as ever.

The council's attempts to clear the waterfront almost immediately met with resistance. On August 30, at the same meeting in which the penalty fines were drafted, a protest letter signed by a number of Sacramento residents was presented to the council, arguing against the council's determination to clear the levee.[55] And while the *Placer Times* endorsed the council's attempts to clear the waterfront as a public service, it cautioned the council against doing so merely to promote the interests of the city's great speculators in the most direct language. "None of your pouncing on the poor man," it warned, "who has pitched his tent to dispose of a few articles to enable him to get to the mines while you let the more wealthy use the public grounds without tax or molestations."[56] Control of the waterfront, however, remained a key issue for the council in the fall of 1849. When a citizens' group petitioned the council to establish a public marketplace on the levee, the council simply tabled the petition and began drafting a more detailed ordinance to regulate the waterfront instead.[57]

In its attempts to control the waterfront, the city's great speculators hoped to gain some measure of control over the chaotic nature of the city's economy. Their concern for ship-based merchants on the waterfront reflected the same concerns. By mid-1849 dozens of ships were arriving at the city, tying up to the bank, and throwing open their holds as floating stores. For these ship-based merchants, undercutting city merchants was simple. One city merchant complained in a letter to the *Placer Times* that he had to pay a 15 percent surcharge to have his goods unloaded in San Francisco and another 10 percent charge to have them reloaded on a launch for Sacramento, while ship captains had none of these expenses. He had also paid $8,000 for a town lot and had paid to have a building erected in which to do business as well. Under these conditions, he claimed, he had no way to compete with ship captains, who undersold him every time.[58] Though the editors of the *Placer Times* disagreed with the anonymous letter writer about the competition ship merchants offered city businessmen, the council quickly condemned the practice and resolved to establish a tax on merchants operating out of ships tied up at the waterfront.[59]

The council's finance committee, like the committee on wharves and streets, was primarily concerned with regulating city businesses. Unlike the council's actions in regard to Front Street and ship merchants, this committee worked more slowly and quietly. Throughout August and September committee members worked to draft a detailed listing of business licenses, setting different rates for each type of business within the city. Part of the committee's hesitation was based on the council's questionable authority to levy taxes. Word of the council's intentions may also have spread, prompting some businessmen to threaten resistance to any business fees imposed by the council. Yet whatever the reason for its caution, the committee's licensing schedule reflects the great speculators' concerns with bringing order to the city's chaotic business dealings.[60]

The business of the council's third committee, designated to find a permanent meeting hall for the council, indirectly indicates the council's sense of itself. Throughout the fall and winter the council met at a number of locations, though most often at the St. Louis Exchange, a restaurant and saloon that hosted a variety of city political and social meetings in the winter of 1849–50.[61] Though the council did not find a permanent meeting hall during these months, it did manage to take care of its own in another manner. Through the winter, turnover within the council was high. Each time a council seat opened up, the council filled the vacancy itself rather than holding a public election. The council, originally composed of nine elected officials, filled eight vacancies and appointed twenty unelected city officials between August 1, 1849, and April 1, 1850, when the council was replaced by a new city government.[62] In most cases, nominations for these positions were supplied directly by noncouncil members such as Samuel Brannan and John S. Fowler.[63] Expedience may have dictated this policy, but the effect was to keep the council firmly under the influence of the city's great speculators.

As for the council's fourth committee, delegated to drafting ordinances for police, trash, health, and general city ordinances, there is no mention in the minutes of any activity on its part until the middle of November, when external forces compelled the council to take a broader view of its duties.[64] Throughout the early days of its administration, the council single-mindedly pursued actions that would organize and regulate the dealings of the city's businessmen while leaving the city's largest wholesalers and investors a free hand. Petitions by citizens' groups and thinly veiled accusations from the *Placer Times* were ignored while the city's great speculators dominated both the issues that the council addressed and the membership of the council itself. Issues of public health, safety, and security rarely even made the council's agenda.

›－‹

Given the precarious authority of California governance in 1849, one should not be surprised that this early city council was in for a prompt and rude awakening. Fifty days after it took office, the council discovered the limits of its authority. On August 21, the council named a committee of its members to draft a formal city constitution. On September 8, the committee presented its draft of the city charter to the council. Over the next week the charter was discussed and amended. On September 12, three hundred copies of the charter were printed and distributed throughout the city, and the council announced that an election would be held on September 20 to ratify it. To the shock of the council, however, the charter was defeated, with nearly 60 percent of the electorate voting against it.[65]

The cause of the charter's defeat is difficult to determine. No copy of this original charter now exists.[66] Several later historians have suggested that the city's gamblers, who opposed the establishment of a city court system, caused the defeat. As one historian noted, "Up to this time there had been no court except that of the alcalde, which, while expeditious, was costly in dispensing justice. The people therefore shunned litigation and this lawless state just suited the gamblers."[67] Without the original charter to examine, this argument is difficult to defend. An amended charter, submitted by the council two weeks after the original charter was defeated, makes no mention of a court system for the city.[68]

Other possibilities for the charter's defeat, however, suggest themselves. The council's refusal even to consider making the embarcadero a public marketplace occurred only five days before the charter was made public. The bulk of the amended charter specified the powers to be vested in the council. Possibly the defeat of the charter was a vote of no confidence in the council members rather than a defeat of the charter itself. The council's actions immediately after the election also implicate the battle that had been brewing over the clearance of the waterfront. On receiving news of the charter's defeat, the council met at Sutter's Fort, a curious meeting place since at the time it was in essence outside the developed city. At this meeting the council conducted only two matters of business: it passed a resolution, reaffirming its support of its earlier resolution to clear the waterfront, and then named a committee to begin drafting a formal series of ordinances that would secure the council's right to regulate the embarcadero. The meeting then adjourned, and the council refused to conduct any official business for over a week.[69]

The charter may also have been defeated because it gave the council the right to license city businesses and levy taxes on city residents. The imposition of taxes and business licenses, a part of the amended city charter, was not popular in the city. Furthermore, the broadside detailing the amended charter and announcing the date for the new referendum on the charter noted that citizens would be given the choice to vote either "Charter" or "No Charter" and should "also express their opinions as to the power of granting licenses: 'License' or 'No License.'"[70] Possibly the council tried to use this vote to lay the foundation for their authority to license city businesses. But they may also have included the vote on licensing to appease voters who had vetoed the original charter.

The defeat of the charter was the first clear indication that the council would need strong public support if it wished to exercise any meaningful authority in the city. Yet the city's great speculators did not share their control of city government easily. Instead council members simply boycotted council meetings. Between the defeat of the original charter and the referendum on the amended charter, eight council meetings were called, but five adjourned without a quorum. Of the three meetings that were held, the first, as already noted, met only to reinforce the council's determination to clear the waterfront, the second to draft a broadside admonishing city residents to approve the forthcoming amended charter, and the third merely to adopt the amended charter and have it submitted to the public.[71]

The tone of the council's broadside, its stubborn resistance to give in on the issue of the waterfront, and its refusal to meet after the defeat of the original charter suggest that the council was completely unresponsive to public disapproval of its actions. The public broadside, published ten days after the charter's defeat, condescendingly demanded that city residents take a more reasonable attitude toward the charter. "We presented to you a Charter for your consideration," the broadside announced, "which you have seen fit to reject. . . . Since then we have been unable to determine what the good people of this city desire us to do; and being Republicans in principle, and having every confidence in the ability of the people to govern themselves, we again request the residents [to assemble] . . . then and there to declare what they wish the City Council to do. If you wish us to act under the Mexican Laws now in force, however inapplicable they may be to our condition, then we must do the best we can; if you have objections to particular features of the Charter, then strike out the objectionable features and insert such as you desire."[72]

The broadside ended on what appeared to be a conciliatory note, but with a dark implication. "The Health and Safety of our City," it warned, "demand immediate action on your part, for in our primitive condition and in the absence of Legislative authority we can, in fact, be of no service to you without your confidence and consent."[73] The final phrase echoed Benton's letter to Californians one year earlier, but the first part of the sentence carried an implicit threat. The council's concern for health and safety and its reference to the primitive conditions of the city are most striking when compared to the council's previous lack of action in these areas and its refusal to meet after the charter's defeat. The combination of boycotted meetings and the patronizing tone of the broadside suggests that the council implicitly threatened to let the baser side of the city's population have their way if the new charter was not passed. Possibly agents for the city's great speculators even precipitated rowdy incidents during these three weeks to dramatize their point. This was the same group, after all, that had only a few months before destroyed McDougal's stock of merchandise in their efforts to make Sacramento dominant over Sutterville.

During the three weeks between the defeat of the charter and the referendum on the amended charter, council members and the city's great speculators established a new political party. The Law and Order Party initially sought the passage of the city charter. As a political organization, the party seems to have been more informal than the title suggests. The reasons for this were straightforward. The great speculators, while holding similar views on business goals and large-scale investments in the city, were still competitors. They could and often did form quick and strong partnerships in a number of business operations, especially when the required capital and potential risks were too high for a single investor to contemplate. Despite these associations, however, the great speculators rarely joined in long-lasting associations that did not promote a profitable bottom line. More interested in business than in community, the great speculators organized the Law and Order Party as another short-term, cooperative partnership with the limited objective of improving their business dealings within the city, in this case by securing the authority of their own, handpicked council. Furthermore, while citizen dissatisfaction with the council was clearly growing, no organized opposition to the Law and Order Party existed. If the party did not meet regularly or create a comprehensive policy vision that would secure the loyalty of a majority of the population, it was because there was as yet no need to do so.

On October 14, city residents voted on the amended charter, and the following day the council announced the passage of the charter, by slightly over 60 percent of the electorate.[74] The charter victory, however, suggests that the Law and Order Party may have done more to influence the election than scold city residents and threaten civil chaos. The number of people who voted against the first charter was 527; nearly the same number, 513, voted to defeat the charter during the second election. The difference this time was in the number of votes cast for the charter: 381 in the first election, 808 in the second. John Morse credited the passage of the charter with the work of the Law and Order Party in securing new voters for the second election. It seems unlikely that the effort of the Law and Order Party did not also rouse at least a few more anticharter voters as well. Ballot box stuffing may have finally secured the Law and Order Party's victory.[75]

The victory ultimately proved to be costly. Two days after its passage, a petition was filed with the city council, protesting the legality of the charter election.[76] Though the council minutes show the council gave the petition little attention, the *Placer Times* also published notices that a number of citizens were protesting the illegal basis of the city's new charter. The leading spokesman against the charter appears to have been James C. Zabriskie, who after serving briefly as legal counsel to the council had resigned in a bitter dispute over his fee.[77] Opposition to the charter, however, was not based on any alleged irregularities in the vote count, but on the legal basis of the charter itself. City charters, Zabriskie noted, were articles of incorporation granted cities by state government; they could not simply be created by cities themselves.[78] Therefore, the council's charter was a meaningless piece of paper, conveying no authority to the council whatsoever.

Zabriskie's argument, although technically correct, ignored the practical problem of providing a viable government for the city in the midst of a growing sense of civic crises. By the middle of October, Sacramento was growing by hundreds of people daily, many of them poor and sick from the long overland trail. The growing population pressed the city's ability to provide food and shelter in sufficient quantity to stave off disaster. The chaos of the city's streets was reaching its height as wintering miners and overlanders began erecting tents on any spot of ground they chose. Few residents joined Zabriskie in undermining the legal position of the council, since by the lawyer's reasoning no government would have been legal. Protests of the charter's illegality thus faded quickly in the next few weeks as city residents spent more time trying to sort out the physical and social chaos that threatened to engulf them.

Zabriskie's argument, however, was not forgotten, and it had a powerful if tacit effect on both the council and city residents. From this point on the council moved much more cautiously, picking its fights with care and weighing its actions against possible public reaction. The council moved forward with its efforts to clear the waterfront and regulate business through licensing requirements. But its actions show a new concern with forging at least a limited agreement with city merchants in regard to licensing requirements and fees, debating the licensing schedules at length over two months before enacting them, and a willingness to consider licensing exceptions and exemptions for prominent enterprising residents both before and after the passage of the licensing schedule.[79]

❯ — ❮

Sacramento's great speculators held significant power in the early months of city development, but their ability to shape their city was limited. Their economic might could build business empires in wholesaling and transportation, but the unsettled conditions of the gold rush frontier still left them vulnerable to disaster. Social prestige seemed to follow economic success, but it was a prestige that turned inward rather than outward, shaping the great speculators' attitudes about themselves more than developing the city's cultural foundations. Political offices in 1849 could still be defined and used to advance business agendas, but the basis of that power was uncertain and growing increasingly contested by the fall of the year.

Walking through the streets of the new and booming city, a great speculator such as Samuel Brannan would likely believe that he had succeeded at last in capitalizing on the great frontier urban boom. With the lucrative profits of his city-building ventures in his strongbox and the apparently never ending stores of gold being uncovered daily in the foothills, he could look at the rising city as both a symbol of his entrepreneurial talents and a promise of future greatness.

Unfortunately, there is no record of what one of these city founders felt when they walked through the streets of their golden city. But one account does exist that might provide a provocative insight into the way early Sacramento City was viewed by its original residents.

During the first week of May 1849, Edward Kemble wrote an editorial extolling the virtues of his new home, Sacramento City. Since arriving in California, Samuel Brannan's former assistant had done well. Though only twenty years old, Kemble was a capable journalist and editor. Himself the son of an editor, Kemble had worked since 1845 in Brannan's New York City print shop. Though not a Mormon, Kemble went with Brannan to California in 1846, where he continued working for Brannan as a printer. In April 1847, Brannan placed Kemble in charge of his new San Francisco newspaper, the *California Star*. Over the next two years, Kemble managed to buy the paper from Brannan and eventually became editor of the *California Star and Californian* and the *Alta California*. When demand for a local paper arose in Sacramento City, Kemble responded by establishing the *Placer Times* in the city in April 1849.[80]

In the paper's second issue, using the effusive style of frontier town boosters everywhere, Kemble described Sacramento as a place of "unexampled prosperity" and predicted "sustained growth and eventual greatness."[81] Yet Kemble's attempt at boosterism quickly became awkward. His difficulty consisted of coming up with an authentic yet accurate description of the new city. He began by calling the city a "town" but then tried to elevate the town into a true city. "Sacramento *City* is no misnomer, indeed,"[82] he wrote, but trapped by that title, he soon became entangled searching for a definition of *city* that would cover Sacramento. Kemble's dilemma sprang from his uncomfortable sense that Sacramento City lacked something subtle but essential for the development of a successful city. Kemble's simple list of the city's principal structures—"two ships tied up at the waterfront, approximately forty stores, a hotel, printing office, bakery, blacksmith shops, tin shop, billiard room, bowling alley, etc., etc., each indispensable in making up the vast compound of a *city*"—merely made Sacramento's rough condition obvious.[83]

"Already the 'outward tokens' are visible," he wrote, "the business hum and bustle of our landing and market places may, upon days of 'driving trade,' be favorably compared to the constant stir and activity peculiar to the business portions of our large Atlantic cities. The river's side presents a scene of admirable city-like confusion."[84]

Admirable citylike confusion. The phrase richly captures the dilemma of early Sacramento. Try as he might, Kemble could not quite elevate Sacramento to the status of a true city. Something essential to the makeup of a city was missing, something that would make the city a community rather than a marketplace, a grand bazaar for the gold rush. Sacramento's business founders had created a shell, in which the outward tokens of urban capitalism had taken root. But it remained to be seen if Sacramento would also attract a population and a civic community that would find life in its busy streets admirable.

It remained to be seen, in other words, whether Sacramento City was or would ever become a real city.

Dr. Charles Robinson. Leader of Sacramento's Settlers' Association and later governor of Kansas, Robinson hardly fit the image of frontier lawlessness usually attributed to Sacramento's squatters. Courtesy of the California State Library, neg. no. 4165.

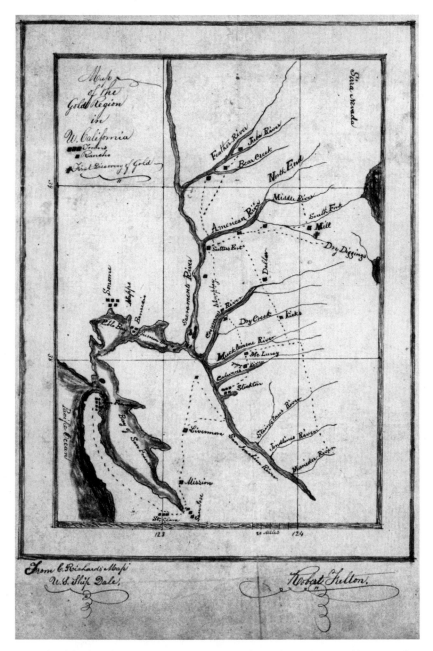

Central California. This early map of northern California shows the central location of Sutter's Fort between San Francisco and the mining camps. Courtesy of the Sacramento Museum & History Division, catalog no. 82/04/78.

John Augustus Sutter. This portrait of Sutter as a young man on the make in California is not as well known as later portraits showing an almost Santa Claus–like figure of frontier benevolence. Sacramento's roots in Sutter's New Helvetia have likewise been romanticized. Courtesy of the California State Library, neg. no. 264.

Sutter's Fortune. Miwok and Nisenan Indians were the builders and mainstay of Sutter's Fort. Long before the Swiss adventurer reached California, he had learned how to manipulate native labor to his own ends. Sutter's successes at New Helvetia rose and fell directly in relation to his ability to control native workers. Courtesy of the Sacramento Museum & History Division, catalog no. 82/05/600.

SUTTER
3 miles below Sac City

Sutterville. Sutter's original urban center for his inland empire saw only limited development before the gold rush. Though situated above periodic flooding, Sutterville was unable to attract the commercial foundations that were also required to make the site viable. Courtesy of the California State Library, neg. no. 7149.

Samuel Brannan. Saint, speculator, and scoundrel: the founder of Sacramento typified the extremes of frontier entrepreneurial spirit. California's first millionaire would make a fortune in the gold rush but would also create many of the problems encountered by Sacramento's early residents. Courtesy of the California State Library, neg. no. 549.

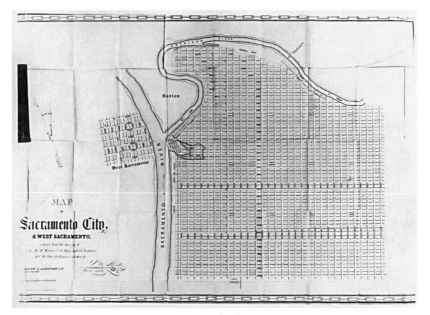

Plat of Sacramento. The vast scale of the planned city suggests Brannan's sweeping vision of Sacramento's future. By acquiring lots in the huge city, Brannan would be certain of a fortune in real estate speculation as well. Courtesy of the Sacramento Museum & History Division, 82/04/68.

Early Sacramento. The first buildings to arise from the wooded banks of the Sacramento River catered to early gold seekers. Note "S. Brannan & Co." to the right of the central tree. Brannan's City Hotel, a former flour mill, is to the left. Courtesy of the California State Library, neg. no. 659.

MINERS' VARIETY STORE.

No. 64 J st., ~~above~~ *below* 3d st.,

Sacramento City.

W. R. PRINCE has constantly on hand the following articles, at the lowest wholesale and retail prices, and will supply Miners and teams for all the mines with implements of every description necessary for their use. GROCERIES, PROVISIONS, and LIQUORS, of all kinds, of the very best quality, put up in proper sized parcels for teams and pack teams. In the assortment are the following goods, viz:

Quicksilver, Retorts, Rockers, Crowbars, Picks, AMES' best Shovels, and others. Camp Kettles, Camp Stoves, and all other cooking utensils, Axes, Hatchets, Handles, and Tools of all kinds. Rifles, Guns, COLT'S REVOLVERS, and other Pistols. Whip, Wood, and other Saws. Spikes, Nails, and Tacks of all sizes, with a great variety of Hardware and Cutlery. Tinware, Crockery Earthen, Stone, and Glassware.--- Powder, Balls, and Shot of all size. 'aps, Flasks, Shot Bags. Magnets, Wash-pans, Miners' Spoons.

Trowels, Scythes and Sneaths, Scythe Stones and Rifles, Hay Forks, Rakes. Garden Seeds of all kinds. Gold Scales of all kinds, and sets of Gold Weights, Counter Scales, Platform Scales, Scale Beams, Spring Balances, and other Scales and Weights of all kinds. Brass, Pewter, and Wood Faucets. Dinner Bells, Mule and Cow Bells. Rope, Twine, Sail, and other Needles, and Palms. Medicine Chests. Bees-wax, Sealing-wax, Letter and Wrapping Paper, Pens, Ink, Stands, Pencils, Blank Books and Stationary. Bar, Hoop, and Rod Iron, Steel in Bars. Clothing, Blankets, Calicoes, Canvass, Duck, Drilling, Ticking, Toweling, Hats, and Caps. Gold and Silver Lever and Hunting Watches, Gold Pens and Pencils. Boots and Shoes, Sole and Upper Leather, Chamois Skins, Gold bags. Corks, Oil Cloth, India Rubber Goods. Tar, Pitch, sperm and Olive Oil, soap, Candles, starch. Saleratus, Cream of Tartar, seidlitz powders, Stoughton's bitters, sarsaparilla syrup. China and other Preserves, Pickles, Flour, Pork, beef, bacon, Hams, Mackerel, salmon, Oysters, Lobsters, sardines, Eggs, Coffee, Tea, sugar, Molasses, Chocolate, butter, Lard, Cheese, Rice, Corn Meal, spices of all kinds, Figs, Raisins, Dried Fruits, Hops, Chile beans, Potatoes, Onions, seed Wheat, Indian corn, barley, split Peas. Beads f·r Indians, Dominoes, backgammon boards, American and French cards. Brooms, P Tobacco, segars. Harness, Riding and Pack saddles, bridles, Hobbles, Whips. ᴀ es; Fiddles and strings; Mexican and American spurs; Knives and Forks, Pockes Knives. Bowie Knives, butts and screws, Locks, bridles and bits, stirrups. Belts and sheaths; Rope of all sizes, bed cords, 'mbrellas; Iron Pumps, Lead Pipe, and all other desirable articles.

Placer Times Press.

Miners' Variety Store. Early Sacramento merchants offered a wide assortment of goods to miners, but within months many realized a greater profit was to be made supplying the needs of a growing city. Courtesy of the Sacramento Museum & History Division, catalog no. 68/110/262.

On the Trail. Immigrants to California faced many hardships on the long trek westward in 1849 and 1850. That they dealt with many problems communally suggests a different orientation than that of many of the individualistic merchants they would encounter in Sacramento. Courtesy of the California State Library, neg. no. 4847.

Encampment at Sacramento. This sketch by John M. Letts in November 1849 shows the typical response of overland migrants on arrival in Sacramento. Having camped along the trail for months, overlanders simply pitched tents in Sacramento, creating a vast encampment that refused to follow the grid drawn up by Brannan and others to organize the city. Courtesy of the California State Library, neg. no. 7143.

Sacramento in 1849. This 1849 lithograph of gold rush Sacramento shows the city as it was beginning to emerge at the height of the gold rush. Trees still remain in the streets, and many of the buildings are made of canvas. The overlanders' encampment surrounding the city is only hinted at by scattered tents. The encampment was centered on the southern (right) and eastern edges of the developed city. Courtesy of the California State Library, neg. no. 5498.

PART TWO

THE ENCAMPMENT

There are in our City a number of men with remarkable principles, who go among those who have newly arrived and offer to sell or lease to them the *PUBLIC LAND* in and about this place, thus imposing upon the unsuspecting. The later are hereby notified that the vacant land in Sacramento City, and vicinity, is open for *ALL,* free of charge.

—Settlers' Association Handbill, June 14, 1850

I am a law-abiding citizen, but if these speculators are ready for a fight, so am I . . . and if they show a fight, give them a battle, and the devil take the hindmost. Let us put up the fences pulled down, *and put up the men who pulled them down!*

—James McClatchy, Settlers' Association member,
late July 1850

CHAPTER FOUR

The Floods of '49 and '50

When newly arrived "Californian" John M. Letts first reached Sacramento in the summer of 1849, he found himself distracted by the gritty reality of the booming city. "Here," he reported, "all was confusion and dust, each generating the other. This is the point from which the first move is made, by land, for the mines, and every man was on the run; mule-teams were moving in every direction, some loading, others preparing to load, each surrounded by a halo of dust which rendered mules and driver invisible."[1] As many would-be miners were discovering, not all the dust in California was golden.

During the fall of 1849, Sacramento City grew from a bustling commercial outpost to a dangerously overcrowded encampment. The change in population may have caught the city's speculative founders by surprise. During its first few months Sacramento had been a crowded place, filled with newly arrived migrants from San Francisco or the California Trail or with returning miners seeking more supplies. Mixed in the throngs on the streets were teamsters with their long trains of pack mules or wagons, on their way out to or in from the mining camps of the central Sierra foothills. The milling crowds of the summer belied the fact that the city's permanent residents—those not on their way to or from someplace else—numbered only a few hundred. But by October and November, a subtle change had come to the city. The streets were still thronged with overland trail migrants and hopeful miners, and strings of wagons and pack mules filled the streets. But by this time the overlander, miner, and teamster traffic was predominantly one-way. Thousands came to the city late in 1849, but few left, and the city population grew in only a few months from a few hundred to an estimated ten thousand.

As late fall became winter, the earlier bustling mood of the city became as dark and threatening as the cloudy skies. The new population brought pressing problems to a city ill prepared to meet the challenge. Overland migrants, especially those arriving late in the season, were invariably exhausted, sick, and poor. Miners, forced out of the mines by the winter weather, entered an extended period of idleness. Even the great speculators felt the pinch: the weather not only reduced the flow of gold from the mining camps and the amount of trade in mining equipment, but also closed roads leading from Sacramento to the mining camps. Teamsters joined the miners in idleness, and goods that might have found a buyer in a distant mining camp sat and invariably rotted in the Sacramento warehouses.

The flood of people out of the Sierra foothills and into Sacramento created an economic disaster. Overlanders, miners, teamsters, and others found themselves cut off from their source of income for several months. Desperate to find a job in the city, they created a labor pool so large that wages were certain to decline. At the same time, the city's great speculators, also feeling the effects of the interruption in mining, were reluctant to invest much money in building projects that might otherwise have provided precious jobs. And caught by the high costs of getting goods to Sacramento and the amount of goods rotting in their warehouses, speculators could not reduce the prices they charged for their goods and even raised many prices to break even. Thus as money grew more scarce during the winter months, prices increased. And as many residents found their resources diminished, piles of goods wasted away unused.

Nature itself, however, provided another focus for discontent. As the city filled up with wintering residents, seasonal rains set in and the city's streets quickly became a swampy morass. During December, nearly thirteen inches of rain fell in the city.[2] The heaviest rains came at the end of the month and continued relentlessly on into the new year. At about noon on January 8, 1850, the American River flooded, spilling over into an abandoned channel, the Sutter Slough, which ran through the northern half of Sacramento City. In less than twelve hours water covered the town, in some places to a depth of twelve feet.[3]

Sacramento's two floods—one of people, one of water—shaped the emerging character and community of the speculators' city. Neither was adequately prepared for, despite clear signs that the city would be inundated. Both floods overflowed the ability of the city to channel the human and natural energies that met in its streets. And as both floods receded in the spring of 1850, they would bring about a major transformation in the social order of the new city.

⇢—⇠

Of the two floods, the human flood started first and would have the greatest long-term impact. Tracing this river to its source, the human flood had two major tributaries: the overlanders and the transient miners.

The first cohesive group to appear in the city after the speculator elite was the overland trail migrants. Overlanders formed a distinct group in several ways. Perhaps half or more of California's gold rush miners took the overland trail. Unlike oceangoing migrants, overlanders did not arrive in a steady stream throughout the year but during the autumn months. The necessity of crossing the plains and mountain passes of the Rockies and Sierras during the summer meant that they generally arrived during the late summer or fall, usually in the months of August, September, and October. Additionally, seagoing migrants usually landed in San Francisco or Monterey and then dispersed to the mines. Many, though not all, came through Sacramento. Most overlanders, however, followed the California Trail and finished their trip at Sutter's Fort or in the central mining region. Thus they came to Sacramento during a concentrated time and in more concentrated numbers than seagoing migrants.

The number of overlanders to enter Sacramento in the fall of 1849 is uncertain. One estimate of the total number of migrants on the California Trail in 1849 is 22,500, with roughly 21,000 actually making it to California.[4] A conservative estimate of overlanders in Sacramento, based on the increase in the city's population in the fall of the year, suggests that the number was at least two thousand and possibly much higher. During the winter of 1849–50, perhaps half to three-fourths of Sacramento's population consisted of overlanders.

Another characteristic of many of the overlanders was poverty and ill health. The arduous journey they finished on entering the city sapped migrants' often slim resources. Coming from frontier farming communities where specie was in short supply already, many migrants raised cash for the journey by mortgaging their farms. Many had purchased mining equipment and supplies in the States, only to abandon the bulk of their supplies on the trail. Few had the abundant cash necessary to buy supplies and equipment once they arrived in California. The exorbitant prices charged for even common items in Sacramento only emphasized the overlanders' poverty.[5]

Though many overlanders sought temporary employment in Sacramento to acquire the funds necessary to survive and begin mining, not all found employment. The number of men looking for employment was initially greater than the number of positions available. Yet even if the newcomers could have found work, many were too ill and worn out from the trail to begin any serious labors immediately. The journey to California had been an arduous trek, sapping physical strength and fitness as it did personal finances.

Though most overlanders brought their supplies and personal belongings in wagons, few rode in them. Horses, mules, and oxen were usually too loaded down with supplies and provisions to add the weight of migrants to the load. Most migrants walked the greater part of the way from the Midwest to California. Many carried packs on their backs as well. The weather on the plains in 1849 was wetter than usual, which brought its own problems. Although the rain helped produce more grass for grazing animals, it also turned paths into muddy quagmires and rivers into raging torrents. Accidents increased as wagon axles and tongues broke and migrants' attentions were dulled by the daily strain of travel. Thunderstorms drove off cattle and weakened travelers' fitness and resolve. On May 29, a tornado swept through the Platte River Valley, upsetting hundreds of trail camps and running off hundreds of cattle.[6]

To sustain them in their journey, overlanders usually lived off a monotonous diet of flour, beans, bacon, and coffee.[7] Diseases found weakened overland parties particularly good breeding grounds. A cholera epidemic swept the United States in 1849, haunting the overlanders as well. Historian Hubert H. Bancroft wrote that five thousand people died of cholera on the trail in 1849, though more recent historians, studying overland trail diaries, suggest the number was closer to five hundred.[8]

The combination of the long trail, poor diet, exposure to the elements, and the effects of diseases took its toll on overland trail migrants. One traveler described his camp near the Truckee River in present-day Nevada as a surrealistic landscape. "Others had arrived here before us. Their baleful camp fires gleamed here and there, and in the pale and misty light, tall gaunt figures, with long disheveled locks, long beards, and tattered garments, perfectly white from the fine impalpable dust which covered them, flitted about in moody silence. . . . The ground was covered with bleached and whitened bones of horses and cattle, the wrecks of other years, and the dried and decaying carcasses of innumerable animals of this, broken carts and wagons, and all imaginable debris."[9]

The trek was especially difficult for those who started late or fell behind during the summer. Throughout their journey they had had to contend with overgrazed land and worsening weather. H. C. St. Clair, traveling overland from Illinois, confided in his journal, "Teams a-continually coming in so near exhausted that they fell down in the road. . . . Some days, after a march of seven miles, I was so near exhausted that I would willingly of laid down without my supper rather than get it."[10] By mid-September, relief parties were already being organized in Sacramento to aid in the arrival of stragglers. One relief organizer recorded the terrible toll that the trail extracted from those who brought up the rear guard of the 1849 migration. "A more pitiable sight I had never before beheld," he wrote. "There were cripples from scurvy, and other diseases; women, prostrated by weakness, and children, who could not move a limb. In advance of the wagons were men mounted on mules, who had to be lifted on or off their animals, so entirely disabled had they become from the effect of scurvy."[11] Many of the survivors of this brutal trek were too sick or weak to begin either gold mining or any other employment. The overlanders needed a period of recovery and convalescence.

Overlanders brought with them health problems that Sacramento had no way of dealing with, and health conditions in the crowded city deteriorated rapidly. By August, Sacramento faced a serious challenge to the continued health of its population. The lack of readily available drinking water, the lack of sanitation services, and the arrival of ill and destitute miners and overlanders threatened to promote widespread disease in the booming city. President of the city counsel A. M. Winn noted that "hundreds are lying sick, rolled in their filthy blankets, without wife, children or friends to nurse them while sick, or bury them when dead."[12] The illnesses brought by the overlanders merely aggravated the city's poor location. "Three fourths of the people who settle in Sacramento City are visited by agues, diarrheas, and other reducing complaints," wrote Bayard Taylor. "In the summer the place is a furnace, in winter little better than a swamp; and the influx of emigrants and discouraged miners generally exceeds the demand for labor."[13]

In addition, their trail experiences set off overlanders as a distinctive group. Having traveled the same trails, overlanders had something in common. When overlanders met in the city, discussions often began with shared observations of the plains and mountains. Migrants compared their experiences crossing the North Platte or other rivers, or landmarks such as Chimney Rock, Independence Rock, and South Pass. Most migrants had spent some time at Fort Kearny, Fort Laramie, Fort Bridger, Fort Hall, or Salt Lake City and could discuss their experiences there. Oceangoing migrants had few such completely common landmarks; characteristics of a particular ship bound only that ship's passengers. Overland migrants, sharing a common path, already had a sense of community when they entered the city.[14]

The sense of community among overlanders, however, reached farther than to a common experience. Dependent on other members of their wagon parties for assistance during the long journey from the East, overlanders already had a keenly developed sense of community responsibility before entering Sacramento. Most wagon parties developed elaborate bylaws governing their journey. Though these bylaws were often abandoned and large wagon parties frequently quarreled and split into smaller groups, the effort originally put into these bylaws points to the migrants' concern with social order on the trail. They expected difficult times, compounded by the lack of true authority on the trail. Only near military posts or Salt Lake City did the travelers come under any formal government, and the military posts were few and far between, whereas few migrants were willing to accept the authority of the Mormon government at Salt Lake. Despite this, they traveled with little conflict, either among the migrants themselves, between the migrants and the Indians, or between the migrants and the Mormons.[15] Unlike the great speculators, overlanders' community sense was often the basis of their very survival.

Nor was the community dependency of the trail a new experience. Many overlanders came from the recent frontier, from the states of Missouri, Iowa, Illinois, and Ohio.[16] With perhaps as many as half of the migrants coming from states north of the Ohio River and west of Pennsylvania, the heart of agrarian culture in the United States, community responsibility was not so much created on the journey as reinforced by it.[17]

In many ways, the California Trail itself became a large community, a kind of traveling city of over twenty thousand people. Men off hunting stray cattle often wandered into wagon camps where they were unknown but were assured of receiving a meal and a night's shelter. Wagon parties often camped in sight of one another, especially near river crossings, where bottlenecks occurred. At times, these encampments might rival the size of many Midwestern towns. A feeling of fellowship united most migrants as they struggled to make their way to California. As one migrant later wrote, "One would suppose that such a close companionship would unite us as a band of brothers. This it did, and as brothers we quarreled, supported and assisted each other to the last."[18]

The community feeling of the overlanders provided a sense of solidarity that eased the harsh conditions of the trail. On arrival in Sacramento, the same solidarity provided overlanders with an infrastructure to deal with the city's undeveloped conditions. Arriving in such great numbers, Sacramento could not possibly provide adequate shelter for these new residents; overlanders responded by forming wagon camps on the edge of the developed parts of the city. When the city was unable to provide adequate medical or health services, overlanders took care of their own as best they could. When the city was unable to provide enough food to feed the newcomers, overlanders shared their meager supplies and organized hunting parties to live off the land.

By the end of 1849, the overlanders had created a new city on the site of the speculators' city. The overlanders' camps, consisting of canvas shelters and covered wagons, was sometimes dubbed the Tent City. The sprawling encampment, estimated to house roughly one-third of Sacramento's total population, lacked the attempted symmetry of the city proper.[19] Bayard Taylor noted the danger attendant in wandering through these informal campsites: "The briery thickets of the original forest had not been cleared away, and the stumps, trunks, and branches of felled trees were distributed over the soil with delightful uncertainty. If [a visitor] escaped these, the lariats of picketed mules spread their toils for his feet, threatening entanglement and a kick from one of the vicious animals; tent-ropes and pins took him across the shins, and the horned heads of cattle, left where they were slaughtered, lay ready to gore him at every step."[20] Life was often harsh in the encampment. Yet it served a temporary need, much as the overland parties had done on the plains.

The overlanders of Sacramento's Tent City represent a separate society within the city. Although they occupied the same location as the great speculators, their values and social organization varied dramatically. The overlanders viewed the city as a vast encampment. Like the large, temporary camps that formed at river crossings on the trail, Sacramento was another bottleneck on their journey toward the mines. To most overlanders, the Tent City provided a place to rest, wait out the winter, and learn the latest news on likely mining sites.

The second great influx of residents in Sacramento in the fall of 1849 had something in common with the overlanders. Late in the fall, as the last wagon parties limped into Sacramento, growing numbers of miners came down out of the foothills to spend the long wet winter in Sacramento, joining the overlanders. Although not as socially cohesive and distinct as the overlanders, the city's wintering transient miners nonetheless shared many of their characteristics.

Sacramento's transient miners represented nearly every state in the Union. In many ways the transient miners represented almost exactly the overall population makeup of the city in general. With an average age of twenty-nine, they also almost directly mirrored the average age in the city.[21] Transient miners, however, had no permanent employment in the city. During the fall of 1849 they were lodged there, not working in it. Thus it is unlikely that they actually represented a community-building faction. They were simply too mobile, too shifting, and had too little invested in the city to contribute to its community. Yet their numbers were large enough, and they were strikingly different from other city residents, so that they constituted a separate group in the city's rough class structure.

The number of transient miners who came to Sacramento in the fall of 1849 is unknown, but a conservative estimate of one thousand to fifteen hundred miners residing in the city throughout the winter would not be unlikely.[22] This number might be doubled if miners who came to the city for only short visits during the winter before heading back to their winter camps were also included.

Though not as united in their origins or experiences as the overlanders, transient miners staying in the city resembled the overlanders in important respects. Miner Charles Moxley illustrates the connections between the miners and the overlanders. Moxley migrated to California overland in 1849 and arrived in the region early enough to engage in some mining before the winter rains set in. After paying expenses, Moxley had only $21 in gold dust, but he and his partner decided to winter in Sacramento. By the time they arrived in the city, Moxley only had $3 left, and his partner was very sick. Moxley and his companion needed shelter, food, medical care, and a job to pay for all of these.[23]

Like the overlanders, they came to the city at about the same time, adding to the strain on the city's meager and undeveloped resources. They also shared in the experience of gold mining, though not to the extent that overlanders shared the trail experience. The miner's world was filled with the backbreaking and monotonous labor of the pick, shovel, and pan. The daylight hours were almost entirely occupied by that single activity, and a day in the gold fields often left men exhausted, sunburned, and muscle sore. Like the overlanders, miners were exposed to the weather and often lacked sufficient food. Thus many were ill or exhausted and sought medical services in the city. And as for the overlanders, the prices charged for basic necessities in the city were usually too high for the miners to rely on them on a daily basis. Although some miners found lodging in a boardinghouse or hotel, many melted into the disorganized Tent City that daily seemed to threaten to overwhelm the great speculators' designed city.

As overlanders and miners flowed into Sacramento, helping to create a tumultuous physical and social setting for the new city, they also brought with them the seeds of a new city. As a raging flood carries with it debris that is eventually deposited when the flood subsides, so, too, the human flood of 1849 carried its own version of flotsam and jetsam to the new city: disillusioned miners and overlanders who had given up the gold quest.

When gold was first discovered in 1848, both the range of the discoveries and the ease of mining fueled the expectations of hopeful miners. Yet on arrival in California, these hopeful miners encountered the increasing difficulty of mining and its diminishing returns. Unlike overlanders or transient miners, the arrival of these disillusioned men in Sacramento went largely unnoticed. They did not arrive during the span of a few short weeks, but entered the city at all times of the year. Their frustrations may have provided some sense of shared experience, but most likely few chose to speak much about their disappointments. On a daily basis, the population of Sacramento grew with the addition of disillusioned miners.

Many sought to return to their homes in the East; others hoped instead to acquire enough of a "stake" to give mining another try. During the summers of 1849 and 1850, when the majority of California's population was roaming the foothills in search of gold, ex-miners who sought employment in Sacramento could generally be assured of high wages. Because of the great labor shortage in the city, clerks, carpenters and other builders, and even unskilled laborers could demand inflated wages for their services. Bayard Taylor noted that "a healthy, sensible, wide-awake man . . . cannot fail to prosper. In a country where Labor rules everything, no sound man has a right to complain. When carpenters make a strike because they only get twelve dollars a day, one may be sure there is room enough for industry and enterprise of all kinds."[24] Samuel Upham, founder of the *Sacramento Transcript,* noted, "Here labor asks its own price, and its beck commands capital. . . . Neither business nor capital can oppress labor in California. Whenever its rights are invaded, the gulches and cañons that lead down the western slope of the Sierra Nevada will furnish a safe retreat, where labor will obtain a rich reward, until its end is gained and the powers that oppress it yield to necessity and consent to do justice."[25] During the winter, however, when the city population boomed suddenly, wages dropped drastically as employers found more potential laborers than could be accommodated.[26]

In traditional agrarian communities, it was not unusual for a farmer to work for a few weeks or months in a nearby town at the end of the harvest to gain enough cash or barter credit to support his family after a bad harvest or to acquire the few necessities that could not be produced at home. Usually these jobs were in the processing or shipment of agricultural produce, areas that faced their highest demands just as farms were demanding less attention. The rhythms of the gold fields, however, were not so friendly to miners. Gold was usually mined from midspring to late fall, depending on the weather. During this time, most towns desperately needed laborers to construct buildings and to work as teamsters and, due to the shortage of labor, usually paid top wages. However, during the winter, when most miners sought city jobs, the urban labor pool swelled just as the demand for workers fell. Without miners in the fields, teamsters were not in as great demand; the foul weather also prevented most new city construction, and with the flow of new gold from the mines temporarily suspended, few businessmen felt inclined to hire extra laborers.[27]

This basic economic cycle had a profound influence on northern California's gold rush population. Simply put, it meant that a person could either work in a city or work in the mines. California mines and cities were both lucrative places in the summer, but both were depressed and nonproductive during the winter. The Californian hoping to make his fortune could either take a chance in the mines or go to work in a city. But the nature of work and fortune seeking between the two locations varied greatly. The choice a person made would have a profound influence not only on his own life, but also on the social development of the region.

While many miners debated whether to continue seeking gold in the mines or to return home, others decided to settle more or less permanently in one of California's gold rush cities. For many of these residents, this decision was unexpected. Most migrants to California in 1849 and 1850 expected to strike it rich and return home as heroes; few expected to seek their fortune in city building, and even fewer expected to make California more than a temporary home.

This change from miners to residents among California's early population dramatically affected California's booming cities. As transient miners became settled citizens, they participated more fully in creating stable communities. However, it is hard to chart precisely when the number of settled residents in a city reached the critical mass needed to generate a civic community. The difficulty comes from the various factors involved in the transformation. How quickly men became discouraged with mining varied considerably. Some may have rejected the idea of working in the mines from the very beginning, choosing instead to make their fortunes by providing services to the miners. Others tried mining for a short period, lasting from days to weeks, and decided that a city-based occupation held a surer promise of wealth than mining. For others, the dream of striking it rich hung on longer. They entered the city searching for work with less of their initial financial resources and with perhaps less enthusiasm than did those who gave up mining more quickly. "I found I could not make only about expenses in mining," frustrated miner Alonzo Hill wrote his parents, "and I did not come here to mine for my expenses. So I just set my face again toward Sacramento City as I knew I could get some wages there."[28]

As miners came down from the foothills and into California's cities, their motivations also varied. Some sought only to get enough to return home; others sought only to make enough to reoutfit themselves for the mines; still others gave up on mining altogether and sought to make their fortunes in the cities. Whatever their motive, these ex-miners sought a wide variety of jobs. Some tried the professions with which they were most familiar—such as doctors, lawyers, and teachers. Others tried their hand at new occupations, especially as saloon keepers, boardinghouse keepers, or merchants. Others worked as clerks or laborers, often working for no more than a day or two.

Many of the argonauts found the temptation to dabble in business too alluring to resist. The miner engaged in long hours of hard physical work, often with little or no reward; businessmen—whether merchants, saloon keepers, teamsters, or hotel keepers—seemed to have more certain odds of success, even if the big payoff of striking it rich was more remote. On his arrival in Sacramento in late November 1849, Thomas Van Dorn wrote to his wife, describing the unusual sight of a large population living in cloth buildings, but he understood the economic activity going on under the ragged appearance. "Everything presents a cheerful and busy aspect," he wrote. "I doubt if any place of equal population would compare in business activity. There is undoubtedly more money in circulation here and greater opportunities for making it than in any portion of the world."[29] David Hewes wrote home, "Being much pleased with the appearance of the place and particularly with its locality, it being the head of ship navigation and the great center of travel to all the mines and to the innumerable little cities and inland towns which spring up in a night, I have thought it best to drive stakes here as I have done. . . . The villages and mountains all around us are literally filled with gold hunters. These people are our customers. Thousands of teams run from this city to the mines."[30] H. C. St. Clair reported the apparent opportunities that awaited such men in the fall of 1849. "Mr. Sanders is making very well teaming. Mr. Maltby is keeping a boarding house. Mr. Nurse has a line of stage," he wrote. "Cook and Eaton started a town. Called it Springfield. 'Twas no-go."[31]

Henry Rice Mann, writing to his wife in the fall of 1849, listed many of the possibly lucrative pursuits that awaited men in California who chose to make their wealth in Sacramento instead of the gold fields.

> Captains of vessels are offering sailors $1000 for their services to New York. . . . [Steamboats] charge $25 for a passenger from here to San Francisco. Blacksmiths do well here: $32 for setting a wagon tire, and the same for shoeing a horse; everything else is equally high. Provisions are very dear. . . . One man made $2000 last winter on two boxes of saleratus that he brought from the Sandwich Islands. . . . All kinds of labor is high; $10 is the lowest wages a common hand can be hired for per day, while mechanics get from 12 to $25 and board themselves. Board is 20 to $30 per week. . . . Teaming is very high. The man I am boarding with pays $4 per hundred for hauling goods from the vessels up, say ¼ of a mile. A good hand with a team will often make $1000 a week. Teamsters are in demand at $3000 per month, and every avenue of business appears to be full—no idlers—all are doing something, if nothing else but gambling. . . . Persons with a few hundred dollars to commence with are rolling up immense fortunes—everyone is full of specie.[32]

George Kenyon Fitch, publisher of the city's first newspaper, echoed the possibilities for new businessmen in the booming city. After publishing for only one week, the *Placer Times* was able to pay its rent, the costs of transporting their equipment to the city, and the carpenter who had erected their building and still have $800 left over. "We made from $3000 to $4000 per month," he later wrote, "and went along that way for 3 or 4 months. Which makes me remark that a new thing in those days was the best thing. The new paper got all the business. The new lawyer got a better business than an old one and the new newspaper got all the business. The new thing was what they were after. The new passengers coming ashore were of more consequence than men that had been there for a week and much more than those that had been there a month. Things were bustling in Sacramento then."[33]

Though of various conditions and dispositions, these residents had one important characteristic in common: they sought to develop business enterprises within the city. Unlike the overlanders and miners, who expected to leave the city in the spring, these enterprising residents expected to remain in the city and to make their livelihoods within its borders. Whereas the overlanders and transient miners threatened to overwhelm the city with their numbers and by their numbers were a powerful influence in the shaping of the city, the enterprising residents formed the city's most stable community-building group. Temporary residents such as the transient miners and overlanders were willing to endure the city's problems; the more permanent residents were not. Expecting to live in the town for a longer period and to make their livelihood from its economy, these residents were forced to confront the city's problems. Like the great speculators, they were interested in the economic development of the city; unlike them, they were interested in more than a profitable return on their investment.

Few had the resources of the great speculators. Trying to make a living on a slimmer margin, enterprising residents more keenly felt the city's problems. John M. Letts, who revisited Sacramento during the latter months of 1849, noted that Sacramento's new entrepreneurs had a booming business in the last weeks just before the weather shut down the city's connections to the mining camps, but saw their businesses decline rapidly as winter settled in. "A season of prosperity had been experienced without parallel," he recalled. "Men were not confined in their operations to their legitimate business, but would invest in anything that presented itself, and everything had been turned to advantage. But as soon as the rainy season cut off communication with the interior, a depression was felt, and soon an entire stagnation in all departments of business. This was not a time when the currents of business could be safely checked; people had been borne to their present positions by one of the most bouyant seas; and should this pass beneath them, the other extreme must inevitably follow as the ebb follows the flood."[34] Economic setbacks notwithstanding, Sacramento's location for entrepreneurs promised to revive in the spring, leading more and more miners to consider settling in the city. Their numbers soon rivaled those of the overlanders and transient miners combined. By the end of 1849, these enterprising residents may have accounted for from one-third to one-half of the city's population.

＋—＜

The human flood of 1849 crowded the great speculators' city with overlanders, transient miners, and new enterprising residents. Each of these groups viewed the city from different economic and social perspectives; each would seek to reshape the physical site and its emerging community. It is in this context that the natural flood of January 1850 is best understood. The waters that inundated the city would touch each group. And when the floodwaters receded, more than trees, tents, and buildings would be washed away; economic and political structures would also flounder, to be replaced by new associations.

Despite the city's low elevation, the long rainfall, and the increasing rise in the Sacramento and American rivers for days before the flood, most residents had believed in the claims of the city's founders that the site was not subject to flooding. John Morse noted in his diary that "everyone was inclined to believe the ridiculous and false assurance of safety. . . . Hence, when the water began to rush in and overwhelm the place, there was no adequate means of escape for life and property."[35] During the early stages of the flooding, many residents hoped they could save their belongings and goods by putting them atop stacks of boxes and barrels. Within hours, however, the rising river threatened to carry away even these precarious towers.[36]

Everywhere across the city, people scrambled to assemble makeshift rafts, and those who could secure a boat of any size made quick fortunes rescuing the goods of their neighbors. James Eaton, an overlander who had found a poorly paying job as a crew cook for an ill-tempered lawyer, land speculator, and lumber dealer, found that the flood actually helped him get back at his employer. Eaton and several fellow workers commandeered their employer's boat in lieu of back wages. Over the next few days the boat crew ferried people and goods to higher land several miles away from the city and "rescued" a number of stranded horses and cattle, which they later sold.[37] Other boats, usually hired out for $30 an hour, sold for $1,000 during the flood.[38]

The waters remained high for over a week, finally receding to their preflood level on January 18. Though residents immediately started rebuilding, the flood had devastated the town. "Very few houses escaped having water on their first floors," reported the *Placer Times,* "while many have been swept from their underpinnings by the strong current."[39] Residents faced terrible losses. "The damage to merchandise and to buildings, and the losses sustained by persons engaged in trade is very great," the newspaper noted. "Vast quantities of provisions and goods have been swept away by the rushing waters. The loss in live-stock is almost incalculable; many persons have lost from 40 to 50 yoke of cattle each, and horses and mules have been carried down stream in great numbers."[40] David Hewes wrote home that "in walking out upon the plains you can count—in a few minutes walk—a hundred beautiful oxen, cows, and horses which were lost by the flood."[41] What the waters did not carry away, boat-rowing "rescuers" often did. Trade with the mines, already limited due to the weather, virtually stopped for the rest of the month. For some small merchants already feeling the pinch of hard times, the flood was the final blow.

Worse still was the continued reluctance of the city council, still controlled by the great speculators, to pass measures for public health and safety. As early as the previous August, president of the city council A. M. Winn had warned that Sacramento faced a serious public health crisis. Yet instead of using his position on the council to provide public assistance, Winn called on the members of the city's fraternal organizations, the Masons and Odd Fellows, to take it upon themselves to visit the sick and raise money for pine coffins.[42] Early in September, the council resolved to call for a meeting of citizens at the St. Louis Exchange to aid in the relief of overland migrants but refused to take any direct action of its own.[43] Not until mid-November did the council take any real action, most likely because by this time the situation could no longer be ignored. By early November, mortality in the city had grown to appalling proportions. At times the death toll reached twenty per day.[44] The council then appointed a committee to meet with the sick who required city aid and began considering paying doctors' fees for the most destitute of patients.[45]

Some physicians felt that the council had not only helped to foster such conditions by its inattention to public health, but actually made conditions worse, especially in its prosecution of squatters living on or near the waterfront.[46] Dr. Morse recorded that the flood increased, but did not create, the suffering. "Some were drowned in their beds, and many died in consequences of the terrible exposures to which they were subjected. . . . Sick men, utterly helpless, were found floating about on cots, and, in the enfeebled tone of dissolution, were crying for help."[47] One man Morse tried to rescue was wrapped from head to toe in a filthy blanket. "The blanket was with difficulty detached," he wrote, "and when drawn off presented a shirtless body already partially devoured by an immense bed of maggots."[48] The man later died, a victim not of the flood, but of the atrocious conditions that existed in the city before the waters rose.

Throughout the winter physicians in the city began submitting medical bills to the council to cover their basic expenses in treating the city's destitute. Generally the council tabled these bills for later consideration; those not tabled they either refused to pay or paid only a reduced amount. After the flood, medical bills from nearly every physician in the city inundated the council. By March the city's physicians, well versed in the city's most pressing problems, had come to know the city's residents and their needs and were generally greatly respected by city residents. In their attempts to force the council to face public health problems they had become politically savvy.

Meanwhile other residents grew increasingly active in prodding the city council to take their interests into consideration. Though businessmen and physicians did not always agree on priorities for various projects, they shared a commitment to living and working within the city, to viewing the city as a home rather than an investment. Furthermore, a few of the great speculators finally joined the call for improved city conditions. Perhaps most prominent among these men was Barton Lee, the city's largest landholder. Unlike Brannan and a number of other great speculators who had investments throughout northern California, including San Francisco, Lee's investments were concentrated in Sacramento. By the spring of 1850, Lee was at the forefront of the city's economic life. His investments would continue to prosper, he realized, only to the extent that all business enterprise in the city did well.[49]

Together a few great speculators and a number of city residents, led by the doctors and the merchants, began to fashion an organized opposition to the city council. Foremost on their agenda was the construction of a new levee to protect the city from further flooding. Early in February a meeting of concerned residents, chaired by Barton Lee, met at Priest, Lee & Company to establish a formal committee to look into raising a levee. Prominent in the meeting was Hardin Bigelow, a businessman and landholder. Bigelow called for a survey to be made of the city to ascertain the correct siting and height of a levee and so that the costs of its construction could be calculated. The committee then named Bigelow and two other representatives to approach the council with their demands. The next day he submitted proceedings from the levee committee to the council. He also submitted an engineer's survey of the city concluding that the city "can easily be protected [from] inundation and that, too, at comparatively a small expense." Under questioning, Bigelow admitted that the actual cost of construction would probably be higher than the report indicated but would still be insignificant compared to what it would save.[50]

The city council had little choice. The organization of the citizens' levee committee, headed by Barton Lee, could not be ignored. Yet the council did not immediately accept either the residents' committee or its report. Instead it instructed the city engineer to make his own survey and cost estimates. It also created a new council committee on the levee, composed of two council members and two citizens' committee members: Barton Lee and Hardin Bigelow.[51]

The establishment of the citizens' committee and its representation in the city council's levee committee mark a turning point for the city council. From this point on, the council could no longer ignore the interests of city residents. Furthermore, the citizens' committee and the push for the levee itself gave residents the organization and focus to begin forging a citywide vision of community interest.

Though residents still remained divided in many ways, the committee grew out of the common interests and experiences that residents shared. As business difficulties had grown in the city, so had residents' attempts to find some order and control in the apparent city chaos. The January flood, which had touched all residents to some extent, demanded an active response to prevent further damage. With the levee committee, residents organized to protect their homes as well as their businesses, to improve living conditions in the city, and to demand that city government be responsive to a wider range of interests than those of the great speculators alone. The organization of the committee also implied a direct warning for the council. By working with the council, residents showed a desire to reform the council rather than abolish it, but by organizing independently and maintaining their own officers and meetings, they implied a willingness to subvert it if necessary.

The transformation of the council from a body representing the great speculators' interests to one embodying enterprising residents' interests as well had developed slowly over the winter, in large part because the great speculators were more organized initially than the enterprising residents. The organization of the citizens' levee committee gave residents an organization that was at least equal to the Law and Order Party that the great speculators had formed to secure passage of the city charter the previous fall. Yet the great speculators still retained control of the council. Despite its sharing of the levee committee with city residents, the council continued to pursue its own interests. For the next six weeks the council virtually ignored the calls for a new levee or tried to join calls for a new levee with its efforts to clear the waterfront, claiming that waterfront obstructions and squatters interfered with its orderly survey.[52] Throughout these weeks, however, the citizens' committee grew more organized as residents' frustrations grew. By mid-March a political upheaval was imminent.

The collapse of the city council came quickly and dramatically. In February the provisional state government had passed an act to incorporate Sacramento City.[53] A new city charter had been written and passed on to the city for the election of a council to conform to the new charter.[54] The council requested revisions in the charter, and the election was postponed. On March 16, the state legislature sent the charter back to the council, calling for a new election to be held on April 1. Voters were to elect a mayor, recorder, marshal, attorney, assessor, treasurer, and nine councilmen.[55] The response was enthusiastic. Three political "tickets" were formed, and in the words of *Sacramento Transcript* editor Samuel Upham, "an immense number of ballots and handbills [were] circulated."[56] Of the many candidates proposed for the various offices, most members of the sitting council were conspicuously absent.

As if resident dissatisfaction with the council were not already strong enough, nature once again underscored the problems facing the young city. During March ten more inches of rain fell on the city, once again swelling the Sacramento and American rivers.[57] Warm weather also caused much of the winter snowpack in the Sierra Nevada to melt. By the end of March the American River reached flood stage once again, threatening the city.

Unable to get assistance from the city council, Hardin Bigelow boldly hired his own work crew and began building a makeshift levee. Bigelow pushed himself and his workers through the night and was soon joined by other volunteers from the business community. The effort succeeded. Though the council appointed a committee to prevent the flood and called on businessmen to help construct the levee at the last minute, its efforts were seen by all as too little and too late. Bigelow was credited with saving the town from a second flood.[58]

Political advertisements published in the *Sacramento Transcript* on the morning of the election gave voice to the frustration of city residents with the previous council. The Democratic Party, which in essence grew out of the citizens' levee committee, published a series of resolutions that denounced the actions of the council.

> *Resolved,* That in Municipal, as well as State and National Governments, the laws should be framed so as to secure equal rights to all, and special privileges to none.
>
> *Resolved,* That honest and honorable competition is the life of trade, and that we are opposed to fostering one branch of business at the expense of another, or building up one enterprise by taxing another. . . .
>
> *Resolved,* That the practice heretofore adopted, of taxing business instead of property, *and which is still authorized by section 5th of the City Charter,* is neither wise nor democratic, but that all revenue necessary to defray the expenses of government should be collected by a direct tax, levied upon property.[59]

Another advertisement also hints at both the passion for the election and the growing organization of city residents in demanding a voice in city government. "The enemy is in the field," cried the Rancho Ticket, "our bills have been mutilated, and in some instances destroyed; but let not your 'angry passions rise' in consequence of the indignity. Imitate as far as in your power lies the example of your leader. Keep cool, work hard and vote early. Remember that abuse and curses, like young chickens, 'will come home to roost.' When once the votes are in the ballot boxes, no appeal can be taken."[60]

Voter turnout on election day was heavy. Upham noted that "polls remained open until late in the evening, and there were lively times around the ballot-boxes. There was no rioting, but a great deal of superfluous gas was ventilated and considerable whiskey drunk."[61] When the ballots were counted, Hardin Bigelow was elected mayor, and Barton Lee was elected city treasurer. No single ticket had carried the election, but few great speculators remained in office. Even the city's squatters had succeeded in electing a few officials, including council member Charles A. Tweed and county attorney J. H. McKune, who also acted as legal counsel for their "Settlers' Association."[62]

Mayor Bigelow summed the vision of the city's new Common Council six days after the election in an agenda set in his first message to the council. "The first and paramount object to be accomplished the present year, and one which involves the deepest interest of the citizens of Sacramento City," Bigelow wrote, "is the immediate construction of a levee, to protect permanently the city from future inundation by water." Bigelow noted that the new charter restrained the city from raising more than $100,000 without direct authority from the electorate. The levee, he noted, was estimated to cost $250,000. Bigelow thus suggested a levee fund be raised separately from other city expenses. Bigelow also noted the need for the establishment of fire companies, for city sanitation, and for the erection of a city hospital and city prison. Further, the mayor pointed out the need to grade city streets, build bridges and sidewalks, and erect a city market house. To accomplish these projects, Bigelow recommended that "just and uniform assessments be made upon real and personal property as the basis of taxation, with such incidental taxation as the circumstances and wants of the city may require."[63] Ten days later, the council approved Bigelow's call for a levee and two weeks later authorized property taxes to raise funds for it.[64]

Bigelow's agenda made little mention of the waterfront, the obsession of the previous council, saying only that he recommended "the establishment of such regulations upon the present levee as will best promote the interest of the business community and yield the greatest revenue to the city."[65] Instead Bigelow gave priority to the problems that the earlier council had so long ignored. To Bigelow and most city residents, Sacramento City was envisioned as a place where midlevel businessmen could earn a comfortable living in a safe and secure setting. The construction of the levee, the establishment of fire companies, and the concern with city sanitation all showed the enterprising residents' commitment to see Sacramento survive despite its many problems. Plans to build a hospital and jail, grade streets, construct sidewalks and bridges, and erect a public market all proclaimed the residents' intention of controlling apparent city chaos while providing public services that would promote business growth.

Though the new council's vision of Sacramento embraced more of the community than had the old council's, the vision still excluded a sizable part of the city population. During the winter nearly half of the city's residents were transients, waiting for the end of the rainy season to leave for the mining districts. By definition, transients had little attachment to the city and generally took little interest in its political affairs. Most miners and overlanders saw the city as little more than a temporary stop on their sojourn and remained outside Sacramento's developing society.

Writing three years later, John Morse noted the rapid improvement of the city after the difficult winter. "The spring and first summer months of '50," he wrote,

> were marked by such evolutions of trade and exchange, such purchases and sales as have seldom been seen by any member of the human family. This season of business developed some of the more substantial mercantile houses and manufacturing firms and, we may say, some of the strongest banking houses of the country. The city improved so rapidly as to astound strangers and beget a lively interest in the prospective importance of the town. The seasons in which this state of business was developed were extraordinarily exempt from disease. The almost innumerable physicians of the previous period of maladies were compelled to abandon pills and powders and take to the less congenial employment of mining. Their calling seemed for a time to be almost gone.[66]

If Morse was correct about the city's doctors, it was an ironic interlude in their Sacramento experiences. Politicized by both the human and the natural flooding the city endured, it was the doctors who led the movement to overturn the old speculator-backed council. But if most of the city's physicians supported city residents in their attempts to bring safety to the streets of Sacramento, at least one doctor took a different course. He would turn his attention not toward levee construction, but toward adequate and secure shelter for the city's transient miners, overlanders, and new residents.

The path Dr. Charles Robinson would take from concerned physician to armed rioter began in the chaotic days between the human and natural floods of 1849 and 1850. It paralleled in many ways the rise of Hardin Bigelow from businessman to political leader. And both paths would end in a sunny, crowded Sacramento intersection, with each man facing the other over the barrel of a gun.

CHAPTER FIVE

The Roots of Community

Late in the fall of 1849, as winter rains were just beginning to move into northern California, *New York Tribune* correspondent Bayard Taylor decided to retreat from the gold fields before the weather made the roads impassable. Taylor found traveling in the gold region difficult. The rugged terrain of the foothills, the many rain-swollen streams, and the muddy ground challenged his ability to find his way safely across the countryside. Eventually Taylor found his way to Sacramento, reaching the outskirts of the city after nightfall. Yet having finally reached his destination, Taylor found the confused urban environment more difficult to navigate than the northern California countryside. Although he had been in the city only a few weeks earlier, the number of overlanders' tents that had sprung up around the city had transformed its streets into a confusing maze. "I picked my way in the dark to Sacramento City," he explained to his readers, "but was several times lost in its tented labyrinths."[1]

Even after he had reached the more organized section of the city, Taylor's disorientation did not abate. "As the day went down dull and cloudy," he explained, "a thin fog gathered in the humid atmosphere, through which the canvas houses, lighted from within, shone with a broad, obscure gleam that confused the eye and made the streets most familiar by daylight look strangely different. . . . The town, regular as it was, became a bewildering labyrinth of half-light and deep darkness."[2]

The city labyrinth that disoriented Taylor awaited all who came to Sacramento during the winter of 1849–50. Nor were the city's streets the only source of confusion. Sacramento's eclectic world of canvas tents and wooden buildings, thrown up with little apparent order, only mirrored its mixed and varied population, which held conflicting attitudes toward money and work, the importance of individualism and community, and the morality of mining, speculating, and gambling. It was, to extend Taylor's description, a bewildering labyrinth of cultural as well as physical half-light and darkness.

The lack of a clear social organization challenged inhabitants to create their order out of chaos. Peter Burnett, one of the city's founders, noted in his memoirs that the city in 1849 had little organization or formal community structure. He saw in the formation of Sacramento society a clear moral lesson.

"I have seen a whole community, for a time, substantially living under the theory of an equal division of property," he wrote. "In California, during the years 1848 and 1849, all men had about an even start, and all grew comparatively rich. At least, they were all *equally* secure of a good living. . . . But within a year or two thereafter the usual inequities in the financial conditions of men began to appear."[3]

The "usual inequities" imply what to Burnett's thinking was the emergence of a *natural* class distinction in Sacramento: divisions of society into economically based classes. During Sacramento's first two years, however, these natural class distinctions did not emerge. Before the gold rush, hard work was generally thought to produce financial success; laziness led invariably to ruin. To a nation composed mainly of farmers, the ethic was based on experience. Yet in the gold rush, this work ethic lost some of its relevance. Hardworking miners could labor for days, weeks, even months without discovering enough gold to cover their basic expenses, while other miners, perhaps digging only a few hours during a single day, could uncover a treasure beyond their wildest dreams. Meanwhile in California's cities, the dirty, impoverished-looking miner might be laden with several heavy bags of gold, while the elegantly dressed scion of a wealthy family might be penniless and working for a living as a steward or waiter in a saloon or restaurant. Further, with the possibility of striking it rich one day only to find a mineral vein run out the next, today's millionaires could easily become tomorrow's paupers. During the earliest days of the gold rush, hard work did not always produce the financial distinctions normally used to evaluate social standing.

In the absence of traditional standards of social judgment, other distinctions came to take on significance in the formation of Sacramento's society. Differences in ethnicity, birthplace, and occupation created distinctions that Sacramento residents used to make sense of their socially chaotic world. On a daily basis, Sacramento residents sought private and public associations, both to survive their stay in the city and to make sense of the chaotic world around them. Sharing their needs, experiences, and reflections of the urban scene, city residents began to lay the basis of civic communities. As in any city, no single, overarching community group or ethic emerged. Nor did city people usually find all their needs met by joining a single community group. But by the fall of 1849, Sacramento hosted enough informal city-based social groups that larger, more formal and organized associations could begin to emerge. And one of the first of these, the Sacramento City Settlers' Association, would soon undermine the economic and legal foundations of the city itself.

>--<

The search for an understanding of Sacramento's bewildering physical and social labyrinth began when newcomers sought out places to get meals, to stay the night, to earn some money, or to enjoy pleasant diversions. The locations where these activities took place became miniature worlds within the city, physical and social landmarks with distinct meanings against the background of apparent urban chaos. In their search for such places and in the building up and repeated use of such places, Sacramento residents laid the groundwork on which their community would rest.

A newcomer's first days in Sacramento were often a lonely, anxious time. During the first day or so people walked the streets, getting impressions of the city, trying to locate and fix as landmarks those parts of the city that seemed most familiar while noting those aspects that were most strange. Initial impressions of the city, recorded in journals and letters, make plain the attempt of newcomers to understand their chaotic surroundings. Dr. Israel Lord, an overland migrant and miner who arrived in the city late in December 1849, was struck by the same sense of confusion that had bewildered Taylor. "The first that strikes one's attention is the want of order—the utter confusion and total disorder which prevail on every hand," Lord wrote. "The streets are not graded, nor is anything done to clear them out, except cutting down some of the scattered trees which five or six months ago were the sole occupants of the ground. The whole town plot . . . is covered with boxes and barrels, empty or filled with all kinds of goods, in passable, indifferent, or bad order, or totally ruined, and wagons, lumber, glass bottles, machinery, and plunder of all sorts, heaped and scattered and tumbled about in 'most admired confusion.'"[4]

The scene Lord described assaults the senses. It leaves the reader much as it must have left Lord, searching for some sense of order among Kemble's "admirable city-like confusion." And Lord provided it immediately. He continued:

> The whole city is literally stuffed, crammed with eatables of every description, so exposed that almost every kind must suffer more or less damage and hundreds of thousands of dollars' damage is already done.
>
> I saw at one establishment alone over 200 boxes of herrings rotting in one pile, any amount of spoiled pork, bacon, cheese, moldy and rotten, pilot bread, and most everything else. The destruction and waste of property here is almost or quite equal to that on the plains, with not half the necessity, and a thousand times the recklessness.
>
> There are a great number of dealers in produce or rather eatables here, but more dealers of "monte." The taverns have usually a large barroom in front—passing to which you will see, on one side, more

display of glasses, bottles, cigars and liquors than in three or four of the largest liquor taverns in Chicago; and on the other, three or four or more tables, literally groaning under piles of silver, with a supply of gold, and a man behind dealing "monte;" and this at all hours from breakfast to midnight.[5]

Lord's observation provides a good opportunity to examine how people began making sense of the city. After describing the confusion of the city, Lord immediately began to classify it. His long list of rotting food and the description of the city's saloons indicate that he had clearly located several sources of food within the city. Furthermore, he had begun to interpret the city's character, describing Sacramento residents as wasteful and disreputable. Given the high cost of food, the difficulty of transporting it to the city in the middle of winter, and the increasing demand for fresh food in the heavily crowded town, it is unlikely that the residents were as wasteful as he wrote. Ignoring the problems inherent in building an instant city, of providing adequate storage facilities, and the heavy humidity caused by the incessant rains and the city's low-lying site, Lord focused instead on the human efforts of city building.

His comment concerning the monte dealers reveals more prejudice than experience. The entire passage is taken from Lord's diary entry of December 22. Lord arrived in the city on the same day in the afternoon; he could not possibly have seen monte dealers in the tavern from breakfast to midnight.[6] Lord's personal prejudices clearly influenced his view of the city, and his understanding may have been in error because of it. However, aside from the degree of error, Lord's diary reveals his first attempts to find landmarks—both nutritional and moral—within the city labyrinth.

Charles Glass Gray, an overlander from New Jersey who arrived in the city early in November, also recorded his initial impressions and his attempts to fathom the chaotic city. *"Sacramento City,"* he wrote on the day he arrived, "should be called *Ragdom* as almost all the dwellings are built of slender joists of wood, covered over with canvas or cloth. Many tents were also in use and they gave the place the look and air of *an immense camp.*"[7] Gray's description, with its shrewd renaming of the city, also conveys a sense of confusion and disorder about it, but unlike Lord, Gray seems much less condemning. To Gray, the city was not wasteful and wicked, but more entertaining. "Had a pretty good look at the city of Ragdom," he wrote on the following day, "with its 'City Hotel' and 'General Jackson House' and 'Fremonts House' and the *'Elephant' who appears to have taken up quarters here.*"[8] Gray also seemed to consider the amount of gambling in the city in a more lighthearted vein. "Gambling is here a perfectly regular business and carried to a great excess, by all conceivable games." "Every possible game here," he wrote, "is to drain the money from one, which however literally flows out of one's pockets in a stream for the absolute necessaries of life."[9] Perceptively, Gray detected the underlying economic basis of life in the city.

Perhaps the best early attempt to understand Sacramento comes from Bayard Taylor, who recorded his experiences more fully than most in order to convey the experience to his newspaper readers. On his first visit to the city, when everything was still new to him, Taylor's description centered on the concerns of most newcomers to the city. He gave a description of the city's physical layout, the high cost of rents, the high wages demanded by workmen, the demographic makeup of the population, and the qualities of restaurants and gambling halls.[10] Remarkably varied, Taylor's observations show his skill as a reporter at gaining detailed information about the city. Though primarily descriptive rather than analytical, his effort shows his attempt to understand Sacramento. He had gathered facts and detailed information about rents, wages, and restaurant fare and had begun to assess these small bits of information by characterizing them.

Throughout his narrative, Taylor defined the city and its people by giving the scenes he witnessed a contextual background that is often more contrived than accurate. His descriptive passages characterize, compare, and contrast Sacramento in ways that provide the reader with clues to the confused environment. His comments were apt: "The Waiters [are] rude Western boys who had come over the Rocky Mountains";[11] "in activity and public spirit it [Sacramento] was nothing behind San Francisco."[12] The original forest trees, which still remained within city blocks and at times in city streets, Taylor called "picturesque";[13] an auctioneer he described as "a quondam New York dandy."[14]

These examples show Taylor's ability to write descriptively. But they are more than just colorful. Each characterization provides a handy stereotype of a complex social scene. Census data show an obvious exaggeration: not all waiters were "Western boys."[15] The picturesque nature of the city's trees was not a view shared by all. Even Taylor admitted that most of the trees were blackened from residents' attempts to burn them out and that one resident was nearly killed when a storm blew over one of the trees, smashing his tent.[16] With his characterizations Taylor was attempting to rationalize the physical and social chaos of the city.

When Taylor returned to Sacramento late in the fall, his account of the city was more analytical. Though still offering up carefully detailed and often strikingly poetic word pictures painting city life, he also attempted to give a broader sense of the city as a whole by describing the rhythm of daily life there. His analysis now recognized growing social divisions within the population. The "working population of Sacramento City," he noted, retired to their beds early. "They were generally worn out with the many excitements of the day, and glad to find a position of repose," he observed. "Reading was out of the question to the most of them when candles were $4 per pound and scarce at that. . . . Men preferred—or rather it grew into a custom—to lie at ease instead, and turn over in the brain involuntarily all their shifts and maneuvers of speculation, to see whether any chance had been left untouched."[17] By nine o'clock the working population had retired.

Another group, however, did not retire but roamed the streets far into the night. Taylor suggested that this group was made up of "a large floating community of overland emigrants, miners and sporting characters." These men visited the gambling halls and theater, looking for the excitement that the city offered. Boisterous and rowdy, the miners made the nighttime streets their own, much as the streets by day belonged to the working residents.[18]

Taylor also described the large encampment of overlanders along the southern edge of the city. "There, on fallen logs about their campfires, might be seen groups that had journeyed together across the continent, recalling the hardships and perils of the travel. The men, with their long beards, weather-beaten faces, and rugged garments, seen in the flickering light of the fires, made wild and fantastic pictures."[19]

Unlike the miners, the overland migrants generally stayed within their own camps rather than spending a lot of time in the city's saloons.

> Sometimes four of them might be seen about a stump, intent on reviving their ancient knowledge of "poker," and occasionally a more social group, filling their tin cups from a kettle of tea or something stronger. . . . The fragments of conversation . . . were narratives of old experience on the Plains; notes about the passage of the mountains compared; reminiscences of the Salt Lake City and its strange enthusiasts. . . . The conversation, however, was sure to wind up with a talk about home—a lamentation for its missed comforts and frequently a regret at having forsaken them. The subject was inexhaustible.[20]

By describing Sacramento, Taylor defined the city, setting up a model of both its physical environment and its social character. Taylor's effort paralleled that of other city residents who tried to understand their surroundings by defining them. Like Taylor, the words they chose to describe their environment helped to shape that environment. Residents noted the confusion of the city and then discussed the basic necessities of living there: food, its condition, and its price; shelter, its condition and price; and job opportunities and wages. Preoccupation with these issues underscores the importance newcomers attached to them.

> ╍╍╍

In seeking food, shelter, and employment, Sacramento's overlanders, miners, and residents utilized and expanded existing private and public associations. Images of gold rushers as individuals without family connections in California and with few social connections other than occasional mining partners and drinking partners disguise the multitude of associations to which the forty-niners belonged. These associations, both intimate and public, predated the formation of the city. Neither private nor public associations were created in Sacramento—they were brought to the city by the groups of people who came to inhabit the physical site. People then expanded, altered, and recombined these associations to fit their needs in the chaotic city, so that in time many of these associations fit Sacramento's unique social landscape. But the associations themselves were part of the cultural baggage residents carried with them. And without these preexisting associations, the city would have collapsed.

One of the most interesting of these preexisting associations was family. Though the common perception of the forty-niner is that of a lone, unattached male, the number of families in early Sacramento is surprising, and gold rush migrants clung to whatever family ties they had. The 1850 federal census shows 392 families living in Sacramento, consisting of 1,120 people, slightly over one-fourth of the enumerated city residents. These families were identified by noting groups of people with the same last name living together in a single dwelling. This method, however, does not identify family groups composed of maternal cousins or extended family relations. Henry Souther, for example, who left Boston for California in the fall of 1849, noted that his party consisted of his son, his brother, his brother-in-law, and numerous friends.[21] Accounts of traveling cousins and relations indicate that it was easier for the family that remained behind to make do without the labor of one son than to get by without the labor of two. Thus many families encouraged cousins or in-laws to travel together as companions.[22] Assuming that this was a common practice, the number of paired cousins should be at least equal to, if not higher than, the number of paired siblings or fathers-sons. If so, it is not unlikely that over 30 percent of Sacramento's population could claim a relative living within the city.

Sacramento's early families can be divided into two basic types: "extended families" and "truncated families." Extended families generally included husband, wife, and children. The classification is subjective, and families coming under this category were not always so complete. I have included here families that appear to represent an attempt to relocate a complete family in California. The term "truncated families" is used to designate migrants who left most of their family members behind and brought only a few along. Predominantly, truncated families were made up of males, usually brothers, cousins, fathers, and sons, or some combination of these.[23]

Of the city's 392 families, 215 were extended and 177 were truncated. However, since many truncated families composed of cousins cannot be easily seen in the census, the number of truncated families was likely much greater, probably greater than the number of extended families.

Differences between extended and truncated family types sometimes extended to the physical conditions of their homes. Census data suggest that many truncated families—brothers, cousins, fathers, and sons—lived in their place of business, whereas extended families seem to have lived in a separate location. The difference was most likely based on needs. Truncated families of men often slept on storeroom floors, on bags of goods, or behind a business counter.[24] Extended families, however, usually felt the need to provide more private quarters for married couples or single women and may have needed to reserve a separated part of the store for children, especially infants. The degree to which business and family spheres were separated depended to a great extent on a family's financial condition and personal inclinations. Still, the sketchy evidence suggests a greater separation of family and work worlds within extended families than truncated ones.

Family bonds had a far greater influence on the population than the number of actual families might at first indicate. Many residents joined fictive families that in many ways were as powerful, if not more so, than actual families. Though fictive families did not have the bond of blood ties, they did have the powerful tie of personal choice. Someone who looked to another person as if he or she were part of the family did so out of choice, not out of obligation.

Fictive families in Sacramento came in several forms. One of the most prevalent consisted of people added onto an actual family. They could be orphans or distant relatives who made their homes with the true core family. The census indicates at least eight children living with families who had different last names. Journals and diaries from the overland trail note that immigrating families often informally adopted children whose parents died on the journey.[25]

Work associations provided yet another source for fictive families. For businessmen, especially merchants, these family additions might have been their clerks who lived in the store with them. Still another source of extended fictive kinship was young men, traveling singly, who attached themselves to a family, originally as a hired hand or as a combination traveling companion/ odd-job helper, and were now considered as a kind of unofficial family member. Such a relationship would not be unusual to Americans in the 1840s, where clerks lived with the families of merchants, apprentices with the families of master craftsmen, and hired hands with farming families. Even in cases where such people lived separately in Sacramento, the associations made during the journey might still provide people with a sense of family, a place of familiarity in the strange new surroundings of early Sacramento.[26]

Comparison of newcomers' experiences shows both how important such connections were and how intensely they were sought out. James Eaton, a young overlander from Illinois, arrived in Sacramento in early November. Though he arrived penniless, he immediately contacted his stepuncle, who was staying at a hotel in the city. The stepuncle bought him dinner, paid for his lodging for the night, bought him breakfast, and then suggested a possible employment for the young man. With the help of his stepuncle, Eaton was well provided for during his first full day in the city and, within less than twenty-four hours, was gainfully employed.[27]

Dr. John S. Darcy, a New Jersey resident who liked to be called "General" and who led the Newark Overland Party to California in 1849, also found his way made easier in Sacramento by old friends who had preceded him to the city. Darcy's friends had made good fortunes in Sacramento and treated him to fine accommodations and to fine foods and dinners among Sacramento's founding elites.[28]

The lack of such connections, however, could lead to misery. Charles Glass Gray was unable to find the same social connections within the city that others had. Though a nephew of Dr. Darcy, he could not, or did not, claim the same hospitality that his uncle received. Unable to afford the cost of boarding, Gray simply encamped "right in the city, say not over one hundred yards from the business part of the place and near the levee."[29] His encampment was spartan: he slept in a wagon, around which he had drawn up several tree branches to try to keep out the rain. After three days, he chanced to run into an old acquaintance, but since his friend had also just arrived, they could do no more than keep each other company.[30]

Exposure to the incessant rain and the privations of the overland trek soon began to take their toll on the young men. Even when Darcy gave Gray and his friend food to help sustain them, Gray noted that they were so famished, the nourishment did not have the intended effect. "[Darcy] received from some of his friends at San Francisco (who he knows not) a present of some pickles, dates and whiskey and he was kind enough to let us into them, which we did with moderation only, on the score of decency, but they were so palatable after our long abstinence and coarse living as to make us more hungry than ever."[31]

Gray soon reached his limit. "I was much surprised today with indications of the scurvy, pain in the ankles and legs, sores breaking out on my hands and bleeding of my gums, when polishing my teeth. God grant it may not be for I have suffered enough already, I think." The following day, Gray decided to depart for San Francisco. Again he hoped to find that important connection that would give him the start he needed. The night before he left, he noted, Darcy "gave me a very kind and somewhat flattering letter of introduction to Messrs Geo. S. Wardell & Co. [a forwarding and receiving company in San Francisco] and for which I feel much obliged to him. These letters are almost invariably miserable affairs, but as I know not a soul at that place it may possibly be of some little service to me."[32]

The need to have some kind of social contacts in the city caused residents who had no blood relatives there to invent them when they did not in reality exist. Men could associate with other men who had emigrated from the same general locale. Though not quite providing the same closeness and intimacy of a family, they could usually provide some similarities of culture and experience. Men from the same state, for example, might be able to talk about similar occupational experiences, speak in similar dialects, and share regional tastes in religion and regional standards, such as food preparation. Perhaps they would also be able to discuss the political and economic scene of their home state in detail. These mutual experiences and attitudes could provide a comfortably familiar setting and basis from which to interpret the world around them.

Finding such associations was not as difficult in Sacramento as one might expect. The first source of such associations would be among one's traveling companions from the trip to California. Both the overland trail and oceangoing ships put numbers of people together for an extended time. Often travelers from a large region found themselves funneled together by the transportation system itself. A ship from Boston, for example, would largely collect people living in Boston's hinterland. Across the nation, as people began streaming westward, the first fellow companions they often fell in with were from a nearby region. Sometimes men from a town, though not related by blood, would agree to travel together, often in some form of a partnership or a joint-stock company. Many of the partnerships and companies fell to quarreling and broke up on reaching California, yet even in these cases the friendships of two or three men might survive. These friendships could provide at least a limited sense of home in the foreign world of the instant city.[33]

In a city with limited housing, people were often forced to live in their place of business and with their fellow workers. David Hewes wrote to his mother of his success in forming a business and an impromptu family as well.

"Since I came to Sacramento City I have been stopping with Moore and Bush from Lowell, who have rented a store in a large brick block now being erected by a Mr. Merritt of New York whose favor, confidence, and good will I have courted and won, and whose store in this half block I have rented. . . . Moore and Bush, Mr. Merritt and myself board ourselves and lodge in the store. . . . We make our own beds, cook our own chocolate and coffee. We have milk usually for dinner."[34] This partnership of business and family shared an Atlantic coast background and most likely the experiences of an ocean voyage to California. Hewes does not describe any friction among these men, living and working together constantly, though some disputes most likely occurred. Instead he seems to value the sense of community as much as the practicality of the arrangement.

Still another important source of fictive family networks was based on the city's hotels and boardinghouses. These businesses sheltered visitors to the city, but quite a few also housed long-term residents. Here men gathered for two of their most basic needs: food and shelter. Since housing was limited, the physical structures may often have been crowded and uncomfortable. Men living in these places sometimes found themselves sharing beds. Meals were served "family style," with boarders seated together, side by side. Daily acquaintances, conversations over dinner, could provide a basis for discussions on the meanings of events in the city as well as insights into how best to succeed there. In general the friendships in these hotels and boardinghouses developed between strangers, but regional associations could foster the process.

Many hotels and boardinghouses took regional names, such as the Ohio House, the Chicago House, or the Southern House. Many of these establishments became informal meeting places for people from the specified region. The Missouri House, for example, advertised that it would open its register so that people from the West and South could find acquaintances.[35] Comparisons of these regional names with census data showing the birthplace of boarders also indicate that sometimes a number of boarders in each house identified with the region mentioned in the hotel's or boardinghouse's name.[36]

The familylike atmosphere that developed within hotels and boardinghouses may have been based on more than the miscellaneous assemblage of boarders. Census data indicate that hotel and boardinghouse operators were more likely to have come from extended families than operators of any other business in the city. Forty-three percent of boardinghouse operators were family members, as were 33 percent of hotel operators.[37] Most likely these families served to some extent as a core family to which boarders attached themselves as fictive members. Boardinghouses and hotels, strong places of community building and sharing, formed the bedrock of the emerging community spirit.

Boardinghouses also provided a sense of traditional gender roles in a strange environment. Examples of working women in Sacramento are few, but the dominant impression is that women who worked followed traditionally established patterns. The majority of women in the city were already married and generally migrated to California with their husbands and children. The majority had also migrated from the western states or from overseas. Most likely they saw themselves as partners with their husbands in the occupation of supporting the family and household.[38] Married women kept boardinghouses, washed clothes, and cooked meals. Thomas Van Dorn noted in his diary that "women are greatly needed and especially, *house wives.* Any industrious woman can make here $12 and $15 per day, aside from her ordinary vocation."[39]

Families were often recruited to run boardinghouses. Lucius Fairchild wrote to his wife and family in 1851 of going into partnership with George Graves in the operation of the Queen City Hotel in Sacramento. "I put in one thousand dollars and Graves has about three hundred and to off set my surplus capital he charges nothing for the services of his wife daughter and son who do most of the work."[40]

Absent women, in fact, were often sorely missed by their husbands for more than romantic reasons. William McFarlin, for example, wrote his wife in 1852 from Downieville, explaining that he had been unable to acquire the fortune of which he had dreamed in the mines. McFarlin's new plan was to open a boardinghouse. However, McFarlin realized he would need help. "You have no idea of the difference it would make if you were here," he wrote his wife. "I would keep a boarding house and all I would want to insure success would be to have some woman to superintend the cooking and table. . . . I am boarding with a Mr. Myers from Newark, Ohio, who has his wife with him. He has from 30 to 40 boarders at $12 per week and one dollar per meal for odd meals, and that amount would bring per week at least $350 and you would have to pay for a cook $30 per week and you will have 175 dollars left after profit—"[41]

Sacramento's boardinghouses clearly acted as domestic havens to many of their boarders. Franklin Buck described his boardinghouse in a series of letters home to his family.

We board at an eating house next door, above us and let one half the upper part of our store to the man and his wife and child for the low rent of $72 per month. . . . The man who keeps the house (Lindley) is a young fellow, all the way from Conn. and with his wife and little girl came across the plains. His wife is much the better half, I guess;

quite a lady and will be quite an addition to our establishment. . . .
Mrs. Lindley does the cooking and we furnish the material and eat it.
The Captain lugs all the wood and water up stairs. We have a parlor and
kitchen and begin to live like rational beings again. . . . In the evening
we have a social game of whist and spend our time very agreeably. Lindley
is a lawyer and his wife a New Haven girl and a lady in every sense of
the word.[42]

James Haines was taken sick in January 1850 and left homeless by the flooding
of the American River. "Finally by a good samaratan I was taken to . . . a log
house built that fall by a Mrs. Merrill, who kept a boarding house. . . .
Fourteen were lodging at the time in the second story and she kindly took me
in and gave me the size of my body in the northeast corner of the house and
nursed me; took care of me for fourteen days and nights. I was delerious,
knowing nothing, but by kind treatment and care of the good lady and her
family, I was brought around."[43]

A substantial number of people lived in hotels and boardinghouses.
Twenty percent of the population lodged in a dwelling containing ten or more
people. Yet even outside of the contrived families centered on the hotel and
boardinghouse, few Sacramento residents chose to live alone. Ninety-seven
percent of city residents lived with at least one other person, and 86 percent
lived with at least two other people. The fact that only 3 percent of the city's
residents lived alone was lost on contemporary observers, perhaps because so
much of the city's housing seemed to be devoted to sheltering single people or
groups of two or three people.[44]

The importance of the city's hotels as meeting places sometimes even stretched
beyond the range of its current boarders. Places that could accommodate large
numbers at once often hosted organized public meetings. On Saturday, December
1, 1849, the City Hotel, the largest hotel, was the site of two public meetings,
one called by the carpenters and joiners to discuss wages and the other by
newly arrived settlers to discuss land titles.[45]

Sacramento's families—real or fictive—gave their members a place to share
their impressions, to compare their findings, and to develop a shared definition of the city, its good points and bad ones, its benefits and drawbacks, its
opportunities and its dead ends. In terms of survival, families found ways to
sustain their members' physical needs; in terms of community, families were
one of the arenas in which shared understandings of the urban environment
were hammered out.

→ — ←

Another arena in which community spirit could be forged was in public associations. As family settings could unite diverse individuals, so could public organizations. In the early years of the city, fraternal, civic, and national organizations were few and weak. However, work associations could reinforce and extend the bonds of community throughout the city. Together with overlapping family associations, work associations could provide the city with the sinews of society. But in early Sacramento, divisions in the workplace could also reinforce cultural diffusions between different family associations. Such divisions could channel private and public associations into the creation of subcultures rather than a citywide community. And in the crowded world of Sacramento during the winter of 1849–50, the creation of a widespread city community was diverted by powerful divisions into the creation of two subcultures.

After securing shelter, Sacramento residents were most concerned about finding employment in the city. Again previous associations often proved crucial. Henry Rice Mann arrived in Sacramento in the fall of 1849, just as the city was beginning to fill with overland trail migrants. "I made fruitless inquiries for work," he wrote to his wife. "Was willing to help unload ships at a dollar an hour, but everyplace seemed to be full. I had given up all ideas of trying anymore today and was sitting in the post office feeling sad and gloomy from a combination of causes . . . when who should pop in but Mr. Bigelow, the father of the student at the seminary who owes me for some work."[46] Bigelow provided Mann with money, a place to stay, and leads on finding a job. Philip Castleman, who also arrived in the fall of 1849, found himself in the same situation. After two weeks, Castleman "chanced to meet Mr. Turner of St. Louis, who had brought the Pioneer Line through." The reunion with Turner proved beneficial. "He said he was a going to open a bakery in a few days and wanted to hire hands and offered me $175 per month. So I thought as I had suffered much inconvenience by being here without a house in the rainy season, I had better take it."[47]

The relationship between employers and employees in the early city, however, was very often strained. In the chaotic conditions of the city, a multitude of factors—age, ethnicity, birthplace, economic standing—could divide workers from their bosses, but the greatest difference between them was residency. Simply stated, employers were attempting to create permanent institutions with transient workers. Merchants trying to hire builders for their warehouses, teamsters to ship their goods, and clerks for their stores found their offers of wages had to compete with the lure of the gold fields.

Building construction—so basic to the creation of the city landscape— shows the difficulty between employers and employees. Carpentry work in the mid-nineteenth century was not necessarily a skilled profession. Many men in Sacramento had at least a rudimentary understanding of building techniques from their experiences in the East, and Sacramento's need for new buildings prohibited too much emphasis on proficiency. Charles Moxley, a miner turned resident, found a job as a carpenter in Sacramento for $12 a day despite his lack of skill. "So much for knowing how to handle tools," he remarked in a letter to his sisters. "But good carpenters make an ounce of gold [valued at about $16] a day at their trade. . . . This is truly a strange country."[48]

Alonzo Hill and an unnamed companion also found themselves out of funds in Sacramento in May 1850. "We thought we must work at something," he wrote his family, "so we offered to let ourselves to a carpenter, who asked us if we could lay shingles. We told him we could lay shingles like a book (who would not) so we made a bargain to work at seven dollars per day and board for myself. We worked one day, and the next we was ordered on [as] 'boss of the job.'" What astonished Hill was that he in fact knew nothing about laying shingles![49]

"We began to lay on the eaves," he continued, "with one or two *Green hands* under our jurisdiction. All things went on like goose grease 'til we got half way up the roof, then it was interrupted by our employer, who wanted to know why we did not lay a double course on the eaves. We felt like as we should pinfeather for a moment, but making the best excuse in our power, we worked on 'till the curtain of night fell on Sacramento, then we took fourteen dollars and with a deceitful 'thank ye' sought a lodging place."[50]

That Hill and his companion could so easily frustrate the demands of their employer illustrates the difficulty employers had in disciplining an unstable labor pool. During the fall of 1849, as wages were falling, the city's carpenters met to form an informal union and agreed to refuse work on any project if wages fell below $16 a day. The carpenters represented a fairly cohesive subcommunity within the city, one that very early began consciously setting occupational standards.[51]

However, the constant turnover in population was often a double-edged sword, and even the carpenters had a hard time keeping wages high. James Barnes, who arrived in Sacramento in the spring of 1850, noted that wages at that time were high. "Work is plenty here [in Sacramento]. I get $12 day. . . . If work is good here this summer, I shall not go to the mines; if they get below $12 a day I shall go to the mines. It is thought by some that carpenter work will be from $12 to $16 a day all summer."[52] The lure of the mines proved too strong, and within a few weeks Barnes was once again trying his luck in them. "I am now in the mines," he wrote his family at the end of May. "I have made up my mind to try the mines this summer. If I make or lose by it, it is healthier up here than in the city."[53] But Barnes found working the gold fields too difficult. Over the next few months he retreated to Sacramento, staked a new claim on the North Fork of the American River, and then returned to Sacramento yet again. As the population of Sacramento swelled in the fall of 1850, wages once again fell. "I came down to the city about a week ago and shall probably not return to the mines. Business here is very dull at present. I am to work at my trade. Wages are from $10 to $12 a day. . . . If I had not went to the mines, I might have been worth some money."[54] As time passed, the economic instability of the city only further deepened the growing gap between employers and employees.

Another example of this gap involved the relationship between merchants and clerks in the early city. The largest single occupation recorded in the 1850 census was "Merchant." With an average age of thirty-one, merchants were slightly older than the average city resident. Merchants came from all parts of the world, yet the number of merchants from New England and the Northeast far exceeds that from every other birthplace. Clerks, after merchants, constituted the second-largest occupational group in the city in 1850. Clerks, however, came from a rather different background than the merchants. Though New York- and Massachusetts-born clerks accounted for roughly one-third of all clerks in Sacramento, the western states of Missouri, Ohio, and Kentucky together accounted for 20 percent. Clerks likewise were noticeably younger than the merchants, averaging only twenty-seven years of age.[55]

Clerks needed at least some education in order to keep accounting ledgers and handle each business's paperwork. Most likely neither requirement was prohibitive among Sacramento's early population. Nor was the basic education required of clerks something that prohibited most people in the city from clerking. Most Sacramento residents in the early years of the rush were literate and probably possessed at least a basic education.[56] Finding a worker with the requisite skills for clerking in the early city may not have been difficult, but the quality of work merchants received from their clerks could be very poor. "Labour—poorest help—is from $6 to $8 per day," David Hewes reported, at a time when clerks "in the States" were often paid half that amount. "Clerks [get] $300 to $500 per month, and the traders get all they can."[57]

Census data show that most clerks lived with the merchants who employed them. Generally these business-households were made up of one or two merchants and one or two clerks. The relationship between merchants and clerks varied. Sometimes clerks were the sons or nephews of one of the merchants. More often, however, clerks were not related to their employers. Merchants and their clerks generally differed in age and birthplace, and cultural differences between these two groups may have left feelings of closeness between merchants and clerks somewhat strained.[58]

Charles Pancoast's experiences as a clerk for a Sacramento druggist suggest the kind of conflicts that often existed between clerks and their employers. Pancoast was a Pennsylvania Quaker who arrived in Sacramento sick and with enough money to provide only a few days' lodging. Having had previous experience in a drugstore, Pancoast set out to find similar employment in Sacramento. Pancoast met a storekeeper who gave him some medicine, and the storekeeper's chief assistant gave him a letter of introduction to a man named Dunbar, who kept a drugstore in which the assistant had a financial interest.[59]

Pancoast went immediately to Dunbar, and though Dunbar had doubts about Pancoast's ability to be of service given his poor health, Dunbar did employ the ailing Pancoast for a one-month trial. At the end of the month Pancoast had recovered his health and announced his intention of leaving Dunbar, but the druggist gave his clerk a $25-a-month raise and his board and thus persuaded Pancoast to stay on. Several weeks later Pancoast again announced that he was leaving, this time to see about buying some livestock out of town with the intention of going into business for himself. Again Dunbar pleaded with Pancoast and offered him a raise. Seeing he would be unsuccessful, he told Pancoast that he could have his job back again at a raise if the stock venture did not turn out as Pancoast hoped. Roughly one week later Pancoast did indeed return; Dunbar then fired the clerk he had hired in Pancoast's absence and reinstated Pancoast at $50 a month plus room and board. Several weeks later Pancoast again left Dunbar, who managed to persuade him to come back, this time for $75 a month. Yet again Pancoast left Dunbar after a dispute over the price Pancoast had charged a customer, and yet again Dunbar persuaded Pancoast to return, this time for $100 and Dunbar's promise to employ another assistant to help with the workload. Several weeks later, Pancoast left Dunbar's employ, this time leaving Sacramento itself for San Francisco.[60]

This quick recital of Pancoast's experiences with Dunbar illustrates the unstable nature of Sacramento's labor pool early in the gold rush. Clerks had too many opportunities to lure them away from their employers, and employers found themselves forced to pay ever greater wages to keep their employees. But what is most interesting about Pancoast's relationship with Dunbar is the personal bitterness that Pancoast held for his employer despite Dunbar's continual accommodating of his unstable clerk.

Pancoast's descriptions of Dunbar, which are lengthy, are uniformly negative. He first portrays Dunbar as "a bristling Jew who had learned his business in New York, but had been a Slave Driver in South Carolina. His hair stood on end; his naturally ugly nose had been twisted and put out of shape; and his whole manner and appearance resembled those of an Employee of a Cincinnati Pork

House." During the first week of his employment, while Pancoast was still ill, Dunbar "pushed me all day in his Nigger-driving style, and I was ready to drop when bedtime came. . . . I found Dunbar continually vicious and ugly, with the breeding of the Pig Sty. He was a drinking man, and would go to bed drunk and arise in the morning, his hair bristling like a Hedgehog, and knock around and displace all my prided arrangement of the articles on the counter." According to Pancoast, Dunbar once intimated that Pancoast had stolen $5, at which Pancoast "pounced upon him and made him apologize." Another time Pancoast gleefully recounted a beating Dunbar received from "a Gentleman," and though the clerk "never could get at the truth of this difficulty, [I] understood there was a Woman involved in it." Still another time Pancoast reported Dunbar's attempt to cheat his way out of a gambling debt. Pancoast also explained that his continual quitting of Dunbar's service was due to his employer's abusive behavior.[61]

What actually happened between Pancoast and Dunbar is difficult to determine. Clearly Dunbar went to rather great lengths to retain Pancoast's assistance. And despite leaving several times, Pancoast always returned. Was Dunbar as vicious an employer as Pancoast reported, or was Pancoast exaggerating Dunbar's behavior to justify his own behavior? Though this cannot be answered with certainty, what is interesting is the manner in which Pancoast paints Dunbar's character. Dunbar is evil in Pancoast's eyes because he is Jewish, a southerner, a former slave driver, a drunk, a gambler, a cheat, a womanizer, and abusive. How much of this litany is accurate and how much is merely adorned is impossible to determine. But the very personal and moral nature of Pancoast's charges suggests the wide cultural gulf that separated Dunbar and Pancoast. Certainly the high turnover of Sacramento's labor pool affected community feelings in more than economic ways.

→--←

Differences in the experiences of employers and employees were aggravated by Sacramento's unique economic base as well as by the cultural differences of its crowded cosmopolitan population. Like the fault lines that underlie much of the California landscape, the issue of land use and ownership ran deep and would violently divide Sacramento's emerging community.

Land title disputes brought the city's cultural divisions to the surface for a variety of reasons. Land ownership had long been a point of heated dispute between settlers and speculators in American history, and contention over land titles was almost certain to arise in California once Americans began settling the state. Large land speculators claimed that their efforts helped to promote settlement. Their speculative operations, while often extremely profitable, were also extremely risky. Many frontier settlers felt that speculators were more often litigious parasites who stole the labors of early homesteaders who had originally cleared and developed the land, which gave the land its real value.

Before the gold rush, the federal government's position was ambiguous. The government sold western lands to speculators to raise federal funds and to promote western settlement and also granted early settlers "preemption" rights to lands that they improved and occupied. Preemption acts throughout the 1830s and 1840s, though only in effect for a few years each, were renewed each time they were about to expire. Seen as a temporary solution, in practice preemption had become a standing land policy. By the late 1840s land reformers were demanding the opening of public lands to settlers rather than speculators.[62]

California land, however, was also subject to the Treaty of Guadalupe Hidalgo, which in addition to ending the Mexican War had guaranteed that the United States would respect and protect land titles made under the Mexican government. These land titles were themselves a source of dispute. Deeds often defined property boundaries in vague terms. Boundaries were usually defined as lines running between landmarks, but often these "landmarks" were groves of trees, a standing rock or skull, or a bend in a river. Many of these landmarks were subject to erosion or misinterpretation. Thus the boundaries of most grants proved difficult to define in later years. Furthermore, a number of Mexican grants were fraudulent, filed in the closing days of the Mexican War or immediately after its conclusion. Many Americans felt no obligation to respect these grants and denied the legality of many grants on this basis.

The problem was in determining which grants would be recognized as legal. Fraudulent claims could not always be easily exposed. Even worse, given the disorganized condition of the Mexican government and California's status as something of a backwater province, not all true grants had been processed by the Mexican government carefully. Americans were left to sort out fraudulent claims that looked legal and legal claims that looked fraudulent, the majority of which had unclear boundaries.[63]

California's new American settlers expected the federal government would be able to solve the state's land problems quickly, once the deadlock over territorial government was solved. Such was not the case. During the spring of 1850, two U.S. agents filed their reports on the general condition of Mexican land grants within the state; the reports almost perfectly contradicted each other's findings. The report filed by William Carey Jones to the secretary of the interior recommended a liberal policy toward affirming the Mexican grants, most of which Jones considered to be valid. The report filed by Henry Halleck to Governor Mason, however, magnified title defects and concluded that most

Mexican grants had not been properly filed and were thus invalid.[64] When the federal government finally did begin trying to determine the legitimacy of the Mexican grants, the process quickly broke down into long and complicated legal proceedings, taking up most of a decade to solve.

Since the federal government had not resolved the problem of providing territorial government for California, residents were left to solve the problem themselves. And to residents, the complicated problems of the grants were not an abstract problem to be solved by fact-finding reports and lengthy legal proceedings. Under the pressure of the gold rush, residents needed immediate answers. To accomplish anything, some sense needed to be made of land titles.

To the city's speculative founders, the issue of land titles was of fundamental importance. Given the huge costs of operating on a frontier far removed from east coast suppliers, the great speculators used the rising value of their real estate holdings to secure their credit. During the early months of 1849, while Sacramento was still competing with Sutterville for regional dominance, land values had not risen rapidly. Even those merchants who committed early to Sacramento were not certain where the city center would develop. Lot sales clustered in three separate places: around Sutter's Fort, at the Sacramento River embarcadero, and at a landing on the American River.[65] When Samuel Brannan and his coalition of merchants persuaded Sutter, Jr., to deed five hundred town lots to them free of charge in April in order to secure Sacramento's success over Sutterville, Sacramento's uncertain future vanished. By April, the city's merchants had realized the importance of the Sacramento River embarcadero as opposed to the other sites and took their free lots from that area. The area of greatest interest to the speculators lay between the Sutter Slough and the southern edge of town, running from the Sacramento River back to Ninth Street. Within this area, town lots were owned primarily by Samuel Brannan, P. B. Cornwall, Albert Priest, Barton Lee, Jacob Snyder, Samuel Hensley, and Colonel P. B. Reading.[66] In control of the city's most valuable real estate, these merchants and other landholders quickly raised the price of land in the city. By summer city lots were selling for $3,000; by winter some lots were going for as much as $8,000.[67] Real estate represented the single greatest source of personal wealth within the city. The scale of such wealth is suggested by data from the 1850 federal census. Thirty-two men in the city owned over $30,000 in real estate; Barton Lee personally owned over $700,000.

It was this wealth that underlay the speculative activities of most of the city's great speculators. Its rising value had created a comfortable cushion of credit for speculators who took chances in other enterprises. City land also lay at the foundation of most city business. Enterprising residents either bought or leased land for their stores and workplaces from the great speculators.

Entrepreneurial interests generally accepted the validity of John Sutter's Mexican grants. Most likely this was not a conscious decision, but one based on the apparently obvious validity of those grants. Speculators expected the government, under the terms of the Treaty of Guadalupe Hidalgo, to recognize Sutter's title. Sutter's grants, however, suited speculators in a number of more subtle ways. Because the grants covered a large amount of land, entrepreneurs could acquire land in large enough quantities to engage in lucrative land speculation. Furthermore, by recognizing the validity of Sutter's grants, entrepreneurs reemphasized their commitment to an admittedly temporary legal system—the city's Common Council—which they expected the United States eventually to recognize.

To many in the city, however, land speculation as practiced by the city's founders was harsh and arbitrary, especially given the recent conquest of Mexico and the policies of land use with which they were familiar, both along the overland trail and in the gold-mining regions. Few newcomers to the city in the fall of 1849 had the money needed to buy a city lot at inflated prices. Unable to purchase or even rent land, many winter residents simply squatted on vacant lots within or near the developed area of the city. When landowners attempted to charge rents or run squatters off, many squatters responded that the land belonged to the federal government as a result of the recent conquest of Mexico. Many disavowed the provisions of the Treaty of Guadalupe Hidalgo, arguing that the recognition of vast Mexican grants was opposed to U.S. land grant practices, which were usually limited to much smaller parcels.

The dispute between speculators and squatters in early Sacramento in many ways echoed similar disputes from the earlier years of American frontier expansion. In Sacramento, however, this dispute took on a more serious demeanor due to two circumstances. First, given the great investments that everyone—speculators, overlanders, miners, and new residents—had made in getting to California and the unstable local economy during the winter, the question of an equitable land use policy quickly transcended from a matter of economics and moved into the realm of morals. Was it moral, many asked, to charge excessive prices on so basic a commodity as land during an economic slump? Second, given the lack of a legal government and the federal uncertainty regarding Mexican titles, would the federal government ultimately recognize Sutter's Mexican grant (thereby upholding the great speculators' titles) or would it declare the grant invalid (thereby making the land in Sacramento public land, available to squatters under the preemption acts)?

The problem of land titles in Sacramento involved both legal confusion and a long-standing cultural debate. It was a complex issue, aggravated by the inability of the federal government to provide a solution when the frantic conditions of the gold rush demanded immediate action. Sacramento's land title disputes thus became the most explosive issue in the city.

During the fall, as hundreds of overland migrants were pouring into Sacramento, city landowners tried at first to force squatters to pay bonus fees for camping on these lands, ranging from $5 to $12 per day.[68] Many squatters who moved rather than pay the bonus fees found only that speculators, who seemed to enjoy a monopoly on all the land in and surrounding Sacramento, also owned their new campsites.

The great speculators' reaction to these sprawling encampments, however, was often harsh. Proclaimed as the source of many of the city's problems by great speculators and enterprising residents both, transients and new settlers were subject to humiliating, and often forced, evictions. One observer of just such an eviction recalled the incident years later. "In the midst of this rainy season, three men, including a Doctor, were passing along the levee between the [Sutter] slough near I Street and the [Sacramento] river, when they met with a pretended sheriff and posse well charged with whiskey. . . . The posse went directly to a structure of logs and canvas, where was a sick man who had been fed and nursed by the Doctor for several days. The man was ruthlessly hauled from his shelter, and the logs and canvas leveled with the ground."[69] Forced to the outskirts of the city, transients and would-be settlers sought some place of refuge, temporary or permanent, in which they could winter unmolested or acquire some land under the preemption acts.

The legal case that brought the issue to the forefront of the city's attention began soon after newly arrived overland emigrants began crowding the city's limited resources. About the middle of October, Z. M. Chapman, a newcomer to the city, cut timber and built a cabin on an unoccupied piece of property outside the city limits. Chapman, like many other newcomers, felt he had "as good a right to any unoccupied lands adjacent to the city as any citizen of the U.S.," and claimed 160 acres.[70]

Twelve days after Chapman began building his cabin, as he was about to put on the roof, Pierre B. Cornwall and another landholder visited him. They claimed Chapman was squatting on land owned by Priest, Lee & Company and demanded that he stop cutting timber. Chapman declared his intention to lay claim to the land through preemption. The confrontation grew heated. Cornwall warned Chapman to get off the land, threatening his life if he refused. Chapman told the landholders that they were all within the jurisdiction of civil authorities; since they had threatened his life, he demanded they turn themselves in to the alcalde's office or he would have them arrested. Cornwall promised under the circumstances to have him ejected legally. The following day Chapman was served with a writ of ejectment and ordered to stand trial.[71]

Many residents and transients attended the trial against Chapman. Cornwall presented his case against the squatter and showed his deed from Sutter for the property in question. The issue appeared to be simple, the evidence overwhelming against the squatter. Chapman, however, then demanded to see the proof of Sutter's original title. Cornwall's title was traced back from himself to Sutter, Jr., and then to Sutter, Sr.

But Cornwall refused, arguing that his own title was clear enough and that Sutter's title, as the original settler of the area, was beyond question. The jury examined the evidence and adjourned without reaching a consensus. Two more juries were called, but neither could agree on the question of Sutter's original deed. Each time the sticking point was the same; each time Sutter's original title was held back. Rumors began to circulate through the town that Sutter's grant had not covered the land on which Sacramento was built. As a result of the prolonged uncertainty of the trial all city land titles began to fall under suspicion, and squatters began settling on undeveloped city lands in earnest. A fourth jury finally decided in favor of Cornwall, and Chapman was ordered to vacate the property.[72]

Meanwhile Chapman's trial sparked a number of settlers' and squatters' meetings and demonstrations. From these grew an informal squatters' association. At first the association seems to have been concerned only with defending the city's settlers, but over the next few weeks the association's organization and vision grew. By mid-December the association drafted regulations and bylaws and adopted the formal title "Sacramento City Settlers' Association."

Observers' responses to the Settlers' Association's meetings and membership were initially mixed. Some thought that they were mostly ignorant and uneducated but were led by men of tact and talent.[73] In mid-December, the *Placer Times* reported that the association had quickly signed up one thousand to twelve hundred members. The *Placer Times'* first reaction was hesitantly positive. "We believe," it observed, "that while there are some unprincipled men connected with this movement, a great majority are honest and deserving citizens."[74] Two months later, however, the *Placer Times* ridiculed the association in strident language. "At several of the assemblages [of the Settlers' Association] *gentlemen* have attempted to make speeches, and succeeded in doing so to their own satisfaction, we presume, and at the same time they satisfied the crowd that they were perfect asses in all respects. Why these bipeds get up and open their heads without knowing what they want to say, or how to say it, or without having the first notion of that which belongs to courtesy or decency, is something we cannot understand. We hope the orators referred to will get out of town as soon as convenient—they can be easily dispensed with."[75] However, a San Francisco reporter, visiting Sacramento at the same time, came away with a more lighthearted perspective. "The numerous meetings held while we were there were very curious; tar barrels, fulminating speeches, peace speeches, war speeches, and law and order speeches, squatters and land holders, whig and democrat, were the characteristics, no distinctive features prevailing in any of them. A more good humored population was never harangued, and if the spectacles furnished no light, the tar barrels did. On the whole, we are fully convinced that Sacramento is bound to *shine.*"[76]

The settlers' organizational abilities were their greatest strength. The Settlers' Association's approach to city governance and community revealed its overland roots. Various accounts suggest that the association was chiefly men from what were then the western states generally or Missouri and/or Oregon in particular. Early organization probably began when a single, extended family, including fictive family members, agreed to help each other out should a speculator or city official confront them. Meetings probably evolved out of informal gatherings as people discussed their concerns around a campfire, over a cup of coffee or a plate of beans. Overland parties often held meetings to discuss problems along the trail; by the time they reached Sacramento, such meetings were almost a conditioned response to difficulty.

The association's most striking characteristic was its community-oriented approach to political leadership. Each meeting began with an election of temporary officers; the chair and secretary of any meeting did not usually succeed to the post at the following meeting, even when the sessions were separated by only a few hours. Offices rotated among association members. The main prerequisite for any post seems to have been a perceived ability to handle the duties and a willingness to serve. Association meetings resembled the overland party governing boards, rural militia musters, and village meetings. All were exercises of community politics familiar to rural settlers.[77]

Accounts of association meetings reveal much arguing and personal bickering, as well as a great deal of rhetoric and debate.[78] Though at times the squabbling appears petty, the arguing was in fact an effective device for arriving at a consensus. The underlying principle in these meetings was the necessity of securing communal agreement. Any course of action had to be adhered to by the full association. Given the vagaries of human nature, such a consensus was often difficult to achieve. Grand rhetoric was used to persuade undecided members; personal attacks could be used to coerce opponents into submission. Flattery and eloquence, humor and drama, accusations and personal slurs not only made the meetings entertaining, but also helped to forge a community consensus.

Under these circumstances, a passionate, eloquent, and shrewd individual could quickly rise to prominence. Dr. Charles Robinson was such an individual, and his actions have sometimes identified him as the guiding spirit of the Settlers' Association. A physician from Massachusetts, Robinson came to California with an overland party in 1849. After only a short time in the mines, Robinson came to Sacramento, where he reopened his medical practice. Appalled by the harsh treatment of other overlanders in the city, Robinson determined to act on their behalf. Reports differ as to whether he was responsible for the formal organization of the association, but his name appeared as its president in a handbill of December 1849, and his actions and writings often lay at the center of association controversies.[79]

However, any interpretation of Robinson's role must be kept within the context of the association's consensus-seeking structure. Though the association often relied on his passion, energy, and eloquence, it just as often placed other men before him in temporary offices. Furthermore, a careful reading of association meeting reports suggests that Robinson did not so much lead the organization as follow some of its more outspoken members. Throughout these meetings, Robinson restated the words put forth by member speakers, usually spelling out the implications of their proposals. Robinson then wrote the association's consensus into a clear and concise statement or resolution. Throughout, Robinson appeared to attempt to quiet or harness membership passions and to direct them toward legal recourses. The problem, however, is that Robinson's search for a legal solution only further led him and the association toward the realization that no such solution existed.[80]

The settlers' vision of community, as embodied in the Settlers' Association, can best be understood by its organization and goals. Its consensus-building approach to governance and policy making worked well among a homogeneous group. Settlers shared rural backgrounds, the experiences of the overland trail, and a common goal. Consensus building had served them well in frontier farming villages, along the overland trail, and in Sacramento's Tent City. But consensus was never easy to achieve, and it would prove to be far more difficult, if not impossible, to organize the entire city in this way. Furthermore, because of the difficulty of winning consensus, the Settlers' Association found it much easier to respond to immediate problems than to formulate long-ranging policies.

The Settlers' Association's rise to prominence in city politics began during the Chapman trial. The association called the trial a sham and backed Chapman's refusal to vacate his claim. According to Chapman's statement made years later, Priest, Lee & Company offered him peaceable possession of 20 acres to relinquish his claim to the other 140. Chapman refused. If anything, the landholders' attempted settlement seemed to betray their nervousness about the title. To Chapman and the Settlers' Association, the offer was meaningless. If Sutter's original title in fact was invalid, the landholders were offering something they did not own. When Chapman refused the offer, the sheriff served him with a writ of ejectment. Chapman refused to leave. The Settlers' Association promised to defend Chapman's claim, but on Saturday night, December 1, while Chapman was alone on his claim, the sheriff returned with a posse of fifty men, who removed Chapman's portable possessions and then tore down the cabin. The Settlers' Association responded on Monday morning by rebuilding Chapman's cabin.[81]

That same Monday, the great speculators called a "law and order" meeting on the waterfront for the following night. The meeting attracted a large crowd. A makeshift speaker's platform was assembled from an assortment of dry-goods boxes, piled against the side of the Gem, a saloon fronting K Street. A board, nailed to the side of the saloon above the platform, supported a row of candles, which according to one observer burned without quivering in the still night air. The meeting began with a series of resolutions condemning the squatters for their lawless action and expressing contempt of city authorities. The resolutions held that Sutter's grant was valid and that a committee should be named to procure a copy of the grant from Monterey to satisfy the doubtful.[82]

But the speculators' resolutions met with loud disapproval, and it soon became evident that members of the Settlers' Association made up the majority of the crowd. The meeting collapsed into chaos, with loud shouts and indignant expressions filling the night air. At this point James C. Zabriskie climbed to the speaker's platform and demanded the crowd's attention. The young lawyer quieted the crowd somewhat with a self-deprecating joke and then said that every man had a right to express his sentiments and that he was determined to express his.[83]

Zabriskie's sentiments were decidedly against the council and the great speculators. Two months earlier, when they had secured the passage of their city charter, he had protested that the council had no right to create its own charter. Only one week before, the council had refused to pay his legal fees for drafting earlier city ordinances. Zabriskie himself was a large landholder and would be expected to align himself more with the city's residents than with its transients. But as Zabriskie took the speaker's platform, his recent fight with the council was a fresh indignity, and at this time city residents were themselves growing increasingly frustrated and angry with the council. Whatever his personal reasons may have been, Zabriskie transformed the "law and order" meeting into a Settlers' Association meeting.

Zabriskie began by holding aloft a copy of one of the handbills that had called the meeting and said he considered it an insult to the people. As to the resolutions' contemptuous allusion to squatters, Zabriskie was most passionate. "Who," he cried out, "who carries the stripes and stars, the institutions and the laws of our land into the far west and have now borne them even to the shores of the far-off Pacific?" The crowd shouted back enthusiastically, "Squatters!" Zabriskie then motioned that the preamble to the resolutions, which used the offending term, be rejected, and the crowd carried his motion. Zabriskie then went through the resolutions piecemeal, altering some parts, rejecting others, adding new material in other places. When Zabriskie and the crowd had finished, the adopted resolutions carried the opposite meaning from that originally proposed by the law and order group.[84]

The confrontation between speculators and settlers escalated quickly. Even while the "law and order" meeting proceeded at the waterfront, Chapman's cabin was burned to the ground.[85] The Settlers' Association immediately rebuilt the cabin on the still warm ashes, and association president Charles Robinson began building his own cabin on speculator-held land between H and I streets near the Levee.[86] On Friday, December 7, Samuel Brannan convened a meeting of the city council. Though Brannan was not a member of the council, he "requested" the council to order the city marshal to remove Robinson's structure. The council then convened. The Settlers' Association brought a suit the following day against the city marshal for his actions in removing buildings on public lands.[87]

Two days later the Settlers' Association drafted its own series of resolutions, which formally defined the organization's principles and guidelines, elected officers to serve for one year, and published a handbill publicizing their stand against the city council. The handbill proclaimed:

> The Sacramento City SETTLERS' ASSOCIATION, believing the ground, generally, in and around Sacramento City, to be Public Land; and desiring to promote the prosperity and harmony of persons settling thereon, has Resolved, that the Association will honorably regard the following Rules and Regulations:
>
> Rule 1st, Every Member of the Association will use his best exertions for the support of his fellow-associates, against any and every innovation of their JUST RIGHTS.
>
> Rule 2d, Every member desiring to obtain a Lot, must have it surveyed by the Surveyor of the Association, whose duty it shall be to record and issue a Certificate for it.[88]

The association's rules and regulations dramatically challenged the precarious position of the Sacramento government. By proclaiming land in and around the city to be public land, the association proclaimed itself to be following American principles rather than defying them. The first rule created a social and political contract in defiance of the city council, whereas the second rule underscored the point by creating a surveyor's office in direct opposition to the city council's recorder. The association stopped short of directly challenging the legitimacy of the city government, as Zabriskie had done earlier. But its actions implicitly denied the authority of the council. Like Zabriskie's argument, the Settlers' Association's stance undermined the legitimacy of Sacramento's de facto government. Its effect sent shock waves through the city's population. A December 1849 *Placer Times* summary of the speculators' and settlers' sides of the controversy ended "by expressing our inability to foretell what will be the result of this agitation, and with the hope that Right will in the end be victorious."[89]

The January 1850 flood only exasperated the already rising tensions. During the flood many residents crowded near the remains of Sutter's crumbling fort and on any other high ground that could be found in Sacramento. As the floodwaters receded, many refused to leave the higher grounds, especially along the riverfront levee, making it difficult for Brannan and other merchants to land their merchandise. Taking matters into their own hands, the merchants decided to force the squatters out. Brannan, "in a condition of frantic excitement, with a piece of manila rope around his waist, in which two revolvers were stuck," led the informal merchant militia. After tearing down the shanty erected by Charles Robinson at the foot of I Street, Brannan's men moved on to another, more substantial structure. When an observer from horseback laughed at the ineffectual efforts of the merchants to demolish the building, Brannan exploded. "Get down here,———you, and lend a hand!" he shouted; the horseman, intimidated by the merchant mob, helped pull down the building with a lasso. When the mob moved to the next structure, its owner confronted the merchants with a shotgun. "You touch this house at your peril! It's mine, and I am going to defend it." Brannan turned to the merchants "and fairly screamed out: 'Warbass, cover that———scoundrel, and if he raises his gun shoot h—l out of him." The squatter watched as Brannan and the merchants demolished the house. By sunset, despite "a regular pandemonium," the levee was cleared.[90]

In the end, however, neither side emerged victorious. Within just a few weeks of Brannan's attack on the squatters, the weather cleared and most of the city's wintering transients rushed out of the waterlogged city and into the gold-laden foothills. Temporarily, the issue of land ownership seemed moot. However, the rise of the Settlers' Association had exposed the deepest division in the city's emerging community.

>---<

As Sacramento's crowded population began to sort itself out during the winter of 1849–50, individuals had relied on both private and public associations to establish shared understandings and a sense of shared obligations among its varied populace. These associations were brought to the city by its new inhabitants, then altered and expanded to meet the unique circumstances of gold rush Sacramento. However, these attempts to create community were often frustrated by the unusual economic cycle in which Sacramento was involved, as well as by the great social and cultural differences within the population. Community building, therefore, took place against a background of growing community divisions.

The issue of land titles galvanized these divisions. Through the Sacramento City Settlers' Association, squatters, transients, newcomers, and those opposed to the questionable or ineffective actions of the city's speculator-dominated Common Council were given an effective rallying point. Based on both the private and public bonds of its members, the Settlers' Association provided its members with a highly effective and meaningful community or, more accurately, a subcommunity within the chaotic city.

As the winter rains subsided, the Settlers' Association had emerged as one of the largest and most powerful organizations in the new city. But then, just as the association was beginning to challenge the great speculators' hold on city power and land titles, the association lost many of its members, who rushed back to the gold fields. The threat of a squatter insurrection seemed to disappear magically, business activity again quickened, and Sacramento seemed to return to the prosperity that it had enjoyed the previous summer.

But the Settlers' Association, though weakened, was not dead. It still provided support for newly arriving residents, a rallying point for those opposed to the rampant speculation in the city, and a legal challenge to the city's landholders. As 1850 wore on and more men decided to give up mining to try their hand at shopkeeping in Sacramento, their strength continued to grow.

CHAPTER SIX

Dangerous Ground

"The chaotic condition in which Sacramento City first sprang into existence, is fast settling into harmony," reported the *Sacramento Transcript* on May 28, 1850. "The disordered elements of a town thrown together with Californian haste here at the mouth of the American River, have been swiftly arranging themselves to consummate a large city of powerful influence. The struggles of her early childhood are over."[1]

Having survived the turmoil of the winter, Sacramento in the spring of 1850 appeared to have finally emerged as a settled and viable city. Its economic base flourished, especially with the reopening of the mines. The city's social organization was more homogeneous after the large transient population left for the mines. City government seemed stable, especially after the election of the new Common Council headed by Hardin Bigelow. Civic officials had begun planning city growth and security, and although they moved slowly in accomplishing their objectives, officials were at least responsive to residents' concerns. F. C. Ewer and G. Kenyon Fitch, the editors of the *Transcript,* reviewed Sacramento's history and remarked with understandable pride that the city's "strength has arisen out of her weakness; stability assumes the place of instability; and, heedless of obstacles, she has trodden steadily on to the commanding place she now occupies."[2]

Yet despite the glowing tribute paid to the city by the *Transcript,* less than one week later the city's other newspaper, the *Placer Times,* warned city residents of a threat to "the rights and interests of the people and the stability of our social institutions. . . . Prudence permits no delay in excoriating a cancer which threatens the very vitality of our body, social and politic."[3] In an article appropriately titled "Dangerous Ground," editor J. E. Lawrence warned that the Settlers' Association was once again growing in strength and that their challenge to city land titles was taking on a very serious character. "Any merely abstract views of this matter do not meet the present occasion, which loudly demands the immediate and summary action of all those who properly consider their own interests, and the peace, welfare and progress of our City."[4]

The sharp contrast between the *Transcript* and *Placer Times* editorials was characteristic of the social mood of the city. As residents looked around them at the city they had built, they could not help but feel a sense of pride and confidence. Out of the chaos of the winter, they had forged stable economic, social, and political institutions that seemed to rival those of any established city in the United States. But at the same time, a sense of unease lay beneath this stability. Though squatter challenges to city lands lost much support when city transients left for the mines, the issue of land titles was not yet settled. Social stability also was more a result of the departure of the transients than any real consensus between residents and transients. And residents realized that within a few months, overlanders and transients would again fill their streets, renewing the social misunderstandings and reinvigorating the Settlers' Association's land title challenge.

Not all of the residents' unease rested on the anticipated return of the city's transients. Prices for goods and land in the city remained high. The new council had yet to prove it could work effectively. The legitimacy of the council also remained unsettled. Unlike the previous council, which had written its own charter, the new Common Council had received its charter from the provisional state legislature. However, since the state legislature was itself not authorized by the U.S. Congress, Sacramento's new charter and city and county government were, strictly speaking, no more legal than the old ones had been.

Thus the great dilemma that faced Sacramento residents in the spring of 1850: order and calm had been achieved, but at any moment disorder threatened to overwhelm the city. And given the unstable foundations of the city—mining, speculating, and gambling—disorder would not just be confusing, but potentially catastrophic. The anarchy that seemed ever just under the surface in 1849 had not been vanquished and, after a year of residents' wrestling with the cultural implications of the gold rush itself, had acquired a more demonic aspect than before suspected. In the minds of most city residents, Kemble's "admirable confusion" had become what his successor called "a cancer which threatens the very vitality of our body, social and politic."[5]

Throughout the spring and summer of 1850, the city's squatters and speculators found themselves in increasingly desperate straits and responded by fighting all the harder to secure their ultimate goals. Both groups attempted to regulate citywide laws and customs according to their own sense of fair play, but both had taken positions that would likely have proven unworkable even without the land dispute. The conflict over land titles dramatically focused the tensions that underlay the city. In the final analysis, the causes of the resulting "Squatters' Riot" were otherwise minor incidents and confrontations that escalated with a quickness that astonished most participants. Yet during the summer of 1850, challenges to the established order rapidly took on the aspect of a moral and cultural showdown, a final clash between the forces of order and anarchy. The specific triggers of these confrontations were of secondary importance. The real struggles were over how to define the boundary between admirable confusion and social chaos. Ultimately neither land titles nor personal fortunes propelled the rioters; rather, the participants sought to define the limits of individual opportunity and social responsibility.

>--<

To most squatters, social responsibility was at the core of the Settlers' Association. After the January flood and the departure of the city's transients, the association seemed to have rapidly collapsed as a viable organization. David Hewes estimated in February that "about two-thirds of the population changes every two days. They are people who are constantly arriving and making but a short stop, then shoot off to the mines."[6] However, the association in fact remained quite active. Once the floodwaters had receded, settlers again began to take up undeveloped lands. When transient miners and recovered overlanders left the city for the mines in March, settlers lost the strength of numbers that they had relied on to protect them against speculator retribution. However, in 1850 the number of real settlers, as opposed to wintering transients, grew spectacularly.

Though most transients left the city for the mines early in the spring, many quickly returned. Placer mining continued to be less profitable, and the average amount of gold that individual miners found daily in 1850 was only $10, down from an average of $20 two years before. For many would-be miners, the gold rush was proving to be a less lucrative opportunity than the hardships of mining warranted.[7] Early placer mining in 1850, after the winter rains, was expected to be good, since it was assumed that the floodwaters would help turn up more gold.[8] Yet placer deposits were not as rich as hoped, and heavy March rains only made working conditions more uncomfortable. As would-be miner James Barnes wrote to his family in 1850, "I went to the mines about the middle of April and stayed about six weeks, and then returned to the city [Sacramento]; the water was too high to work. Then I laid a claim on the North Fork. I returned about the middle of July to work but it proved a failure. . . . I came down to the city about a week ago and shall probably not return to the mines."[9] The number of disillusioned miners returning to the city grew steadily beginning in the early spring.[10] The Settlers' Association welcomed these returning miners. The Tent City surrounding Sacramento, which almost disappeared with the coming of good weather, quickly began growing again.

The Settlers' Association also saw potential members coming over the horizon from the east. Despite the decline in individual mining profits, gold rush fever was still high in the States: in 1850 roughly forty-four thousand migrants set out for California, nearly twenty thousand more than the previous year.[11] Throughout the summer, Sacramento residents heard reports of the thousands of emigrants heading their way, of their difficulties, sicknesses, and poverty.[12] Unlike the previous year, 1850 would prove to be a dry year on the plains. Water and grazing would prove more difficult to obtain, and many migrants had been warned not to carry as many provisions as migrants from the previous year. The result was often desperation and starvation.[13] When they arrived, their numbers would swell the Tent City once again. The Settlers' Association looked forward to their arrival, both with concern and hope, again believing that with their numbers and needs they would help convince the federal government to settle the land title dispute quickly and in their favor.

In the meantime, city settlers tried to keep the validity of the land title dispute before Sacramento residents. In a letter published in the *Placer Times* on February 2, John Plumbe, an engineer seeking to build support in the city for a transcontinental railroad, tried to present the legal precedents on frontier land titles and to draw a conclusion about the title dispute. Plumbe admitted that an easy solution could not be found. He argued that the U.S. Congress should intervene and suggested that no one be granted a title until Congress ruled on the legality of Sutter's grant. He concluded, however, that Congress should lean toward the settlers' arguments and award them those lots that they had developed.[14] Plumbe's argument drew a sharp response from an unidentified resident who defended the Sutter grant and ridiculed his cautious attitude as being impractical.[15] Further discussion of the land dispute did not appear in the *Placer Times,* and the Settlers' Association was left to establish its claims in other forums.

Association rallies and demonstrations brought some attention to the settlers' cause. The impassioned rhetoric of these meetings grew increasingly inflammatory as the year progressed. Attacks on land speculators soon included attacks on members of the Common Council as well. The aspersions settlers flung at the council had also been directed at the old council, since it had been under the direct control of the city's great speculators. Although the new Common Council did not as directly represent the views of the great speculators, most council members owned substantial amounts of city land.[16] Furthermore, city funding, so necessary to the construction of the proposed levee and other city improvements, was dependent on taxing personal property.[17] The council thus tended to assume the validity of Sutter's grant, since to deny it robbed them of needed funds. Settlers turned their invective on civic leaders as well as great speculators, and association spokesmen most severe in their judgments against the Common

Council usually received the most applause.[18]

Settlers' Association meetings, however, made little impact on the city in general, if newspaper reports are any indication. On April 20, the *Transcript*, ignoring previous land disputes, editorialized on the wondrous state of society despite the excitement caused by the gold rush. "Never has a country been more orderly," it reported, "never has property been held more inviolable, or life more sacred, than in California for the last twelve or fourteen months."[19]

However, events were rushing forward that would force the editors to reconsider their judgments. On April 23, an advertisement appeared for the first time in the *Transcript* offering for sale a "translation of the papers respecting the grant made by Governor Alvarado to 'Mr. Augustus Sutter,' showing that said grant does not extend any further *south* than the mouth of the Feather river, and, therefore, of course, does not embrace Sacramento City."[20]

The pamphlet, written by John Plumbe, hit the town like a thunderbolt. The arguments made against Sutter's grant were numerous. According to the pamphlet, Sutter's grant was invalid, since there was no evidence that the central government in Mexico had ever sanctioned it. The grant was made out to "Mr. Augustus Sutter"; the pamphlet questioned whether this was in fact the same man known as Captain John Sutter. The grant specifically excluded land overflowed in winter; clearly the Sacramento site could not have been included. Finally, and most convincingly, the grant specified that its eastern boundary was the Feather River, and its southern boundary was stated as latitude 38° 41' 32." This would place the southern boundary of Sutter's grant some miles north of the city, crossing the Sacramento River near the mouth of the Feather River. Sacramento land had not been covered by Sutter's Mexican grant; the Captain's only claim in the area was that of a squatter himself. As such, he had a right to 160 acres, but no more. Since Sutter by then had taken up his residence at Hock Farm, roughly forty miles north of Sacramento City, Plumbe argued that even as a squatter Sutter's claim could not have covered city lands.[21]

During the Chapman trial, Sutter's grant had not been produced; speculators had merely testified to its authenticity. Just the rumor that the grant had not in fact been valid or had not covered city lands had led to increased squatting in the city. Now, according to the pamphlet, the rumor was true, and squatters rushed to take up any remaining undeveloped lots in the city. In the following weeks the Settlers' Association rode an exhilarating wave of confidence. Membership rose dramatically. The association established its own recorder's office, hired Plumbe as surveyor and register, and began issuing certificates of title to city lots.[22] Assured of their legal position, the association organized and circulated a petition that it forwarded to Congress, asking for a distribution of the public land among actual settlers.[23]

The association's efforts, however, did not go unnoticed by the city's great speculators. As Dr. Israel Lord noted in his diary, "When the emigrants with families first began to arrive in the city . . . , [Samuel] Brannan, a notorious gambler and pickpocket but great land owner here, stuck up a flaming hand-bill giving notice that he would lease for one year without charge a lot to each family which might apply. Now these lots were one and a half to two miles out of the city or at least from the levee where all business is done, in short, where nobody then desired to locate. One hardly knows which to admire, the unblushing effrontery and consummate impudence of the offer or the infinite simplicity and ignorance it evinces."[24]

To counter Brannan, the association began circulating its own handbills among newcomers to the city, outlining their position and warning prospective residents not to accept land titles based on the Sutter grant. "There are in our City a number of men with remarkable principles," the handbill warned,

> who go among those who have newly arrived and offer to sell or lease to them the *PUBLIC LAND* in and about this place, thus imposing upon the unsuspecting. The latter are hereby notified that the vacant land in Sacramento City, and vicinity, is open for *ALL,* free of charge; but, they can make either of the following gentlemen a present of a few thousand dollars, if they have it to spare. Such favors are eagerly sought and exultingly received by them. In fact, some of them are so solicitous in this matter, that, if they are not given *SOMETHING,* they will *ALMOST NOT LIKE IT,* and even threaten to *SUE* people who will not contribute to their support.

The handbill then went on to list the most "notorious" of these "gentlemen," boldly naming over twenty of the city's leading landholders and city government officials.[25]

The effectiveness of the Settlers' Association campaign shocked the city's great speculators. The continued challenge from the association brought a slowdown in the city's growth. Residents hesitated before buying city lots from speculators, whose title might not be valid. City land values, which had been rising so dramatically since the city's founding, now had reached a plateau and even begun to drop off in value. Concern over land values rippled through the city.

✦ — ✦

The great speculators struck back quickly and forcefully. Speculators countered that the boundaries of Sutter's grant had in fact covered the Sacramento City site: that the latitude line given in the grant had merely been a surveyor's error. Jean Jacques Vioget, the Swiss sailor, tavern keeper, and surveyor who had conducted the survey of the grant, signed an affidavit in San Francisco confessing his error. According to Vioget, the latitudinal error had been constant throughout the entire survey. The northern boundary, Vioget pointed out, was also in error, as a close reading of the grant would show. The northern boundary was described as being the "Tres Picos," today's Sutter's Buttes. No one disputed this boundary, despite the incorrect latitude given for it. The southern boundary survey was off by the same amount and was meant to be about four and a half miles south of Sutter's Fort. Vioget's argument was published in both the *Placer Times* and *Transcript* and prompted lively debates between settlers and "Sutterites," as landholders under the Sutter grant came to be known.[26]

Landholders hardly contented themselves with the flurry of newspaper debates. Throughout the spring landholders throughout the state had demanded that the legislature take some kind of action to stabilize land titles. On April 22, the day before the pamphlet appeared, the transitional legislature passed "An Act concerning Forcible Entry and Unlawful Detainer." This extraordinary act gave justices the right to eject, fine, and seek restitution from squatters according to a judge's discretion. Plaintiffs bringing charges against squatters were under no obligation to present proof of their own title; only defendants were required to show legal title to the land.[27] Under normal conditions, such an act would have been patently illegal. But given the uncertain nature of Mexican grant titles and the lack of federal confirmation, the act represented an attempt to impose some order on California land disputes.[28]

Armed with this piece of legislation, Sacramento's great speculators next forced a city ordinance through the Common Council forbidding anyone to erect tents, shanties, or houses on any vacant lot belonging to a private person. In May, city speculator and councilman John P. Rogers brought suit against John F. Madden, a Settlers' Association member squatting on a vacant lot belonging to Rogers on the southeast corner of Second and N streets. The suit against Madden not only sought to test the enforcement of the Act of Forcible Entry and Detainer, but also sought to push settlers' claims outside the city limits. Hemmed in by the Sacramento River to the west and Sutter's Slough and the American River to the north, city development was moving east and south. Madden's claimed lot lay in the transition zone between the developed city and the sprawling Tent City encampments south of the city, directly in the path of city growth. Madden's case both symbolically and realistically came to represent the essential struggle between the landholders and the Settlers' Association.

When the case came to trial, County Attorney J. H. McKune represented

Madden and the settlers. Though the court ruled against Madden, McKune appealed the case to the county courts. Neither the Settlers' Association nor McKune expected to find justice in the city recorder's court but hoped to continue appealing their case until it reached a U.S. court outside California. There the Settlers' Association hoped to force the U.S. government to deal with California's unsettled land titles.[29] In the meantime, Madden refused to vacate the disputed lot, and the Settlers' Association continued to provide Madden with legal counsel.

Frustrated by their inability to stem the growing number of squatters on their lands, the city's great speculators resurrected their old political organization, now called the "Law and Order Association." Notices printed in the papers announced their intention to defend their property under the Sutter title to the last. The Law and Order Association also began to form and to drill companies of militia.[30]

On June 21 and 22, speculators personally began upholding their land titles by force. On the first day, four or five landholders demolished a squatter's home erected on a lot belonging to one of the party. The Law and Order Association celebrated its victory well into the evening and early the following morning set about renewing their attacks. At four in the morning a policeman "found Mr. Brannan breaking off boards from the front of a building."[31] Several hours later twenty-five to thirty landholders, armed with picks, shovels, and crowbars, went to the levee just above J Street and began demolishing a squatter's shanty. When their work was nearly completed, the party shoved the remaining structure over onto an adjoining lot, causing the collapse of another squatter's tent. They next moved on to a third lot, surrounded by a fence, which they tore down, and then to another squatter's house, which they completely demolished. Though a crowd quickly gathered, no one offered any resistance to the demolition. As the party was about to disperse, one of the raiders called out that he owned two lots on J Street, outside the developed part of the city. The party promptly accompanied him to the site, removed the fences the squatter had put up around the property, and then returned to town. By this time a crowd of squatters had begun to form, who grew increasingly loud and threatening. But in the face of the landholders' determination, the squatters avoided a fight.[32]

The landholders' raids on squatters' homes late in June were the culmination of the speculators' attempts to secure their land titles in the city. Although the Settlers' Association's challenge of Sutter's grant had certainly affected the legitimacy of land titles in the city, the great speculators had continued to acquire every possible bit of Sutter's original grant.

Analysis of land deeds granted by Sutter and Sutter, Jr., from 1848 to 1850 reflects the land title dispute in the city. During the initial period of the city, the last week of 1848 and the end of January 1849, the number of town lots acquired was high. A drop-off in sales during February most likely reflects the uncertainty over Sacramento's future, for during this month the competition between Sacramento and Sutterville was most intense. The rise of deed grants in March and April corresponds to Sacramento's success in its struggle with Sutterville; April's grants include the large land deeds given to Sacramento merchants for staying in the city. The reduced interest in Sutter land in May probably represents something of a saturation and reorganization period. During this month land transactions were high, but speculators seem to have been more interested in trading lots among themselves than in acquiring new Sutter lands.

Acquisition of Sutter lands increased during the summer of 1849, reflecting both the growth of the city and the election of the first city council in August. Throughout the winter of 1849–50, sales of Sutter lands almost perfectly mirrored the city's population level, rising in the fall as more people came to the city, gradually declining early in 1850 as transient residents left for the mines, reducing pressure to open new areas for development. A dramatic drop in sales in January most likely was caused by the great flood, which disrupted all city business throughout most of the month.

The dramatic drop, sharp rise, and then cessation of interest in Sutter lands during the following summer appears to be the result of the Settlers' Association's attempt to invalidate Sutter's grants. A drop in land sales in April occurred when Plumbe's pamphlet appeared on the streets of Sacramento. The pamphlet's carefully reasoned argument did even more than the Chapman case in undermining confidence in Sutter's grant. Though supporters of Sutter's grant responded quickly, the lack of interest in Sutter lands during April and most of May seems to reflect an uneasiness over purchasing deeds that might not convey legal title.

A sudden upswing in grants late in May and throughout July represents a desperate move on the part of the city's land speculators. Their renewed interest in Sutter lands was sparked apparently by two incidents: the legislature's passage of the Act of Forcible Entry and Detainer and the Common Council's Private Property Ordinance, and the Settlers' Association's initial defeat in Sacramento's courts, which reinforced the validity of the Sutter grant. The sudden rush to acquire Sutter grants, however, came when Sutter agreed to surrender his remaining lands free of charge to anyone willing to clear squatters from the lands.[33] Thus, just as the case for upholding Sutter's title was apparently growing stronger, Sutter offered his lands to speculators at almost no cost. During late May and early June, speculators in essence acquired every remaining piece of Sutter's original grant. The precipitate drop in new grants made in July does not reflect speculators' disinterest in Sutter lands; by July,

Sutter simply had no more lands to sell.

These purchases of land in Sacramento, however, reflected a serious concern of the great speculators. In fact, the challenge of the Settlers' Association to city land titles only marginally affected property values. Much more troublesome was the speculators' own financial irresponsibility. Clearly city land values were inflated far beyond their real worth and would eventually fall again. Speculators, however, ignored this inevitability and instead based the bulk of their business dealings on the inflated value of their real estate holdings. During the summer, the city assessor's report on the value of property, real estate and personal, listed a combined total value of $7,968,985; real estate alone was assessed at $5,586,000. Dr. John Morse, however, later estimated that the report was probably $5 million *over* the true intrinsic value of the property at that time, making the reported values inflated by 1,000 percent. "Yet such was the inflated and ruinous estimates of the day," he wrote, "such the unbounded confidence in the prevailing standards of calculation, that men skilled in the science of money lending regarded property at this enormous valuation as a sufficient guaranty of payment."[34]

Throughout 1849 and the first half of 1850, the city's great speculators had sold city lands to individual businessmen at inflated prices, then allowed them credit based on the inflated values of the businessmen's new land. Wholesale goods, which speculators then sold to the businessmen on this credit, already inflated by the costs of shipping them to California, were further inflated by the market manipulations of the great speculators. Thus the ability of the great speculators to dominate the city and amass a fortune rested on the grossly inflated property values of the lands they held in the city. Although this concentrated profits in the hands of the great speculators, the whole structure was a fragile house of cards. And by the summer of 1850, the cards were beginning to wobble.

During the difficulties of the winter of 1849–50, a number of small businessmen began going out of business, and the great speculators found it impossible to collect the debts owed to them by these small merchants. During the spring, while business in general resumed its earlier energy, the great speculators still found it difficult to collect their debts. The proliferation of businesses in the city did not so much increase the gross amount of city business as simply spread it thinner. The establishment of more cities in the mining fields further reduced Sacramento businessmen's profits. Individual businessmen made good livings, but hardly the spectacular gains of the previous year. Prices for all commodities fell in the city, and businessmen had a difficult time repaying the great speculators' inflated loans.[35]

Furthermore, as Morse pointed out, "many of the business men of Sacramento were persons whose education and experience unfitted them for the positions

they occupied. This was probably peculiarly the case with the banking houses.
. . . Men who had for years confined themselves to the tedious rounds of their
particular business at the East regarded this as a good opportunity for changing
their pursuits, and hence the unutterable compound of lawyers, doctors, ministers,
merchants, mechanics, and laborers that in a few months became so entangled
in the labyrinths of trade as to require a general train of rebuking bankruptcies
to restore them to their sense and their legitimate callings."[36]

By midsummer 1850, the great speculators were themselves being hard-pressed
by eastern suppliers. Pressuring local businessmen had little effect, leaving the
speculators to foreclose on mortgages, which at best often returned less than
one-quarter or one-eighth of the principal invested.[37] Under these circumstances,
it was only a matter of time before many of the great speculators would begin to
declare bankruptcy. The immediate solution was thus to acquire more land on
which to shore up a shaky investment empire. By the summer of 1850, however,
there was no more land to be had. It is in this context that the Settlers' Association
threat was understood by the great speculators. Land title challenges, in that
they reduced land values, at the very least weakened an already tottering financial
structure. Should the settlers succeed in overturning the validity of the Sutter
grant, the great speculators faced utter ruin. Furthermore, should the great
speculators fail, they would pull down with them the entire financial structure of
the city, ruining enterprising residents as well. The great bazaar would become
bankrupt, and Sacramento would collapse. Thus the great speculators saw the
Settlers' Association challenge as a direct threat to their fortunes, to their ability
to direct city affairs, and to the city. Increasingly they viewed the Settlers'
Association's challenge to land titles as a revolutionary act against the city itself.

To many residents in the city, however, the land dispute still seemed a less than
serious threat. Although the city's newspapers reported on the confrontations and
residents' letters and journals commented on the various merits of both sides, few
residents took an active role in either defending or defeating Sutter's grant. Alonzo
Hill, who wandered back and forth between the mining camps and Sacramento,
described the dispute in sarcastic, cynical terms in a letter to his family. "The
aristocracy in this country like all other countries are bearing down on the poor
and unfortunate," he wrote early in the summer of 1850. "The speculators pretend
to own all the land whereon the city of Sacramento now stands. They say they have
a title from 'Sutter' but the class not so wealthy contend that 'Sutter' has no claim
or title and one man has as good a right to the soil as another. So they settle a land
claimed by the aristocracy and the result is lawsuits, and fights with bloodshed.
But the 'Settlers' as they are called, knowing that Theocracy and Democracy
are combined, they are determined to sustain the just right of Autocracy. Aye,

even if it cost the price paid is Stratocracy."[38]

Like other residents in Sacramento, Hill did express concern over the possible escalation of the conflict. He noted:

> Yet a little while, and I think it will appear that the down-trodden "Settlers" are powerful in their Imbecility, and are not to bow the knee to the land speculators and brigands, Jews, gentiles or whatever name of loathing some can imagine. The spirit which declared the American colonies free and independent, is bursting forth like the flood of a torrent. And even now is a crisis which calls forth the noblest attributes of manly character. Here is soil where American citizenry rights and possessions lie buried seven feet deep under invalid Spanish claims and those claims sustained by aristocracy, who have so many gold rings on their fingers they can't get them into their breeches pockets. But a party is organized to attack this monopoly and is augmented day by day. I hope for peace, but ah! me, I do not know what the Historians will need to chronicle on the page of 1850.[39]

$$\rightarrow-\leftarrow$$

To members of the Settlers' Association, the struggle over land titles in Sacramento was serious business. The validity or invalidity of city land titles called into question the broader issues of political and social order. To the settlers, the Sutter grant was a fraud, instigated to deprive American citizens of their constitutional rights. Proclaiming the invalidity of Sutter-derived land titles quickly brought the settlers into conflict with any agency that tried to validate Sutter's original grant. Since the local government and its recorder's office recognized the validity of the Sutter grant, settlers believed an illegitimate local government was victimizing them. One of the settlers' key beliefs was that the Sacramento government was not acting under the principles of U.S. law. Their overall strategy, therefore, was to find a way to appeal their case beyond the local courts to a federal court. The process, however, was certain to be difficult.[40]

Following the landholders' raids on settlers' claims in late June, the Settlers' Association held a number of crucial meetings to determine their course of action. Early in July, the association began making arrangements to provide all squatters in the city with a legal defense. Before this time, each squatter had defended himself individually, "on his own hook," as one association member put it. Many newcomers, however, were too poor to afford their own counsel. To solve this financial problem, the association proposed to form a contract among all association members, raise funds through a community-based subscription drive, and employ a team of lawyers to defend their rights. One member objected to the proposal, arguing that since Sutter's grant was illegal anyway, it was unnecessary to go through the courts. A member identified only as "Milligan," who apparently proposed the plan, argued back that "the object was to keep their enemies at bay until the question could be brought before a legal tribunal, where justice would be done." Milligan further claimed that "squatters were only aiming at justice; *satisfy them* that Sutter's title was good, and they would leave the *land as quick as a flea would jump off a hot griddle!*" Milligan's plan was adopted.[41]

At a subsequent meeting, Charles Robinson announced that he had found a legal team, the law partnership of Tweed, Aldrich, Mayhall, and McKune, who were willing to represent the squatters. However, they wanted $4,000 for their services: $2,000 down payment was required, $2,000 needed to be secured through a bondsman, and if the lawyers were successful, the settlers were "to do what they could afford to do in addition to the $4,000."[42]

Raising the needed funds proved difficult. After two days of soliciting, an association committee reported that it had raised only about $1,200 but admitted that many potential subscribers had not been at home or had been too poor to contribute to the defense fund. Milligan himself admitted that the fund-raising had been "no pleasant task"; on approaching a man he had been told was "a brother-squatter," the man had replied "that he had known people to make money by minding their own business!" After hearing the committee's report, one of the association's leaders, James McClatchy, offered to join the subscription committee himself, especially when he heard that the committee had refused to take less than $25 from any individual.[43]

Even more troublesome, however, was the role of new settlers in the fund-raising process. Robinson pointed out that "if the immigrants are expected to pay a part, some plan must be adopted to let them into the benefits when they come, by paying a fee." Otherwise the newcomers would feel cheated by the association's lawyers and refuse to pay their share, and the lawyers might quit. The membership debated various securities for the lawyers, failed to reach a consensus, and agreed to postpone the discussion while they continued soliciting.[44]

Finally, during the middle of July, Robinson devised an at least temporarily effective legal conundrum to turn the tables on the landholders and provide some measure of financial security for the association. Previously, when settlers arrested for squatting proved unable to pay court bails, they faced a long and difficult stay in prison. To counteract this, Robinson staked off several blocks of land near the outskirts of the city, put up a large tent, and moved in. When the next settler trial was brought before the courts, Robinson offered this property, valued at $100,000, as bail. When the court asked him about his title, Robinson responded that his was as good as any in the city. The move was brilliant: under prevailing laws, instituted by the speculators, the judge could not rule against Robinson simply because he could not show a clear title. Robinson's title could only be challenged if someone with a prior claim filed suit against him. Since no one expected Robinson to use his claim in this manner, no one had yet filed against him. The judge's hands were tied. Ruling that he could not try land titles, the court was forced to accept Robinson's assertion of his legal right to the property offered. The maneuver not only worked to secure the release of squatters awaiting trial, but also illustrated the deficiencies that undermined the courts' ability to enforce anyone's land titles.[45]

While trying to devise an effective strategy to deal with the landholders, the Settlers' Association also gave vent to the feelings of frustration and rage members felt over the "Sutterite" raids of late June. Rhetoric was an essential part of association meetings, used to persuade and cajole members into taking unified action. During the meetings in July, the rhetoric grew increasingly heated and pushed the association toward radical actions. When Milligan proposed his plan that the association provide a legal defense for all squatters, he reinforced his proposal with "an eloquent appeal about the sacred right of the homestead—a right which every man was bound to protect in justice to himself."[46] Milligan further announced that "squatters were men of firmness; their cause has reached the States; [and] they had many hearty sympathizers on the Atlantic shores."[47]

Robinson argued that if the speculators were upheld in their titles, it would result in the oppression of poor men throughout the state. "Was this right? Was it a blessing? If so, Ireland was blessed, and all other oppressed countries. Would any Anglo-Saxon endure this? The Southern slave was not treated worse."[48]

Robinson pointed out that the Common Council, through its ordinance on private property, had undertaken to legislate public property, an action that only the legislature could take. "Has the Mayor any right to say what is *my* property and what is not?" Robinson asked. The Common Council was destitute of common sense, he argued, and should be regarded accordingly. "It has been said, 'answer a fool according to his folly,'" Robinson noted, "and if a man showed himself too low to be respected, don't respect him." For his part, Robinson

> looked down on the Council—way down—down so low that he could not see them. They were far out of sight of decent men. For his part, he meant to imitate the Mayor, meant to be a big squatter! It was just as easy to squat on one hundred and sixty acres as on one acre, and what he didn't need he would give to the poor squatters who are coming along by and by. It was as easy to defend a big piece as a small piece, and

far better to take it themselves than to let the big landholders get in and sell it.[49]

Robinson's disdain for the council inspired similar outbursts from other members, and in subsequent meetings, association members became more daring in their defiance of the council. By the end of July, association speeches began openly calling for civil disobedience. McClatchy, one of the most vociferous of association speakers, proclaimed that "he was a law-abiding citizen, but if these speculators were ready to fight, so was he. He would rather fight than collect subscriptions, any day; and if they showed fight, give them battle, and the devil take the hindmost. Let us put up the fences pulled down, *and put up the men who pulled them down!*"[50]

McClatchy pointed out that God's laws were above man's laws and that God gave man the earth for his heritage. In this case, McClatchy continued, U.S. laws were on the side of the settlers, and the Supreme Court would second God's laws once their case finally reached that jurisdiction. In the meantime, "if the land-holders act as they do, we shall be obliged to lick them."[51]

These examples of rhetoric show the gradual shift in the association toward outright defiance of the city government. By the middle of July, Robinson declared that "we should abide by all just laws, [but] not unjust," and his defiance heartened members. At the end of one meeting late in the month, one member announced that he "was proud to feel that by their language that evening they had already been violating those city ordinances which forbade assemblages for unlawful ends. 'A fig for their laws; they have no laws!'"[52]

Up to this point the Settlers' Association had accepted the existing framework of city order. Though it protested the landholders' titles to city lands and correctly claimed that city courts were merely vehicles controlled by the speculators, the association felt that they could win their struggle by working within the existing, if corrupt, system. They continued staking out claims to city land, filing these claims with their own recorder's office and petitioning Congress to come to their rescue. When members were arrested, they endeavored to defend them, knowing full well that local courts would decide against them, setting their hopes on an appeal process that would eventually bring them justice.

But as the summer progressed, the association grew increasingly frustrated and disheartened in the face of speculator laws, courts, and militia raids. Believing their cause to be just, they were forced to live under a government that they felt represented speculator greed rather than American principles of justice. The rhetoric of association meetings, searching for a consensus for action, instead served to inflame passions.

As the summer stretched into August, the Settlers' Association's reliance on consensus solutions to urban problems forced its leaders to abandon the existing city government entirely. Association leaders were not revolutionaries at heart. Their progress toward rebellion consistently attempted to instill what they considered traditional rural American values and laws into the chaotic physical and moral environment of a gold rush city. Their denunciation of Sacramento government and its practices did not denounce American government and principles but sought to reaffirm them.

By the beginning of August, both the great speculators and the settlers felt they had reached a point of no return. To the settlers, their legal attempt to bypass the local courts was nearing success, and their confidence in their ability to resist the local government grew daily. To the great speculators, the growing challenge of the Settlers' Association threatened them with utter ruin unless it was stopped quickly. To the settlers, success lay in moving boldly ahead; to the great speculators, disaster could only be avoided by a decisive move against the settlers. Then, within the first two weeks of August, two unrelated incidents pushed both sides into open conflict.

The first incident undermined the great speculators. On Saturday, August 3, Barton Lee published a small notice in the *Transcript* announcing his retirement from Barney, Blossom, and Company. Lee's retirement from the large firm sent an ominous chill throughout the city's financial network. Two days later Lee, the city's largest landholder and a prominent member of the great speculators, announced his bankruptcy.[53]

The news stunned the city. The managers of Lee's estate tried to reassure residents who held Lee's notes that they would be made valid. The day after Lee's announcement his managers published a notice claiming that Lee's liabilities amounted to $1,000,300 and that his property was worth $1,400,000. Lee's monthly income was estimated at between $55,000 and $80,000.[54] Lee's property, however, was figured at the inflated prices of the summer, and much of his income was derived from real estate rents, leases, and sales. If Lee's bankruptcy and settler unrest triggered a collapse of land prices, Lee's creditors could be ruined.

To try to forestall the city's economic ruin, Lee published a notice in the *Transcript,* asking his creditors to have faith, assuring residents that his estate would make good on all his debts. "It is my sincere determination to pay every cent of my liabilities," Lee wrote. "All I ask, is to rest assured that I do not mean you an injury, and to bear with me patiently for awhile, so that I may recover from the immediate pressure." Lee asked his creditors not to sell his notes for less than face value.[55]

Lee's collapse, in retrospect, seems inevitable. Because the financial power of the great speculators rested on inflated landholdings, the first speculator to fall would be the one with the largest holdings. Lee's bankruptcy dramatically demonstrated the Achilles' heel of the great speculators. And because so many of the great speculators' investments were intertwined, Lee's bankruptcy threatened all the great speculators. Thus, following Lee's announcement of his intention to pay every cent, a number of the city's largest speculators and businessmen printed notices in the *Transcript* offering to take Lee's notes at full value as cash.[56]

This act of faith by the buyers was really an attempt to preserve the city's land values as much as it was a display of confidence in Lee's personal honesty. Lee's ability to pay his notes was based on the inflated value of his property holdings. If Lee were forced to sell them at a reduced value, land values all over the city would drop and likely produce more bankruptcies in a chain reaction. If, however, the great speculators bought Lee's notes at face value, they could keep land values high and so protect their own financial base. Purchasing Lee's notes amounted to whistling in the dark, an act of self-delusion intended to hold off a very real threat by pretending it simply did not exist.

By the middle of August, the threatened collapse seemed to have been averted. Confidence hesitantly returned, and the trick seemed to have worked. On Wednesday, August 14, the *Transcript* published a short editorial noting the revival of business and the renewed confidence of the city. "Nothing can be more gratifying to the Sacramentan than the present aspect of our city," it proclaimed, noting that the city "is a different town from what it was ten days ago."[57] Yet the great speculators' house of cards was falling rapidly about them. The result was to leave the great speculators more determined than ever to crush the Settlers' Association. The *Transcript* editorial, in hindsight, is deeply ironic. On the same day that the editorial appeared, settlers and city officials opened fire on each other in the commercial heart of the city: the "Squatters' Riot" had begun.

→ — ←

The other incident that led to the riot had undermined the settlers. And as Lee's bankruptcy struck directly at the root of the greatest speculators' fears, so, too, would this strike directly at the settlers' greatest hopes. The incident involved John Madden's appeal of his indictment under the Act of Forcible Entry and Detainer. Following his defeat in B. F. Washington's City Recorder's Court in May, Madden's attorney, McKune, had appealed the decision to the county court. Neither Madden, McKune, nor the Settlers' Association expected the court to rule in Madden's favor. According to the Settlers' Association strategy, however, Madden's lawyers planned to continue the appeal before a territorial or federal court. On Saturday morning, August 10, Judge E. J. Willis, one of the prominent landholders in the city,[58] sustained the lower court's verdict.

What happened next is uncertain. Settlers' Association attorneys apparently declared their intention to appeal and asked the judge whether the appeal would go next to the Supreme Court. Willis later declared that he had responded that "if there was any law providing for an appeal in such cases, it was hoped that the case might be carried up." But on further questioning by the lawyers, Willis declared that he "knew of no law providing for an appeal."[59]

Whether or not such a law existed in the muddled state of California government, the Settlers' Association took Judge Willis's comments to mean that he denied any further appeal from his court. Association members were enraged. Denied a right to appeal beyond the local courts, the settlers felt they were being denied the only course to justice open to them. Robinson sent out handbills calling for a mass meeting of squatters and other interested parties that same evening on Madden's disputed property. A large crowd attended the meeting. A report in the *Transcript* described the proceedings as "characterized by great excitement, with a mixture of mirth and sparkling wit, which made the meeting decidedly 'rich and racy.'"[60] From the description of the debate that followed, it is clear that both squatters and landholders attended in roughly equal numbers. With Lee's bankruptcy only a week old, both sides of the confrontation understood the meeting's importance.

The settlers seized the initiative. The meeting began with the presentation of a series of resolutions by Robinson designed to resist decisions made by Judge Willis. A motion was made that the resolutions be considered separately, but at this point the crowd began shouting for various speakers to make their views on the subject known. A settler named McClure took the stage first, and for roughly forty-five minutes he outlined the deficiencies of Sutter's title and the long struggle of the Settlers' Association against the city's speculators. But when McClure stated that Sutter's homestead was Hock Farm and not the fort, Samuel Brannan shouted up from the crowd, "False!" and the crowd interrupted McClure with loud cries and demands for a new speaker. McClure retired.[61]

Brannan and a man identified as "Judge Wilson" attempted to co-opt the meeting and took the stage. Wilson claimed to have just arrived in the city with a complete translation of the Mexican laws on land titles, which he said would prove that the association was "vastly mistaken in regard to one or two of the arguments they use in support of their rights." The crowd erupted in disorder and confusion, and Brannan launched into his comments. Brannan called McClure's statements "false, untrue," and defended his use of force in ejecting squatters from his land, "land that had been paid for, with money he had earned by hard work."[62]

The crowd next demanded the appearance of Colonel E. J. C. Kewen, the attorney who had represented the great speculators in their case against Madden. After "considerable tumult," Kewen took the stage, where he described himself as "a man who is not afraid to face any populace, or give expression to the honest convictions of his heart, at any time, or under any circumstances."

"Are you a land-holder?" the crowd shouted.

"Yes, I have a few acres of land, which I have honestly acquired—land which I bought and paid for." Kewen charged the squatters for being honest men who "had been deluded by designing persons." When someone in the crowd interrupted him with the cry, "Soft Soap!" Kewen, referring to settler complaints and Robinson's resolutions, replied "Yes, I believe there is a little too much LIE in it, and I will forbear." The crowd again grew noisy, some approving of Kewen's remarks, others disparaging them.[63]

At this point the meeting threatened to dissolve in complete chaos. When one element in the crowd called for a rereading of the resolutions, Robinson not only obliged, but also attempted to regain control of the meeting by launching into his own lengthy defense of the resolutions. He closed with the remark that "as for himself, he meant to defend the property he had settled upon at all hazards, and that his corpse would be found there, rather than yield in this matter—that in his earlier days of squatterism he had recommended moderation, but the day was past." Robinson then took a vote on the resolutions; despite a loudly mixed response, he declared them carried.[64]

The following day, Robinson drafted a manifesto to accompany the resolutions, carefully trying to spell out the legal position of the association and the dramatic stance it was taking. Robinson reminded residents that California had not yet been admitted as a state and was thus still a territory. Therefore any laws passed by the legislature in San Jose, formed in the last year by a grassroots movement in the state, were merely advisory; Congress alone made the laws governing territories. Some of the laws of the San Jose legislature were clearly unconstitutional. Now the courts, which this legislature had set up, refused appeal from their decisions to higher state and federal courts.[65]

Robinson then announced the association's break with the Common Council. "The people in this community called settlers, and others who are friends of justice and humanity," he wrote, "in consideration of the above, have determined to disregard all decisions of our courts in land cases, and all summonses or executions by the sheriff, constable, or other officer of the present county or city touching this matter. They will regard the same officers as private citizens, as in the eyes of the constitution they are, and hold them responsible accordingly."[66] In addition, Robinson warned, Settlers' Association members "have deliberately resolved to bear arms, and protect their sacred rights, if need be, with their lives."[67]

When the Settlers' Association finally took this irreversible position, the action followed a train of logic and precedent that had been building since the Chapman trial nearly ten months earlier. First the association had pledged to uphold settlers' rights to public land. Next it had investigated and proven Sutter's grant to be invalid in regard to city land. Since the city recorder had not recognized their claims, they had established their own title office. When city government continued to deny settlers justice under American law, the association declared the government to be acting illegally. The ambiguous basis of California government further undermined the Common Council's authority. Pushed by passionate rhetoric, bitter frustration, and apparently unjust opposition, the association found itself with very little room for political maneuvering.

When the Settlers' Association proclaimed its defiance of the Common Council, Sacramento residents had mixed feelings for the association. Early newspaper coverage had generally condemned the organization, but by July there is some evidence that the editors of the *Transcript* had begun to sympathize with the settlers.[68] And although settler meetings and letters produced a flurry of verbal opposition, many residents generally stayed out of confrontations between settlers and landholders. When Sutterite parties demolished squatters' homes, most residents did not interfere, but they also did nothing to prevent settlers from establishing new claims.

The association's challenge to the Common Council, however, would mean very little without broad public support. The fate of the Settlers' Association's revolt against the Common Council was in the hands of city residents. To secure their support or even their involvement, however, would not be easy. Robinson himself understood the importance of public support for the settlers' cause. In a letter to his fiancée in Massachusetts, Robinson worried about the precariousness of the association's position. He noted that after drawing up his argument he had taken it to a lawyer, "to see if my position was correct, *legally,*" before having the document printed and distributed. Yet his doubts, he admitted, remained. "What will be the result?" he wrote to his confidante. "Shall I be borne out in my position? On whom can I depend? How many of those who are Squatters will come out if there is a prospect of a fight? Will the Sheriff take possession [of Madden's lot], as he has promised, before ten o'clock A.M.? How many Speculators will fight? Have I distinctly defined our position in the bill? Will the *world,* the *Universe,* and *God* say it is just?"[69]

On Monday, August 12, Robinson and the Settlers' Association distributed the printed manifesto and resolutions. As the manifesto spread throughout the town, Robinson himself went to the lot in question, making speeches to passersby, gathering a crowd of about two hundred. Settlers' Association men enrolled the names of volunteers among the listeners who were willing to fight for the cause. A military commander was chosen, John Maloney, a veteran of the Mexican War, and soon some fifty men had pledged to support the association's cause with arms.[70]

The sheriff was expected to serve a writ of ejectment on Madden, but instead Mayor Hardin Bigelow appeared, riding to the edge of the gathering on horseback. Robinson, hoping to impress the mayor with the seriousness of the situation, managed to keep his volunteers mingled with the spectators so that the mayor would believe more men were flocking to the association's cause. The mayor never dismounted but advised the crowd to disperse. Robinson responded that the men would be peaceful if left alone, that they were on their own property and had no hostile intentions if not molested. Mayor Bigelow returned to his office but was soon followed by Robinson and a committee of squatters. The squatters wanted no mistake, according to the committee, and were anxious to avoid bloodshed. Robinson and the committee begged the mayor to use his influence to prevent the service of the court writs. Robinson understood the mayor to promise to use his influence in a private way, as a peace-loving citizen. However, the committee of squatters assured Bigelow that if the writs were served after the armed men went home, they would hold the mayor and sheriff responsible.[71]

The afternoon passed peacefully, though many squatters still remained around the disputed lot. The Settlers' Association's threatening proclamation and public show of force seemed to have won the day. That evening, however, rumors began to circulate that there were warrants out for the arrest of Robinson and other Settlers' Association leaders.[72]

The next morning the *Placer Times* printed the mayor's assurances to the Settlers' Association, and the squatters dispersed from the disputed lot.[73] A small fire broke out in the city and was quickly extinguished, but a rumor circulated that the squatters were attempting to set fire to the city.[74] Then Settlers' Association leaders James McClatchy and Michael Moran were arrested, charged with resisting or attempting to resist the sheriff in the execution of a judgment of forcible entry and detainer by the county court.[75] The two were brought before Justice Fake, charged, and in default of $2,000 bail were placed in the city's new prison ship, *La Grange*. The county attorney, McKune, who was sympathetic to the settlers, was also arrested. A warrant was issued for Robinson as well, but he could not be found.[76] That afternoon, despite the assurances of the mayor, the sheriff quietly served the court's writ on Madden and put Rogers in possession of the disputed lot.[77] Reports of the arrests circulated rapidly in the city, and resident Benjamin Stillman wrote in a letter to his family that evening confessing, "It is rather difficult to keep out of the excitement."[78]

Robinson and Maloney met that night in a cabin six miles outside the city limits. Together they issued a call to all the volunteers who had pledged to defend the settlers' claims. Volunteers were told to meet early the next morning under an oak tree on the outskirts of the city. When the two leaders arrived at the appointed rendezvous early Wednesday morning, the site was deserted. After four or five hours, the two men had managed to rally about fifteen others, who spent a short time drilling on the outskirts of the town. At noon, under Maloney's direction, the "army" was given orders to march. The plan, devised by Robinson and Maloney the previous night, was to retake the disputed property and hold it by force.[79]

Robinson and Maloney's plan of taking the lot by force was a clear violation of the law. Robinson had already devised his legal stance on local land laws, and thus he could rationalize the planned takeover of the lot. However, Robinson realized that the takeover must appear as official and "legal" as possible. Further, the action would have to be bold and popular enough to ensure that the local government would be unable to prevent it. This presented Robinson and Maloney with a problem: if the settlers seized the lot at night, coming as thieves, they would undermine the open justice of their actions. Besides, if they had waited till nightfall, Robinson might have been arrested, or the sheriff and Rogers might have fortified the lot. Clearly Robinson had hoped to take the lot at the head of a citizens' militia, one that by its numbers and discipline would convey both popularity and power to the local government. But after five hours of waiting, only a handful of men had shown up.

To compensate, Robinson and Maloney picked their path into the city carefully. Forming two ranks of seven and led by Maloney, who was mounted on Robinson's horse, the settlers' force-marched down N Street from the eastern edge of the city. The route that the association's troops chose to enter the city, which ran through squatter encampments rather than the developed part, was designed to protect the volunteers as much as possible while encouraging others to join their ranks. The device worked: the army soon attracted an organized following, some unarmed, some armed with rifles, shotguns, and revolvers. It was a motley following and probably did not project the sense of officiousness and authority that Robinson would have liked. But it was a more powerful group than the one he had started out with.[80]

As the settlers' army neared the disputed property, however, a disagreement broke out between Maloney and Robinson about the army's aims. It quickly became evident that Maloney intended to use his ragtag militia to go beyond Robinson's initial goal. Maloney announced that he planned to order the home of A. M. Winn destroyed. Winn had been the president of the former city council and one of the most outspoken foes of city squatters. Maloney may also have had a personal grudge against Winn. As Maloney led the army toward the house, Robinson shouted from the ranks that destroying Winn's home would permanently discredit the association. Maloney, however, remarked, "We will never have a better time," and prepared to order the house torched. At this point Robinson left the ranks, confronted Maloney with rifle in hand, and shouted: "If you order that house destroyed, I will blow your brains out!" Maloney relented, and the army continued on, but growing more aggressive both in appearance and in disposition.[81]

When the army arrived at the disputed lot, the sheriff's deputy assigned to watch it was nowhere in sight. The lot was quickly retaken. Madden's furniture and personal property were moved back into the house without opposition. Robinson, however, realized that Maloney and the ragtag army could not be easily controlled and, fearful of passing by Winn's home again, began casting about for some way to get the squad back out of the city by another direction. He suggested that they visit another lot on I Street, where lumber had been deposited on a settler's claim without the owner's permission.[82]

Robinson's choice of an exit route again showed a measure of awareness of the city's neighborhoods. By marching up Front Street, the army defied the speculators' exclusive control of the waterfront. At the same time, it would put the army across town from the encampments of the overlanders, who were now beginning to rally in an uncontrolled fashion around Maloney's erratic leadership. Furthermore, the route would avoid the city's commercial heart, taking them through the more neutral public-space corridor of the embarcadero. From there, Robinson hoped to persuade Maloney to march the army out of the city by following I Street, a sparsely settled edge of the city since it lay alongside Sutter's Slough.[83]

As the marchers and their growing number of armed followers marched along the levee in the early afternoon, a growing crowd of hundreds of residents watched the procession with a mixture of amusement and apprehension. Unfortunately, city residents misread the army's intention, for at the foot of I Street lay the city's prison brig, which confined Moran, McClatchy, and McKune. A rumor quickly circulated that the settlers were going to storm the prison ship. Mayor Bigelow next appeared, riding his horse up and down J Street, calling on citizens "to take up arms for the defense of the laws of the city and of California." A number of residents scrambled for guns and began to assemble on Front Street near the prison ship. Rather than causing the dispersion of the settlers' mob, its trek along the waterfront had given rise to an equally unruly opposition mob.[84]

On reaching the lot on I Street, Maloney announced that the lumber on the lot belonged to a friend of his who had left it there merely as a matter of convenience and that it implied no claim on the land. At Robinson's suggestion, Maloney now led the squatters' army up I Street. Despite the tension at the waterfront, Robinson still hoped that a confrontation could be avoided. Yet Maloney resented his retreat from the city.[85]

As the squatters bypassed the prison brig and turned up I Street, the spectators and the citizens' posse began to laugh and jeer at the ragtag army. One block up I Street, Mayor Bigelow appeared on horseback, where he attempted to address the squatters. Maloney, however, marched the squatters on past, ignoring him. Bigelow then turned to the trailing crowd of residents, warning that the city needed protection from this armed band, again encouraging those who had not yet done so to go home and return with their guns. The mayor received three cheers. Bigelow then promised to lead the citizens' militia himself, and together the crowd started moving toward the settlers.[86]

When the settlers' army reached Third Street, Maloney suddenly wheeled his volunteers to the right, leading them directly into the busiest part of the city. The cause of this action is unknown. Possibly Maloney intended a show of force right through the middle of the town. On reaching J Street, Maloney turned his followers about once more, taking them directly up the city's principal business corridor. Yet at the corner of Fourth and J streets, Maloney wheeled about again, directing the army toward the south, possibly planning to leave the city and gather more followers among the overland encampments. Shortly after making this move, however, Maloney discovered that the citizens' militia led by Mayor Bigelow was following him. Maloney ordered his followers to turn about and form a line across the southern opening to the intersection, with the overlanders' camps approximately four blocks behind him. The mayor, now joined by Sheriff McKinney, brought their impromptu deputies to a halt opposite the settlers.[87]

For a few moments both sides faced each other. The retaking of Madden's claim and the bold march through the heart of the city encouraged the squatters. City residents, thinking they had thwarted an attempt to storm the prison ship, believed the squatter army was already retreating. In the heat and dust of the afternoon, amid the excited tempers on both sides of the intersection, Robinson and Maloney on one side and Bigelow and Sheriff McKinney on the other tersely discussed how they could resolve the standoff. Nearby, city assessor J. M. Woodland remarked to a friend, "Oh, it's too bad for these men to take such a stand, for they will certainly be shot down; I will go up and advise them."[88] At the same time, Bigelow and McKinney ordered the squatters to lay down their arms and surrender and also started forward. Maloney, already spoiling for a fight and possibly believing the approach of Bigelow, McKinney, and Woodland was the beginning of a charge on his army, shouted out loudly,

"Shoot the Mayor; shoot the Mayor!" Maloney's followers leveled their guns and fired. The mayor's militia, caught somewhat by surprise, hesitated only a moment before returning the fire.[89]

Woodland died instantly. Bigelow fell on the neck of his horse and was then thrown to the ground by the startled animal. He had been wounded in four places. A squatter discharged his revolver six times at the sheriff; miraculously, not a single shot struck him. Meanwhile Robinson was struck by a bullet that passed within two inches of his heart. Maloney was wounded in the arm. Since the squatters had discharged their guns in a volley, the citizens' return fire caught them with unloaded weapons, and they began to disperse. Seeing the squatters breaking up and running, the citizens charged. Maloney, whose horse was killed in the melee, was chased several blocks and received a second wound in the back. City recorder B. F. Washington caught up with him in an alley and killed him with a shot to the head.[90]

The violence lasted only a few moments. Benjamin Stillman, who was watching the standoff when the shooting started, reported that he raced home to get his gun, a distance of only half a block, but that when he returned, the fighting was over and the streets were empty.[91] Three squatters were dead, one wounded; one of the citizens' party was killed, four were wounded.[92] Bigelow, despite the number of wounds, still lived but was unable to continue his duties as mayor. One ball had grazed his cheek, while another had penetrated his thigh. A third had nearly torn off his thumb and shattered the bones of his hand; the thumb was amputated later that day. Infection set in, however, necessitating the amputation of the arm as well. The fourth wound was the most serious, passing through his body in the region of the liver. Three months later, while recuperating in San Francisco from his wounds and the amputations, the weakened Bigelow was stricken by cholera and died.[93]

Robinson, wounded and finding himself abandoned by the settlers' army, managed to crawl into a nearby restaurant.[94] On learning of his whereabouts, B. F. Washington ordered Stillman to procure what help he could and "take him, dead or alive."[95] Stillman found the restaurant owner standing watch over Robinson with a shotgun and threatening to shoot anyone who tried to apprehend the association's leader. Two men who accompanied Stillman threatened in return to make "a large hole" in the owner's body, and the proprietor backed down.[96] Robinson was placed on a cot and carried to the prison ship, where he was not expected to survive the night. The following morning, however, a doctor announced that Robinson's condition had stabilized and that unless inflammation set in, he would recover.[97]

→ — ←

The rebellion of the Settlers' Association ended on the afternoon of August 14 with the violent confrontation at the intersection of J and Fourth streets. After the outbreak, the association was largely discredited and leaderless. Maloney was dead; Robinson, Moran, McClatchy, and McKune were in jail; association members, who had only reluctantly joined Maloney's army that morning, either fled the city or went into hiding in the warren of tents and wagons of the overlanders' encampments. Residents remained somewhat sympathetic to the settlers' cause but condemned the association itself and the violence it wrought.[98]

Yet despite this, the violence was not over. The events that led to the second outbreak did not originate with the squatters, but with the city's great speculators. For months, Settlers' Association challenges had undermined real estate titles at the same time that the great speculators' financial empires, based on real estate values, were crumbling. In reality, the settlers' challenge neither provoked nor probably even significantly contributed to the speculators' financial ruin. Yet their shanties and cabins, meetings and marches, gave the speculators a focus for their own apprehension and frustrations. When settlers and city officials began firing on one another on August 14, the entire population was thrown into a panic, but it was the great speculators who demanded that city officials take further actions to quell the disturbance. Teetering on the brink of ruin and blaming the squatters for their problems, the great speculators proceeded as they had done since the town was founded. Under the slogan of law and order, they used city government to crush their opposition.

Influencing the city government did not prove difficult. When the Common Council met shortly after the shooting, it was in no mood to entertain thoughts of leniency toward any squatters. Council president Demas Strong was named acting mayor. City recorder B. F. Washington, who now proudly proclaimed that he had dispatched Maloney, was placed at the head of the city's police force and granted the authority to raise up to five hundred men to patrol city streets. The council then agreed to arm themselves and place themselves under Washington's charge. Another company of volunteers raised by J. Sherwood also placed themselves under Washington's orders.[99] Strong, Washington, and Sherwood were among the city's leading speculators.

Led by members of the old Law and Order Party, Sacramento residents were called on to patrol their streets in an atmosphere of increasing hysteria. "The ladies were nearly frightened out of their wits," Stillman recalled; "they all retired into their cozy little cottages, and securely bolted the doors."[100] Stillman admitted to his own nervousness as he and six hundred other armed men patrolled the dark city streets, on guard against the expected squatter attack. "It may seem strange to you," he confessed in a letter to his family, "but I did not like the idea of going out to shoot at squatters in the dark, when a fellow might just as well get shot himself by mistake for some more maliciously disposed person. . . . We patrolled up and down the lonely streets, with fixed bayonets; stopping every man for the countersign, and if he could not give it, marching him home."[101]

In such a panicky environment, it is remarkable that more violence did not take place. Yet the watchmen found little evidence of defiant squatters on their streets. Augustus Moore, who worked packing supplies for teams in Sacramento, recalled the edge of anxiety among the patrollers that could easily turn to absurdity in the aftermath of the riot. "One little Dutchman was arrested for being found with firearms in his possession," he wrote.

> He was marched by a file of big soldiers to headquarters of the party operating against the settlers and there charged with the carrying of deadly weapons for the purpose of resisting authority. He denied this and then the valiant soldiers produced the evidence of his guilt. There were a great many miners present and a burst of merriment went around when they saw that the evidence consisted of two Allen revolvers, which were considered among the most harmless things in the country. When called upon to explain, he said he had been so foolish as to bring them over to sell. He would have done just as well had he taken ice to Sitka. Those fire-arms (called by the miners old pepper boxes) could have been picked up at that time in the mines by the hundreds.[102]

The city's elite leaders, however, knew the type of person they were after and insisted on making a clear and harsh statement. Shortly after nightfall, Henry Caulfield was arrested and charged with the murder of Woodland. Initial reports say he was intoxicated at the Five-Mile House.[103] Stillman, however, reported that he was not easily apprehended, taken only after a struggle between Caulfield and his captor while both were mounted and riding very fast. Stillman further noted the prisoner's battered condition when he was finally brought back to town. "The party came down J Street at a furious rate," he wrote, "with their prisoner tied in the saddle; his feet under the horse's belly, his hat off, arms tied behind him, and his face covered with blood and dust. They swept on down to the levee, and it was said that they were going to hang Caulfield on a tree."[104]

Little is known of Caulfield beyond this brief appearance. Like many members of the Settlers' Association, Caulfield was Irish. Whether or not he was a squatter is uncertain, but he "was known as a carpenter and joiner, and was active in Democratic politics."[105] What "active" meant is unknown, but given the carpenters' early informal unionizing to keep wages high and a general antiforeigner bias among city residents, it is likely that Caulfield was arrested and paraded through the city for reasons only marginally related to the squatters. Caulfield most likely fit the squatter stereotype—Irish, an outsider, and leader of an organization that frustrated enterprising residents' attempts to make a clear profit. Though kept in the prison ship for days, Caulfield was never convicted of Woodland's murder.

When the sun rose the following day, few people in the city had slept. Other than Caulfield, no squatters had been apprehended during the night. That afternoon Assessor Woodland was buried in the cemetery south of the city. Since the funeral procession would proceed through the overlanders' encampments, Sherwood's volunteers and Washington's deputies escorted the long procession and stood watch over the burial services. The Reverend Dr. Grove Deal, also one of the city's leading speculators, presided over the ceremony. Woodland had many friends in the city, and the *Transcript* reported that "not a heart present but sympathized deeply, feelingly, in the loss his family has sustained—the breach his death has made in society—and the void his absence has created in the ranks of the business men of the city."[106] The funeral ended late in the afternoon, leaving those who attended in a heightened state of emotion.

After the funeral, Sheriff McKinney and a number of others rode out to Sutter's Fort, where he announced his intention to go out to the surrounding countryside and arrest any squatters that he could find. McKinney's decision caught several of his party by surprise, who had come out unarmed and who decided to turn back for the city. As city sheriff, his jurisdiction ended at the city limits, just past the limits of the crumbling Sutter's Fort. His announced intention of going as far as Mormon Island, a gold-mining camp east of the city, and the surprise his intention caused several of his party suggest that his action was not premeditated. That other men were armed indicates a possible premeditation on their part. Who most of these men were is unknown, but when McKinney set out from the fort, he organized his posse into three squads of six men each, giving command of one squad to A. M. Winn and the other to Henry E. Robinson. Both men were prominent speculators and former members of the old city council.[107] Other speculators known to be members of the posse were Eugene F. Gillespie, E. J. C. Kewen, David Milne, and John S. Fowler.[108]

The activities of the great speculators, like those of the Settlers' Association, underscored their basic approach to the city and its problems. Time after time, the great speculators had demonstrated their belief in individualism. In city affairs they disdained community responsibility in favor of their own economic betterment. They involved themselves in community organizations only if they held positions of individual importance. In the city's social turmoil they staged elaborate balls and grand soirées to emphasize their prominence in the community as opposed to their participation in it. They expected to lead and to be followed, and their goals were more personal than community oriented.

If the great speculators labeled their actions "law and order," it was not because they sought to disguise their real goals. The great speculators believed in a form of law and a social order that defined the rules governing an individual's actions. In their view society by definition demanded a hierarchical class structure based on wealth. Laws reinforced the natural order but did not create it. Activities such as destroying competitors' goods, ballot stuffing, and government manipulation were not illegal but extralegal if they served "law and order," that is, were undertaken to preserve the natural social order and its impartial laws. Illegal activity, by contrast, was any activity that defied this order.

The difference between the great speculators' vision of social order and that of the settlers could not be more striking. To the great speculators, settler meetings were chaotic, utterly lacking in social distinction, and susceptible to the unregulated passions of personal eloquence and shifting standards. The association's violent outbreak proved it to be an illegal organization and a menace to all of society. The great speculators responded by taking command of city government, city police, and volunteers and by prodding supposedly impartial city officials, in this case the sheriff, to uphold the natural order of society.

Setting out from Sutter's Fort, Sheriff McKinney's posse galloped in rank of four to the Five-Mile House, a tavern east of the city. Finding no squatters there, they next proceeded toward the Pavilion at Brighton, six miles outside the city. Along the way, however, the party met a man who told McKinney that a contingent of squatters was staying at Allen's, a saloon two or three houses past the Pavilion.[109]

Approaching Allen's at twilight, McKinney sent his three squads to surround the house, one to approach from the left, the other from the right. McKinney led the third squad to the front of the house, pretended that his men were simple travelers, called out jokingly that this looked like a good place for a drink, and led his men into the house. McKinney and a couple of his men entered while the rest lingered outside to tie up their horses.[110]

In the gathering darkness, what happened next is uncertain. Sheriff McKinney apparently found armed men inside, waiting for him. Identifying himself, he ordered them to lay down their arms. Allen, whose sick wife lay bedridden in the adjoining room, may have declared his intention of defending his home. Gunfire erupted. A general melee ensued, and brisk firing was kept up both by the occupants of the house and the posse outside. After several minutes of confused battle, McKinney got to the doorway of the house. Silhouetted against the faint evening light outside, a man inside the cabin fired at him. McKinney turned and staggered about ten steps outside the house, crying, "I'm dead, I'm dead, I'm dead!" before collapsing.[111]

The melee continued for a few minutes longer before the posse finally gained control of the scene. Surveying the disheveled cabin, the posse took a grim reckoning. McKinney and two squatters lay dead; one posse member and two squatters were wounded. The posse took four men prisoner, but Allen escaped. Kewen was sent back to town to get reinforcements, and various law and order parties broke into the house at several times in the evening. Allen's wife was not injured by the gunfire and was left behind to be tended by a servant. The battle and the boisterous comings and goings of "reinforcements" throughout the night took their toll, however, and the woman died during the night.[112]

News of McKinney's death renewed residents' fears. The great speculators increased their demands for action. Brannan in particular seems to have demanded continued force against squatterism and "talked mightily of law, order, and blood."[113] Stillman encountered Brannan and other speculators later that night at the Law and Order Association's informal headquarters at Warbass & Co. "All were eager for the fray," Stillman observed, "and I thought if they fought as well as they swore, the country would be safe."[114]

For days following the shoot-outs on J Street and at Brighton, residents seemed ready to believe any rumor, no matter how wild. Reports circulated through the streets that an army of squatters was gathering to attack the city, that they numbered seven hundred strong, that they intended to set fire to the city, that they had already set fire to the city, although no one knew where.[115] One of the most revealing rumors regarded Allen, who, it was said, had reached the mining camps and was leading an army of miners to the city to join the squatters in burning down the city.[116] One city official even approached former Settlers' Association president Charles Robinson, recovering in the prison ship, and begged him "to send word to the miners that he did not wish to be rescued, as he thought this would quiet the town and allay the excitement."[117]

Yet as time passed, none of the fears proved to be founded, and city residents regained some of their composure. Public opinion also began to turn against the great speculators and their own violent response to the squatters' violence. Stillman noted that the speculators at Warbass & Co., who now commanded city security, might be as little interested in justice as the squatters. "I heard threats," Stillman later wrote, "that a young man named McKune, who had been acting as an attorney for the squatters, should hang before sunrise. Here was law and order for you, with a vengeance!" Listening to the threats and plans, Stillman, like many others throughout the city that night, began edging away from the speculators' law and order position. "I knew where McKune's office was, and hurried down to give him the alarm," Stillman recalled, apparently unaware that the attorney was already under arrest. "I thumped away at his door, but could get no answer; so I concluded he had left, and that, if he was with the squatter force, the others might go and get him, and bide the fortunes of war."[118]

The great speculators' attempt to reestablish their authority in Sacramento by crushing the Settlers' Association thus backfired. Far from being seen as civic leaders, the city's economic leaders appeared to be just as misguided as the squatters. Neither did the attempt to stop the squatters forestall the speculators' own economic collapse. Rather, the riot acted as a check on any further speculation in city lands.[119] The great speculators had woven financial confusion throughout the city and by August were inextricably snarled in their own knots. Within the two weeks following the riot, two more banking houses in the city, Hensley, McKnight & Hastings and Warbass & Co., closed their doors. A number of leading merchants followed the bankers, and as Morse recalled, "In a few weeks the intoxicating progress of the city was arrested by a perfect prostration of confidence, an utter skepticism in the value of real estate, and a general excitability of the public mind as it vibrated between the ever changing points of hope and fear."[120] Sacramento's economy had collapsed.

→—←

As the disastrous month of August 1850 ended in Sacramento, the city was left bitterly divided over the actions of the settlers and the great speculators. The violent confrontations between the government and the settlers forced residents to confront the city's social confusion and to take immediate, straightforward action in the face of long-simmering complex problems. That the conflict would come between the Settlers' Association and the Law and Order Party is understandable. Both groups formed at polar opposites of the political and cultural spectrum. Perhaps more important, however, both groups were relatively small. As such, they were able to organize more effectively than the majority of city residents, for whom the issues had less clarity, and could thus offer clear visions and goals to their members.

Following the riot, however, neither the squatters nor the speculators carried much authority in the city. Speculators and settlers were in many ways indistinguishable; "law and order" vengeance led to needless violence; golden fortune had left a swath of business ruin. Bereft of these two extreme views, city residents would have to define more inclusive visions and goals for their city. But in the aftermath of the bloodshed, it remained to be seen how Sacramento's enterprising residents could find or construct anything admirable in the chaotic urban environment.

Flood. On January 8, 1850, the American and Sacramento rivers flooded, sweeping away much of the city and worsening the poverty, malnutrition, and sickness of thousands of the city's newly arrived residents. Courtesy of the California State Library, neg. no. 5491.

Hardin Bigelow. An early city hero, Bigelow saved the city from flooding a second time in March 1850, was elected mayor, and then set out to improve public health. As one of the city's major land speculators, though, Bigelow had little sympathy with the Settlers' Association. Courtesy of the California State Library, neg. no. 5033.

NOTICE
TO
IMMIGRANTS!!

As there are in our City a number of men with remarkable principles, who go among those who have newly arrived and offer to sell or lease to them the *Public Land* in and about this place, thus imposing upon the unsuspecting. The latter are hereby notified that the vacant land in Sacramento City and vicinity, is open for *ALL*, free of charge : but, they can make either of the following gentlemen a present of a few thousand dollars, if they have it to spare. Such favors are eagerly sought and exultingly received by them. In fact, some of them are so solicitous in this matter, that, if they are not given *something*, they will *almost not like it*, and even threaten to *sue* people who will not contribute to their support. Those who have made themselves the most notorious, are

Barton Lee,
Burnett & Rogers,
Hardin Bigelow,
Pearson & Baker,
Thomas M'Dowell,
R. J. Watson,
J. S. Hambleton,
Starr, Bensley & Co.,

Prettyman, Barroll & Co.,
A. M. Winn,
S. Brannan,
Hensley, Merrill & King,
Conn. Mining and Trading Co.,
Paul, White & Co.,
W. M. Carpenter,
R. Gelston,
John S. Fowler.

Warbass & Co.,
J. Sherwood,
James Queen,
Dr. W. G. Deal,
Eugene F. Gillespie,
T. L. Chapman,
Dewey & Smith,
E. L. Brown,

Sacramento City, June 14, 1850.
"Sacramento Transcript" Print.

By order of the Settlers' Association.

Notice to Immigrants! The Settlers' Association posted notices warning newly arrived gold rushers that they might be charged for public lands that they believed should be free to all and listed the major city land speculators "who have made themselves most notorious." The association's aggressive litigation called into question the city's land titles, threatening the economic stability of city businesses. Courtesy of the Sacramento Museum & History Division, catalog no. 82/05/5641.

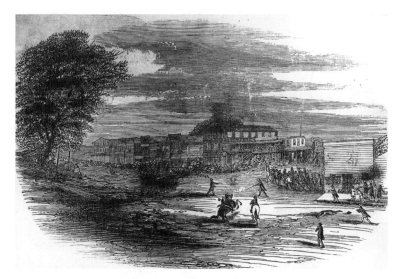

Riot scene. This woodcut shows the initial volley of shots that brought down Hardin Bigelow. Written descriptions of the riot indicate that the streets were crowded when the shooting began; the woodcut not only makes it easier to see Bigelow being wounded, but also hides the mob the mayor was leading against the Settlers' Association. Courtesy of the Sacramento Museum & History Division, catalog no. 82/04/672b.

On the road to recovery. Disillusioned miners often became teamsters to earn their fortune. For many the experience was the first step in making the transition from miner to Sacramento businessman and resident. Courtesy of the California State Library, neg. no. 99.

THE GRADE.

The Horse Market. A famous early Sacramento institution, the corner of Sixth and K streets rapidly became the scene of informal livestock trading. The market gave everyone in the city—newly arrived immigrant, anxious miner, or old-hand teamster—a taste of the medium-scale entrepreneurship that characterized Sacramento. Courtesy of the Sacramento Museum & History Division, catalog no. 67/38/01.

Miner and Speculator. In the early days of the gold rush, these two men would have been indistinguishable. But by 1851, Sacramento residents increasingly would make the distinction between the miner with the gun on his hip and the speculator dressed in fashionable clothing. Courtesy of the California State Library, neg. no. 26,904.

A WELL-KNOWN BANKING HOUSE.—See page 47

VIEW OF THE INTERIOR OF THE EL DORADO. SACRAMENTO.

Democratic State Journal print

The Eldorado. The gambling hall symbolized much of the gold rush experience for the forty-niners. Though usually condemned in letters home, writers also noted the universal attraction of gambling. Courtesy of the Sacramento Museum & History Division, catalog no. 82/04/457.

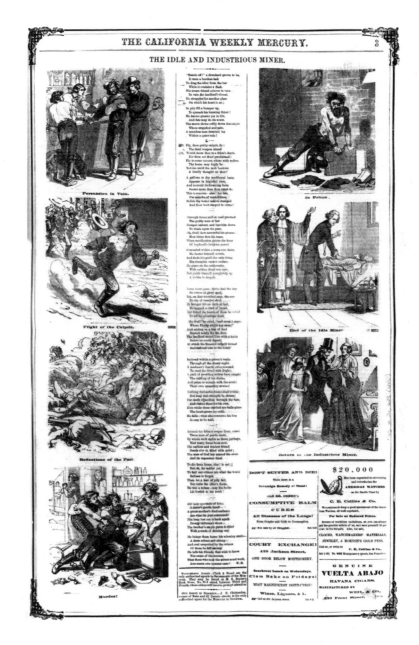

The Idle & Industrious Miner. Alonzo Delano's poem, illustrated by Charles Nahl, dramatically draws the difference between the miners who were hardworking and reunited with their families and those who were not. Publications like these both reflected and shaped public attitudes toward the city. Courtesy of the California State Library, neg. no. 26,902.

The Happy Family at Home. For most Sacramento businessmen, success only created a new dilemma: how to resolve a lengthy residence in California with the family waiting at home in the East. After having gloried in the macho adventure of the gold rush, how could they convince families that California was indeed a safe place for women and children, too? Courtesy of the California State Library, neg. no. 26,903.

Huntington, Hopkins, & Co. Collis Huntington, Mark Hopkins, and William Carpenter all successfully made the transition from miner to Sacramento merchant and foresaw the future business advantages that living in Sacramento would offer. Carpenter, however, was unable to overcome the objections of his family to his continued stay in California. Courtesy of the California State Library, neg. no. 26,905.

John Frederick Morse. As editor of the *Sacramento Union,* Morse's articles mapped out the city's social development in the early 1850s. His photograph shows his fashionable attire, suggesting that Sacramento was no longer home to the wild and disheveled miners of the gold rush. Courtesy of the California State Library, neg. no. 22,449.

✦ -- ❖ ❖ -- ❖ ❖ -- ❖ ❖ -- ❖ ❖ -- ❖ ❖ -- ❖ ❖ -- ❖ ❖ -- ❖ ❖ -- ❖ ❖ -- ❖

PART THREE

IMPROVISATION

✦ -- ❖ ❖ -- ❖ ❖ -- ❖ ❖ -- ❖ ❖ -- ❖ ❖ -- ❖ ❖ -- ❖ ❖ -- ❖ ❖ -- ❖ ❖ -- ❖

The character of our people, the success
of our city, and above all, the safety and
peace of the community demand that
the laws should be regarded as supreme,
and their acknowledgement a requisite
to citizenship.

—F. C. Ewer, editor of the *Sacramento Transcript*,
August 16, 1850

I more particularly look at it with great
interest, for have I not seen California
in its infant days, and now fast verging
into strong and vigorous manhood?

—William Carpenter, Sacramento resident,
to his wife, Lucretta, February 25, 1855

Civic Middlemen

In the aftermath of the riot, Sacramento's residents were divided as to whether the great speculators or the Settlers' Association had been in the wrong. Resident merchant David Hewes noted in a letter to his mother that there had been "a civil war in our midst," but that "civil law has triumphed." Regarding the combatants, Hewes reported, "One party who styled themselves *'Squatters'* claimed that they had a right to go and squat on any lot or piece of land and hold it as their own, notwithstanding someone else had bought it and had paid their money for it."[1] Hewes had reason to support Sutter's title. Having paid $2,000 in rent for three months, Hewes had at last purchased two city lots; his own title was dependent on the validity of Sutter's title. Furthermore, Hewes not only needed the lots to avoid rent payments; they were needed collateral in his attempts to acquire the merchandise he hoped to sell to gold rush miners. Hewes calculated that he could "take one thousand dollars advance on the two lots whenever I wish."[2] Thus Hewes, like many enterprising residents, sided with the great speculators in the land dispute.

Responses to the Squatters' Riot from city residents, however, varied widely, for the riot dramatically pointed to the differences between those with a developing stake in the city and those who merely saw the city as a temporary home. Other residents who leased and paid the high rents current in the city may have had more reason to sympathize with the squatters. James Haines and his partner started a store in Sacramento in the spring of 1850 by squatting on a lot at the corner of Eleventh and J streets. Haines bitterly wrote about the behavior of the city's officials, especially the sheriff, and afterward worked to elect former Settlers' Association members to the state legislature.[3]

Shopkeeper William Prince also showed his growing disgust with the antidemocratic attitudes of the great speculators in a letter to his wife several days after McKinney's death. Calling the sheriff's raid on Allen's "a kind of spree," Prince reported, "it now turns out there were no Squatters there at all. One man had been sick a month that they killed and the others were Allen's family and some hired laborers and neighbors. A more needless act of wrong, arising from erroneous impressions and from neglect of proper enquiry cannot be instanced." Prince concluded that the confrontations had ended, "except the probable unjust punishment of the prisoners. . . . The local courts here are dead against the Squatters and they can get no justice from them." Prince accused the "Yankee Speculators" of manipulating Sutter merely to gain false land titles. As Prince explained to his wife, "This Sutter is a good meaning, pleasant man, but the most sappy-headed fool you can conceive of, and excited with wine usually and half drunk; the Yankees have used him and flattered him and made him believe that he owns the greater part of California . . . [and] the amoral Speculators have got him to give deed for all."[4] Prince, in debt to several speculators, may have been giving vent to private frustrations.

Reading over the many responses to the riot as well as the many comments made by residents about the brewing troubles before the fighting, it is easy to see that the issues of land titles, rampant speculation, and the responsiveness of the city council to democratic demands were major events in Sacramento in the summer of 1850. But this attention to the riot tends to obscure another, and ultimately far more important, development that was taking place at the same time. Looking back again over Hewes, Haines, and Prince's comments, one sees another subtle concern in evidence. No matter which side of the debate these men took, all three were influenced by their business concerns in the city. All three, and many other city residents as well, viewed the riot and formed their opinions about the struggle from the perspective of their own business situation—either because they needed city land as collateral for credit or because rents and leases were too high to run their own business operations.

What makes this so remarkable is that so few of Sacramento's residents in the summer of 1850 had set out for California the previous year with any intention of establishing and operating a business in the West. The vast majority had come to California assured that after a year (or less!) of simple mining, they would be able to return to their eastern homes with a fortune. Yet one year later, mining seemed to be as far from these men's minds as were their families in the eastern states. Rather than making a quick fortune and returning home, many men found themselves struggling to build businesses that would certainly be profitable but would require a much longer stay in California. As Sacramento was being divided into lots by the great speculators and redivided by the Settlers' Association, the characteristics of the growing number of city residents were themselves changing. That change—from miner to merchant—would eventually play a more profound role in the development of the city than any previous event.

In its own quiet way, this transformation should be given the real credit for the establishment of a stable city. Sacramento City, in a very real sense, was founded not by a Swiss adventurer, a Mormon entrepreneur, or a passionate

New England doctor, but by thousands of ex-miners who were flexible enough to adapt their dreams of striking it rich quick in the gold fields to building a stable fortune out of the chaos of the gold rush in an urban environment. By men, in other words, who sought to fashion something admirable out of confusion.

$\rightarrow$ — $\leftarrow$

The great transformation of miners into businessmen was not an event restricted to Sacramento, but one felt throughout California beginning in 1850. At its heart was a simple geologic fact. The sources of gold in the Sierra Nevada, the so-called mother lode, were veins of gold buried deep in granite. For millennia, streams washing down the mountains had dug canyons into the rocky ground and washed out some of the gold, depositing it along the sandy banks downstream from the mother lode. Early gold seekers found these nuggets in abundance along the stream banks or only lightly buried in gravel and streambeds. But this easily accessible gold was limited, and by 1850, the third year of the rush, most of this easy gold, or placer gold, was gone. Plenty of gold remained in the granite mountains—indeed, the majority of the gold still lay untouched there. But this gold was unreachable by the single miner with a pick and pan. Beginning around 1850, mining increasingly called for more equipment, expensive equipment, more and more men, and modern deep shaft mining techniques. The romantic adventure of the single miner striking it rich in a single afternoon was giving way to the harder realities of mining companies paying wages to gangs of employees in dark and dangerous tunnels.[5]

The shift to corporate mining was not sudden or even. Lone prospectors still held out hope of finding a valley awash with placer gold, and from time to time such valleys were discovered. And before giving up entirely, many miners formed partnerships with three or four others who did some deeper digging and washing or even partnerships of dozens or more to build dams to divert streams out of their gold-lined beds. But as time passed, the amount of work increased while the payoffs fell. Gold rush historian Rodman Paul estimated that a miner's daily wage—that is, the average that a single miner might earn from his own placer mining—was $20 in 1848, the first year of the rush, but had fallen to half that by 1850 and would level out at about $3 a day by the mid-1850s.[6]

For many men who had crossed the length of the continent to get their hands on a pile of gold, the wall of granite separating them from their prize was too hard to breach and the realization of this too bitter to bear. Many discovered that they had mortgaged their farms, left their families, and wasted their health on a gamble that did not seem likely to pay off. To miner Franklin Langworthy, the gold rush quickly turned from a golden dream to a base nightmare. "A residence here at present," he wrote, "is a pilgrimage in a strange land, a banishment from good society, a living death, and a punishment of the worst kind, and the time spent here ought to be considered as a blank period in existence, and accordingly struck from the record of one's days."[7] Songs of the gold rush also suggest the disillusionment of many miners. The song "Oft-Told Tale" depicts a poverty-stricken, ruined miner, stranded in the mountains alone, pondering his fate:

> I had no *sense* in coming here,
> I've gained no *cents* by coming.
> I have not sinned as some folks do;
> I pick but do not *steal,*
> And though my ways of life are *hard,*
> My heart is *soft* to feel.[8]

Deep in debt from the high costs of the trail and mines, exhausted and weak from their labors in the mines, and bereft of family support, many miners felt a sense of having been cheated and looked for someone or something to blame for their misfortunes. Sometimes they blamed themselves: suicide ranked as one of the leading causes of death in the mines. Others sought to blame their hard luck on those who they felt had misled them into joining the gold rush. Bernard Reid, a hopeful miner who spent a fortune just trying to get to California, found that the gold rush was nothing but a high stakes lottery and wrote in his journal, "Oh! how bitterly do many curse the day they left home, and swear vengeance upon the whole tribe of editors who deceived them!"[9] Most miners eventually left the gold fields, bitterly disappointed in their inability to acquire a fortune.

Many of those who left, however, did not leave California, nor did they easily give up on their initial dreams of gold rush fortune. Instead they looked for other opportunities in gold rush California. Mining, Dr. Israel Lord concluded late in 1850, "is a losing business." But he noted the example of "the Fosters," a team made up of a father and his two sons, who had made over $20,000 "but not by mining. They have bought and sold and packed and ranched and dealt in any and everything that would turn a penny into their pockets."[10] For some, the shift from mining to shopkeeping was rapid, especially if the would-be miner had been a shopkeeper in "the States" and had ready access to credit and a supply of goods to market. For the majority, however, the transformation was less abrupt, a very gradual shift involving new ideas, new experiences, and new expectations.

The first step for many miners wishing to get out of mining was in hauling goods. Miners journeying from their claims to a mining camp or perhaps to

Sacramento for supplies soon realized that they could make a bit more money—and make it more securely—by picking up items for other, neighboring miners. Once they had made several such trips, many realized the profits to be made and became teamsters, either for a merchant or on their own hook. Moreover, such profits, while less spectacular than those from an imagined gold strike, were far more stable and certain than the gamble of placer mining. For many, teamstering or other part-time jobs in a mining camp or in Sacramento were initially seen as a way to supplement their income while pursuing mining or merely as short intervals in which to gather enough money to resupply them for another attempt in the gold fields. But over time, these part-time sojourns proved attractive. Not only was the income more certain, but the work itself was often more enjoyable than hard-rock mining.

The letters of Mark Hopkins to his brother Moses suggest the thinking of many miners turned merchants in gold rush California. Though older than most of the hopeful argonauts of 1849—Hopkins was already in his late thirties—he embarked on the adventure with almost boyish enthusiasm. Leaving New York on the ship *Pacific,* he had first been a member of a partnership of twenty-five men. On reaching California, the partnership dissolved, but he quickly joined a new partnership of only six. Together they had gathered mining equipment and set off up the Sacramento River, eager to make a fortune. Like many other miners, however, Hopkins quickly became disillusioned with mining. Writing to his brother, he complained, "It is outright folly for merchants, clerks—mere indoor men—to think of working with their hands in the mines—The daily tasks of the Irish laborer on your canals and Rail Roads is VERY easy work compared to it."[11]

Leaving mining, he decided to become a teamster, hauling goods between Sacramento and the mining camp of Placerville, where he also set up a small store dealing in mining equipment. Yet Hopkins seemed happiest on the road, hauling goods. He was amazed at the sense of power and accomplishment in contrast to mining that came with teamstering. "I have certainly done some things almost incredible," he wrote, "things I could not have believed myself, possessed of strength and endurance to perform while in the Atlantic states." Hopkins exuberantly detailed his experiences as a teamster, "driving from six to twelve oxen in my team, buying my load here and selling in the mines 50 to 100 miles distant—& such roads, and hills, and rocks, and gullies to run a wagon over would astonish you. Although I never drove an ox until I came here, I believe I can perform the most difficult feats in that sort of navigation." Hopkins playfully explained that he had become a teamster "not because I chose it as delightful pastime, but because it was ELEVATING—Elevating in the sense that climbing a hill may elevate one in passing to a greater eminence beyond."[12]

Hopkins's elation likely came, at least in part, from his release from the frustrating labor of mining. Teamstering provided a psychic salve to gold rush disappointment. For men who had boasted of crossing the continent, braving the elements, and digging up a fortune, only to find that fortune still out of reach, teamstering would still allow a miner to boast of having stood up manfully to the same elements as a miner but provided the extra incentive of a more secure profit. As a teamster, a miner might give up the dream of the big strike but could still earn a fortune and do so in a manner equally as manly and adventurous as that of any prospector.

Teamstering may also have provided an easier transformation from mining to urban business pursuits. Given the amount of goods that needed hauling in the early years of the gold rush, teamsters could easily acquire enough money to start a business of their own. And hauling goods between California's towns and mining camps also gave teamsters both the practical knowledge of trade flows and the needed business connections in a variety of towns and camps that would suit them well as middlemen. In the spring of 1850, while hauling goods, Hopkins chanced to meet on the road one of his former colleagues from the *Pacific*, and the men agreed to open a grocery in Sacramento.[13] On July 1, 1850, the firm of Hopkins and Miller, retail and wholesale grocers, opened in Sacramento.[14] Within the next few weeks, Hopkins and Miller were doing more business than they could have hoped. Writing again to his brother in October, Hopkins noted that he and his partner "with no help, not even an hours labor in doors or out, in buying or selling goods, have turned out over twenty two thousand dollars worth of goods this month. Our sales have steadily increased every month since we commenced, exceeding up to this time $70,000 since the first of July. How many more than seven hours we get to sleep, out of twenty four you may guess, but I will tell you we sleep well, and feel quite well."[15]

Hopkins's success was not isolated. The experiences of James W. Haines were probably typical of the activity required of would-be miners turned businessmen. Like Hopkins, Haines first built up a bit of working capital by doing some hauling in the region. Then he opened a small business in a forty-foot-long cloth boardinghouse, for which he paid $50 rent a day. "I had a table made of wagon beds and supported by small oak trees driven into the ground and cut off at the right height and strips of wagon covers formed the table cloth. I used to feed from 50 to 200 persons a day, charging them a $1.00 a meal. The fare would consist of such as the market would afford. . . . The front room was rented for a gambling room for a Spanish doubloon equal to $16.00 per day. The size of the room was about 16 x 20 feet. The bar had a wagon box for a counter and it would be a poor day when we did not take in $500 from the bar."[16]

Haines's store was washed away in the January 1850 flood, but he had managed to save about $10,000. Soon after the flood, he went into business again and with a series of partners remained in business in Sacramento for two years. Then, like many of the fortune hunters, Haines decided to leave his urban version of a gold mine. "Webster [his partner] and myself, being both young, concluded that we had made about all the money we really required and that it was best that we should return to our native home and get married and return again; so the following spring [1851] we rented our store and public house so that it was bringing us in an income of $550 per month," and Haines left California for the East.[17]

Haines's success story, however, belies the numerous obstacles that threatened would-be businessmen at every turn in the frontier city. A number of disasters courted new businesses early in the California gold rush. One of the difficulties was in ordering goods. Would-be merchants either had to buy from the great speculators of Sacramento or San Francisco or try to arrange for the shipment of goods from across the continent. Edward Austin's frantic letters from Sacramento give some sense of the urgency with which he tried to get his family to send goods for his store. In the fall of 1849 Austin asked his friends to send him pickaxes, water bowls, padlocks, brass tacks, shovels, a cooking stove, red flannel undershirts, fine-tooth combs, toothbrushes, moccasins, deerskin bags, onion and parsley seeds, gold scales, and a *building* to be used as a store! Austin was quite specific about the dimensions of the store: "By all means have it 20 feet front—and 40 or 50 long—And our extra boards for counters. Have three windows on the sides, two on the back. . . . I should like to have the front open . . . to hoist up on hinges to open every morning and put up as an awning . . . and leave everything exposed to view." Austin drew a sketch of the proposed building, as well as a sketch of a gold scale. He gave detailed instructions to have the goods shipped across the Isthmus of Panama, noting to "lock the goods in the trunk, the more spurs and seals the better. You must not send poor seals; have them neat and good." Austin's optimism, despite the difficulty of getting goods, remained high. "There are chances here every day to make money on a small amount, and in many cases small chances are the best, for a man won't mind them. . . . If Frank is ready to come out he can do well much better than he can at home. . . . If Ned Draper will come out I will offer him the same chance. . . . I am going to have a pile in two years, they can do the same."[18]

Some merchants hoped to find more captive customers by relocating their businesses in the mining camps. Yet this, too, had potential dangers. Goods were even harder to come by in the foothills, transportation costs were higher, and

"settled" mining camps often proved extremely mobile, especially when a rich strike
was rumored to be just over the next mountain ridge. Henry Rice Mann, who had
earlier listed the many opportunities available in Sacramento, summed up a year's
experience in a Valentine's Day letter to his wife in 1851. "One year ago and I had
just commenced laying the cornerstone of my fortune on the Pacific. Thousands
have passed through my hands, but how they have eluded my Grasp. . . . In that
short year how varied have been my fortunes." Mann recounted how he had gone
from working in Sacramento for $7 a day to opening a boardinghouse in a
mining camp where he made $1,200. Believing the camp to be stable, he opened
another house, but within three weeks he had to sell out both establishments
and was forced to return to Sacramento. After several weeks working, he had
saved enough to buy a stock of goods and returned to the mining camps, where
business remained uneven. "You may censure me for my varied movements,"
he explained to his wife, "but I could not help it—one has to move in this
country as the miners move, if they wish to do business, and I find that I must
do something else but dig for gold as I am not able to endure the labor."[19]

Perhaps the best example of the life of an urban fortune hunter can be
found in the pages of the diary kept by George Underhill. Though Underhill
established his operation in Stockton, California, rather than Sacramento, the
story of his rise clearly illustrates the workings of these men. Stockton stood in
much the same position as Sacramento: as a distribution point between San
Francisco and the southern mines. Economically, Stockton served the same
role in northern California's urban hierarchy as Sacramento.

George Underhill sailed from New York to California in 1849 as a member
of the Greenwich and California Mining and Trading Company. The company
was dissolved by the time Underhill reached California, but he arrived in the
gold region in the company of his brothers, James and William, and still retained
close ties with many of the former members of the company.[20]

Though Underhill and his associates tried their hands at mining in the fall
of 1849, their returns were somewhat meager. When the winter rainy season set
in, Underhill quit mining altogether and formed a partnership with his brother
James and John McCracken, formerly vice president of the association, to run
a small freighting business. Acquiring the animals was easy, as many overlanders
gladly parted with them on their arrival in California.[21] With two wagons and
seven yoke of cattle, the men began transporting goods between Stockton and
the southern mining camps, charging between fifty and sixty-two cents per
pound. The work was hard and tedious. Roads were treacherous, muddy, or
washed out—if they existed at all. The men sometimes got lost and spent many
a night exposed to the wind, rain, and snow, struggling to get their wagons

back and forth between their appointed stops. By early February 1850, the partners were ready to quit the business.[22]

Their timing was good. Underhill noted that "the business of carting and packing to the mines had paid so well through this winter that many persons that had accumulated gold determined to invest it in that business, the consequence was that there were many buyers and that prices for all kinds of animals was high." Underhill and his partners sold their ox team and wagons for $1,000 more than they had paid for them in the fall; their mules and other equipment sold for three times their previous value. With this money as working capital, the men set up a store in Stockton.[23]

Underhill's original store was "a very poor affair," a small tent on a city lot that they rented for $100 per month, but the partners "felt confident that we should make a show after a while." Indeed, the men were to make quite a show. They proved very successful in attracting important customers for their goods. "The teamsters and packers that we had become acquainted with on the road considered us as belonging to their clan, and gave us the preference. They also worked with us against others." Underhill thus used his connections among the freighters to ensure that his goods would be shipped regularly to the mines, increasing his market base substantially.

Underhill was determined to carry a large variety of goods for the lowest prices. To do this, the partners decided to send George to San Francisco as a purchasing agent while his brother James and their partner, McCracken, ran the store in Stockton. They would deal only in cash, thus getting the lowest price possible. James would send the cash receipts of the store to George each day, with new orders for goods, which George would endeavor to ship up the next day. In this way, the partners hoped to maintain a well-stocked store.[24]

To retain the teamsters' loyalty, Underhill and his partners built on their relationships with the miners by giving them added incentives to trade, providing free meals and board for the teamsters while they were in town. The teamsters soon developed a strong loyalty to the Underhill partnership. As Underhill noted, "To show the confidence that the Teamsters and Packers had in James and McCracken, I will state that it was their custom when they arrived in Stockton to go to the store, hand over their bag of gold dust to be placed in the iron box, hand out their list of goods wanted and tell them to get them ready, and perhaps not ask the price of more than one or two articles in a bill that would amount to two or three hundred dollars. When the goods were ready they [James and McCracken] were directed to weigh out gold enough for the balance of the bill." With such confidence in "Underhill & McCracken," the business grew rapidly.[25]

Over the next year, the business changed partners and names on several

occasions. McCracken left for "the States" in September 1850 and was replaced
by William Underhill, the firm then becoming known as "Underhill & Bros."
Three months later William also returned home, and James and George continued the business under the name "Underhill & Brother." For many would-be
merchants, the turnover of partners might have proven difficult, if not disastrous.
Yet for the Underhill brothers business appears to have proceeded smoothly.
During this same year, they replaced their tent with a wooden building, leased
two additional city lots adjoining their first, and erected wooden buildings on
these as well. The rent on these three lots now totaled $4,800 per year, and the
cost of constructing the wooden structures was also high. Yet at the end of
March 1851, the same month in which they began to lease the third lot, George
was able to send 125 ounces of gold dust home, with instructions that it be
invested in government bonds for the two brothers. Over the next year, George
would attempt to make regular shipments of gold back east.[26]

So far, the Underhill brothers had managed to secure a variety of goods at
a low price, maintain a steady operation despite partnership turnovers, and
nurture a loyal and wide customer base. But the unstable frontier conditions of
California threatened the firm in a variety of unseen and uncontrollable ways.
The brothers' business could still be destroyed by a multitude of disasters. The
teamsters they so needed could go out of business; the mines could play out
and the miners move too far away to make their operation worthwhile; theft
was always a possibility; and fire, either in the Stockton store or among the San
Francisco suppliers, could ruin them.[27]

Disaster threatened the Underhills in May 1851. On May 4, a fire swept
through San Francisco, destroying many of the city's businesses. George
Underhill was not in the city; having taken sick several days earlier, he had
returned to Stockton to be cared for by his brother. The fire in San Francisco
made it harder for all inland merchants to get an adequate supply of goods for
their stores, and George's absence threatened to increase further the difficulty
for the firm. Then on May 6, fire swept through Stockton as well. As the fire
neared their stores, the brothers desperately sought to remove as much of their
goods as possible, but the fire was too strong. Surveying the damage the next
day, the brothers calculated that they had saved $3,000 worth of goods from
the fire but had lost $15,000.[28]

Fortunately, the Underhills seem to have been born under a lucky star.
Their "iron box," which survived the fire, contained $10,000 worth of gold
dust. As George confided in his diary, "If I had not taken sick the most of this
gold would have been invested in goods, and have been burned up with the
other goods, which would have left us in a very weak condition." George was

immediately dispatched with the gold to San Francisco to purchase a new stock of goods. Here George's prior connections with his San Francisco suppliers paid off. Though nearly all of the city's stores had been destroyed, George knew which merchants had goods stored on ships in the bay that had escaped the blaze. His suppliers commiserated with him over the loss of their goods and offered to give George credit to purchase some of the few remaining goods left in the city. This offer alone showed the respect with which the suppliers held the Underhills, a benefit acquired in part due to the long period of doing business by cash.[29]

Underhill, however, announced that he had cash for his purchases and managed to assemble a shipment and have it shipped upriver to Stockton that same day. When the goods arrived in Stockton the following day, the demand was so high that they were all purchased from the steamboat dock by other merchants in town for one-third down in cash. This cash was then sent back to George in San Francisco to prepare the next shipment. "This was continued for weeks," wrote Underhill, "until our brother merchants, who had lost nearly everything by the fire, could make arrangements to commence again. Our business was so much improved by the little competition that we had after the fire for a considerable time, and the increased profit, that at the end of three months from the time of the fire we had made up our entire loss." By December of that year, Underhill and Brothers' inventoried worth stood at about $30,000.[30]

George and James Underhill illustrate the challenges that faced resident merchants of Sacramento. Problems facing any business were heightened in the unsettled gold-mining frontier of California. Sacramento merchants also faced the problems of finding regular customers, steady suppliers, and stable partnerships in an unstable environment. Yet the Underhills showed the possibility of success in such an environment. George's diary indicates that he regularly sent gold home for investment for himself and his brother. During the year between March 1851 and March 1852, George recorded having sent 1,368 ounces of gold home for himself and his brother, plus another 188 ounces for his father, valued at nearly $25,000.[31]

Then, despite having built up the business from nothing and rebuilding it after the fire, George and James returned home to New York. On March 1, 1852, George and James sold their business to the firm of Trembly & Harold. The conditions of sale suggest the strength of their business at that time. As part of the sale, George and James advanced Trembly & Harold $10,000 and agreed to divide the profits of the store equally through the next ten months. George and James could thus expect to profit further from their business even after they returned to the East Coast.[32]

>--<

This shift from disappointed miner to expectant businessman occurred throughout the mining region. Gold rush camps and towns grew increasingly crowded with men other than miners, offering a broad variety of goods and services. Urban development throughout northern California blossomed as a result. But given Sacramento City's recent events—the flood and the riot—it might be reasonable to expect that the city would not attract its share of newly inspired entrepreneurs. In the aftermath of the city's violence, how could Sacramento draw new residents?

Unfortunately, the weeks following the riot only showed that the city's dangers were far from over. As Dr. Israel Lord noted in his diary, "This is certainly the filthiest city I was ever in and worthy of all execration. . . . The cholera is approaching us slowly from both east and west. It will make a charnel house of Sacramento when it comes."[33] Cholera broke out in Sacramento late in October and swept through the city with devastating results. An overlander who signed his name only as "Philo" described to his sister the horror of the disease-ridden city. "Almost every case as yet has proven fatal. Some days there were more than one hundred deaths. Five who came through in our train have died within the past two weeks. One died about six weeks ago. One or two more are not expected to live. . . . It is thought that the cholera will abate as soon as the winter rains set in. Nine tenths of those who came in this year have been sick for a few days or weeks with a disease of the stomach and bowels."[34]

Estimates of the death toll varied, ranging from seven hundred to two thousand.[35] W. B. H. Dodson later wrote, "The death rate was fearful, I have seen as many as twenty-four coffins picked up and hauled at one time for burial, packed up like so many boxes of goods."[36] Resident James Barnes noted, "It was a rich harvest for the undertakers; they were kept very busy from morning to night. The hearse was kept going all the time."[37] Dr. Israel Lord, who kept his own tally and compared it with the number of new graves in the city cemetery, estimated the death toll to be about eight hundred.[38]

By early November, as many as 150 new cases were being reported daily. The fear of cholera had an even bigger impact on the city than the disease itself. Many residents fled. By mid-November, Morse estimated that only one-fifth of the regular population remained. Barnes noted, "Our City, before the Cholera broke out, contained between nine and ten thousand inhabitants and in three weeks after it broke out hardly three thousand people were left. The people fled in every direction; public houses that were crowded to overflowing were closed for the want of customers. There were fifteen gambling houses doing a good business before the epidemic broke out; they were all closed except two. Our streets that used to be crowded with people and wagons were left almost desolate."[39] Newspaper editor George Kenyon Fitch agreed: "It [cholera] interfered with business very much, and damaged our business very much. Instead of making 3 or $4,000 a month it was a question if we were making anything; from that time on, the business ceased to be profitable."[40] A number of outside observers predicted the city was dead and would never rise again.[41]

Yet as if to defy belief, Sacramento quickly rose again. In fact, compared to its earlier growth, the city's population boomed following the epidemic. After its initial founding in January 1849, Sacramento grew slowly. By the summer of 1849 the city's permanent population—as opposed to the floating population of transient miners visiting the city for provisions—probably numbered only a couple of hundred people.[42] With the arrival of overlanders and wintering miners in the fall of 1849, the city grew to an estimated population of thirty-five hundred.[43] But this population shrank dramatically as good weather returned in the spring of 1850. Slowly, throughout that year, the city's permanent population rose to an estimated ten thousand but then, as Barnes noted, fell to roughly three thousand during the epidemic. Yet within only a few months, Sacramento's population was back to its previous level of nearly ten thousand,[44] making it the second-largest city in the West barely two years after its founding.[45] If the reported estimates of the dip, then rise in the city's population are accurate, the weeks at the end of 1850 and the beginning of 1851 saw a tremendous boom in city residency. Despite the flood, bloodshed, and disease, something was drawing people to the city in great numbers.

The reasons for its rise were rather subtle—no single event suddenly gave the city a new lease on life. But the logic of the greater transformation of miners to businessmen worked in the battered city's favor. New entrepreneurs in the gold fields could theoretically set up operations in any camp or town they chose. But the realities of geography and geology proved to push them toward Sacramento. Merchants who set up shop in a mining camp soon discovered that their operations were still too vulnerable to the limits of geologic abundance: when the placer gold was gone, the camp packed up and disappeared. Worse still, merchants who had extended credit to miners in a camp could suddenly find themselves overextended when placer mining failed. Businessmen who focused too closely on the hoped-for returns of a single camp found that they shared too closely the fate of the camp's frustrated miners.

Meanwhile, if the Sierra Nevada proved stingy with its gold, the mountains of the coastal ranges to the west blocked the easy landing of ships on the California coast. Thus the vast majority of goods shipped to the gold region came in through the Golden Gate. Gold rush businessmen had to secure their goods eventually from the Bay Area. The combination of geography and geology suggested that a business could be best operated midway between the bay and the unstable mining camps. Here entrepreneurs were close enough to secure goods for resale and could shift their retail sales from camp to camp as conditions warranted. Better still, such midlevel businessmen could simply sell goods in bulk to merchants in the camps, reducing their own risk of loss.

While pushing entrepreneurs toward cities such as Sacramento, Stockton, and Marysville, however, the nature of the shift from miner to merchant tended to discourage nascent businessmen from locating in San Francisco for a variety of reasons. First, as the shift to mercantilism was not imagined before coming to California, few former miners were prepared to secure a large stock of goods from eastern suppliers. Even if they could write requesting such goods to a wholesaler in the East, few ex-miners had the available capital to buy a ship full of goods and pay for its transportation. For many who gave up on mining to try operating a small business, the grand-scale operations of San Francisco wholesalers were simply too far above their reach. At the same time, locating an operation in San Francisco removed them too far from the mining camps, where many of these new entrepreneurs had their best contacts. Sacramento's disasters could not be ignored, but the logic of rising entrepreneurship in northern California proved insurmountable.

And though fears of flooding, riots, and disease still lingered, other events suggested that by the end of 1850 Sacramento might finally be conquering some of its more fearsome monsters. In September the city received rumors that the long deadlocked Congress was nearing a resolution on the issue of slavery in the West. On October 15, the riverboat *New World* arrived in Sacramento, carrying with it New York newspapers reporting on California's admission as a state. Though the news coincided with the cholera outbreak, its significance was cause for celebration. The admission of California as a state, bypassing the territorial stage, gave residents immediate access to clearly defined federal and state powers. The legal system, and the traditions that it carried, now covered the city. For the first time, residents who debated community values and real estate titles in Sacramento could do so in a traditional and secure legal setting.

Sacramento residents lost little time in taking advantage of this setting. Admission to the union opened the way for federal review of the state's Mexican land grants. In the spring of 1851, Congress passed the California Land Act, establishing a commission to review titles and ascertain the validity of Mexican grants. The commission's work lasted most of the decade, and its findings were controversial. Throughout the state its proceedings tended to encourage rather than discourage squatterism. In Sacramento, in the fall of 1850, however, all of this was in the future. For the time being, the promise of federal intervention and a quick resolution to the land question brought relief to Sutterites and settlers alike.[46]

With the coming of statehood, Sacramento also saw the emergence of local branches of the Democratic and Whig parties. Dr. Israel Lord sarcastically noted, "There is a great deal of noise and hurrahing down street. The 1001 are gulling the people with blarney and making promises which they not only can't fulfill and never intend to but which they do not even understand."[47] Lord's derision of the candidates to the contrary (noting that the coverage of one political speech by the local press was flawed: "The reporter does not do Tom justice. He has made him merely ridiculous while he is infinitely below that. He never aspired so high"[48]), his journal is full of comments on the increasing level of political activity, betraying the new importance of local political participation in the city. Official and unofficial party organs were also established rapidly: the Whig *Sacramento Index* in December 1850 and the Democratic *Placer Times and Transcript* in June 1851.[49] What is most remarkable about these organizations, however, is that they did not exist before statehood and that they co-opted and absorbed both the Law and Order Party and the Settlers' Association. Political expression in the city took on forms that were in essence those of other states rather than the rough forms of a wild frontier. Sacramento politics provided a traditional framework for expressing political disagreements and working toward solutions.

And ironically, even the cholera epidemic would eventually give way to a new sense of security. Before the cholera outbreak, unsanitary conditions in the city had been a focus of concern and had fostered the formation of a civic-minded subculture. By the summer of 1850 the city's doctors had begun to emerge as one of the few stable elements of Sacramento's society. These doctors had their own view of the gold rush, colored by the cholera that dogged overland travelers and the scurvy that haunted seaborne immigrants. Living conditions in California's cities and mining camps bred exposure, disease, and death.

Throughout the gold rush, doctors were called on to minister to dying men and to do so with a minimum of medical supplies or community support.[50] Unlike miners or speculators, the doctors worked with little hope of vast riches. Although the demand for their services was sometimes high, the ability of patients to pay was often limited. Most doctors made a living, but few became rich from their practice.[51]

Originally the reputation of Sacramento's doctors did not rate high. Horace Rice Mann recounted in his diary his tribulations with ineffective doctors in the fall of 1849. "The poor miserable physician that gave me the medicine yesterday morning has called to see me yesterday evening. He has been figuring around all day, done me no good, and tonight I have sent for another physician.

The first one made out his bill at $12, and I paid it and let him go."[52] Over the next week Mann would go through a series of doctors who would charge him $38 for ineffective treatments.

Health in Sacramento had long been a concern of city residents. The election of Hardin Bigelow in April 1850 had been supported not only because Bigelow had saved the city by erecting a levee, but also because he supported the movement toward establishing a viable city hospital. The hospital had been established, but sanitary conditions in the city had not improved much during the year. In May, sometime miner Alonzo Hill had written to his parents, "This Sacramento City is the biggest sink of Filth I suppose in the known world being overflowed so much, [and] will this summer probably give birth to some contagious epidemic which will shovel the people without distinction into eternity."[53] The following month, Hill again predicted an epidemic, noting that "Chronic Dysentery and Typhoid fever I expect will be the popular disease this season."[54] What was obvious to Hill was most likely obvious to others: Sacramento was a disaster waiting to happen.

Sacramento's professional doctors were the toughest critics of the city's medical community. In the spring of 1850, thirty Sacramento doctors formed the Medical Chirurgical Association of Sacramento in order to curtail the fraudulent doctors who were practicing medicine in the city and to better regulate the city's medical practitioners.[55]

Attempting to establish a viable and effective medical response to the gold rush, several doctors took positions on the city council, pushing for the involvement and support of government aid for hospitals and the sick.[56] As physicians, they circulated throughout the length and breadth of gold rush society, doctoring to the rich and poor, city dweller and transient miner. In the tumultuous conditions of the early gold rush, the doctors were perhaps the only ones who had such a broad exposure to the city's varied population.

Still, other issues seemed more important—the settlers' land claims, the ebb and flow of business, the ever present lure of instant wealth in the nearby foothills, and the city's financial ups and downs. Sanitation in the city was usually ignored, and conditions there formed a perfect breeding ground for disease. Newly arrived overlanders, already weak from the difficult trip across the plains, were perfect victims. Given the setting, a horrifying epidemic was practically inevitable.

Yet in the aftermath of the October outbreak, Sacramento residents found a sense of unity. The cholera epidemic ended late in November; drier weather, combined with increased sanitation, dramatically improved city health. The cholera outbreak widened the growing gap between settled residents and transient miners. During the epidemic, miners avoided the city, trying to avoid the dreadful disease themselves. As a result, many of the miners' chief attractions in the city also suffered. "It had the effect of pretty much closing up business," Fitch recalled, "principally of that kind called gambling and saloons—hotels where the understory was a saloon where they sold liquor for gambling at the tables. It closed that business."[57] With the absence of the miners, city residents found themselves united by both their fear of the disease and their commitment to the city.

Unlike the land title dispute, the epidemic carried no ideological disputes. The epidemic was a citywide threat, and its end brought citywide relief. In this sense, it gave residents a common foe and at least temporarily united people who had previously disagreed with one another. During the outbreak, many left the city, but many remained. Foremost among those who stayed were the city's doctors, seventeen of whom lost their lives to the disease.[58] Most were widely praised as heroes who saved the town from complete ruin. Dodson recalled, "I was in Sacramento and practiced medicine. The cholera scourge was terrible; I was almost worked to death. All other physicians worked with the energy of brave noble-hearted men. . . . I shall never forget the kind, noble, and generous aid extended to the afflicted by the men and women of Sacramento."[59] That the doctors were middle-class professionals, many of whom had earlier helped lead the residents to their victory in the Common Council, only further enhanced their authority and leadership in city affairs.

→--←

Following the cholera outbreak, enterprising residents tried to rebuild Sacramento along the broad commercial interests of middle-class businessmen. At first the city economy seemed to falter. Alonzo Hill wrote home on September 27, "I received a letter from Luther, he wants advice in relation to coming to California. I think it is all folly to come now unless with *considerable* means—There is now a great many heavy failures, both here [Sacramento] and in the 'City of Conflagrations' [San Francisco]."[60]

Commerce and stability remained residents' primary concerns, especially when trying to reopen communication with mining camps after the banking failures and the epidemic. On December 30, the city's levee was finally completed, and though it was not needed that winter, it promised to keep the city secure.[61] One of the most important topics of conversation was the attempt to have Sacramento declared a port city in order to facilitate trade. Residents also expected fiscal responsibility from the Common Council; one of the most heated editorials in the *Transcript*, published under the title "To What Have We Arrived?" demanded an accounting of the city budget and lambasted council members for taking salaries when funds were running behind for building the levee.[62]

As was the case the previous spring, recovery was not so much the result of careful planning as of fortuitous circumstances. Despite the near collapse of the city's financial houses, the gold rush still worked its magic. Merchants in towns and mining camps that had sprung up in the central mining district depended on Sacramento for supplies. The previous winter those who had stayed in the foothills had gotten cut off when the winter rains set in. During the winter of 1850–51 mining camp merchants were determined not to be caught empty-handed again. Instead of avoiding the city, these merchants pursued trade vigorously, laying up heavy stores of goods in the fall. Their business, coming on the heels of the financial panic, soon had the city's economic pulse racing again.[63]

This time, however, enterprising residents found themselves in a more secure position. Lacking loans from city speculators, city merchants required full payment in gold for the goods delivered to the foothills. When possible, firms also sent representatives to eastern suppliers themselves, who negotiated cargoes to be sent directly from Atlantic ports to the city's waterfront, thus eliminating not only great speculator wholesalers, but also transshipment fees from San Francisco. The results quickly became evident. When the winter proved to be exceptionally mild, a number of foothill merchants actually found themselves oversupplied and sold their stores at ruinous sacrifice. Yet the setback did not engulf most city merchants, who continued to prosper.[64]

As the city's economic pulse quickened, the city's new merchants saw their business prospects revive. Mark Hopkins continued to make his business grow, in part because he understood the conditions of business so well. "A few goods at California prices amounts to 'a heap' of money. . . . In New York the great trouble is to find sale for goods—Here it is the reverse, our greatest trouble is in buying goods, they sell themselves."[65] David Hewes wrote home that "all branches of enterprise are moving on with electric speed. In our public improvements, and in building generally; durability, convenience, and ornament are most anxiously cared for. We have some fine three story brick buildings and blocks. Our streets are now planked, which will render the city much more convenient in passing about. . . . The cholera disappeared a week or two since, and the City and Country around here are at present very healthy."[66]

The economy of the Sacramento region also began to diversify as dreams of instant success in the gold fields subsided. The original attraction of the Sacramento and San Joaquin valleys had been agriculture. The gold rush had initially hindered agricultural development. Late in 1849, Van Dorn had noted the effects of the gold rush on regional agriculture. "As might be expected, every branch of agriculture is abandoned, nor will this pursuit prosper until the return from the mines falls back to a moderate price per day."[67] However, while the amount of gold an individual miner might hope to find decreased after 1849, the total amount of gold produced in the mines remained high and in fact continued to rise. Thus while individuals would make less at mining in 1851, the amount of gold in circulation would continue to increase.[68] The stage was set for an economic boom outside of the mining profession. Merchants would make more money, and so would nearly any other business. Agriculture took time to develop: crops take time to grow, animals to raise and fatten for market. Yet by early 1851 the region around Sacramento City began to be more intensely utilized for agriculture. The diversification of the city's economy thus helped to give it a more stable footing.[69]

Many residents began to realize Sacramento's potential dominance of northern California's commerce. As Morse pointed out, "The entire northern mining population, dependent upon us in a great measure for the necessities of life, must always render this city the depot from which they will draw their supplies. And as the mines are inexhaustible, so will the demand be unceasing as long as there are laborers to work in them."[70] Yet Morse's visions were far broader than those of the city's founders. "The tributaries of the Sacramento also bring to us the steamboat and schooner laden with garden vegetables, hay, the products of the dairy, and every variety of "fish, flesh, and fowl, and return as deeply laden with passengers and merchandise."[71] By looking beyond the needs of miners alone, Morse was rekindling Sutter's old scheme of building a town at the junction of the Sacramento and American rivers that would dominate trade in the Sacramento Valley. By enumerating goods not usually associated with mining, Morse suggested the possibility of establishing a city economy based on more than mining.

He also hinted at potential industrial pursuits in Sacramento. In a city of such size and so far from eastern manufactories, craftsmen and mechanics were in high demand in every field. Morse pointed out that much of the chaos in local trade originated in the lack of sufficient goods, a problem that could be remedied with local industry. The city's needs were great, and experienced workers were few. The situation was ripe for anyone to try his hand at any occupation. Sacramento's enterprising residents had few restrictions on choice of employment in the city.

The occupations people chose in the booming city suggest something of the opportunities that awaited ex-miners who decided to relocate in Sacramento. According to the census of 1850, half of the city's workers were engaged in consumer-oriented services. Twenty percent of the population serviced the city: transporting goods to or from the city, building it, or governing it. Manufacturing in Sacramento was still in its early stages but probably represented a huge leap over the state of city manufacturing in the fall of 1849.

The range of occupations within Sacramento at that time and listed in the census is quite large. Over 240 occupations were listed, ranging from the city's

numerous merchants and clerks to its single chambermaid, interpreter, uphol-
sterer, and professor. Occupations directed primarily toward providing services
to individual consumers far exceeded those of other categories, accounting for
nearly 50 percent of all city workers.[72]

Analysis of the census suggests that in most respects Sacramento's occupations
were open to anyone, regardless of their age, birthplace, or ethnicity. Generally
each occupation's demographic characteristics mirrored those of the overall
population. This finding corresponds to a peculiarity noted in several accounts of
the early days of the city. John Morse later observed that during the first year or so,
Sacramento business was in a wild state of instability because it included a great
number of people who had never been in business before.[73] Business opportunities
in the early days of the city were too tempting to resist. Nor did these opportunities
initially require a great deal of business acumen. As Morse noted, this easy
environment did not last long, and soon many erstwhile businessmen found
themselves facing sharp and canny competitors, declining profits, and eventual
bankruptcy. Morse himself started in California as a miner, switched back to
his profession of medicine, then tried his hand at banking, real estate speculation,
auctioneer, and editor before returning again to medicine. Most remarkable of
all was the brief period of occupational experimenting: Morse tried all these
professions within a space of only three years.[74]

Morse, however, was encouraged by indications that many Sacramento residents had already begun to seek out their old familiar livelihoods. "Men are
resuming those places for which nature, education, and former habits have
fitted them," he wrote.

> The learned professor, now teamster, now speculator in lots, is again
> engaging the exploring qualities of his mind in the development of the
> hidden treasures of our country, which can alone be revealed through the
> media of science. The accomplished lawyer, now delver and digger in the
> mines, now trading, now cooking, is again assuming his legitimate place
> at the bar, re-perusing the huge works of the old guides to the principles
> and practice of law, and vindicating those interests around which law
> builds up its equitable support. The grave minister, who from theology
> went successively into mining, trading, speculating, and town-making, has
> again resumed the habits of a parson, and now may be seen contending for
> the supremacy of Truth, and defining the obligations of moral law.[75]

Part of the city's new stability also came from a peculiar weeding out of the
city's population. John Morse noted that by 1851 Sacramento had rid itself of

"those individuals whose mental constitution always leads them to look at the gloomy side of things. . . . We certainly do not regret their absence. They were incapable of hope—they possessed not energy, and therefore were totally unfitted for a country whose bright prospects are in the future—whose richest resources are yet to be developed."[76]

The ease with which men seemed able to get start-up capital in gold rush California towns astounded newspaper reporter Bayard Taylor. "Men were not troubled by the ordinary ups and downs of business, when it was so easy for one of any enterprise to recover his foothold. If a person lost his all, he was perfectly indifferent; two weeks of hard work gave him enough to start on, and two months, with the usual luck, quite reinstated him."[77] Though Taylor undoubtedly underestimated businessmen's concerns about the instability of business, he accurately captured the mood of many city residents.

Nor did starting businessmen need the expense of a building in which to transact their trade. Two of the biggest and best-known business sites in Sacramento, the Front Street Embarcadero and the Sixth Street Horse Market, sprang up without planning or organization. Both places, however, provided an open, comfortable location in which people could gather, and these places quickly became recognized and accepted locations to conduct particular kinds of business.

The development of the Horse Market at the intersection of Sixth and K streets began with the fortunate combination of a comfortable arena and nearby related businesses. "This was one of the principal sights in the place," Taylor wrote,

> and as picturesque a thing as could be seen anywhere. The trees were here thicker and of larger growth than in other parts of the city; the market-ground in the middle of the street was shaded by an immense oak, and surrounded by tents of blue and white canvas. One side was flanked by a livery stable—an open frame of poles, roofed with dry tule, in which stood shivering mules and raw boned horses, while the stacks of hay and wheat straw, on the open lots in the vicinity, offered feed to the buyers of animals, at the rate of $3 daily for each head.[78]

The site naturally drew Sacramento's transient miners and overlanders. Newly arrived overland migrants and miners sought to sell their livestock, either to avoid the costs of stabling their animals or to raise enough money to provide a start-up stake for living in the city. Miners on their way to the gold fields sought new mounts. Taylor watched the various people who gathered at the site but noted the common characteristic of past experience with the mines or the overland trail: "The ground was usually occupied by several persons at once—a rough, tawny-faced, long-bearded Missourian, with a couple of pack-mules which had been starved in the Great Basin; a quondam New York dandy with a horse whose back he had ruined in his luckless 'prospecting' among the mountains; a hard-fisted farmer with the wagon and ox-team which had brought his family and household goods across the continent."[79]

Buying and selling probably took place outside all the city's livery stables to some extent, but the comfortable shade of this site made trading most attractive. Storekeeper Franklin Buck recorded the colorful activity that took place at the Horse Market on a daily basis. "Right below our store is one of the most busy scenes you ever saw," he wrote to his sister in Maine. "It is a large livery stable where they sell horses, mules, oxen and carts at auction. The auctioneer gets on an animal and rides him up and down the street, shows him off to the best advantage and frequently four or five are selling at once. Such a Babel of sounds! There is always a large crowd and some rare sport."[80]

James Haines also profited from the Horse Market. "The Horse Market was in front of the house, and horses could be bought for from $5 to $10 a piece from parties coming from the mines and the same were readily sold to parties coming from San Francisco for $150 a piece. We carried on that kind of business all that fall. I had made $1000 per day in buying and selling horses."[81]

Perhaps even more impressive was the daily gathering of buyers and sellers on the city's waterfront, the old embarcadero landing that now was incorporated into the city as Front Street. The site was a natural place to buy and sell goods since ships unloaded their supplies here. Ships also unloaded passengers here, bound for the gold fields. Many of these people were eager to buy equipment and provisions for the mines before heading out of town, while others were anxious to sell whatever personal goods of value that they had at their disposal to raise enough funds to get to the mines in good order. Thus Front Street brought buyers, sellers, and goods into contact in a concentrated site.

Like the Horse Market, the embarcadero operated without overall organization and with much apparent confusion. Wholesalers bargained for ships' cargoes, while retailers bargained with wholesalers and looked for a chance to beat the wholesalers to a prize shipment. Passengers disembarked, bewildered looks on their faces as they stumbled across the crowded waterfront. Would-be miners tried to make a quick sale out of whatever excess baggage they had brought with them—old newspapers, combs or brushes, an extra coat or valise—in order to collect enough money to buy mining equipment before heading for the mines. Street hawkers and auctioneers wandered through the crowds, hoping to make a daily living. A San Francisco newspaper writer visiting the city wryly recorded one waterfront auctioneer trying to make his livelihood selling shoes and socks. The auctioneer had little luck with the socks and so tried offering a pair of pegged brogans. "Every peg was dwelt on in the most glowing terms, and the large number of them properly represented; but they went off at a bargain, which should be good evidence that boots and shoes are coming down a peg."[82]

What makes this site most interesting, however, is that it not only sprang up without overall organization, but continued in the face of active measures to discourage it. The city's founding merchants owned most of the lots facing Front Street and had acquired title to the street as well. According to the provisions of their title, Front Street was in effect private property: only the cross streets were open to public access.[83] Time and again throughout 1849 and 1850 the Front Street landholders tried to clear the embarcadero of competitors and small merchants. Laws forbidding loitering and the storage of goods on Front Street were passed but ignored. At times cargoes left on Front Street were confiscated by the sheriff or by representatives of the early merchants, acting outside the limits of the city's laws. Yet the embarcadero continued to be a popular gathering place.[84]

For many would-be miners who became new California merchants, the gold rush had taken an unexpected but still lucrative direction. Mark Hopkins celebrated those men who came to California and set out to establish stable businesses despite the disappointments of gold mining.

> Very many came here with extravagant expectations founded on an indistinct something (a kin to nothing) in the distance, which vanishes like vapor when they approach the realities of a pick and shovel under a midday sun. Notwithstanding this sad disappointment, there are some who soon recover from it and set themselves about something and do well. Much better than they could do at home. Industry of every kind here is well rewarded. Common laborers, mechanics, and good businessmen *I think can gain a thousand dollars surplus money as easy here as they can a hundred in the States.*[85]

Over the next year, Hopkins became a careful and insightful observer of Sacramento business conditions. Long before even dreaming of his future as a transcontinental railroad mogul, he assessed his activity in California optimistically: "I think the second best move of my whole life was my coming here—I have never for one moment doubted it since I have been here—Though if I had been alone it would have been much better for me—But now I believe all are doing well."[86]

The Death of Frederick Roe

Frederick Roe died on February 25, 1851, at nine-thirty in the evening, on Sixth Street, between L and K streets, under one of the old oak trees that had still not been cut down from along the city's streets. Perhaps the last thing he saw was one of the bare branches of the now leafless trees, starkly illuminated by lantern light. More likely, his dying eyes saw the mob of over five thousand people—the majority of the city's population—who less than thirty minutes before had stormed the jailhouse where he was incarcerated, paraded him down the street, and then put a noose around his neck and hung him from one of the old oaks. Before his death, Frederick Roe's ears were assaulted by shouted arguments, the pounding on the jailhouse door, cheers, cursing, whoops of triumph, and pleas for mercy. But as he jerked with the weight of his own body, spasmed, then swung lifelessly, the carnival-like noise of the mob suddenly stopped, and the people remained silent as the death of Frederick Roe began to register in their minds.[1]

The silence of that night remained nearly unbroken. Although *Sacramento Transcript* editor F. C. Ewer reported the lynching in painstaking detail, his account is nearly the only evidence remaining of what happened that day and night. Though Sacramento residents wrote of the Squatters' Riot in letters, journals, pamphlets, and memoirs, they remained silent on their thoughts or feelings about the death of Frederick Roe.

Lynchings were not uncommon in the California gold rush, but the sudden taking of a life by a mob still demands a historical explanation. The commonplace observation that the West was wild and untamed and thus a place where people often took the law into their own hands simply does not answer for the peculiar conditions of a given lynching at a specific time and place. The death of Frederick Roe had specific, local causes and repercussions. To explain it away as simply a typical Wild West scene or to ignore it entirely—as many of the city's participants later tried to do—is to hide an important event in the city's development.

In the death of Frederick Roe, Sacramento City crossed an important, perhaps even critical threshold. In their transition from would-be gold miners to settled businessmen, California's frenetic population needed to shift not only goals and expectations but behaviors and attitudes as well. It is typical to think of such confrontations in the West as being between those who sought a wild, irresponsible freedom and those who sought to establish a civil and settled community.[2] The mistake in this stereotype, however, is to suppose that these represent two different groups of people. In reality the lines between these groups ran not between them but *within* them, and those lines were usually blurred, shifting, and contradictory at best. The death of Frederick Roe dramatically and forcefully defined at least some of these inner divisions in a powerful public setting. As such it broadened a personal transformation into a public evolution. In the aftermath, few in the city may have been willing to preserve the lynching for posterity, but the hanging body of Frederick Roe swaying in the lantern light on that cold winter night, and the account of his death published in the *Sacramento Transcript,* would mark a critical turning point in the city's development.

⤍ — ⤎

During the first few years of the gold rush, the distinction between Sacramento "settlers" and foothill miners was ill defined. Miners might stay in the city for extended periods, either to await the end of winter or simply to work long enough to gather enough money to buy supplies to head back for the gold fields. Settlers themselves might leave for other towns or return east after only a few months. The loose association of city people and miners, in fact, gave the Settlers' Association much more perceived power than it probably ever enjoyed in reality. Following the Squatters' Riot, rumors swept the city that the owner of the Brighton tavern where the shoot-out between the sheriff's posse and suspected squatters had taken place had escaped and made his way to a mining camp and that the miners were marching on Sacramento to burn it to the ground.[3] The rumor turned out to be false, but the belief that the miners were allied to the settlers suggests that the city's "settlers" still comprised a substantial number of transient miners as well as permanent residents.

Though many of its leaders were either dead or jailed, the Settlers' Association published its first issue of the *Settlers and Miners Tribune* on October 30, 1850. The paper only lasted for about two months, but its publishers were determined to keep the matter of land titles before the residents of Sacramento.[4] Issues reported on the developing trial against Charles Robinson and other association members, supported pro-settler candidates for local elections, and carried notices for public "Settlers and Miners" meetings.[5]

The paper's greatest triumph came with the nomination of association president Charles Robinson to the California state legislature at a time when Robinson was still in prison and undergoing a trial for his part in the August riot. The trial gained a further complication when Robinson actually won election to the state legislature. Then, in a move loudly criticized by the *Settlers and Miners Tribune,* the trial against Robinson was moved to the city of Benecia, either to inconvenience or to intimidate defense witnesses from coming forth on Robinson's behalf. Ultimately the courts dropped the charges against Robinson and the other association members, and Robinson took his seat in the state legislature. Since the paper's goals seemed primarily to be protecting association defendants and helping elect pro-squatter officials, both objectives were in essence reached by the end of November. Shortly afterward, the *Tribune* ceased publication.[6]

During these same weeks, however, Sacramento's more permanent residents began to disassociate themselves from the Settlers' Association. Support for the association is suggested by the list of advertisers in the *Tribune's* pages. Though the paper was short-lived, the number of advertisers grew during the paper's life. A comparison of advertisers in the *Sacramento Transcript* and the *Settlers and Miners Tribune* suggests that to a certain extent, merchants expressed their approval or disapproval of the settlers' land title claims by placing their advertising with one paper over another. Few merchants advertised in both papers.[7] The type of ads that merchants ran in the *Tribune* suggests the demographic makeup of the "Settlers and Miners." Ads for mining equipment, gold shippers, saloons, and hotels made up the largest part of the advertising. Several ads were addressed "To Miners, or any others." Attorneys' ads also made up a large part of the paper's advertising.[8] Evidently many Sacramento businessmen came to associate the *Settlers and Miners Tribune* with miners alone, rather than settlers and miners.

As the months passed following the riot, the gap between the city's transient miners and city residents grew ever larger. John Plumbe, who became the register of the Settlers' Association after the riot, wrote a lengthy tract to James Gordon Bennett, editor and proprietor of the *New York Herald,* and published his work in booklet form in Sacramento early in 1851. In this work, Plumbe not only tried to clear the association of any wrongdoing, but also tried to enunciate the association's vision of Sacramento society. Plumbe pointed to the social divisions between settlers and speculators. The settlers, he wrote, "made no pretensions to being leaders of fashion; nor to any right to a place in the 'first circles' of Sacramento exclusiveness. They could not boast of being the sole possessors of all the 'wealth and respectability,' the talent and refinement, and the 'law and order,' in their community. . . . At the same time," Plumbe continued, "they were not able to comprehend why those who appropriated to themselves all these high attributes, embraced individuals whose *conduct* was so strikingly at variance with everything that the plain, unpretending settlers had always, *before,* been accustomed to regard as constituting the character of a *true gentleman.*"[9]

These passages point to the wide differences between the city's great speculators and the Settlers' Association, but they also represented a voice that was becoming increasingly marginalized after the riot. Although Plumbe's attacks were strident, there is little indication that his argument was popular among city residents. For almost immediately after the riot, the composition of the Settlers' Association changed. Quietly yet unmistakably, Sacramento's resident population was beginning to incorporate many of the elements of the old Settlers' Association. New, more permanent residents wanted clear title to city lands, but at least some of them increasingly felt that the federal government should invalidate many Mexican land grants. Most seemed to favor the recognition of Sutter's grant in order to avoid more conflict but also favored opening more land around the city as "public land."

In this transformation from miner to resident, the term "settler" came to be appropriated by many city residents. The shift is especially apparent in the election of pro-squatter officials to local offices. As the term "settlers" came to cover more and more residents, it was also subtly pulling away from describing the miners. And as the fall of 1850 passed, the easy connection between "settlers and miners" became more strained. For as more and more residents sought to make their fortunes in the city, they co-opted not the simple claims of the settlers, but the more elaborate claims and gentlemanly behavior of the speculators, previously rejected by Plumbe and the Settlers' Association.

In addition, the city did not provide many avenues to bring entrepreneurial city people and transient miners together. For the great speculators, home was most often a hotel. Analysis of the city's richest men shows that the majority lived in large hotels. Furthermore, the great speculators did not cluster in one or two hotels, but lived in different hotels.[10] Here the great speculators lived divorced from their workplaces and offices. New enterprising residents stayed in the widest variety of places, including tents, boardinghouses, and hotels. Perhaps the majority of enterprising residents, however, lived within their place of business.[11] Samuel Upham, founder of the *Sacramento Transcript*, noted in the spring of 1850: "Sacramento City being in its infancy, . . . hotel accommodations were limited. We lodged in the office . . . and [I] slept on the soft side of the office counter, with a roll of paper for a pillow."[12] Bayard Taylor found similar quarters in the city: "I was indebted for quarters in Sacramento City to Mr. De Graw [a merchant]. . . . I slept very comfortably on a pile of Chinese quilts, behind the counter."[13] Surrounded by the daily trappings of work, their home given over largely to the work space, enterprising residents clearly drew the values of business from their home environment. Business came first; family support went toward the continuing success of the business. Family businesses predominated.

Transient miners, on the other hand, tended to pitch tents in the sprawling overlander camps to the south and east of the city. Here they were more likely to strike up meetings with newly arrived migrants, who like themselves still hoped to strike it rich in the gold fields. These informal camps themselves even served some of the functions of the city itself. Visiting miners needing wagons, oxen, or horses sometimes could find them available from migrants looking to dispose of their trail rigs. Overlanders usually welcomed visiting miners, as they were sources of information about conditions in the gold fields. Overlanders and miners shared many characteristics in the large shadow city of canvas that surrounded Sacramento, but their attitudes and behaviors more often resembled those of the trail and mining camp than the settled attitudes of the developing city proper. During the city's first two years, the lines between city residents, transient miners, and overlanders were almost indistinguishable. But by the spring of 1851, these differences were beginning to be felt in the physical structures of the city as well as in the attitudes and behaviors displayed in the city's dusty streets.

>--<

As Sacramento residents grew more conscious of the differences between their goals and experiences and those of visiting miners, one of the most troubling attitudes that they continued to share was that toward gambling. *Sacramento Transcript* editor John Morse eloquently recorded the popularity of gambling in Sacramento. Describing the "Round Tent," one of the earliest and most popular of the city's gambling establishments, Morse wrote that

> music and a decorated bar and obscene pictures were the great attractions that lined this whirlpool of fortune and coerced into the vortex of penury and disgrace many an American who had come to California without his morals or the decencies which he was taught at home. . . . The toilers of the country, including traders, mechanics, miners, and speculators, lawyers, doctors, and ministers, concentrated at this gambling focus like flying insects around a lighted candle at night; and like such insects seldom left the delusive glare until scorched and consumed by the watch fires of destruction. . . . The gaming at this time was of a most Herculean grade so far as boldness and amounts hazarded were concerned. Every saloon, every table devoted to betting contingencies were literally crowded and sometimes so completely overwhelmed as to make it physically dangerous to be even a spectator of the scenes.[14]

Alonzo Delano had been shocked by the amount of gambling that was pursued in early Sacramento. "I regret to say, that gambling formed a prominent part in the business of the city; and there appeared an infatuation, if not unprecedented, certainly not excelled in the annals of mankind." Delano reported the tale of a young man who had mined $19,000 worth of gold and started for home when he decided to spend some time at gambling. So as not to lose his fortune, he deposited $16,000 with friends before heading into a gambling hall with the remaining $3,000. "He soon lost this, and under the excitement which it occasioned, he drew the sixteen thousand from his friend, notwithstanding all remonstrance, and determined to retrieve his luck. He returned to the table, and continued playing till he had lost every farthing, when, instead of making his friends happy, by returning to their embrace with a competence, he was compelled to return to toil and privation in the mines."[15]

Gambling halls epitomized gold rush realities better than any other culturally sanctioned entertainment, and this in fact may best explain their overwhelming popularity. Californians entered gambling establishments with the same sense of adventure as they had experienced when they embarked on the gold rush itself. Like the country they had crossed, the gambling hall was an exotic, mysterious environment. The hard drinks sold there served as a kind of initiation into manhood, much as migration hardships served to separate men from boys. The rich and ornate furnishings of many halls, which patrons could enjoy temporarily but not own, seen through the clouds of smoke and the intoxication of liquor, were similar to the dreams of fortune experienced by migrants on their way to California. Prostitution reminded gold rush migrants that they had moved beyond the settled world of traditional morals. Furthermore, the ease with which men could buy the companionship of women perhaps mirrored their own hopes of buying patriarchal authority and respect when they returned to their families and communities with their fortunes.

Gambling required that men "ante up," contribute an initial investment to the game just to take part, much as the gold rush had required an initial investment before would-be miners could get in on the gold rush experience. Gambling, like the gold rush, required further bets, or investments, if players wished to stay in the game. Moreover, gambling required that men invest in possibilities that they could not see. Poker challenged players to bet on cards that lay facedown, much as mining required betting on the possible wealth hidden under a gravel bank. Like the frenetic world of speculating, players at roulette gambled their money on the final resting place of a ball spinning in one direction around a wheel spinning in another. Games such as these concentrated all the experiences of gold rush life in a compact moment. If they conveyed the bitterness of defeat to players, they also surrounded the gamblers with music and brilliance, warmth and whiskey, and, most important of all, the companionship of other gamblers, most of whom continued playing. For as in mining and speculating, gambling's "logic" was all luck, and bad luck that took one man's fortune away could as quickly become good luck, showering him with a new fortune.

Games of chance, like mining or speculating, played on the ambiguities of the gold fever ethos. Miners and speculators expected to be governed by rules in their daily lives and sought them in trying to understand the underground logic of mineral deposits or the complicated workings of the commodity market. Games were attractive because the rules were clear, spelled out, easy to understand. They offered a security of underlying order and hinted that mining and speculation also had underlying rules that could be understood.

As a concentrated and accurate parable of the miners' daily experience, it is no wonder that gambling was so popular and during 1849 everyone gambled. The pervasiveness of gambling seemed to know no bounds. "Even boys of twelve and sixteen years of age were sometimes seen betting," Delano noted. "But little else could be expected, from the extent of the demoralizing influences thus set before them."[16] "Not one man in ten," Morse testified, "if one in twenty, either by his absence or denunciation, condemned the universal mania for gambling which swept the country. Two ministers of the Gospel, very soon after these saloons opened, could be seen, one of them piously engaged in dealing monte, and the other, with less concentration, running about trying his luck now at faro, now at monte, anon at poker, and next, perhaps, at vantoon or the legitimately named sweat cloth."[17] And why should ministers have been exempt from gambling? They more than others may have sensed that gaming spoke more to the experiences of their flocks than any gospel.

The significance of gambling in Sacramento went beyond the gambling hall. The games that took place in gambling saloons merely echoed the speculative activities of miners and businessmen alike. Gambling lay at the heart of Sacramento's emerging commercial community. Businessmen gambled so that they could make a profit in the city, acquire the goods needed to stay in business, or even to corner the market on a particular item and win the commercial jackpot. Collis P. Huntington, who like Mark Hopkins would later be numbered as one of the railroad barons of the Central Pacific, came to Sacramento in 1849 as a midlevel businessman determined to make a fortune. Later in life he described his business philosophy at that time in terms of pure speculation: "I made my money by commerce; kept my ware-house full when prices were low, when they went up I sold out. Prices go up and down as sure as the days come so regular, but just as sure nothing stands still in this world—as somebody said: 'There is a time in the affairs of man if taken at flood tide leads on to fortune.'"[18]

In a speculative move that rivaled Samuel Brannan's ride through San Francisco, proclaiming, "Gold!" on the American River after buying all the mining

equipment he could lay his hands on, Huntington clai
the market on all the shovels in California in 1850. A
sold by manufacturers for $12.50 per dozen. Hunti.
hundred shovels for only $2 to $3 per dozen, then bou
eight hundred shovels for $25 per dozen. Having purchased nea.
available, he then publicly bought a few dozen shovels through a San
broker at the astronomical price of $125 per dozen. This public purchase,
greatly inflated price, set off a panic in the mines, where shovels were a vital
piece of equipment. Then, after having conditioned the market for such a high
price, Huntington sold two thousand shovels for *only* $120 per dozen—making
a profit of $100,000. At the same time, Huntington made another $100,000 in
speculations on potatoes.[19]

In the fall of 1850 Sacramento society was largely grounded on the activities of
middlemen, especially those who sold their goods to miners. Following the floods,
rioting, and cholera epidemics of 1850, Sacramento businessmen seemed finally
to be in a secure position to reap fortunes from the gold rush trade. Opportunities
were abundant, especially with winter closing in on the foothills. Foothill town
merchants realized that they would have to lay in a large overstock of goods in
the fall to last them through the winter, when northern California's roads were
once again expected to become impassable. As a result, Sacramento merchants
did a brisk business in the fall.[20]

Such opportunities, however, did not necessarily eliminate the pitfalls to
doing business in Sacramento. The highs, the lows, and the sheer volume of
business presented a chaotic world to Sacramento's merchants. Under these
conditions, many did incredibly well, but others failed abysmally. "All who are
settled in business are making money," wrote Dr. Benjamin Stillman in his
diary, "but, alas! for the many unfortunates. You have heard of the *Battle of
Life*—it is a reality here: the fallen are trampled into the mud, and are left to
the tender mercies of the earth and the sky."[21]

Following the example of the city's leading speculators, speculation by smaller
merchants grew rampant in Sacramento. Bread sold for fifty cents a loaf; butter
fetched between $2 and $3 a pound. Board, without lodging, ran between $16
and $49 a week. A glass of liquor at a first-class bar cost a dollar, a cigar fifty cents.[22]
Even drinking water commanded a high price. Since the city had no adequate
water service, river water was filtered through charcoal on the anchored bark *Eliza,*
then retailed for twelve and a half cents per pail.[23] City merchant Thomas Van
Dorn noted in his diary, "Everything [is] ruled by high or exorbitant prices—
there is but one scale here, and that is *High*."[24] And to his wife he wrote,
"Everything is conducted upon the High Pressure system. Cities spring up like

brooms. High prices in every department of labor and high rates for every ..icle of consumption. Such rates as would astonish anyone in the States."[25]

Even the most basic transactions of the city's economy were so unstable as to make a man rich beyond his dreams and then stone broke, all in a single day. The need to get their goods on time in order to realize a profit kept many merchants on constant edge. Storekeeper William Prince wrote his wife detailed accounts of his business ups and downs. "Mr. Cornwall came up on the 30th, the 2nd day after I had moved in, and found matters going on bravely. He brought about $400 of Goods with him, half of which are already sold. We purchased next day 800 lbs. Zinc at 40 cents that had arrived the night before and of which I got the refusal before I went to bed, knowing there was none other here, and in one week it will be all sold at $1, making about $500 profit on it. . . . I was sick for one day about losing the $7000. I found out by chance here that such a lot [of unclaimed goods] was at San Francisco onboard a ship in the bay, and wrote Cornwall [to purchase the shipment for him] but was a day too late."[26]

Many businessmen found the dynamics of Sacramento's gold rush economy stimulating; others, however, were less enthusiastic. The economic chaos provided opportunity for spectacular profits but also for bewildering ruination. As the city's businessmen committed themselves to making a fortune in the city, they also sought to understand the ups and downs of their fortunes and to seek ways to order the economic chaos. Many joined business associations or the Masons or the Independent Order of Odd Fellows; others sought the passage of laws to rationalize the chaos of many of the city's business practices.[27] Yet as they looked around them, many saw evidence that perhaps the greatest problems they faced were of their own making.

The quest for individual profits challenged the obligations of community bonds. John Morse, in a three-part editorial titled, "I Came to this Country to Make Money," attacked the destructive ruling ethic of the early gold rush. His eloquent and passionate attacks on speculation fever echoed similar attacks on the ruinous effects of gambling:

> Under the pressure of such a wild and irrational system of speculation, such vicious and frenzied sentiments of enterprise, who would stop to recognize or treat with the stipulations of law—to award a moment's support to general government—to think of spending 24 hours to the building of a house when a tent could be pitched in 10 minutes—to dream of an expenditure of money in erecting harbors and wharves to save a half dozen cargoes of merchandise, which might not be wanted for 48 hours—to

think of spending a week in repairing a steamboat, when a new one could be bought for $150,000 to $200,000? Who could wait for the slow and plodding returns of a cultivator of the soil? Would any body be so silly as to think of merging their energies into the development of permanent departments of mechanical industry? Who could afford to spend their time in providing hospitals for the sick, asylums for the poor subjects of insanity, churches where the sublimest maxims of truth could be best portrayed to the human mind—or school-houses, where the living elements of the soul are the most beautifully and substantially developed? . . . And churches, which are not at all essential to an exclusive purpose to make money, might produce much inconvenience by giving rise to inadvertent references to an antique and somewhat obsolete DECALOGUE, and especially to the seventh commandment of the series.[28]

Morse saw social instability in the philosophy "to make the most money in the shortest possible time, out of the least capital, and with perfect indifference to the consequences so far as the State was concerned; and also without any very fastidious notions of honor or propriety."[29] His editorials describing the causes and effects of speculation served not only to educate Sacramento resident merchants, many engaging in trade for the first time, to the economics of trade, but also sought to instill morality into the hearts of gold rush merchants.

Yet his attacks were never on business or profit making itself. In an editorial titled "Reflections upon Commerce," Morse made his objections to speculation clear. "As a people," he wrote, "we must make a strong effort to divest ourselves from that impetuous, restless, and wild spirit of speculation, which is too often predicated rather upon extravagant conjectures and unsound theories than upon the basis of careful and systematic calculations." Morse praised the "slow and accumulative results of patient toil" and vilified only the personal gain that came from "the overreaching and shrewdly pulled wires of morbid and violently forced business evolutions," representing them as "a constant reproach of illegitimate trade."[30]

In the transition from miners to residents, Morse sought to establish a respect for sound and stable business practices that would build a community up rather than tear it apart. Like many others in the region, Morse viewed the acquisition of a fortune in moral as well as economic terms. "Fortunes acquired in a day or year," he noted philosophically, "are not often freed from the taints of injustice, or from associations of loss and concurrent misery, which diminishes their value and makes them more the sources of anxiety than enjoyment." But he applauded men who made their fortunes in more traditionally sanctioned ways. "In the breast of every man there is a feeling of unmingled satisfaction in contemplating fortunes which have been attained by the operations of methodical, calm, and progressive industry. . . . We must abandon those rough-and-tumble, headlong, rash, and impetuous habits of business, which have marked our character heretofore. We must settle down in our own legitimate spheres, and be content with the profits of a trade conducted somewhat after the fashion of business that obtains in the established houses of the Old World."[31]

Morse's critiques of business and urban development nearly always came down to personal, moral, behavioral solutions. In his crusade against those people who merely "came to this country to make money" Morse concluded by pleading with his readers to adopt public-spirited values and actions.

> Have we not the means of relief in our own hands? Can we not let our favor, our support and interest, be chiefly appropriated to those who are contemplating years of business in California and are careful to cherish the resources of the country? Those who engage in building up instead of destroying—those who are disposed to add to, as well as take from—those who take an interest in the government, assist in the administration of law, and help to establish society upon a good and enduring basis. These are the men of California, who, if principally sustained, will make it a State unequalled in wealth, position or power. They are the men who will roll back the tide of calamity which has been let in upon the country by the prevalence of that adage, which in an unjust and objectionable sense has been excised in the incipient settlement of California as a State.[32]

To Morse, true manhood was defined not by private gain but by public involvement. Sacramento needed the public involvement of its business leaders if it hoped to build a community based on the ethic of gambling. What Morse and other civic leaders sought was some sense of controlling the speculative fever of the gold rush. Through appeals to honor, morality, and manhood, Morse tried to instill in city residents a sense of social responsibility to balance individual quests for power and profit. Not all gold rush Californians, however, understood the significance of gambling in the same light.

➵—➴

For many miners, the gambling nature of the gold rush led in a different direction. For many of these men, the speculative nature of gold rush mining mocked traditional cultural notions of a steady reward for hard work. Having invested their fortunes, time, and health in working the California gold fields, most men expected to reap a fortune as their due. James Barnes, who drifted back and forth between mining and carpentry work in Sacramento, vented his frustration and anger in an impassioned letter home that for many caught the essence of the gold rush: "Mining is a lottery; a man may sink a dozen holes and not get a cent, and he may sink another and get paid gold. . . . You wanted to know if there was any chance of speculation for you here; I think your chance is better where you are. There are hundreds of just such looking fellows as you are here prowling about the streets every day looking for something to do, out of money and a good home. Stay where you are and be contented."[33]

Though gambling lay at the heart of the gold rush experience for the miner, overlander, resident, and speculator alike, each group experienced gambling in a different way. For the miner, mining was a gamble that could be won only by repeated gambling; if one claim did not pay off, a miner had to try another one. The more miners who "played," the more likely that new deposits would be discovered. For urban speculators, however, speculation was a gamble that could provide an individual a fortune but at the same time create a hellish environment, hardly conducive to community building. As time passed, many urban merchants found it necessary to curb their speculative instincts; miners, on the other hand, often needed to apply the "rules" of gambling to ever increasing areas.

One of the basic acts of gambling is the transfer of personal property. Indeed, another way to look at gambling is as a system of property transfer. Players gamble an investment, then, if lucky, reap the benefits. That an entire system of living could be based on such a system was troubling. A miner, speculator, or gambler might lose all on the turn of a card and gain it all back again on the next turn of a card, only to lose all again in the next game. Property shifted from person to person through luck. Luck could be influenced, but as long as chance remained the underlying basis of property rights, cultural sanctions toward hard work and private property were challenged.

Given the harsh conditions of mining, as well as the loosened concept of property, it is not unusual that theft would take on a more ambiguous meaning in the gold fields than under other circumstances. Dr. Israel Lord noted late in 1849 that one of his traveling companions visited his camp and reported that a cow had been killed several miles down the river. "Did Bob kill it? If nobody owns the cow he did. If anybody owns it he didn't. It is probably a wild cow, and not marked and of course, not owned. No matter, we must have something to eat."[34] One of the sharpest illustrations of this type of ambiguity concerns the "Honest Miner" of gold rush songs who turns to theft in order to survive in the mines:

When first I went to mining, I was uncommon green,
With a "gallus" rig I went to dig, and claimed a whole ravine;
But when I could not make my grub, with implements to gag,
An honest miner might have been seen at night with a pig in a bag.
As he lugged it away from the pen,
Was thinking how lucky he'd been;
Went into a hole, dug deep after gold,
With pig in the bag tumbled in.[35]

The humorous depiction of the "honest" miner engaged in theft is a consistent theme of gold rush songs. Repeatedly the miner finds himself in a position in which theft is the only way to survive. To early miners, mostly middle-class men who originally saw themselves on a historic quest and who would not normally have engaged in any criminal activities, the humor of these songs worked as a salve to an uneasy conscience. In essence, the truly "dishonest" man was not the miner, but the merchant who had robbed him of his meager earnings or who profited from the difficult circumstances.

City speculators and merchants also provoked the miners' aggressiveness by charging exorbitant prices for needed supplies. This growing sense of confrontation often exaggerated other differences between transient miners and city people. Philip Castleman migrated to California overland in 1849 and arrived in Sacramento at the end of October. It took him several weeks to find a job, but he was eventually hired to work in a bakery. When the bakery was washed away in the 1850 flood, however, Castleman's boss was unable to pay his wages but gave him a note instead. Castleman tried his hand at mining and later gave his note to a trader headed back to Sacramento to collect for him. The trader, however, "collected and swindled me out of [the money] afterwards." Castleman, a rural Kentuckian, pointed out caustically in his diary that the trader was from New York.[36]

Miners' songs were nearly unanimous in their portrayal of city people's mistreatment of miners. As shown in the song "When I Went Off to Prospect," many overlanders and miners were looked down on by city residents:

The town was crowded full of folks,
Which made me think 'twas not a hoax;
At my expense they cracked their jokes,
When I was nearly starving.[37]

Sacramento City particularly came in for its share of disapproval. Sacramento was the nearest place miners could send or receive mail in the early months of the gold rush. This alone brought many miners to town on a somewhat regular basis. But miners had to wait in long lines, and mail at the post office was not sorted regularly. Some miners spent a day or more in line, waiting for mail that could not be found or that had not arrived. Chief among miners' complaints was their difficulty in getting mail, and disappointments and frustrations associated with the post office disorganization likely extended to the city itself.[38]

Gold miner H. C. St. Clair recorded his reluctance to even visit the city in the fall of 1849. "They [his partners on the overland trek] are upon a stand whether to go up or down to the mines. They all have to go down to Sacramento City to buy provisions. Let them go where they will." St. Clair only visited the city when it was his turn to buy provisions and then found the city to be expensive, disorienting, and unfriendly.[39] His experience could have been summed up in the song "Crossing the Plains," telling of the would-be miner who found city residents far from sympathetic:

> When you arrive at Placerville, or Sacramento City,
> You've nothing in the world to eat, no money—what a pity!
> Your striped pants are all worn out, which causes people to laugh,
> When they see you gaping round the town like a great big bindle calf.[40]

The feelings of contempt that city people showed transient miners and overlanders, however, were often returned in kind by the miners. Though Sutter's Fort had earlier had a high reputation among overland migrants as a friendly shelter at the end of the long trail, gold rush miners in the song "Hunting After Gold" soon came to resent the pompous attitudes of Sacramento's city fathers:

> When I left old New York, to go hunting after gold,
> Chunks bigger than my head I could pick up, I was told;
> I stopped at Sacramento, on a devil of expense,
> And they sent to the mountains, where I've not been sober since.
> The first man I saw in Sacramento Valley,
> Was his Honor lying drunk, on a ten-pin alley,
> With half a dozen more, some whose names I dare not call,
> If you'd rolled for the center you'd been sure to got them all.
> I went to eat some oysters, along with Captain Sutter,
> And he reared up on the table, and sat down in the butter;
> The Mayor and Recorder, they were drunk as ever,
> So the next day they sent me fluming on the river.[41]

Miners' songs give an impression of the growing confrontations between miners and California's newly minted city people. To the miner portrayed in "Seeing the Elephant," the entire gold rush experience was a confusing, demoralizing event:

When I left the States for gold,
Everything I had I sold;
A stove and bed, a fat old sow,
Sixteen chickens and a cow.
Refrain:
So leave you miners, leave, oh, leave you miners, leave,
Take my advice, kill off your lice, or else go up in the mountains;
Oh no, lots of dust, I'm going to the city to get on a "bust."
Oh no, lots of dust, I'm going to the city to get on a "bust."
On I traveled through the pines
At last I found the northern mines;
I stole a dog, got whipt like hell,
Then away I went to Marysville.
There I filled the town with lice,
And robbed the Chinese of their rice;
The people say, "You've got the itch,
Leave here, you lousy son of a bitch."
Because I would not pay my bill,
They kicked me out of Downieville;
I stole a mule and lost the trail,
And then fetched up in Hangtown Jail.[42]

As one "greenhorn" discovered, Sacramento was a world run according to different standards. In this song, the miners' experience in both the cities and the mines was aptly summed up in an overused but appropriate cliché:

When I got to Sacramento, I got a little tight,
I lodged aboard the Prison brig, one-half a day and night;
I vamoosed when I got ashore, went to the Northern mines,
There found the saying very true, "All is not gold that shines."[43]

By the spring of 1851, many residents had come to view the disorder that seemed inherent in their lives as bad for business as well as dangerous for society.

Violent confrontations in the city's streets sometimes claimed the lives of innocent residents. During the Squatters' Riot shoot-out between the Settlers' Association and Mayor Bigelow's informal militia, a shopkeeper's daughter had been seriously wounded.[44]

Sacramento newspapers reported a rise in violence in the city during the winter of 1850–51. From December on, the *Transcript* carried increasingly numerous reports of assaults, robberies, and shootings. Stores were broken into, and residents were attacked on the streets.[45] Crime in the city seemed to be rising and growing bolder. Only five watchmen patrolled the city's streets at night; in mid-February two prisoners escaped from the city's prison brig, an event the *Sacramento Transcript* editor called "almost a weekly occurrence."[46] Sacramento newspapers increasingly began to report the growing use of lynch law in California mining camps.

Possibly crime did not actually rise in the city, but was merely reported more attentively. More likely, the greater difficulty in and diminishing personal returns from mining provoked bitter disillusionment and caused more miners to turn away from it. Poor, often desperate, some of these men may have seen the city as an easy target. Certainly not all miners, or even a great majority of miners, turned to a life of crime. Yet miners had by now acquired reputations for transience, rowdiness, and thievery. Whether the reputation was deserved or not, or whether the increase in crime was real or only perceived, is not important. Far more important is that residents believed that miners were a threat to the fragile order that had finally come into their lives.

It is against this background—of a growing division and suspicion between residents and the city's transient miners, merchants' growing sense that gambling must be controlled, and the rising perception of crime and violence in the city streets—that the death of Frederick Roe ironically became such a focal point in the development of Sacramento's commercial community.

➢--➣

At about two o'clock in the afternoon of February 25, 1851, a miner stood beside a monte table in front of the Mansion House on the corner of J and Front streets. The scene was not uncommon: games of chance were so popular in the city that many gamblers often set up "tables" on sawhorses and barrel tops, crowding the busy city sidewalks. Many city residents, however, distrusted such games. Monte was played with a special deck of forty cards, with the player betting against the dealer on the color of the cards to be turned up from the deck. The game was regarded as one in which it was very easy for a dealer to cheat a player, resembling a shell game.

The miner evidently had his suspicions too and was watching the dealer closely but not playing. Also standing at the table was Frederick Roe, another monte dealer who in this case was playing, not dealing. Possibly the monte game was honest, and Roe was either playing to pass the time or simply visiting a fellow gambler at the time. It is also possible Roe was playing a rigged game, which the dealer let him win to sucker in other unsuspecting players. Whatever the case, it is known that Roe was intoxicated and that his inhibitions were down. He took offense at the miner's suspicions and told the miner to ante up and play or leave. The miner refused, telling Roe to "go to hell." A fistfight erupted quickly.[47]

The fight lasted roughly five minutes. The two men were parted by their friends several times, but each time the men broke away and continued fighting. Then, when one of Roe's friends felled the miner with a blow to the head, Roe fell on the miner, brutally beating him in the face. The crowd that had formed to watch then began shouting for Roe to stop. At this point Charles Myers, a wheelwright who had just picked up a load of lumber on the waterfront, stepped in, physically pulling Roe off the battered miner. Roe struggled against the stouter Myers, shouting to Myers to let him go. Myers shouted back at Roe, "For God's sake, don't three or four of you kill a man—fair fight," and released him. Roe then pulled a gun, aimed it wobbly at Myers and the crowd, and fired, shooting Myers in the head.[48]

With the shocked and outraged crowd shouting, "Kill the man or take him," City Marshall Cunningham arrived, arrested Roe, and took him to the police station house on the corner of Second and J streets. A growing crowd carried Myers up the length of K Street to the blacksmith shop of his former partner, Joseph Praeder. Though Myers had not yet died, his wound was quickly determined to be mortal. The dramatic procession up K Street soon spread the news of the shooting throughout the city and crowds began forming at both the station house and Praeder's blacksmith shop. In front of Praeder's, city councilman Dr. McKenzie climbed on top of a wagon to address the crowd. Decrying the shooting down of peace-loving citizens in the streets, McKenzie demanded an investigation and punishment. Soon the crowd was calling for "lynch law."[49]

The crowd at Praeder's marched back to and joined the growing crowd at the station house, while "some of the most prominent and respectable men in the city," according to *Sacramento Transcript* editor F. C. Ewer, also began meeting to discuss the incident and to join the crowd. By late afternoon the growing mob numbered over two thousand people. Again people began speaking to the crowd from wagon beds and soon formed a jury to "let justice be done both to the people and the person implicated." The city marshal addressed the crowd in an effort to quiet the excitement. He said he believed Roe to be a scoundrel but was in favor of letting the law take its course. Others argued against the marshal and formed a committee to investigate the killing and to take action. The crowd was becoming a lynch mob.

At this time in California, vigilante justice was a growing phenomenon, and given the recklessness and brutality of Roe's actions, it is understandable that passions would quickly be inflamed. But at the same time, lynch law was brutal and morally troubling; though their thinking was often clouded and inflamed by passion, few participants in a lynching took part without serious reservations. That fiery speakers were needed to whip the mobs to fury and to keep them at that level suggests the general reluctance of even a mob to take such a fatal course easily. Even in the heat of the moment, mobs needed to be emotionally convinced to take or support an illegal act.

The mob's committee dramatically focused the emerging Sacramento commercial community. The case against Roe was simple and obvious, leaving little room for disagreement. The likely verdict, had the law been operating, was also widely acknowledged: death. On these two aspects everyone could agree. The case thus provided one of the requisites for community: shared understanding. And in the gathering mob outside the station house, it was clear that this sharing was citywide.

However, another requirement for community—shared obligation—was less clear. Was it the obligation of the community to take the law into their own hands or to let the legal system take its course? Sacramento residents were of two minds. Some, like McKenzie, called for lynch law; others sided with Cunningham, defending the legal system. As the mob began to form its "committee," some in the crowd argued that the jury was a sham and the prisoner, who was still in the station house, was not safe. Dr. G. Taylor was nominated to examine Roe and to attest to his safety.

Taylor addressed the crowd shortly afterward and apparently was overcome by mob mentality. For the next few hours, while the committee interviewed witnesses and deliberated Roe's fate, Taylor addressed the crowd on several occasions, whipping them into a frenzy. Long before the committee finished its work, Taylor had become the mob's leader.[50] Taylor demanded lynch law, exhorting the mob to give the committee "half an hour—if a decision is not made in that time I will head the crowd and take this prisoner out. A peaceable man has been shot down. If those who are now guarding the prisoner mean to shed blood, let it be so. The people are supreme and will be so now." Later, while waiting for the committee to finish its work, Taylor again inflamed the mob. "Taylor called on every citizen to arm himself," Ewer reported. "If the officers of the law thought proper to interfere and seek to protect the prisoner, when a jury had decided on the case, then said Dr. T., let the streets of Sacramento be again deluged with the blood of her citizens. Dr. T. was ready to sacrifice his own life, if necessary, to carry out the ends of justice."[51]

Yet despite Taylor's rhetoric, several residents tried to stop the demands for lynch law. One of the foremost of this group was the lawyer Charles Tweed. Tweed was prominent in the city, having run for local office and performed several legal functions for the city council. When the mob first formed, it initially called on Tweed to chair the "committee" to investigate Roe's guilt. Tweed, however, after stating that Roe was "a grand scoundrel, and should be hung," declared that he was for letting the legal system run its course and took his place beside the city marshal, trying to keep the mob from seizing the prisoner. During the committee investigation, Tweed acted as much as possible as Roe's legal counsel.

The composition and actions of the committee itself suggest the sense of uncertainty and disunity of many of its members. Myers, the victim, was a wheelwright, and his former partner and close friend was a blacksmith. Ewer suggested in *Transcript* stories on the lynching that the city's blacksmiths and wheelwrights would come out in force for Myers's funeral. Yet in the lynching itself, not a single blacksmith or wheelwright played any part. Ewer was remarkably detailed in his account of the lynching, giving the names of people who addressed the mob, who were on the committee, who guarded the prisoner, who were called as witnesses, even of people who were asked to serve and who declined. In all, seventy-three names of participants were included in the stories. Of these only Myers and his former partner, Praeder, were blacksmiths or wheelwrights, and Praeder played no active role in the lynching that was recorded.[52]

Yet patterns do exist among the lynching participants. The committee that investigated the shooting was composed almost entirely of merchants. Of the fourteen people who eventually served on the committee, nine listed themselves as merchants, one was an auctioneer, three were among the city's great speculators, and two were doctors.[53] Ewer was asked to be on the committee but begged off in order to report the story impartially and was excused. No miners or laborers, wheelwrights, or blacksmiths were included.

The committee members represent a striking pattern. Not only were they overwhelmingly merchants, but they were predominantly members of the rising resident group. All of the committee members were listed in the January 1851 city directory, a listing by subscription of midlevel businessmen. Of those with known origins, all but three were from New York. Six owned real estate, and all the men tended to be in their late twenties to midthirties, thus older than the average age of the population. Of the ten whose living situations are known, only one lived with his extended family, three lived with male relatives, and six lived with their business partners and clerks. The committee thus almost perfectly reflected the resident merchant group demographically.[54]

As such, their actions in regard to the lynching are interesting. Unlike the Settlers' Association or the Law and Order Party earlier, these merchants had no strong organization and no clear ideological vision. They also had the example of the danger caused by the other two groups during the Squatters' Riot. Sacramento's residents sought to continue business as usual but to avoid the brutal and bloody excesses of the previous August riots. In fact, the committee was formed not to decide broad or abstract ideological points, but to bring a murderer to justice and a degree of safety and peace to their streets.

Yet in doing so, they were taking the law into their own hands, an action that must have been profoundly troubling to a citizenry that had already endured two years without a legal government. The city had rejoiced when California had finally been admitted as a state and Sacramento received its charter from a legal government. But now the mob was bypassing that legal system, in a sense reverting to its earlier ambiguous legal status.

A frenzied mob may be able to ignore such finer points, but individuals acting as an illegal jury had the time to consider their actions more carefully, and apparently the committee members did so. The first dilemma involved the simple step of swearing in the committee. This largely symbolic act, however, caused some turmoil. Clearly no officer was present in the mob who would legally swear in an illegal jury. One juror argued that the solemnity of the occasion was enough; another argued that the jury had to be sworn. Finally the committee president administered the oath, under the authority of his position. The difficulty over the swearing in seems almost humorous at such a distance, yet it reflected the very real dilemma of the committee. And at the very least, it served to remind the committee that what it was about to do would not have the sanction of the law.

The committee's next problem also lay in the legality of their actions. One of the first actions of the committee was to allow Roe a legal counsel before the committee, to be selected by his friends (as Roe himself was still in the station house). After the president of the jury administered the oath, one jury member argued that since Roe had a legal counsel, so should the state. Yet after three men were nominated to act as counsel, all three declined to serve. Obviously the three lawyers realized that they could not uphold the laws of the state of California while taking an active role in the lynching. The problem was resolved when committee member Spaulding argued that since they were not a jury, but a fact-finding investigation, there was no need for counsel for either side.[55]

During the committee's deliberations, delegations from the mob interrupted several times, demanding that the committee finish its work more quickly.

Each time, members of the committee objected, and eventually two members resigned over this issue. Their reason: that by its actions, the mob was pressuring the committee. The members resigned not because the mob was trying to push them into the wrong verdict, but merely because the mob was not allowing the verdict to be reached in a calm manner.[56]

The mob's committee interviewed a string of witnesses despite the simplicity of the facts in the case. The witnesses all agreed that Roe had shot Myers, though several of Roe's friends testified that Roe did not know Myers, had been drunk and quarrelsome, had not aimed at Myers, and probably had not intended to hurt him. This testimony, however, probably did Roe more damage than good; Roe's drunkenness meant that Roe could have killed anyone in the crowd. That Myers, a hardworking businessman and would-be peacemaker, had been killed only further damned Roe in the committee's eyes. At about half past eight o'clock, the committee announced its findings, declaring Roe guilty of shooting Myers without provocation.

The investigation further unified members of the city's commercial community by establishing agreement over the facts and the verdict in the case. Further, it gave a symbolic meaning to the crime. Myers came to symbolize the recklessness of gambling and the casual and even random violence that city residents had grown to fear. By embodying the vague anxieties that troubled so many residents, Roe focused those anxieties. And the simple facts of the case made it easier for residents who might have disagreed over details on other, related issues to agree absolutely. Finally the emotions aroused by the murder momentarily pushed residents to go farther in their agreement than they might likely have gone under less emotional circumstances.

Reaching a verdict, however, was still not the same as taking the action, and several residents still argued against the lynching. After the committee reached its verdict, Tweed begged the mob to postpone the execution until the next day, hoping that by then cooler heads would prevail. Getting nowhere with the mob, Tweed asked Dr. Taylor, as the mob's leader, to examine Roe once more.[57]

At this point, Taylor suddenly switched his position and came back agreeing with Tweed that the execution should be put off. Taylor, who shortly before had pledged his life to seeing Roe's immediate execution, now advised the mob to wait. The mob would have none of it. Taylor was overthrown and a new leader appointed.[58]

What had happened? During the investigation, Roe had sobered up and was now quite repentant. The combination of Roe's repentance and Tweed and Cunningham's arguments that the law be allowed to take its course apparently swayed Taylor. In the midst of the excitement over the lynching, even the mob's most fiery leader could be persuaded to take a more legal course of action.

The marshal warned that he would not give up the prisoner and pleaded, "I have a duty to perform. Sacramento has a duty to perform." The crowd continued shouting its disapproval and continued to grow. The *Transcript* later reported that "at this time there could not have been less than twenty-five hundred or three thousand spectators. Second Street from J to K was jammed— windows on each side, and up J Street were crowded—porticos and awning posts occupied at every point."[59] By nine o'clock the crowd had grown to over five thousand. Thirty minutes after the committee reached its verdict and shortly after Taylor's plea for restraint, the crowd acted. Tearing down an awning post to use as a battering ram, the mob broke down the door to the station house, seized Roe, and carried him past Praeder's blacksmith shop, where Myers lay dying, and then to Sixth Street, between K and L, where a number of large oaks still stood. At nine-thirty, Roe was hanged "amid a profound silence which pervaded the vast multitude."[60]

>--<

In the aftermath of the lynching, the silence of the mob remained nearly unbroken. F. C. Ewer wrote a detailed description of the event, two short notices about the lynching were published by two of the participants, and Ewer then followed up with an editorial, trying to put the lynching into perspective. Other than these there is little to go on to estimate how city residents responded to Roe's death. Yet these few sources hint at how city residents may have interpreted the incident.

The first notice was published by Dr. Taylor two days after the lynching, denying that he had been bribed and bought out by gambling interests. Taylor argued that he had changed his mind about Roe based solely on moral grounds, and not on personal greed. Either people were talking about Taylor, or he feared that they would. Charles Tweed, Roe's defender, wrote the other notice at Taylor's request: an affidavit testifying to Taylor's honesty! Not only had the leader of the mob changed positions near the end of the lynching, but he called on his victim's lawyer to defend himself from the very public opinion he had helped to inflame. The irony was not lost on Tweed, who responded bitterly. "For your conduct during the first of the excitement, I blame you," Tweed wrote. "For having been influenced by feelings of humanity after seeing the prisoner, all good men will applaud you. That any pecuniary consideration was offered to, or received by you, I am certain is wholly untrue."[61] These notices suggest both the sensitivity and the ambiguity that remained after the lynching. Clearly the Roe case was not ignored and was associated in the public mind not only with violence, but also with the pernicious influence of gambling on society.

One other public reference to the lynching is found in the same issue of the *Transcript* as the Taylor and Tweed correspondence. According to the *Transcript,* placards were posted all over town, calling for a meeting at the Orleans Hotel in order to create a standing vigilance committee in Sacramento. Again Ewer indicates the widespread participation of the city's residents, claiming the meeting itself "was the largest that ever assembled" there. Yet the first speaker to the crowd was Samuel Hensley, one of the founding fathers of the city. According to Ewer, Hensley "arose, and after a few pertinent remarks, moved an adjournment. This very wise motion was put and carried almost unanimously."[62]

No record of Hensley's "pertinent remarks" exists. But given the size and apparent disposition of the crowd, Hensley's comments must have been dramatic. Whatever he said, however, he certainly touched on the ambiguity of the entire event. For just as the mob had risen to take the law into its own hands, one man apparently found a way to stop it. This single action differentiates Sacramento from San Francisco and a number of other western mining towns, where vigilance committees arose and instituted a reign of terror in their streets.

The last clue to how city residents responded to the lynching is Ewer's editorial. The writing strikes the modern reader as a biased rationalization for mob violence. "Our city has returned to a complete state of quiet," he reported. "The manifestations of the American Mind as it has presented itself within the last two days—its deliberation—its fixedness of purpose—its majesty, is such as can not fail to inspire the profoundest admiration."[63]

Majesty? Admiration? The words strike us today as antithetical to lynching. In fact, they might have struck Ewer's readers initially the same way. Only six months before, in the aftermath of the Squatters' Riot, Ewer had called for strict adherence to the law. "Our heterogeneous population," he then wrote, "gathered as it is from all quarters of the globe, entertaining diverse and conflicting opinions, must not be allowed to decide the questions by muscular force or an appeal to arms." Shocked by the violence of the disturbance, Ewer candidly admitted that it was "impossible for a whole community to think alike anywhere, and peculiarly so here; for our people have heretofore lived under a variety of institutions and laws. Their ideas of what is proper and right must differ widely."[64] In a city as large and diverse as Sacramento, a harmonious community would not likely emerge easily. "Our only safety, then," he concluded, "is to compel all classes to submit to the laws under which we live. . . . The character of our people, the success of our city, and above all, the safety and peace of the community demand that the laws should be regarded as supreme, and their acknowledgment a requisite to citizenship."[65]

Yet only half a year later, adherence to law gave way to taking the law into community hands. "A certain set of men were beginning to conceive the vain idea that they could run rough shod over the community," Ewer explained. "Some have called the assemblage of Tuesday last a mob, but in that assemblage we recognized the same order-loving spirit which induced our citizens prior to that time to abide the workings of our legal tribunals. It appeared in a different phase, but it was the same spirit. . . . It loved order and quiet in the community, and above all, security of life."[66]

The lynching itself did not inspire Ewer's support. What he admired was that people "did not conduct the affair with blind outrage. Under the circumstances, the whole was done with moderation." The people had conducted a "calm investigation," had "listened patiently and attentively" to all witnesses, even those for Roe. When the verdict was reached, "the culprit was taken out and led without violence to the gallows. The scene at the gallows was solemn, but all was conducted with the strictest propriety. . . . They were firm, moderate, and determined that all should be conducted with order." Most impressive of all, to Ewer's thinking, was that the following day, when a meeting was called to consider instituting a standing "citizens' guard" to guarantee the continued suppression of crime in the city, the meeting adjourned in less than four minutes. "The same people who had the day previous voted for Lynch law, knew that punishment had been inflicted—felt that they had done their duty—that when it was necessary they would do it again, and that there was no more need of any more excitement."[67]

Ewer's editorial deserves attention. After the lynching, many residents may have wondered about the morality of what they had done. The notices by Taylor and Tweed and Ewer's editorial suggest that "gambling interests" were given the blame for creating a roughshod community. In a city where gambling and speculation were too often blurred, Ewer separated them by condemning the rough violence of gambling interests while praising the deliberateness of city builders. Read together, the editorials of Ewer and Morse are a public manual on how to behave properly in a booming city. Neither condemns speculation in itself, but both call for restraint. Confusion, they might have noted, provided opportunities—was indeed admirable—only if it did not cross over the line to chaos. The lynching of Frederick Roe dramatically and publicly brought these inherently personal issues into the public arena.

The residents of Sacramento City, gathered from a diversity of backgrounds, challenged by the uncertainties of a mining economy, had come together as a community. They had built a viable city, composed of solid buildings, a stable economy, a responsive government, and a dawning sense of shared understandings.

Gold rush expectations had promoted individualism over social responsibility. Sacramento residents sought neither to deny individual opportunities in favor of squatters or settlers, nor to limit those opportunities to a limited class of capital-rich speculators. Yet they refused to allow individualism to go so far as to undermine the security of an orderly society. Roe's lynching, as Ewer explained it, "was not a reckless mob overriding the courts and law . . . it was an assemblage assisting the courts in the great end for which they were formed." If Ewer correctly perceived the events (or if he was successful in convincing Sacramento residents that what he reported was indeed how they felt), Roe's lynching had symbolic qualities. By their participation in the execution, residents signaled their acceptance of a community-defined boundary between the admirable confusion of gold rush opportunity and the immoral anarchy of gold rush irresponsibility.[68]

The Buildings Most Needed

"There are about 250 persons on board, and I am as well acquainted with them as though I had seen them on land for twenty years," wrote hopeful miner William Carpenter. The twenty-seven-year-old Carpenter was writing to his fiancée, Lucretta Spencer, from the deck of a ship bound for California in 1850. Carpenter came from a family of pioneers: his ancestors had helped settle Massachusetts, Connecticut, Vermont, and New York. Now in the midst of a new historic migration, Carpenter described his own companions as "doctors, lawyers, mechanics, farmers, in fact men of all and every profession from the cobbler to the Texas duelist. . . . The variety is great and the characters as different as there are persons in number. Each person is different in speech, action, walk, build, dress . . . the young, the old, the middle aged, some with dyspepsia, some with rheumatism, and some with the blues; some with children, some ladies with their husbands going to California . . . yet all have the same end to obtain by this voyage: their fortune."[1]

Like thousands of others who came to California in the gold rush, William Carpenter would encounter a chaotic world and attempt to give it order. In part this effort would include buying land, digging for gold, driving a mule, and opening a store in Sacramento. As miner, teamster, and shopkeeper, Carpenter helped to reorder northern California's physical landscape. During his first two years in the gold fields, he would join almost anonymously with the anonymous multitude that transformed Miwok and Nisenan hunting lands into mines, a former Mexican province into an American state, and Sutter's Embarcadero into a booming city.

Yet there was more to building Sacramento than erecting buildings. Through both public and intimate connections with his fellow residents, Carpenter also attempted to establish a new home for himself in California. To succeed, he and the other city residents had to forge the shared understandings and obligations required of a community. Many residents would succeed in this task; Carpenter was not fated to be one of them. But in trying to understand Carpenter's attempts at creating a future in Sacramento, we can see best how others succeeded in establishing a strong and vital community.

Like Carpenter, most of Sacramento's early residents had not originally planned to stay and build a community in California. They had started instead with dreams of finding a fortune in gold as miners. After turning their backs on mining as a way to an instant fortune and their homes in the eastern states, these residents needed to find a new vision. Their goals and expectations had changed, but their old dreams of golden success still beckoned. As these residents turned in a practical manner to new forms of moneymaking and social success in Sacramento, they also needed to adapt their old aspirations. Sacramento needed to support more than just a great business opportunity; it had to support home and hearth.

Sacramento's new residents found that the decision to create a new life in California involved more than changing their own minds. Community, by its very definition, required decisions made by more than one person. At its most basic level, community involved social connections—the bonds of understanding and obligation between men and women. If business partnerships and connections defined the public bonds of Sacramento's commercial community, the private bonds of community would be forged in the intimate relationships of its population. Love, marriage, family—these relationships would have as much to do with shaping Sacramento as its storefronts, saloons, and city council.

Social historian Thomas Bender has urged historians to see community as a social network characterized by a distinctive kind of emotional bond and mutuality. Specifically, a community involves a limited number of people in a somewhat restricted social space or network, held together by shared understandings and a sense of obligation. It encompasses a wide range of concerns, rather than a narrow set of interests. It is not always harmonious, but tends either to contain or adapt itself to conflicts within its membership, and its values, structures, and purpose change over time. A community is best understood as being organic, rather than as a fundamental, unchanging set of values and relationships. Instead a community responds to the holistic needs of its members—physical, economic, political, social, cultural, moral—as these needs are understood in a unique historical moment.[2]

The rise of Sacramento during the gold rush was chaotic, but not only because so many young men converged on a city ill prepared to accommodate their needs. Confusion was also rooted in their ambivalent attitudes toward what represented a true community itself. The lynching of Frederick Roe had been one step toward establishing community standards, but it was a crude and extreme measure of behavior. The workplace could provide some basis for community development, but few Sacramento residents would feel at home in a world based only on such public associations. In the mid-nineteenth century, Americans trusted the inner associations of family more than the outer world of professional organizations and defined themselves more by local customs than by any national standards. It was precisely these family relationships and local standards that Sacramento residents longed for. To finish the transformation of Sacramento from a gold rush marketplace to a true and stable city, residents needed to establish the trusted and familiar local routines that the gold rush had denied them.[3]

William Carpenter's torturous attempt to find and strengthen these bonds in Sacramento suggests both the difficulty and importance of such connections in the early city. Yet before turning to his story, we need to consider the roles that family played in America in the mid-nineteenth century. The California gold rush must be set into the context of these roles. For Carpenter, as well as for thousands of others, the gold rush involved not only individual wealth, but also family goals and community standing.

→ — ←

Gold rush literature is so full of the stories of men seeking golden fortunes that to ask what motivated these men seems a foolish question. But perhaps the question should be rephrased: What would cause thousands of young men, mainly between the ages of twenty and twenty-five, to leave home and family and undertake a long, dangerous, and expensive journey? Certainly the dreams of golden wealth beckoned, but were they enough to offset the deferment of other dreams? The gold rush historically took men from their homes and families during the years when they were most expected to be courting and marrying, starting a family, and getting settled in an occupation. If enough gold could be found, of course, the forty-niner would return able to establish himself financially (or at least, so he hoped). But would this advantage alone offset the sacrifices required in such intimate areas as love and marriage? Or more significantly, were there other advantages beyond economic ones to be gained from the gold rush?

Letters and journal entries written by hopeful miners long before they ever reached California reveal an interesting mind-set. To many, the very adversities that made the trip dangerous appear to be the very reason why they chose to undertake the journey. On the one hand, these young men appear to be caught up wanting to playact a role in a great historic drama. By 1849, Daniel Boone and Davy Crockett were well-known legends, and western adventurers such as Jim Bridger and Kit Carson were popular heroes. The late 1840s particularly elevated such men. John Charles Frémont's exploration of the Oregon and California trails promoted the young topographical engineer to national prominence, and the recent Mexican War elevated its own share of heroes. The gold rush thus offered young men something besides wealth: the possibility of celebrity status.

The motivations of the forty-niners, however, may run deeper. For if California's argonauts were determined to become social heroes in the East, we should ask why they felt this need so strongly and in such great numbers. The quest for social status was not unique among young men in mid-nineteenth century America. But this particular form of advancement was unique, as were the particular conditions of life in "the States" at midcentury.

The period in American history in which the forty-niners were born and raised was one of tremendous social and economic upheaval. As children, the future gold rushers were witness to an unprecedented expansion of American enterprise. Families moved west, filling in and developing the trans-Appalachian region, and began settling a new tier of states west of the Mississippi River valley. Technological developments gave Americans a new industrial base from which to trade commodities both nationally and internationally. Transportation improvements—canals, steamboats, and railroads—made this expansion of people and goods both possible and profitable. Political expansion, in the form of universal white manhood suffrage, led to the formation of mass political parties. And the reform movements of the 1830s and 1840s increased the dynamic tempo of social and cultural change. The tremendous energies unleashed during the antebellum period, however, also brought a great deal of physical and social dislocation.

The majority of Americans in the middle of the nineteenth century lived on farms, and the environment in which they were raised shaped their attitudes toward work and life. Hard work generally resulted in a predictable yield. Farm laborers, however, were often difficult to secure, and those who did hire out could demand high wages. Agrarian families responded by producing large families. Children were useful laborers for as long as they remained on the farm. To ensure the continued labor of children, paternal authority reigned supreme in agrarian culture, and family patriarchs held the reins of community power firmly in their hands. Agrarian culture stressed the mutual dependence of people on each other. Transactions between farmers rarely involved cash payments but were bartering arrangements, with neighbors exchanging labor as well as farm produce. Hard work and strong kinship ties shaped many agrarian Americans' view of their world.[4]

In the first half of the nineteenth century, however, this agrarian world was in crisis. By the 1830s, the plentiful supply of "free" farmlands on the frontier was dwindling, especially in the northern states, and many farm children faced a bleak future. At the same time, an expanding transportation system of canals and railroads pushed the world of the commercial market into the heartland of American agrarianism. This intrusion, however, did not necessarily elevate the "common" man. Many young men found it increasingly difficult to find farmland of their own within the nearby region. Unable to make a traditional living on a family farm, many young adults left their homes, seeking to re-create old patterns on new lands farther to the west or searching for more urban occupations in the growing cities of the new Midwest. Establishing new lives in growing urban centers, however, often meant choosing individualism over the bonds of kinship, economic dependence over agrarian independence, and a continual acceptance of a greater degree of social and economic instability than many had known before. Upward social mobility—the rise from rags to riches—did not often accompany this transformation: more often, young men fell from wealth, sometimes into poverty.[5]

To the young men of the antebellum period, social mores were in flux. In the new towns and cities they sought to find new homes and a new way of life. Courtship and marriage customs changed. Without the background of a long-established, tightly knit community, courtships lost the context of relationships between allied families. Young men and women more frequently made courtship choices outside of the influence of their families. In some ways this was a liberating experience. But it also lacked the sense of security of a match approved by knowing family members.

Furthermore, the objectives of marriage were becoming less certain, further confusing courtship customs. For example, the large families expected of farm families were detrimental to many town and city folk, to whom children were not productive laborers but nonproductive consumers. Even the expectations of gender roles were changing. Women in agrarian families, though expected to be subservient to their husbands, still managed and produced a great deal of the household economy. In the new patterns of town and city labor, however, men increasingly were called to occupations outside of the household, shifting the economic production of the family away from the home. The increasing division between men's and women's spheres denied women a meaningful place in the household economy.[6]

As men were expected to compete in an increasingly public world of market and business transactions, however, women were expected to maintain a moral and stable home as a shelter from the immorality of the outside world. Having achieved moral authority in the home, many women extended their influence outside of it by extending the limits of their moral authority. Women were major players in many of the morality crusades of the early nineteenth century, such as the temperance and abolitionist movements. Thus, as men found a world of bewildering moral and economic dilemmas, women increasingly became the arbitrators of morality. A young man, starting to make his way in the world in the late 1840s, knew that he would have to determine his own way in a bewildering world and would have to be ready to explain his moral decisions according to a yardstick held by women.

In such a world, young men must have faced a series of difficult choices. Clearly their traditional role in the family and community would be diminished, a situation that may have left many men questioning the role of maleness in an urban world. At the same time cities, while offering new opportunities, reserved most of those opportunities for men with capital. To many young men, the gold rush offered a stake to play in the market world of capitalism, as well as the social prestige that was missing in their new world. Best of all, the road to social prestige was a peculiarly male road: young men would acquire social prestige not by redefining their gender roles but by reaffirming them through the grand and historically sanctioned act of western adventuring.

For many men, as their diaries, journals, letters, and memoirs make clear, the trip to the gold fields was such a heroic undertaking that the journey itself would clearly enhance their status. Their letters home and their diaries reveal their awareness of their participation in a noble and historic event. Many argonauts viewed their California sojourn as an adventure that would elevate them socially as well as financially in the eyes of their families and hometowns. Especially in the first years of the rush, young men wrote of dangers faced in heroic terms.

Enos Christman, for example, wrote home that "every difficulty should be met with manly fortitude, and my intention is to meet them in such a manner that I need never be ashamed. I now boldly turn my face toward the celebrated Sierra Nevada."[7] As Lorenzo Sawyer reported with pride to his family,

> I have crossed the broad American continent from shore to shore . . . and have seen human nature under a great variety of circumstances, and in every stage of development. . . . I have a more enlarged, a more comprehensive view of the works of nature, a more accurate conception, and a nicer appreciation of their beauty and grandeur. I am sensible that I have obtained a more thorough knowledge of mankind, of their character, their energies and capabilities, of the motives and springs that govern human actions. In short, I am thus far satisfied with my enterprise, though, in some respects it may not turn out as favorable as I could wish.[8]

To many men, the adventurous quest itself seemed as important as actually finding a fortune.

Early gold rush songs also bear out this feeling. One of the first songs written about the gold rush was "Oh, California," a parody of "Oh! Susanna." The verses tell of the argonaut who meets many tribulations on his way to California, such as seasickness, bad food, and homesickness. The hardships are manfully faced, however, and the miner returns home with his pockets full of gold, "so brothers don't you cry!"[9] The plea to face difficulty without crying seems to be addressed to the singer's fellow gold seekers. What is so interesting about the song, however, is that it was written in November 1848 by John Nichols, who was just *beginning* his trip to California.[10] Nichols in effect is promising to live up to difficulties that have not yet occurred! Clearly he knew the difficulties; the song indicates that facing them only adds to his eventual triumph. This refrain is also echoed even more directly in the refrain of another adaptation, "O! California":

O! California
We'll see you bye and bye
If we've good luck, and if we don't,
Why, bless you, don't you cry.[11]

Still another song, "Ho! For California!" goes into even more detail regarding the dangers and difficulties that will be faced and manfully endured, comparing the gold rush to the days of old foreseen by the prophets—images especially appealing to young men seeking to recapture the authority of agrarian patriarchy. In this song, however, the men are not expected to be homesick, but rather tell the women they leave behind not to cry for them.[12]

Not surprisingly, many gold rush songs deal with the relationships between men and women. One of the best-known songs from the gold rush is "Sweet Betsy from Pike."[13] Even today schoolchildren learn this song as a "folk song." The original verses to "Sweet Betsy," however, raise many questions regarding the proper gender roles of men and women during the gold rush.

The song tells of the journey of Betsy "and her lover," Ike, as they leave Pike County, Missouri, headed for California. Ike and Betsy bring with them a few farm animals. Here is a stock partnership from the American agrarian frontier: a young man and woman setting off to start their own home in the West. Like many agrarian couples, Ike and Betsy are not married, but appear to be eloping— one of the resorts that agrarian children often used to force their parents to let them leave the farm and go out on their own. An early verse suggests that Betsy is expecting a baby, but the storyteller of the song assures his audience that everything is straight—that is, the couple has probably not had sexual intercourse yet.

Ike seems to be firmly rooted in agrarian culture. But Ike is a comical figure because he is an ineffectual male. Throughout the song he seems peculiarly unable to take a dominant role, a point made clear both by the title of the song and its first lines. Ike is clearly attracted to Betsy but seems unable or unwilling to take any measures to provide for her. When their provisions run out on the trail, he does not go out hunting, but gets discouraged; when Brigham Young attempts to seduce Betsy, she must flee on her own—Ike, apparently, takes no part in her defense; when in the desert "Betsy gave out, / Down on the sand lay rolling about," the ineffectual "Ike, half-distracted, looked on with surprise, / Saying Betsy, get up, you'll get sand in your eyes." While most songs celebrated the heroism of the male adventurer, Ike in contrast is unable to manage the role. As the first verse reminds the listener, Betsy crossed the mountains with Ike, not vice versa.

Betsy, however, is undergoing an interesting transformation of her own. She begins firmly rooted in the agrarian tradition but seems to have more ability than Ike. When Ike gets discouraged, she gets mad. And when she is told to get up in the desert by an inattentive Ike, she "gets up in great pain" and declares that she will go back to Pike County—back to an agrarian world, and very likely to a more effective husband.

This scene becomes the critical moment of the song. Ike apparently manages to live up to the ideal, if momentarily, and the couple embraces and crosses the mountains arm in arm. Yet the crossing is a symbolic one: Betsy is going forward, not back to Pike County. On arrival in California the couple go to a dance. Ike "wears a pair of his Pike County pants," but Betsy instead wears "ribbons and rings," products of an urban rather than an agrarian homestead. Furthermore, Betsy now exclaims she is willing to dance with miners other than Ike. Betsy, in a way, has crossed a cultural divide; Ike is still in Pike County. At the end of the song, Ike is jealous and obtains a divorce. Betsy shouts at him, "Good bye, you big lummox, I'm glad you backed out."

The initial audience of the song was gold rush miners, men who could laugh at Ike's ineffectiveness and at Betsy's transformation and conclude that both sides were comic. That they are not to be taken too seriously is suggested in the first line of the song: "Do you remember sweet Betsy from Pike." These characters are forgettable, to be recalled merely for amusement. Yet the themes of the song deal directly with the core issues of gender at midcentury. Ike and Betsy are not just going to California, but also leaving an agrarian past for a new economic and social world that in its way was every bit as challenging as the trip to California and whose potential benefits were equally bright. Betsy reaches this new promised land; Ike does not. The underlying message for the male audience in California is strong: If you are trapped in the past, like Ike, you will become a comic anachronism.

As many gold rush diaries and songs indicated, some gold rush adventurers sought a patriarchal status with women as a result of their trek to California. By following in the footsteps of earlier western heroes, men hoped to attain a level of personal heroism themselves. Yet after a few years in California, many men began to realize that such status depended on the willingness of women to appreciate men's heroic undertaking. Simply put, men expected women to admire their acts of western bravado, but they worried that women in fact might not respect their actions.

The melancholy many miners expressed for lost sisters, mothers, and wives was certainly increased because of their separation by many miles. Yet the separation could be measured in more than physical distance. The women and family scenes many miners mourned were also receding into the past. A close examination of many miners' words themselves suggests a longing not just for riches and women, but for a particular kind of success and woman. In the fall of 1849 miner Lewis C. Gunn wrote in his journal,

> I tried a place by myself but with no success, and this made me thoroughly heartsick. I thought of home, of wife and children, how they used to hang about my neck, and sit on my knees, and laugh and enjoy themselves, and how I used to enjoy myself, and became homesick. Every effort I have made to obtain a support for my family since 1845 has failed, and even the bright prospects of the mines have proved a disappointment. I threw myself on the ground under a tree in the woods and cried.[14]

Certainly Gunn was homesick and disappointed, but the homesickness was for a subservient wife, and his misery is based on his inability to fill a traditional agrarian role before as well as during the gold rush.

Alonzo Delano, a would-be miner turned chronicler and poet of the early years of the gold rush, captured the general longings of many miners to become responsible yet patriarchal husbands and fathers in *The Miner's Progress,* a poem published in Sacramento in 1853. Delano's miner is a wretched sight, a man broken physically and spiritually by his journey to the California mines. This miner is trapped in his quest, as the poet cleverly reveals:

I saw, in dreams, a pile of gold
Its dazzling radiance pour:
No more my visions are of gold,
Alas! my hopes are *ore.*
Thrice have I left this cursed spot,
But mine it was to learn
The fatal truth, that "dust we are,
To dust we shall *return.*"

However, he dreams of "His wife, whose smile hath cheered him oft, / And rendered light his care," and of "wailing babes at home, / Unrocked, an orphan band." These images torment him at night; when the next morning he finally uncovers his fortune, the miner has learned his lesson, and "Vamoseth the Diggings" back to "the Bosom of his Family":

> His wardrobe changed, behold him now,
> In affluence and pride,
> Surrounded by the forms he loves,
> With joy on every side!
> Pressed closely to his heart he holds
> His wife and children dear,
> The latter shouting madly, while
> The former drops a tear.[15]

This image of men gaining status by facing the hardships of the trip repeats itself in many early songs of the gold rush. As an "Emigrant from Pike" made abundantly clear, he expected both status and marriage when he returned home, whether he had found gold or not:

> When I go home with an empty sack
> I'll show them where the Indians shot me in the back,
> And how my mules laid down and died
> And I nearly starved to death beside.
> Hokey, pokey, wiker wun, We're all good fellows, we'll have some fun,
> And all get married when we get home, so what's the use of talking.[16]

Perhaps the most interesting song to make the connection to male social expectation is "Crossing the Plains." Like many other songs, the singer tells of his difficulties in journeying to California, difficulties that the singer faces bravely. Yet there is a not too subtle subtext to the song, which makes the narrative a dramatic lesson for the miner's wife. The song begins with the narrator preparing for the trip and buying so many weapons that "there's not a man in town, but what's afraid of me." After this beginning act of machismo, the narrator immediately is seen *returning* from California to his family, to his mother and "lovely Jane." Their reaction to his return is instructive: Jane is surprised, but his mother first cooks him some food and only afterward asks of his trip. The narrator only then launches into his tale of the rigors of the trip. The song concludes with two apparently unrelated incidents. One verse tells of women who went on the trip to California with their husbands but found the trip too difficult and proceeded to "jaw their husbands round"; these women, the miner hopes, will get "a turn of di-a-ree." In the last verse, however, the miner points out that the hardships men endure can be cured at the Sacramento post office, where "you'll find a line from ma' and pa', and one from lovely Sal. / If that don't physic you every mail, you never will get well." Most important, the song makes no mention of whether the man has returned rich or ruined.[17]

The subtext of "Crossing the Plains" appears to be an elaborate lesson to women. The woman who supports her husband by writing regularly can cure him of his discomforts, even from a distance. This vital support is qualified: the letters come from home, a woman's proper sphere, and are only part of the greater array of support offered by the entire family. But although the lesson in the song is aimed squarely at Jane and implies that she must take up the traditional gender role of the agrarian wife, the moral of the song is aimed elsewhere. Because the song was originally sung in California, to a largely male audience, it is not so much a lesson for "Jane" but an expression of the effect the miners hoped the gold rush would have on their lives.[18] The song glorifies the macho trek, reminds men that the task they are engaged in is heroic, and plays out a return home where the miner will have attained a more elevated social standing while reinforcing an image of women's more subservient role. Significantly, this role is based on the experiences the man has had on the trip, not on his success or failure to return with gold.

The warning is put even more directly, though not as eloquently, in a less well known song called "Joe Bowers."[19] Joe introduces himself as the brother of Ike from Pike County and makes reference to Ike and Pike County several times in the song to reinforce its connection to "Sweet Betsy from Pike." Joe has fallen in love with Sally Black, but Sally will not marry him until he can provide "a little home to keep your little wife." Joe thereupon declares:

My dearest Sally, oh! Sally for your sake,
I'll go to Californy, and try to raise a stake.

Joe works hard in California but without regret, for his work is literally a labor of love:

I worked both late and airly, in rain, and sun, and snow
But I was working for my Sally, so 'twas all the same to Joe.

The irony of the song is that even though Joe succeeds as a miner and saves a pile of gold for Sally, he fails as a man. In the end his brother, Ike, a potent symbol of doom in his own right, sends Joe a letter telling him that Sally has married the butcher, because he had red hair, and she now has a red-haired baby. Significantly, the acquired gold did not solve the problem—it is, in fact, irrelevant. The impact of this less than memorable song on its audience was memorable: the miner is not in California only to get gold, but to get his manhood; gold will not substitute for success if he loses the girl he left behind him.

⇁—↽

Certainly many of California's young men missed the companionship of women, and as many letters, journals, and stories of the gold rush make clear, women in the mining region were often treated with exaggerated respect. Yet something about these sources suggests that men treated women in California with respect as a group more often than individually. Miners idealized womanhood rather than individual women. The rare presence of women in Sacramento seems to have reminded men of wives, mothers, sisters, and daughters left behind in the States. As such, women served as reminders of home, of an ideal of womanhood, and of the men's distance from both.[20]

Women's company and companionship were eagerly and actively sought out in Sacramento, and because of the scarcity of women, those who were present received more attention, no matter their status otherwise. Yet those women who did live in Sacramento often failed to live up to the ideal set by many gold rush residents. For example, when two celebrations of the Fourth of July were held in 1850, women from far and wide were invited. Within the city, the celebration was held by the Sons of Temperance, and it was reported in the *Transcript* that "the presence of the ladies gave éclat to the occasion, and under their inspiring influence no one present marveled at the enthusiasm manifested, while the toasts were being drunk with cold water." The presence of the women was remarked on in several of the toasts, including, "The Ladies—The great moral stimulus to prompt man to noble deeds and lead him onward on the paths of virtue," and, "The Ladies and Cold Water—To dream of living without either would be considered insanity."[21]

At the other celebration, however, where alcohol flowed more freely, women again were the subject of attention. "The most gratifying circumstance of the whole occasion was the beautiful array of the fairer sex, who lent the enchantment of their presence and encouragement to the scene of patriotic remembrance of the good old Fourth." Yet the toasts made near the end of the dinner suggest the occupation of these women. The first few toasts were serious, but soon they began to take on humorous undertones. The final toast may thus have had sexual undertones: "The Ladies—If Congress would comply with their wishes, our admission would no longer be procrastinated—for they, as Californians, are in favor of Union."[22] In general, then, women in Sacramento were often seen as a double-edged sword: they reminded men of home, as well as how far they had come from it.

One sense of difference between early Sacramento and eastern homes was the openness of prostitution. Details on early Sacramento prostitution are scarce, and in the earliest days of the city prostitution may not have been very prominent. The 1850 census suggests the presence of three brothels in the city and possibly a number of prostitute's cribs, though this accounting probably underrepresents the actual number. Before 1854, Sacramento had no antiprostitution law on its books, an omission that a number of prostitutes used to evade legal prosecution in the early years of the city.[23] But early reports of the insignificance of prostitution in the early days of the city may have some validity. Certainly prostitution existed, and the census figures provide only a poor accounting of women engaged in this profession. However, it is likely that prostitution during the earliest days of the California gold rush was less significant than in other mining rushes. The rush of 1849 was without precedent in U.S. history, and it occurred at an extreme distance from "the States." As time passed, prostitution undoubtedly flourished, and during succeeding mineral rushes western prostitutes, as individuals or in organizations, were well positioned to travel quickly to newly discovered mining regions. Thus accounts of prostitution on the mining frontier may suggest a seemingly pervasive and well-established institution that in fact had not developed in the earliest days of the first rush.

Not all of the concerns over women centered on prostitution. Physical distance between residents and the women they left behind them underlay fears of a growing cultural distance. The appearance of store-bought clothing and goods often represented the first wedge of the intrusion of the market revolution into agrarian society, an intrusion many women welcomed gladly.[24] "Sacramento Gals," for example, who bedecked themselves in the latest fashions, were viewed ambiguously at best:

> They're pretty gals, I must confess,
> Nipping 'round, around, around;
> And "Lordy-massy" how they dress,
> As they go nipping 'round.
> On J Street they are to be found, . . .
> Their bustles lift them off the ground, . . .
> Their hoops will reach around a dray, . . .
> They're "airy" on a windy day, . . .

There's many a gal from Ar-kan-saw, . . .
Who well remembers hollowing "haw," . . .
Their faces covered with paint and chalk, . . .
Their hoops take up the whole sidewalk,
As they go nipping 'round.[25]

The images of Sacramento women are comical and irreverent but also suggest a deeply subtle disdain. References to paint, chalk, and airy skirts may refer to fashions out of place in the rough city or to prostitution. The gal who remembers "hollowing 'haw'" may be of a rural background or may have been wildly inebriated "as she went nipping 'round." The word *nipping* itself is ambiguous; definitions include stealing, a stinging remark, or to check the development or growth of something. The connotations of *nipping* in "Sacramento Gals" could thus suggest that Sacramento women, in miners' eyes, were vain, biting, or drunken and/or fallen. However the individual miner interpreted the song, the image was almost certainly of women who had broken with the traditional behavior expected of them.

California's gold seekers, who were predominantly young men, understandably showed a great degree of interest in marriage. Nearly all of miner John Ingalls's letters to his stepbrother asked for information on who had gotten married to whom since he had left and how married life was suiting his friends. "I suppose Thomson is taking lots of comfort with his wife—" he wrote; "ask him, for me, the next time you see him how he enjoys *married life*. If you can in any way put *it off* you must not get married till I get back for I want to go to your wedding— won't we have a high time?"[26] Despite the distance and the delay in letters reaching his stepbrother, Ingalls wrote in a personal, even gossipy style regarding affairs of the heart in Hartford, Connecticut.

> So Kate Morris is about to be married—well that seems rather funny but I suppose such things are bound to happen in the natural course of events. Give her my love and tell her I wish her joy—she is a nice girl. Frank B. is also going to *taste* the joys of *connubial felicity*—I don't think a bit strange of that for all she told us she was going to live and die an old maid. I hope she will make her husband as happy as I think she is capable of doing. . . . Morris is about to take himself a spouse. I really believe the folks in the States are getting crazy and you are enquiring about Fanny Talcott. . . . Fanny is a fine girl and we are first rate friends. For that reason if no other it would be pleasant to see you united in the *holy bonds of wedlock*. . . . [27]

Families worried that men in California might make unacceptable marriage arrangements. Franklin Buck teased his sister,

> You seem very anxious about my getting married. Well, I will put your mind to rest on this subject. I intend to stay here until I make some money and stay single, and then I am going down to Lima and marry one of those beautiful dark-eyed senoritas and bring her to Bucksport! What do you think of my plan? And how would you like one for a sister? I think there are some advantages in it. They are easily wooed and won and love with all their hearts when they do love.[28]

Franklin Buck teased about getting married in California more than once. After Buck's companion and his wife left, he was left alone and forced to cook for himself. "Just got through supper. Confounded hot work this cooking," he wrote his sister. "A real bore, isn't it? If you don't send out that serving girl I'll get married and have somebody to keep house."[29]

The attraction of California's Mexican or California women was a subject of at least some discussion in letters between gold rush miners and their families. John Ingalls responded to a letter from his stepbrother on the subject by noting, "The idea of your being proof against the shafts of cupid is really laughable. I would not trust you one night alone with a bewitching Senorita—I know you too well."[30]

Despite the playful remarks regarding marriages made in California, gold rush miners quickly discovered a trap largely of their own making. Having come to California to prove their manhood and having written of California as if it were a wilderness, men often found they had created a mental world in which women—or at least, their idealized vision of womanhood—could not exist. Franklin Buck's letters to his family seem particularly confusing in his remarks about Sacramento's women.

> At the Foster House where I boarded were quite a number of ladies: Mrs. Towers, whose husband is landlord, Mrs. Foster, Mrs. Covilland and Mrs. Haight. Mrs. C. and Mrs. F. are two of the party who came over the mountains in 1846 and came so near starving. You recollect the horrid sufferings they endured, even to *eating each other*. They are the elite of the place, of course. Mrs. Covilland is quite young and pretty but there is not the least refinement or taste about them. The fact is that there is no woman who can come to this country at present and have any refinement. Their finer feelings, if they have any, will soon get blunted with the life they must live here.[31]

Franklin Buck told his sister of a woman who left a Sacramento boardinghouse

ıout paying two months' rent. "O woman, woman!" he complained. "They
about men losing all honor, and self-respect when they arrive in this country!
ı .ıis is in some measure true but in regard to *women* it's certainly holding
good. All that keeps them up at home is the rules of society. No sooner do they
get out of that restraint than they show out their natural dispositions. Among men,
some few retain all their principles in this country and are the same here as at
home, but of all the women of my acquaintance there is none, no, not one."[32]

John Ingalls's concern for affairs of the heart in Connecticut may have been
related to concerns of his own heart. Nineteen days before leaving Connecticut,
Ingalls had married Anne Smith. Ingalls's letters express his thanks to his
stepbrother, Trumbull, for taking care of Anne but also suggest his concerns at
their separation. "Anne says she had a nice ride with you through *love lane!*
Look out or you will make me jealous and then Coffins and Pistols would be
the result. Nevertheless I am very much obliged to you for showing my Anne a
little attention when I am so far away."[33]

Fears of losing women to rival suitors left behind, of widening cultural gaps
between men and women, and of a loss of manhood all underlay calls to bring
wives and loved ones to Sacramento. And ultimately this transformation was the
most difficult for many Sacramento residents to make. The shift from seeking a
fortune from mining to earning a fortune in a booming gold rush city was
relatively easy. Both involved acquiring wealth, though the method was dramatically different. But bringing a wife, family, or loved one to California represented
a fundamental shift in gold rush sensibilities, and one that the miner could not
make alone. To men who left eastern states in search of gold and family status
and who had found not a portable fortune, but a business fortune rooted to a
western city, the only way to achieve success within the family was to have the
family join him in the West. But to women who had watched their fiancés or
husbands set off with the promise to return within a year or two, requests to
journey west were a dramatic departure from previous expectations.

Letters from residents to wives in the East increasingly called on women to
make the difficult trek to California and to reunite their families there. Rarely
were these negotiations short or simple. Usually couples exchanged a series of
letters, sometimes over the course of a year or more, debating the advantages and
disadvantages of permanently relocating in California. Despite the difficulties
and dangers of the journey, however, many eastern wives did eventually join
their husbands or fiancés in Sacramento.

John Ingalls's concerns were lightened in the fall of 1850 when his wife,
Anne, agreed to join him in California. Apparently Anne's ship arrived a day or
two early, causing a mix-up.

Anne arrived at San Francisco on the 4th of March in excellent health and spirits having made a fine passage and enjoying it very much. The next day she left for Sacramento and I left this place [Sacramento] to meet her there. You can judge of my feelings on my arrival there when I was told that Mrs. Ingalls had gone up the river. You may bet your life I was on hand for the first boat bound for Sacramento where I arrived at two in the morning—*but I didn't sleep on board that night.* The papers here had quite a pathetic article telling how a young married lady had just arrived from the east expecting to meet a *loving husband* and what must have been her feelings to find on her arrival here that her lord and master had *vamosed.* Of course it had not any reference to us.[34]

Not every woman who arrived in California, expecting to join her husband, had the fortune of finding her spouse. For Henry Rice Mann, who left his wife and four children behind in Michigan, the separation became unbearable. Mann began calculating how much it would take to send for his wife as well as their chances at making a living together in California. In 1852, Mann's family left Michigan to join him in California. Unfortunately, a bear killed Mann while his family was en route.[35] What happened to Mann's wife in California is unknown, but her situation was probably not unique. Accidents on the trail or in California probably left a number of women to care for families on their own.

The importance Sacramento residents placed on family was often critical to their ability to make a home in the new city. The decision to remain there began with the individual miner turned businessman, but it eventually involved family, friends, and sweethearts left behind in "the States." The experience of William Carpenter dramatically illustrates not only the progression from miner to resident that many of the residents made, but also the difficulty the resulting tensions created for would-be residents and their families.

→ — ←

William Carpenter arrived in California awestruck by the variety of his traveling companions, aware of the historic role he and they were playing, and hopeful of making his own fortune in gold. But he also looked at California with the eyes of a farmer, one leaning toward entrepreneurial possibilities. "Climate here first rate," he wrote his fiancée shortly after his arrival in September 1850. "Cloudless days and nights. Air pure . . . [But] farming can be done here in spots only, save on the banks of the River Sacramento and San Joaquin." Like many miners, he described California society as a wilderness fit only for men. "What a place for a woman to be in! I pity those women here. . . . I expect to become almost a barbarian before I come back, for society is indeed a blank here."[36]

In evaluating the gold fields, Carpenter quickly equated a miner's success with his moral capacity for hard work. "The mines as I find them are filled to overflowing—plenty gold, but not enough to be got by all the thousands come to the mines." He looked disparagingly on those who "are not courageous enough to strike among all the difficulties that beset them on the first onset, and so go back discouraged and disheartened to their homes, if they have money enough to get them home. . . . You may understand how it affects most men here by one fact I can give you. In the vessel we came in from Panama to San Francisco were about 250 passengers. They came in to the mines, and 130 of them returned on her when she sailed back, which was in about four weeks." Carpenter, however, was more optimistic, especially about his own abilities. "I find the longer I stay here the more I find I can do well. The prospects are better than I first supposed. There will be more gold taken out this year than last by two to one."[37]

However, the disillusionment that eventually overpowered most miners also overtook Carpenter late in 1850. In a dark and discouraging letter written after only a few months of mining, Carpenter had few good words to say about anything in California. "I have nerved my heart and steeled my hand to write to you from this barbarous land," he began.

> And sure it is a barbarous land, for vice of every kind, dissipation, sloth, and crime, men of every nation, rank and station, name, shape, color and hue abound. All ages from children to the gray-haired man just tottering into the grave are here. No place in God's creation like this self same California. Men at home of respectable habits and standing come here and soon become reckless and dissolute from want of the success they dreamed of, expecting to make their fortune without any effort; too indolent to work or make the necessary efforts in this country that are required in any country. The consequence is vice, immorality, gambling of every kind abound. Liquors of every kind, not used as drink but poured down these worse than brutes, making society a perfect sink of pollution. One cause of this is the want of woman's restraining influence after a day of toil or to cheer one after disappointment and misfortune.[38]

This letter stands out among Carpenter's letters as unusually melancholy. Carpenter clearly finds California society objectionable and, like *Sacramento Union* editor John Morse, believes that men in California do not care to do the work required of a stable community and that the want of women is partially to blame. Carpenter continued, in other words, to view the gold rush environment in moral terms. However, he also rejected farming as an alternative to mining.

"California will never be used to any extent for farming purposes, in spite of what Butler King says of her farming qualities in his celebrated report last winter. The country will be a mining country and that will be its chief characteristic. Who ever heard of a mining country being a desirable country to live in? I never did. Neither is this. Nor will I stay after I get a decent sum of its glittering dust."[39]

Thus by the end of 1850, Carpenter's attitude toward California was probably typical. Initially he had seen the gold rush as both a financial and a moral quest. The disappointments of mining, however, forced reconsideration. Carpenter portrayed California as a place where men fell from grace due to their disappointment and laziness. Yet such a view was a trap, for if other miners failed due to personal failings, how could Carpenter explain his own failings? In letter after letter, Carpenter reexamines his motivations and his goals in coming to California. "I know that if I had been in possession of a competence I should never have come to this place, and now with my knowledge I can advise no one person to come to this barren country, though there is gold enough; yet but few get it."[40] Carpenter, however, was unwilling to consider farming as an alternative. "As for the farming country in California, well, I had rather have one good county in [New] York state than all the farming country in this barren land. So much for the farming part of California and so much for the famous report of Col. Frémont and Butler King in regard to this part of it."[41]

Unable to make his fortune mining and unwilling to consider farming, Carpenter began casting about for other work. His ability to find lucrative employment brightened his mood considerably. "I have got an M.D. attached to my name," he wrote mischievously in April 1851, "but it stands for quite a different thing in California than it does at home. I have turned MULE DRIVER and am in the city [Sacramento] every week buying goods to take to the mines."[42] Over the summer of 1851, Carpenter gave up mining completely, using his "pile" to invest in his growing entrepreneurial activities. During the summer, he bought and sold mining claims, purchased goods for sale in the mining camps, and eventually started a small store in Sacramento, the neighbor of a hardware store run by Collis Huntington and Mark Hopkins. Carpenter's success may be surmised by a short note he sent home in August 1851. "Business takes all my time, for I am hard pressed to keep up with the demands of trade."[43] And with an improvement in fortunes, Carpenter's descriptions of "barren" California improved considerably. "I might almost say that this is a fairy clime, so pure, so bright and so full of wonders. No sky like California's. No clime like hers. Pick in the best season of the year the most beautiful day at home and then it will not equal our sunny days here."[44]

Gradually Carpenter's disappointment in the gold rush was fading and his original dreams of gold rush success shifting. It was a shift he probably came to subconsciously, but one that apparently troubled his fiancée in New York. Carpenter, the farmer, who had gone to California to get a stake, presumably to buy or expand a farm, had given up on mining, rejected farming, and now seemed to be making a more permanent home for himself in Sacramento. The tension between returning home to farming and his fiancée and staying in Sacramento as a rising merchant began to underlie many of his letters. "You fear I may be overdoing," he wrote to his fiancée, who apparently only expressed this concern when he had turned from mining to other pursuits.

> I think not, although I am busy all the time. I wish to get away as soon as I get a snug little pile, for of all the lives to lead the California one is the most freezing and deadening to all the higher and finer feelings of man's nature that can be thought of, one that makes the soul shrink within itself. Yet it is a country to make money in. It is a fast country, a very fast one. A year here is worth four at home. . . . The miners are doing better this summer than last and the prospect for another summer is good. Sac City is growing to be a fine city.[45]

The ambiguity in the passage is striking, and it continued in later letters.

Carpenter's success was enticing. By November 1851, he was well on his way to making the fortune he had originally hoped for. "I am in trade here and doing well. Have made (since I sent home some 800 dollars to Brother Augustus) in the neighborhood of four thousand dollars. . . . I can tell you our amount of business by saying that I have paid out for the last three months from eight to fifteen hundred dollars every week for goods in gold dust."[46]

However, Carpenter's success was not based on gold found in the ground and carried away without strings attached. He had made his fortune at business. Unlike a mining claim, which would one day run out, Carpenter's business, if well managed, would continue to produce profits. Carpenter's earlier rejection of farming may also have been based on his feelings toward farming in general, for despite his rejection of Butler's report, California's agricultural prospects were good, and agriculture was developing well at the same time that Carpenter ridiculed it. Carpenter apparently had come to prefer mercantile success in Sacramento over plowing his gold rush fortunes into an upstate New York farm.

The difficulty facing Carpenter now, however, was his fiancée. Since success was defined as much by family status and traditional gender roles of family, Carpenter would now have to convince Lucretta of the worth of his new goals as well. A few days before Christmas 1851, barely a year after Carpenter had disparaged California's environment and society, he began broaching what he suspected

would be a difficult topic. "It seems to me now, from being acc'
beautiful clime and genial skies, as though it were impossible
that cold bleak country as we do in this sunny clime. Ol
climate to live in; scenery which none can surpass. Would you see ι.
its grandeur, it is here. . . . California is bound to be a great state."

After describing California's sunny climate during New York's winter, Carpenter
hinted at his eventual goal. "If you were only here I could live contented for three
or four years at least; but it is a poor society to bring a woman to as yet, although
the prospect is that next year will bring an influx of ladies into this country that
will change society in great measure. . . ." Carpenter stated he would not return
home just yet. "I am in business in Sacramento and shall be for the next year. I am
in the iron foundry business and hope to do well." Carpenter then explained
that it would be "inadviseable" to return home at the moment, chiefly because
of the difficulty in finding a trustworthy partner to manage his business in his
absence and because of "the extra expense and time lost in the journey, and
time is worth from $6 to $8 dollars per day—this is no small item."[47]

Lucretta would have none of it. Early in 1852, she apparently refused to join
Carpenter in California or to wait any longer on his return. Carpenter instead
convinced his brother, Augustus, to come to Sacramento to manage his business,
something that must have galled William as Augustus had himself just gotten
married. On his brother's arrival, William showed him the ropes, including the
management of his store as well as a few mining claims. William then set out for
New York. Before leaving, however, he sent Lucretta a detailed accounting of his
fortune in California. "You would be pleased to know something of my business.
Well, I have some six thousand dollars in foundry property, in connection with
my partner in the mines; and some five or six river-shores that are worth as
many thousand dollars; and our goods in our store. So that if I have any decent
fortune this summer in our business I shall be worth from eight to twelve
thousand dollars this fall; but cannot tell in this uncertain country. But am
expecting to come home this coming December with about five thousand dollars
and leave about the same amount in good property here."[48]

Clearly Carpenter was proud of his business success and hoped to return to
it. Yet on the way home he wrote Lucretta a reassuring letter, possibly in response
to a letter from her about his recent mercantile success. "Who would not rather be
first in the whirl of life, and his highest and best occupation agriculture, than be
one who apes to be a man but cannot because he does not follow an independent and noble occupation. Thus may a farmer feel, free from vexations and cares
of him who is less independent of his fellow man. As for myself I will be a farmer
as soon as possible, for I like it and deem it all I have written yea much more."[49]

Carpenter arrived back in New York in 1853 and finally married Lucretta. The negotiations over William's future, however, only intensified. Lucretta became pregnant while William was in New York. William, determined to return to Sacramento, considered bringing his family to Sacramento with him but was concerned that the trip would be too hard on his wife and the baby. Still, he apparently discussed the idea with Lucretta. At this point, however, Lucretta's parents got involved, and William was forced to promise them that if Lucretta came to Sacramento, she would return to New York no later than three years afterward. William left for Sacramento alone, apparently hoping Lucretta would join him within a year or two.

On his arrival in California, William set up a new store in Roses Bar and wrote to his wife, perhaps still hoping to persuade her to join him. "Business here has better prospects for three years to come than it did have last year, for the development of these old hills shows that they are full of gold; and I am acquainted here and deem it the place for me to stay. . . ."[50] Yet only one month later, William wrote Lucretta not to come to California after all, that he would return home within six months.

What happened to change William's mind is not known. His remaining letters, however, suggest that William was by now torn between his family in New York and the attachments he had formed to California. "Do not blame me for thinking it best for you to come here, for consider how hard it is to start in business at home; prostrated as it is with you, can you wonder I deem it best to stay where a man can know how much he makes and get his pay in gold that does not fail as banks do with you."[51] As he was preparing to return home, William briefly considered the potential represented by a plan to link California to the East by railroad, a project that his next-door neighbor in Sacramento, Collis Huntington, would become intimately associated with. "We may well look at one of the greatest enterprises of the day with marked interest," he wrote Lucretta,

> the Pacific Railroad, for it is one of vast magnitude to all the earth, and to America's sons in particular, and perchance to you and me. . . . I more particularly look at it with great interest, for have I not seen California in its infant days, and now fast verging into strong and vigorous manhood? What she will be with this road is not distinctly seen, but that it must be of great utility to her is plain. That I should think of this state as much or more than any other is a natural result of being with her in her infant days and having seen her progress to its present state.[52]

Carpenter returned home in the fall of 1855, made one last trip to California, driving a herd of horses there to market in 1856, and then gave up any notion of staying in California. It is interesting to speculate on what might have happened had Carpenter stayed in Sacramento, had his enthusiasm for the railroad led him to join his neighbor's partnership in the Central Pacific. Torn at last between his gold rush successes and his family, Carpenter tried for years to manage both but ultimately decided to live with his family. Such were the ambitions of California's gold rush dreamers. Most hoped to have wealth and family status. The wealth, originally envisioned as gold, might become instead marketplace profits. Yet wealth itself could not make up for family ties.

The decision to give up on his California dreams, however, was not an easy one, as the letters of William Carpenter illustrate. In 1892, William revisited California with his son and daughter-in-law. Together they toured the gold fields and the city on the Sacramento River that Carpenter had once known so well. Gazing at the great progress that state had indeed made, progress Carpenter had himself envisioned years before, he remarked to his son that he regretted not making California his permanent home.[53]

>--<

The year 1851 seems to have been a turning point in the social history of Sacramento, as more and more women began arriving there. *Sacramento Union* editor John Morse, in addition to trying to educate city residents on the dangers of speculative business practices, also sought to encourage Sacramento businessmen to bring their wives and families to the city. His editorials often gave residents the arguments they would need to convince wives and families to move to Sacramento. "The society of this city," Morse wrote, "is as intelligent, refined, and social as in the most highly favored communities of the eastern States." Morse delineated Sacramento's advantages: "its natural position, the rich agricultural and mineral region which surround it, and the salubrity of its climate, and the commercial facilities it possesses, united to a society which is unsurpassed for intelligence and refinement, render it an attractive and desirable place of residence . . . for the man of business and his family."[54]

But Morse's editorials on this subject suggest what family bonds meant to Sacramento's commercial community. By the spring of 1851, Morse argued that the city's future advancement would depend not on "the wants of masculines, who, bent upon the accomplishment of a fortune in a few months, become indifferent to the social and intellectual embellishments of humanity." Far more important was the business "of organizing social circles, developing intellectual resorts, opening the various avenues of science, of establishing and maintaining good and efficient laws, without which we can afford no guaranty of security and happiness to the mothers, wives, and daughters who are now daily arriving in our country."[55]

Morse's understanding of Sacramento society was made clear in a March 1851 editorial. Sacramento society, which Morse often struggled against, was too chaotic and unstable because of the rampant speculative business practices engaged in by many of its residents. How could this be remedied? "The only elements that can make a Home, keep men in civilization, or adorn and embellish human society," Morse wrote, "are chaste and virtuous females."

The idea that women would "keep men in civilization" was in many ways a product of the reform movements that had been sweeping the country for over two decades. Morse's concern that women come to Sacramento was not new. But Morse faced the dilemma of how to get women to come there, given its rough reputation. The only way, he argued, was for men to begin to make their society fit for women. "No state in the world ever entailed so difficult a task upon men as Californians have now to respond to," he noted.

> If we expect to realize the benefits of Home—if we expect to enjoy the sweet-toned pleasures of quiet firesides, around which thought lingers and affections revel in the only true bliss of earth—we must turn our attention to a judicious construction of society. . . . We are called upon, by every consideration of chivalry and humanity, to organize and maintain a society in which the rights of chaste and virtuous females will be held inviolate and sacred. Can we do it? . . . Every arrival from our old homes brings us new and accumulating inducements for the development of law and order, civility and refinement. . . . We must endeavor at least to prepare for them an unoffending condition of social life.[56]

It is a cliché that the wild western frontier was tamed by women settlers, who encouraged the establishment of churches, schools, and temperance clubs and fought against the influences of gambling, prostitution, and drunkenness. Yet Morse forcefully argued that men—not women—must begin this process in order to encourage the first women to arrive at all.

How should men begin this process of civilizing themselves? Appropriately for a commercial community, one of Morse's arguments suggested that bringing families to Sacramento could be profitable. "The Buildings Most Needed in Sacramento," Morse wrote, were those that would house

> families brought to this country, with a view of taking up permanent residence. It is not to be denied that there are great deficiencies in respect to neat and comfortable cottages in our city, and we imagine that men will do well who will respond to the necessities of the new coming

families, by selecting desirable locations, and erecting on them houses, which while they contemplated neatness and elegance, would at the same time not be beyond the reach of the moderate incomes received by the heads of families.[57]

Sacramento needed women and families to set a moral tone, Morse argued, and providing adequate housing would soon become another profitable business.

Most encouraging to Morse, however, was that such a transformation in Sacramento society was already taking place. He noted the appearance of "men now controlling the bulk of trade who seem to take pleasure in throwing the security of a good brick wall around their merchandise and contemplating the solid and substantial comforts of a permanent home—who have their families with them, or have sent for their families, or who, if unmarried, are seen exhibiting no small degree of tender and solicitous interest in the future welfare of the dear creatures who make up the lively and inspiring circles of our forming society."[58] As more and more of these families settled into Sacramento and stabilized the chaotic public environment, Sacramento would finally and truly emerge as an admirable city.

Morse was not alone in noting the changes taking place in the city. Even Franklin Buck, who used to tease his sister about his marriage prospects in Sacramento, noted the shift in social attitudes. Writing on January 1, 1852, Franklin reported: "Society is improving in some respects. Gentlemen are not seen in gambling saloons as formerly, banking at monte. Nor is it hardly respectable to be seen riding out Sunday with a Mexican Senorita. . . ."[59]

Franklin Buck did not believe that Sacramento had reached a magical utopia, but he clearly felt an attachment to the city. After noting that the number of women and families in the city had grown dramatically, Buck admitted: "There are a good many things yet to be reformed but they will be accomplished in time. Sacramento is the most like home to me of any place in this country and it is the prettiest city and the most orderly in the state."[60]

John and Anne Ingalls made the adjustment to life in Sacramento rather easily, though they continued to miss friends and family in Hartford. "Anne is getting to like California better and better though she don't think it quite equal to Hartford yet. We have frequent rides on horseback which she enjoys very much. Last week we spent gadding about. We went to San Francisco and from there to Stockton and back with Bro George. . . . Anne gets a little lonely once in a while and says 'lets go home' but there is no telling when we shall get started."[60]

During the early years of the gold rush, as the city was in its infancy, would-be miners tended to see everything in California in terms of its orientation to mining. The mining region received most of people's attention; Sacramento was an interesting but clearly supporting player in the great drama of the gold rush. Leander V. Loomis, who visited Sacramento in the fall of 1849, looked at the city and its surroundings with the eye of an entrepreneurial farmer and concluded that there was "some fine farming land around it, and it will probably some day be a rich settlement. . . . It is now and ever will be the great center of business for all of north Cal." Like many of Sacramento's earliest visitors and residents, however, Loomis saw Sacramento's potential as tied directly and solely to the potential of the mining country. "It is bound to improve as long as there can be good wages made in the mines," he wrote, "but after the mines fail, the improvements of Sacramento City will be very few and small."[62]

Yet as time passed, the growth of Sacramento came to be recognized as the historic accomplishment it was. Alonzo Delano, who would eventually publish poems of life and morals in California, traveled throughout northern California, visiting Sacramento several times. On his second visit to the city, in the spring of 1850, Delano was amazed at the magical rate of progress that the city exhibited in just a few months.

> Before returning to the mines, I visited Sacramento, and the improve-
> ments not only in the city, but in the country around, which a few months
> had produced, astonished me. Along the road hotels and dwellings had
> been erected at convenient distances; and where we had traveled the
> previous fall without seeing a human habitation, was now the abode of
> civilized man. . . . Sacramento City had become a city indeed. Substantial
> wooden buildings had taken the place of the cloth tents and frail tenements
> of the previous November, and, although it had been recently submerged
> by an unprecedented flood, which occasioned a great destruction of
> property, and which ruined hundreds of its citizens, it exhibited a scene
> of busy life and enterprise, particularly characteristic of the Anglo-Saxon
> race by whom it was peopled. An immense business was doing with
> miners in furnishing supplies; the river was lined with ships, the streets
> were thronged with drays, teams, and busy pedestrians; the stores were large,
> and well filled with merchandise; and even Aladdin could not have
> been more surprised at the power of his wonderful lamp, than I was at
> the mighty change which less than twelve months had wrought, since
> the first cloth tent had now grown into a large and flourishing city.[63]

Delano's description suggests the wonder that many Californians felt in watching Sacramento grow. Its growth soon became part of their historic experience, an experience characterized by its scale. The journey from the East, whether by wagon or ship, was a long and dramatic one, accomplished by thousands of people. The gold that they hoped to find in abundance was spread over hundreds of miles and hundreds of campsites. That large cities should arise magically from nothing was another example of the scale of the gold rush, another example of the historic accomplishments of the miners. Just as the miner who gathered somewhat less gold than he had hoped could take some comfort in the heroic and historic accomplishments of his journey, so too could he take some measure of pride that he had, directly or indirectly, participated in California's magic urban growth.

By the late summer of 1851, Ledyard and Margaret Frink had also decided to make Sacramento their permanent home. The Frinks had started with a small boardinghouse in Sacramento. Late in 1850 Ledyard had purchased dairy cows and was providing fresh milk to his boarders. Though other hotels offered milk, none offered it free to guests, making "Frink's Hotel" popular in the city. In May 1851 Ledyard purchased an established dairy, raising his dairy herd to twenty-five cows; in August he sold the hotel and bought another dairy, doubling his herd to fifty head. "We had by this time," Margaret wrote in her memoirs, "given the land of gold a fair trial. We had come here as gold-seekers only, not as settlers. But after a year's residence in the delightful valley of the Sacramento, we had satisfied ourselves that no pleasanter land for a home could be found, though we should roam the wide world over. We gave up our plan of further travels. . . . The future of California seemed to us full of promise, and here we resolved to rest from our pilgrimage."[64]

As time passed, Sacramento's pioneer settlers reinforced these ideas of future greatness, ideas originally conceived in the excitement of the gold rush. The hardships endured for the sake of a personal fortune in retrospect became hardships endured for urban greatness. Looking back over the years, Margaret Frink concluded that the promise of California had indeed paid off. "As the years passed on the mushroom city of tents and rough board houses grew, in defiance of fires and floods, to be the capital of the state, and one of its most prosperous, beautiful, and wealthy cities. . . . The progress of time only confirmed us more strongly in our choice of a home, and we never had occasion to regret the prolonged hardships of the toilsome journey that had its happy ending for us in this fair land of California."[65]

A More Rigid
Adherence to Fashion

Two weeks after the Roe lynching, *Transcript* editor F. C. Ewer wrote an editorial pointing out a change in the nature of Sacramento life. His remarks on this occasion did not attempt to unravel thorny questions of law and order, to protest or proclaim justice and lynch law; he wrote not of flood or cholera, political corruption or financial distress. Writing in plain language, Ewer nostalgically turned his attention to the good old days.

"One year ago there seemed to be only one kind of circulating medium," he wrote. "It was 'dust,' and nothing else. The miner, when he came to the city, hauled out his huge buckskin purse and paid for his 'section of gingerbread,' or meal at a restaurant, in 'dust.' . . . Gold dust seemed to have lost its conventional value in his estimation, and the free spirited miner parted with it without a sigh, a why or a wherefore. How things have changed in one year."[1]

The spring of 1851 saw Sacramento well established and reasonably secure in its newfound political, economic, and social stability. Yet having achieved this stability, something seemed to have changed, a subtle shift in the landscape of city life. Ewer, despite his calls for law and order, community unity, and financial good sense, looked back nostalgically at the earlier spirit of the city. "Those were good old times," he wrote,

> when the miners paid for everything in dust—when the red-shirted gentry were the nabobs of the land—when the dirty shirt and coatless party were worth their thousands. It may seem strange, yet it is not less true, that thousands of persons in this State last fall a year did not own a coat, and yet they may have had several thousand dollars in the pocket. The fact of it was, coats were a sort of useless appendage, and but few seemed willing to trouble themselves with packing them about. Last September a year, a floating population of at least six thousand persons were in and around Sacramento, yet out of this entire number there were not over one dozen coated persons. As for "tiles," we doubt if there were a dozen

respectable looking hats in this city—they were a perfect mongrel breed—of all shapes, sizes, and conditions—some crownless, some rimless, and so patched and worn that the looker on could not have told whether they had originally been "plush" or "wool." . . .

Those days have passed, and with the change has come idleness, vagrancy, and coin as a circulating medium. Instead of that free and don't care spirit of spending money, men now regard dollars as much as they once esteemed ounces. They grip a dollar with more tenacity than they formerly did their pounds of dust. Instead of old time apparel, nothing will do now but clothes of the fanciest hue and finest fabric, and "tiles" of the latest and most fashionable style. We doubt indeed whether there is a more rigid adherence to fashion anywhere, than is now visible in the resident population of Sacramento.[2]

Ewer's lament for the fashionless days of the past, appearing so soon after the city was founded, reminds the modern reader of just how quickly Sacramento "grew up." In its first twenty-six months, the city endured dramatic population shifts, two major floods, a general land riot, a disease epidemic, and a brief episode of mob rule. Yet despite this, Ewer is already critical of the new "rigid adherence to fashion" evident in the streets of Sacramento.

Ewer was not the only one to note the change in the city at this point. Two years later, when *Sacramento Union* editor John Morse attempted to write the first history of Sacramento, he noted that the "introduction given to 1851 can find no parallel in history, and it seems almost impossible that its counterpart can ever appear in the future." And though he intended to write a longer history of the city, a project he never completed, in his short history Morse was content to end the story in the spring of 1851, when the "delightful comminglings of business and pleasure" took hold of the city population.[3] Morse, evidently, agreed with Ewer: Sacramento's frontier period was over. Or, to put it another way, Sacramento was now a dull place!

Dull might be overstating it, of course, but it does seem to categorize the attitude of many later historians, who found Sacramento too dull—too ordinary, unremarkable, or unexceptional—to warrant in-depth study. To many researchers, the California gold rush was an exciting period of American history, one filled with mass migrations, excited young men, dashed dreams, and epics of financial speculation, city building, and state building. Furthermore, because of the gold rush, California could early on lay claim to being "the great exception," a place where history was interesting, but so different from the American norm as to be almost irrelevant.[4] Indeed, this attitude underlay much (though certainly not all) of

American historiography on the American West in general. Sacramento did not fit this framework, and its larger history lies waiting to be written.

Yet if this is in fact the case—if Sacramento is not exceptional in the California tradition—then it may be more deserving of study. Given the physical environment, the historic rush, its distance from "typical" cities in the East, and its wildly unstable demographic base, what is astounding is just how "normal" Sacramento became and how quickly it achieved that character. And if Ewer truly did miss the good old days that he waxes so nostalgically over, why did he not lend a hand in making Sacramento a more unique, a more coatless and tileless city, a city where red-shirted gentry could establish a new social order?

Opportunities to establish a truly unique world in Sacramento did exist. Sutter had envisioned a feudal imperial city on the site. The city's later entrepreneurial founders certainly entertained rather unusual economic visions for their creation. And Settlers' Association members fought and even died to bring about a new egalitarian society with the power to redefine the city. All of these alternative visions competed on the site within the space *of less than three years,* during the period when Sacramento went from a small frontier outpost peopled primarily by Sutter's Native American workers to a city of over ten thousand people, becoming the second-largest city west of the Missouri. Given these alternatives as well as the chaos of the gold rush, how can we account for Sacramento's *atypical* typicality?

Finding the answer to this question brings us back to the questions originally asked in the prologue to this book. The clues lie in the unique history of Sacramento itself. But they are also found in a reconsideration of the California gold rush and in the larger experiences of American urban and social history.

Sacramento was not simply a smaller version of San Francisco. The logic of the city was dominated by trade patterns, as was San Francisco. But with the rise of San Francisco as the region's major port, Sacramento quickly assumed a different role, that of a distribution center for regional trade rather than the regional urban core. This meant that the city rapidly lost many of its early entrepreneurial founders, who saw bigger opportunities in the city by the bay. Sacramento was an ideal place for miners, turned teamsters, turned midlevel merchants to rise to stable positions of profitability. It also gave the city a middle-class community ethic, which began to make itself felt in city politics and civic attitudes.

However, this development in the city, making it distinct from San Francisco, did not necessarily distinguish it from such cities in the second tier of urban hierarchies in the rest of the nation. In fact, Sacramento's development here is remarkably unremarkable. Northern California did not produce one great city in the gold rush; it produced an urban network, a hierarchy of cities and towns directed at funneling gold into camps, towns, and cities, ultimately reaching San Francisco, while at the same time creating a flow of goods from San Francisco back through its cities, towns, and mining camps. These flows only look unique when one identifies the items traded as gold or when one considers the high prices charged for the distributed goods. However, if one considers the gold to be a raw material, transformed into a commodity—as agricultural produce was in the East—the "geography of capital" was remarkably similar.[5] Indeed, given the distance from the eastern core, it is hard to imagine a commodity better suited to this distant frontier. California without gold would have had to establish an economic system based on some commodity that would have kept its value for the long journey back east. Before the gold rush, American traders saw much to admire in California, but only cowhides and tallow held up as solid commodities. Gold, based on its value and durability, allowed a capitalistic urban network to form rapidly at a similar level of complexity to that of an eastern urban hierarchy, comparable to one based on Boston, New York, or Chicago. In such networks, the pinnacle city had the financial and cultural resources for urban distinctiveness. Secondary and tertiary cities, however, played roles that were more practical.

Sacramento's development has more in common with other cities within these urban networks than an economic function: it also matched many of the demographic and social elements of these cities. Much can be made of the demographic imbalance of the gold rush, the arrival of so many young, middle-class men in the city at once. But who left the farms of the East and Midwest to crowd the growing cities of older states? Although Sacramento's demographic imbalance may have been extreme, the new urban residents of America's other cities were also primarily young men of moderate means. Like the gold rushers, they came to the cities to make their fortunes. Like many argonauts, they often had little experience in urban businesses but found in the growing cities new opportunities for profitable enterprises. Sacramento's young businessmen had to convince their girlfriends, wives, and families to come to stay in the West permanently, but how many young men in eastern cities and towns also had long and difficult conversations of the heart over relocation from rural communities to booming cities? The shorter distances may have made the transitions easier, but given the state of transportation and communications at midcentury, a separation of only a few hundred miles could be as distant in many ways as a relocation across the continent.

And how might these new rural transplants to city life have responded to the new sensibilities of urban confusion? On the one hand, city ways may have elicited troubled protests as an impersonal business ethic replaced previous rural community ties. The Settlers' Association provides an extreme example of this kind of backlash, but the underlying feelings of dislocation and distrust of the new urban order may have been more common. In fact, civic order in the United States in the 1850s had remarkably strong elements of disorder.[6] In the face of this transition, communitywide demonstrations of public attitudes and accepted values could take on deadly serious roles, whether the citizens were trying to create a citywide prohibition on alcohol or a citywide intolerance for gambling.

Sacramento's early development suggests not the ways in which California was different, but the ways that its development was mainstream. It suggests that the gold rush was not so much an exceptional dream, but more a variation on a theme. In addition, it provides a window into the evolution of an urban network and an urban hierarchy that a study of San Francisco by itself cannot provide.

Which perhaps brings us back to Charles Robinson's troubled question in the dark: "Will the *world,* the *universe,* and *God* say it is *just?*"[7] Perhaps answering for the world, the universe, and God is a bit presumptuous, but it is possible to begin to answer the question for Robinson's peers: the men and women who by 1851 had created a city in the Sacramento Valley. It was a city that was at times chaotic, troubled by natural and human violence, economic and political disruptions, and social and cultural transience. To many walking its streets, it must at times have presented a scene of utter confusion. Yet in that confusion city residents established new identities, new businesses, and new families— erecting by choice permanent institutions in the midst of one of the most unstable and chaotic environments of the nineteenth century. They clung to family ties and familiar institutions, but they saw in the confusion around them admirable opportunities. As time passed and the city grew, city residents enjoyed the fruits of their efforts—stable institutions, a booming economy, and the formal trappings of their newfound status: the coats and "tiles" of Sacramento's postfrontier days. But as Ewer's editorial suggests, they continued to cherish a nostalgic feeling for "the good old days," for the admirable confusion that had shaped their new lives.

Notes

Prologue

1. Don W. Wilson, *Governor Charles Robinson of Kansas* (Lawrence, Manhattan, and Wichita: University Press of Kansas, 1975), 1–4; Frank W. Blackmar, *The Life of Charles Robinson* (Topeka, Kans.: Crane & Company, Printers, 1902), 40–42.

2. Letter published in *Sacramento Transcript*, August 16, 1850.

3. W. W. Robinson, *Land in California, the Story of Mission Lands, Ranchos, Squatters, Mining Claims, Railroad Grants, Land scrip [and] homesteads* (Berkeley: University of California Press, 1948), 114–16.

4. Josiah Royce, "The Squatter Riot of '50 in Sacramento," *The Overland Monthly* 6, no. 33 (San Francisco: California Publishing Company, September 1885): 235–36.

5. *Sacramento Transcript*, August 16, 1850.

6. J. Horace Culver, *1851 Sacramento City Directory* (Sacramento: 1851), 71.

7. Stephen G. Helmich, "K Street Landing, Old Sacramento, and the Embarcadero," *Golden Notes* 26 (Sacramento County Historical Society, fall 1980): 10–12.

8. Mel Scott, *The San Francisco Bay Area: A Metropolis in Perspective*, 2d ed. (Berkeley: University of California Press, 1985), 23–29; Roger Lotchin, *San Francisco: 1846–1856: From Hamlet to City* (New York: Oxford University Press, 1974), 32–33; and Gunther Barth, *Instant Cities: Urbanization and the Rise of San Francisco and Denver* (Albuquerque: University of New Mexico Press, 1975), 134.

Chapter One

1. See Thor Severson, *Sacramento: An Illustrated History: 1839 to 1874* (San Francisco: California Historical Society, n.p., 1973); Myrtle Shaw Lord, *A Sacramento Saga* (Sacramento: Sacramento Chamber of Commerce, 1946); and William Holden, *Sacramento* (Fair Oaks, Calif.: Two Rivers Publishing Company, 1987). Lord calls Sutter "number one pioneer of Sacramento" (1), and Holden begins his book by noting: "This book commemorates the 150th birthday of Sacramento. . . ."

2. Iris H. W. Engstrand, "John Sutter: A Biographical Examination," in *John Sutter and a Wider West*, ed. Kenneth N. Owens (Lincoln: University of Nebraska Press, 1994), 76.

3. Howard Lamar, "John Augustus Sutter, Wilderness Entrepreneur," in Owens, *John Sutter*, 28.

4. Richard Dillon, *Captain John Sutter: Sacramento Valley's Sainted Sinner* (Santa Cruz: Western Tanager, 1967, 1981), 76.

5. Erwin G. Gudde, ed., *Sutter's Own Story* (New York: G. P. Putnam's Sons, 1936), 25, 30–31.

6. Ibid., 25.

7. Richard White, "John Sutter and the Natural World," in Owens, *John Sutter*, 95–96.

8. Albert L. Hurtado, *Indian Survival on the California Frontier* (New Haven, Conn.: Yale University Press, 1988), 14–20.

9. Gudde, *Sutter's Own Story*, 29; Hurtado, *Indian Survival*, 34.

10. Hurtado, *Indian Survival*, 32–37; White, "John Sutter and the Natural World," 97–98.

11. Hurtado, *Indian Survival,* 39–43.

12. Ibid., 46–47; White, "John Sutter and the Natural World," 99.

13. Engstrand, "John Sutter," 76–79.

14. Dillon, *Sutter,* 46.

15. Gudde, *Sutter's Own Story,* 8–26; Engstrand, "John Sutter," 79–80.

16. Lamar, "John Augustus Sutter, Wilderness Entrepreneur," 33.

17. Ibid., 27–33, 35–36.

18. See Howard R. Lamar, "From Bondage to Contract: Ethnic Labor in the American West, 1600–1890," in *The Countryside in the Age of Capitalist Transformation: Essays in the Social History of Rural America,* eds. Steven Hahn and Jonathan Prud (Chapel Hill: University of North Carolina Press, 1987).

19. Albert L. Hurtado, "John A. Sutter and the Indian Business," in Owen, *John Sutter,* 54–56.

20. Gudde, *Sutter's Own Story,* 25.

21. Ibid., 42–44.

22. Ibid., 44–48; Hurtado, "John A. Sutter and the Indian Business," 59–60; Hurtado, *Indian Survival,* 48.

23. Gudde, *Sutter's Own Story,* 55–56; Hurtado, "John A. Sutter and the Indian Business," 59–60; Hurtado, *Indian Survival,* 49.

24. Hurtado, *Indian Survival,* 49–50; Gudde, *Sutter's Own Story,* 55–60; Lamar, "John Augustus Sutter, Wilderness Entrepreneur," 35.

25. Gudde, *Sutter's Own Story,* 97. A number of studies have detailed the hardships faced by migrants on the overland trail. See George R. Stewart, *The California Trail* (Lincoln: University of Nebraska Press, 1962); John D. Unruh, Jr., *The Plains Across: The Overland Emigrants and the Trans-Mississippi West, 1840–60* (Urbana: University of Illinois Press, 1979); and John Mack Faragher, *Women and Men on the Overland Trail* (New Haven, Conn.: Yale University Press, 1979).

26. Gudde, *Sutter's Own Story,* 64–65.

27. Ibid., 64; Oscar Lewis, *Sutter's Fort* (Englewood Cliffs, N.J.: Prentice-Hall, 1966), 28.

28. David J. Weber, *The Mexican Frontier, 1821–1846: The American Southwest Under Mexico* (Albuquerque: University of New Mexico Press, 1982), 204–5.

29. Gudde, *Sutter's Own Story,* 53, 91–99.

30. Weber, *The Mexican Frontier,* 205.

31. Lewis, *Sutter's Fort,* 35.

32. J. Peter Zollinger, *Sutter: The Man and His Empire* (Gloucester, Mass.: P. Smith, 1967), 271–72.

33. Hurtado, *Indian Survival,* 43–44.

34. Ibid., 50–51.

35. Ibid., 51–52.

36. Ibid., 78–91.

37. Gudde, *Sutter's Own Story,* 207, 217–18; Zollinger, *Sutter,* 272–74.

38. Zollinger, *Sutter,* 274–75.

39. Hurtado, *Indian Survival,* 91–99.

40. Ibid., 97, 101–3.

41. *Sutter's Fort State Historical Monument* (State of California Department of Parks and Recreation, n.d.), 19–20.

42. *New York Tribune,* December 9, 11, 1848: the quotation is a composite of the two days' editorials.

43. *Sutter's Fort State Historical Monument,* 20.

44. Gudde, *Sutter's Own Story*, 212.

45. Ibid., 213.

46. Quoted in Lewis, *Sutter's Fort*, 175.

47. Ibid., 183.

48. Zollinger, *Sutter*, 261–70.

49. Ibid., 264.

50. Ibid., 261–70.

Chapter Two

1. Brannan's activities in California, while important in the building of both Sacramento and San Francisco, have been extremely difficult to document. Though several short biographies exist, they are heavily fictionalized when dealing with Brannan during the gold rush. As Will Bagley noted in his collection of Brannan's papers, the merchant's personal written record in essence disappears during this period. Yet Brannan appears to have had an interest in nearly every trading partnership at Sutter's Fort and in early Sacramento. See, for example, John F. Morse, *The First History of Sacramento City* (Sacramento: Sacramento Book Collector's Club, publication no. 3, 1945 [1853]), 22; and William Ladd Willis, *The History of Sacramento County* (Los Angeles: Historic Record Company, 1913), 67. The details of Brannan's story previous to the founding of Sacramento are most thoroughly documented in Will Bagley, *Scoundrel's Tale: The Samuel Brannan Papers*, vol. 3, *Kingdom in the West: The Mormons and the American Frontier* (Spokane, Wash.: The Arthur H. Clark Company, 1999); and in Florence McClure Dunlap, "Samuel Brannan" (master's thesis, University of California, Berkeley, 1928).

2. Bagley, *Scoundrel's Tale*, 23–25, 37; Dunlap, "Samuel Brannan," 5.

3. Bagley, *Scoundrel's Tale*, 37.

4. Ibid., 25, 41–44.

5. Dunlap, "Samuel Brannan," 6; see also P. A. M. Taylor, *Expectations Westward: The Mormons and the Emigration of Their British Converts in the Nineteenth Century* (Edinburgh and London: Oliver and Boyd, 1965).

6. Bagley, *Scoundrel's Tale*, 37. Italics added; whether Brannan misspelled the word or was being ironic is unknown.

7. Ibid., 51–59.

8. Parley P. Pratt, *Autobiography of Parley Parker Pratt*, ed. by his son, Parley Parker Pratt (New York: Russell Brothers, 1874), quoted in Dunlap, "Samuel Brannan," 11.

9. Bagley, *Scoundrel's Tale*, 50, 66–69, 274–76.

10. Ibid., 75–128.

11. Ibid., 121, 132–33.

12. Ibid., 114–28.

13. Ibid., 133.

14. Ibid., 142.

15. Dunlap, "Samuel Brannan," 23–24, 26–27, 30–32, 62; Bagley, *Scoundrel's Tale*, 135–36.

16. Bagley, *Scoundrel's Tale*, 169.

17. Dunlap, "Samuel Brannan," 48–51; Bagley, *Scoundrel's Tale*, 183–84.

18. Bagley, *Scoundrel's Tale*, 186.

19. Dunlap, "Samuel Brannan," 53–54.

20. Bagley, *Scoundrel's Tale*, 213.

21. Ibid., 225.

22. Dunlap, "Samuel Brannan," 54–58; Bagley, *Scoundrel's Tale*, 255.

23. Bagley, *Scoundrel's Tale*, 222.

24. Ibid., 229.

25. Dunlap, "Samuel Brannan," 60–62; the quotation is by William Glover, "The Mormons in California, with Narratives of Kemble and Eager," ms. in Bancroft Library, University of California at Berkeley. See also Bagley, *Scoundrel's Tale*, 234.

26. Dunlap, "Samuel Brannan," 74; quotation from *California Star,* January 22, 1848.

27. Dunlap, "Samuel Brannan," 74–75. Bagley, *Scoundrel's Tale*, 255.

28. Bagley, *Scoundrel's Tale*, 239.

29. Dunlap, "Samuel Brannan," 75–76. Bagley, *Scoundrel's Tale*, 240–41.

30. Dunlap, "Samuel Brannan," 77; *California Star,* May 20, 1848. Bagley, *Scoundrel's Tale*, 264.

31. Dunlap, "Samuel Brannan," 78; Bagley, *Scoundrel's Tale*, 266–67.

32. Dunlap, "Samuel Brannan," 78–79.

33. Bagley, *Scoundrel's Tale*, 285.

34. Ibid., 297. The story of Brannan's response to Young in regard to tithing moneys is explored by Bagley in detail. In fact, Brannan did repay tithing funds and loans to the church but refused to turn over receipts from the mine, which he saw as a tax or rent but not as a tithing. Furthermore, Brannan's disfellowship does not mention the failure to turn over church funds. Bagley believes Brannan himself made up the story in order to further distance himself from Young.

35. Bagley, *Scoundrel's Tale*, 266.

36. Willis, *History of Sacramento County,* 123.

37. Peter H. Burnett, *Recollections and Opinions of an Old Pioneer* (New York: D. Appleton & Company, 1880), 287; Zollinger, *Sutter,* 261–70.

38. Zollinger, *Sutter,* 270–74; John W. Reps, *The Forgotten Frontier: Urban Planning in the American West before 1890* (Columbia and London: University of Missouri Press, 1981), 61.

39. Zollinger, *Sutter,* 273–74.

40. Burnett, *Recollections and Opinions,* 1–287; see also "Peter Hardeman Burnett," in *Dictionary of American Biography,* vol. 3 of 20 vols., eds. Allen Johnson and Dumas Malone (New York: Charles Scribner's Sons, 1928–37), 300–301.

41. Reps, *Forgotten Frontier,* 61; Rodman W. Paul, *California Gold* (Lincoln: University of Nebraska Press, 1947), 22–24.

42. Zollinger, *Sutter,* 273–74; Burnett, *Recollections and Opinions,* 287.

43. Ibid., 287.

44. Ibid., 293.

45. Ibid.

46. Morse, *First History,* 23; Willis, *History of Sacramento County,* 835. See also John A. Sutter, Jr., *Statement Regarding Early California Experiences,* edited, with a biography by Allan R. Ottley (Sacramento: Sacramento Book Collector's Club, publication no. 2, 1943). The struggles between Sacramento and Sutterville from January to April 1848 and the land deals between Sutter, Jr., and the Sacramento merchants have not been fully explored. Sutter's biographers and Sacramento City and County historians have discussed each of the incidents described here, but dates and details have been vague or contradictory. The following reconstruction of events is based primarily on Morse's history.

47. Morse, *First History,* 23–24; Willis, *History of Sacramento County,* 835.

48. Morse, *First History,* 24.

49. Ibid., 24–25.

50. Ibid., 25. Reps, *Forgotten Frontier,* 61, suggests this was a canny move on Sutter, Jr.'s, part to secure the merchants for the town and that the practice was common in other speculative towns. Morse, however, claimed that the young Sutter was "unsophisticated and

plastic" (25) and implies that the young man was basically swindled. Most biographers of the Sutters agree with Morse. Given the original goal of selling town lots in order to retire the Sutter debt, it is hard not to believe that the deal was in essence forced on Sutter. What is not clear is the exact amount of land that Sutter lost by the deal. Morse claimed that Sutter was left with one-fifth of Sacramento (p. 25). Deeds on file in the Sacramento County Recorder's Office suggest that the merchants actually got much less than four-fifths. The figure of five hundred lots, however, matches both Morse and the land deeds. However, the lots that the merchants claimed do make up approximately four-fifths of the area of the city that was settled during the early years of the city's history. Morse's claim that Sutter was left with only one-fifth of the city, for practical purposes, is accurate.

51. Gudde, *Sutter's Own Story,* 221–24; Zollinger, *Sutter,* 275–80.

52. *San Francisco Morning Call,* 1852, quoted in Severson, *Sacramento,* 108–9.

53. *Nevada Transcript,* 1852, quoted in Severson, *Sacramento,* 109.

54. Letter from Lansford Hastings to John Bidwell, October 11, 1853, ms. in California Room, California State Library, Sacramento.

55. Reps, *Forgotten Frontier,* 61, mentioned the rise in lot prices from $250 to $3,000. Bayard Taylor, *Eldorado, or Adventures in the Path of Empire* (Lincoln: University of Nebraska Press, 1949 [1850]), 164, valued the lots in Sacramento's best locations during the summer of 1849 as ranging between $3,000 and $3,500. However, a letter to the *Placer Times,* July 14, 1849, complaining of the high cost of land in the city, gives the figure of $8,000.

56. Sacramento *Placer Times,* June 26, 1849.

57. A. J. Moerenhout, quoted in Lewis, *Sutter's Fort,* 175.

58. Thomas Van Dorn, diary, entry for November 19, 1849. Thomas J. Van Dorn Papers, Western Americana Collection, Beinecke Rare Book and Manuscript Library, Yale University.

59. The City Hotel was something of a landmark in 1849 and is mentioned in most accounts of the early city. See the *Placer Times,* June 26, 1849; Culver, *City Directory,* 72; Taylor, *Eldorado,* 164.

Chapter Three

1. *Placer Times,* April 28, 1849.

2. *Placer Times,* May 5, 1849.

3. Morse, *First History,* 28.

4. Ibid., 30.

5. Helmich, "K Street Landing," 12–13.

6. Taylor, *Eldorado,* 163.

7. Helmich, "K Street Landing," 12–13.

8. Taylor, *Eldorado,* 163.

9. Culver, *City Directory,* 5.

10. Robert D. Livingston, "Sacramento's First Bankers," *Golden Notes* 30 (Sacramento County Historical Society, winter 1984): 1–3.

11. Sacramento *Placer Times,* May 5, 1849.

12. Ibid., May 12, 1849.

13. Ibid.

14. Ibid., May 19, 1849.

15. Ibid., June 6, 1849.

16. Ibid., April 28, 1849.

17. Ibid., May 26, 1849.

18. Ibid., February 1, 1850, and March 2, 1850.

19. Bruce Cornwall, *Life Sketch of Pierre Barlow Cornwall* (San Francisco: A. M. Robertson, 1906), 12–13, 28–30, 44–47.

20. Morse, *First History,* 29.

21. Sacramento *Placer Times,* May 12, 1849.

22. Ibid., July 14, 1849.

23. Ibid., August 11, 1849.

24. Joseph A. McGowan and Terry R. Willis, *Sacramento: Heart of the Golden State* (Woodland Hills, Calif.: Windsor Publications, 1983), 22; Morse, *First History,* 30; Willis, *History of Sacramento County,* 66.

25. Burnett, *Recollections and Opinions,* 337–38.

26. Sacramento *Placer Times,* July 14, 1849.

27. Derived from "Free Inhabitants in Sacramento City in the County of Sacramento, State of California, enumerated by me, on the day[s] of October 1 through November 19, 1850. William W. Johnson, Assistant Marshal," dwellings numbered 1 through 1069 (U.S. Bureau of the Census), Original Schedule of the Seventh Census of Population for California (Microfilm No. 432, National Archives Microfilm Publications), hereafter abbreviated as "1850 U.S. Census manuscript."

28. Derived from "1850 U.S. Census manuscript"; Culver, *City Directory,* 83; Settlers' Association broadside, "Notice to Immigrants!" June 14, 1850, New York Public Library.

29. Derived from "1850 U.S. Census manuscript."

30. Ibid.

31. W. B. H. Dodson, biography: ms., 1885, Bancroft Library.

32. Samuel C. Upham, *Notes of a Voyage via Cape Horn, Together with Scenes in El Dorado, in the Years 1849-'50,* (Philadelphia: S. C. Upham, 1878), 291–92.

33. Ibid., 291–92.

34. Ibid., 295.

35. Katherine A. White, compiler, *A Yankee Trader in the Gold Rush: The Letters of Franklin A. Buck* (Cambridge, Mass.: Houghton Mifflin Company, 1930), 69.

36. Upham, *Notes of a Voyage,* 297.

37. *Niles National Register,* Philadelphia, October 18, 1848.

38. Burnett, *Recollections and Opinions,* 294.

39. Morse, *First History,* 26. Morse noted that the "sovereigns assembled" included Samuel Brannan, Barton Lee, Samuel Hensley, and John Fowler, among others (25).

40. Culver, *City Directory,* 73.

41. Morse, *First History,* 25.

42. Burnett, *Recollections and Opinions,* 294.

43. Morse, *First History,* 26.

44. Burnett, *Recollections and Opinions,* 296.

45. Morse, *First History,* 25.

46. Sacramento *Placer Times,* May 5, 1849.

47. Morse, *First History,* 25.

48. Ibid., 26–27.

49. Culver, *City Directory,* 73; Willis, *History of Sacramento County,* 71.

50. Sacramento City Council Minutes, 1849–50, Book A, p. 1.

51. Ibid., 2.

52. Ibid., 3.

53. Ibid., 5.

54. Ibid., 7.

55. Ibid., 5.

56. Sacramento *Placer Times,* August 25, 1849.

57. Sacramento City Council Minutes, 1849–50, Book A, pp. 8, 12.

58. Sacramento *Placer Times,* July 14, 1849.

59. Ibid.; Sacramento City Council Minutes, 1849–50, Book A, p. 4.

60. Reports of the finance committee in the city council minutes for August and September merely state that the committee was working and needed more time. The first report of the licensing schedule was referred to on October 17, the first presentation of the schedule to the council was made on November 5, and the schedule was not accepted and published for the public until December 3. See Sacramento City Council Minutes, 1849–50, Book A, pp. 17, 19, 49.

61. Sacramento City Council Minutes, 1849–50, Book A, p. 28.

62. See Sacramento City Council Minutes, 1849–50, Book A, entire.

63. For example, see Sacramento City Council Minutes, 1849–50, Book A, p. 8.

64. See November 12, 1849, meeting, Sacramento City Council Minutes, 1849–50, Book A, p. 25.

65. Sacramento City Council Minutes, 1849–50, Book A, pp. 2, 8–11; McGowan and Willis, *Sacramento,* 28.

66. Though the original charter was printed on the presses of the *Placer Times* and distributed among the residents, it was not printed within that newspaper. Searches in both the Sacramento City and Sacramento County archives have failed to uncover a copy of the charter, and early city council documents contain neither a copy of this charter, an earlier draft of the charter, nor even a detailed account of discussion on the amendments made to the original charter during the week of September 8–12, 1849.

67. Morse, *First History,* 52–54; Willis, *History of Sacramento County,* 71; see also McGowan and Willis, *Sacramento,* 28.

68. "Proclamation by Order of the People of Sacramento City," 1849, broadside in the Sacramento City Archives.

69. Sacramento City Council Minutes, 1849–50, Book A, pp. 11–13.

70. "Proclamation by Order of the People of Sacramento City," broadside.

71. Sacramento City Council Minutes, 1849–50, Book A, pp. 11–16.

72. "Proclamation to the People of Sacramento City, By Order of the President and City Council," October 1, 1849, broadside in California State Library, Sacramento.

73. Ibid.

74. McGowan and Willis, *Sacramento,* 28.

75. Ibid., 28; Morse, *First History,* 52–54.

76. Sacramento City Council Minutes, 1849–50, Book A, p. 17.

77. Sacramento *Placer Times,* October 25, 1849; Sacramento City Council Minutes, 1849–50, Book A, p. 42. Zabriskie charged the city $2,500 for his work on the council; the council, which noted that they served without pay, refused to grant more than $680.

78. Sacramento *Placer Times,* October 25, 1849.

79. Sacramento City Council Minutes, 1849–50, Book A, pp. 17–55.

80. Fred Blackburn Rogers, "Preface," in *A Kemble Reader,* ed. Fred Blackburn Rogers (San Francisco: California Historical Society, publication no. 37, 1963), iii–x.

81. Sacramento *Placer Times,* May 5, 1849.

82. Ibid.

83. Ibid.

84. Ibid.

Chapter Four

1. John M. Letts, *California Illustrated: Including a Description of the Panama and Nicaragua Routes. By a Returned Californian* (New York: William Holdredge, Publisher, 1852), 61.

2. Willis, *History of Sacramento County,* 21.

3. James Eaton, "From the Memoirs of James Eaton," *Golden Notes* 32 (Sacramento County Historical Society, summer 1986): 2–11.

4. Stewart, *California Trail,* 231–32, 292.

5. Ibid., 221, 237–38.

6. Ibid., 226–29.

7. Faragher, *Women and Men on the Overland Trail,* 78.

8. Stewart, *California Trail,* 227–28.

9. Ansel McCall, quoted in Stewart, *California Trail,* 267.

10. H. C. St. Clair, journal, entry for September 25–30, Beinecke Library.

11. John H. Peoples, quoted in Stewart, *California Trail,* 290–91.

12. Quotation in McGowan and Willis, *Sacramento,* 35.

13. Taylor, *Eldorado,* 163–64.

14. Ibid., 208.

15. Stewart, *California Trail,* 240–44; see also John Phillip Reid, *Law for the Elephant: Property and Social Behavior on the Overland Trail* (San Marino, Calif.: Huntington Library, 1980).

16. Stewart, *California Trail,* 232–33.

17. Ibid., 232; Taylor, *Eldorado,* 208; see also Faragher, *Women and Men on the Overland Trail,* and Reid, *Law for the Elephant,* for discussions of community in overland trail parties.

18. Joseph Stuart, quoted in Stewart, *California Trail,* 240.

19. David Hewes, letter to his mother, February 24, 1850, Bancroft Library.

20. Taylor, *Eldorado,* 204–5.

21. Derived from "1850 U.S. Census manuscript."

22. According to the 1850 census, taken in the fall of that year, 204 miners resided in the city. That figure, however, must be adjusted since the 1850 census was admitted to be inaccurate by the census taker. To get a more accurate figure for the fall of 1850, it would be better to calculate the number based on the percentage of miners counted to the total population counted and then the number of miners extracted from the estimated population total, which was 150 percent higher than was counted. This would translate into a total of approximately 500 transient miners in the city. Next the actual number of miners should be enlarged somewhat again. Like the overlanders, many miners could not afford the high costs of rooms in Sacramento and most likely threw up their tents in the overlanders' Tent City, where they probably eluded the census taker's count. Thus a rough estimate of 750 transient miners in Sacramento during the winter of 1850–51 is not unreasonable.

However, the estimate of transient miners in the city during the winter of 1849–50 must be revised again still higher; certainly there were more miners in Sacramento during that winter than during the winter of 1850–51, when the census was taken. During the earlier year, the first big year of the gold rush, mining region towns were fewer and less developed—much like Sacramento. Poor weather, extensive rainstorms, closed the muddy roads to teamsters during the winter, and the mining region towns and camps were thus particularly inadequate during the first year of the rush. Sacramento's winter weather, though wet, was milder than that of the mining region, and the city had better and more varied stockpiles of supplies than most mining camps. Sacramento would therefore have been a more inviting wintering site at the close of 1849. The following year, however, the mining camps were more developed and were capable of providing for larger populations.

Given a more equal choice, most miners would probably have elected to stay in the mining region. Furthermore, Sacramento had gained a notorious reputation by the fall of 1850. A riot, financial collapse, and a cholera outbreak in the city in the fall of 1850 kept many miners from returning there even for short visits. Thus the number of transient miners in Sacramento during the winter of 1849–50 was probably much greater than the 1850 census figures indicate.

23. Charles G. Moxley, letter to his sister, December 16, 1849, Beinecke Library.

24. Taylor, *Eldorado*, 165.

25. Upham, *Notes of a Voyage*, 307–8.

26. Culver, *City Directory*, 72–73; Taylor, *Eldorado*, 165.

27. See Sacramento *Placer Times*, October 1849 through April 1850. A number of articles discuss attempts by several occupations, especially carpenters, to form a union to keep wages at summertime levels.

28. Alonzo Hill, letter to his parents, April 17, 1850, Beinecke Library.

29. Thomas J. Van Dorn, papers, Beinecke Library.

30. Hewes, letter, February 24, 1850, Bancroft Library.

31. St. Clair, journal, entry for October 10, 1849, Beinecke Library.

32. Henry Rice Mann, diary, Beinecke Library.

33. George Kenyon Fitch, "Journalism in San Francisco and Sacramento," ms., 1887, Bancroft Library.

34. Letts, *California Illustrated*, 133.

35. Quotation from Severson, *Sacramento*, 72.

36. Eaton, "Memoirs," 2–3; Buck, *A Yankee Trader*, 58–59.

37. Eaton, "Memoirs," 3–11.

38. Morse, *First History*, 62.

39. Sacramento *Placer Times*, January 19, 1850.

40. Ibid.

41. David Hewes, letter to his mother, February 24, 1850, Bancroft Library.

42. McGowan and Willis, *Sacramento*, 35.

43. Sacramento City Council Minutes, 1849–50, Book A, p. 8.

44. Culver, *City Directory*, 78.

45. Sacramento City Council Minutes, 1849–50, Book A, pp. 19–28.

46. Blackmar, *Life of Charles Robinson*, 57–59.

47. Morse, *First History*, 61.

48. Ibid.

49. Derived from "1850 U.S. Census manuscript"; Culver, *City Directory*, 83.

50. Sacramento City Council Minutes, 1849–50, Book A, p. 67.

51. Ibid., 67–70.

52. Ibid., 72–81.

53. McGowan and Willis, *Sacramento*, 28.

54. See Sacramento *Placer Times*, February 9, 1850, for the full text of the new charter.

55. Sacramento City Council Minutes, 1849–50, Book A, pp. 66, 82.

56. Upham, *Notes of a Voyage*, 278.

57. Willis, *History of Sacramento County*, 21.

58. Sacramento City Council Minutes, 1849–50, Book A, p. 85; Morse, *First History*, 65.

59. *Sacramento Transcript*, April 1, 1850.

60. Ibid.

61. Upham, *Notes of a Voyage*, 278–79.

62. Ibid., 282; Willis, *History of Sacramento County,* 42–43.

63. Hardin Bigelow, "To the Honorable the President and Council of Sacramento City," reprinted in Upham, *Notes of a Voyage,* 283–88.

64. Sacramento City Council Minutes, 1849–50, Book B, pp. 5, 11.

65. Bigelow, "To the Honorable," 285.

66. Morse, *First History,* 67.

Chapter Five

1. Taylor, *Eldorado,* 202–3.

2. Ibid., 204.

3. Burnett, *Recollections and Opinions,* 337–38.

4. Israel Shipman Pelton Lord, *A Doctor's Gold Rush Journey to California,* ed. Necia Dixon Liles (Lincoln: University of Nebraska Press, 1995), 192.

5. Ibid., 193.

6. Ibid., 192–93.

7. Charles Glass Gray, *Off at Sunrise: The Overland Journal of Charles Glass Gray,* ed. Thomas D. Clark (San Marino, Calif.: Huntington Library, 1976), 149.

8. Gray, *Off at Sunrise,* 150.

9. Ibid., 151.

10. Taylor, *Eldorado,* 163–69.

11. Ibid., 165.

12. Ibid.

13. Ibid., 164.

14. Ibid., 168.

15. Derived from "1850 U.S. Census manuscript."

16. Taylor, *Eldorado,* 164.

17. Ibid., 205.

18. Ibid., 205, 209.

19. Ibid., 208.

20. Upham, *Notes of a Voyage,* 208–9.

21. Henry Souther, Entry for October 30, 1849, "Journal of Henry Souther Begun October 30th 1849." Western Americana Collection, Beinecke Library.

22. See J. S. Holliday, *The World Rushed In: The California Gold Rush Experience* (New York: Simon & Schuster, 1981), 57; when William Swain decided to go to California, his brother, who would have been an otherwise ideal companion, stayed behind to watch after William's farm and family. Swain thus turned to several neighbors for traveling companions.

23. Derived from "1850 U.S. Census manuscript."

24. Comparison of "1850 U.S. Census manuscript" and Culver, *City Directory,* makes this arrangement apparent.

25. Faragher, *Women and Men on the Overland Trail,* 36–39.

26. Ibid.; see also Jack Larkin, *The Reshaping of Everyday Life, 1790–1840* (New York: Harper & Row, 1988), 9–15.

27. Eaton, "Memoirs," 1.

28. Gray, *Off at Sunrise,* 149–53, 168.

29. Ibid., 149.

30. Ibid., 152–53.

31. Ibid., 153.

32. Ibid., 154–56.

33. Holliday, *The World Rushed In,* 50–52; see also Reid, *Law for the Elephant.*

34. David Hewes, letter to his mother, February 24, 1850, Bancroft Library.

35. *Sacramento Transcript,* August 1, 1850.

36. Derived from "1850 U.S. Census manuscript" and from Culver, *City Directory.*

37. Derived from "1850 U.S. Census manuscript."

38. Ibid.

39. Van Dorn, diary, entry for November 19, 1849, Beinecke Library.

40. Joseph Schafer, ed., "California Letters of Lucius Fairchild," in *Western Historical Publications Collection* vol. 31 (Madison, Wis.: 1931), 109.

41. William H. McFarlin, letter to his wife, Margaret, Beinecke Library.

42. Buck, *A Yankee Trader,* 52, 56.

43. James W. Haines, "Life and Experiences in California," ms., 1887, Bancroft Library.

44. Derived from "1850 U.S. Census manuscript."

45. Sacramento *Placer Times,* December 1, 1849.

46. Mann, diary, Beinecke Library.

47. Philip F. Castleman, journal, entry for November 11, 1849, Western Americana Collection, Beinecke Library.

48. Moxley, letter to his sister, December 16, 1849, Beinecke Library.

49. Hill, letter to his parents, May 1850, Beinecke Library.

50. Ibid.

51. Taylor, *Eldorado,* 165; Sacramento *Placer Times,* November 24, 1849.

52. James S. Barnes, letter to his family, March 21, 1850, Bancroft Library.

53. Ibid., May 29, 1850, Bancroft Library.

54. Barnes, letter to his mother, August 24, 1850, Bancroft Library.

55. Derived from "1850 U.S. Census manuscript."

56. The 1850 U.S. Census ledgers contained columns in which census agents were supposed to note whether or not a counted person was illiterate. This column is blank for the Sacramento City entries, supposedly indicating that most of the population was literate. However, both agents who counted the Sacramento population indicated that the population count was rough at best and that the rest of the information was impossible to ascertain—which might mean that they made no attempt at all to determine this category. The best evidence that a majority of the population had a basic education is circumstantial and is based on the middle-class origins of the residents and on the city's ability to support two daily newspapers less than eighteen months after the city was founded.

57. Hewes, letter to his mother, February 24, 1850, Bancroft Library.

58. Derived from "1850 U.S. Census manuscript"; Morse, *First History,* 28.

59. Anna Paschall Hannum, ed., *A Quaker Forty-Niner: The Adventures of Charles Edward Pancoast on the American Frontier* (Philadelphia: University of Pennsylvania Press, 1930), 362–63.

60. Ibid., 363–71.

61. Ibid.

62. Western land speculation and public land policies have been discussed in numerous studies. See, for example, Benjamin Horace Hibbard, *A History of the Public Land Policies* (Madison and Milwaukee: University of Wisconsin Press, 1965); Robert Tudor Hill, *The Public Domain and Democracy: A Study of Social, Economic and Political Problems in the United States in Relation to Western Development* (New York: Columbia University, 1910); and Roy M. Robbins, *Our Landed Heritage: The Public Domain, 1776–1936* (Princeton,

N.J.: Princeton University Press, 1942). The best recent survey of public land policy as it related to California in the 1850s is Donald J. Pisani, "Squatter Law in California, 1850–1856," *Western Historical Quarterly* 25 (autumn 1994): 277–310.

63. Robinson, *Land in California*, 60–132; Pisani, "Squatter Law," 286–88.

64. Robinson, *Land in California*, 91–98.

65. See Sacramento County Recorder's Office, Book of Deeds, vol. A, pp. 4–5, 7–8, 10–16, 18–22, 24–25, 66, 68, 85, 123, 164, 169, 221, 283, 390, 571, 656, 679; vol. B, pp. 9, 205; vol. C, p. 171; vol. D, p. 60.

66. See Sacramento County Recorder's Office, Book of Deeds, vol. A, pp. 27, 28, 36.

67. Hubert Howe Bancroft, *History of California* (San Francisco: History Company, 1888), vol. 6, 329.

68. Ibid.

69. Blackmar, *Life of Charles Robinson*, 58; quotation from Charles Robinson, *The Kansas Conflict* (Lawrence, Kans.: Journal publishing company, 1898), 37.

70. Bancroft, *History of California*, vol. 6, 329.

71. Ibid.

72. Ibid.

73. Willis, *History of Sacramento County*, 49; Bancroft, *History of California*, vol. 6, 328; Royce, "Squatter Riot," 228–29; Theodore H. Hittell, *History of California*, vol. 3 (San Francisco: N. J. Stone, 1898), 667.

74. Sacramento *Placer Times*, December 15, 1849.

75. Ibid., February 16, 1850.

76. Ibid., February 23, 1850.

77. See accounts of Settlers' Association meetings detailed in the *Sacramento Transcript*, July 2–6, 1850; Upham, *Notes of a Voyage*, 335–41; Hittell, *History of California*, vol. 3, 669–75; Blackmar, *Life of Charles Robinson*, 58–67.

78. For best accounts of Settlers' Association infighting, see Upham, *Notes of a Voyage*, 335–41.

79. Robinson's role as the organizer of the Settlers' Association is vaguely described in Blackmar, *Life of Charles Robinson*, 58–60. However, other accounts of informal settler meetings preceding Robinson's involvement suggest that he did not organize the association.

80. Robinson's role in the Settlers' Association has been discussed by Royce, "Squatter Riot," 235–42.

81. Bancroft, *History of California*, vol. 6, 329.

82. Hittell, *History of California*, vol. 3, 670–71.

83. Ibid.

84. Ibid.

85. Bancroft, *History of California*, vol. 6, 329–30.

86. Morse, *First History*, 52–54.

87. Sacramento City Council Minutes, 1849–50, Book A, pp. 51–52.

88. Sacramento City Settlers' Association, "The Sacramento City Settlers' Association, believing the ground . . . ," handbill, in the Bancroft Library.

89. Sacramento *Placer Times*, December 15, 1849.

90. Bagley, *Scoundrel's Tale*, 309–10.

Chapter Six

1. *Sacramento Transcript*, May 28, 1850.

2. Ibid.

3. Ibid., June 3, 1850.

4. Ibid.

5. Ibid.

6. David Hewes, letter to his mother, February 24, 1850, Bancroft Library.

7. Paul, *California Gold,* 120.

8. See Sacramento *Placer Times,* January 19, 1850. In the midst of its report on the January flood that devastated Sacramento, the *Placer Times* conjectured that the flood might actually uncover more gold and build up new nugget-rich gravel bars in California's streams and rivers.

9. Barnes, letter, August 24, 1850, Bancroft Library.

10. Royce, "Squatter Riot," 230.

11. Unruh, Jr., *The Plains Across,* 120.

12. Newspaper reports of the coming trains of California migrants appeared in almost every issue of the *Placer Times* and *Transcript* from the early summer to the late fall of 1850. Typical of these reports, which dwelt on both the size of the migrant parties and their sickness and poverty, is the report appearing in the *Sacramento Transcript,* August 2, 1850.

13. See, for example, Reid, *Law for the Elephant.*

14. Sacramento *Placer Times,* February 2, 1850.

15. Ibid., February 16, 1850.

16. Derived from "1850 U.S. Census manuscript."

17. Culver, *City Directory,* 83, reprints 1850 City Tax Rolls; Upham, *Notes of a Voyage,* 286–87.

18. Hittell, *History of California,* vol. 3, 671.

19. *Sacramento Transcript,* April 20, 1850.

20. Ibid., April 23, 1850.

21. Royce, "Squatter Riot," 232.

22. Bancroft, *History of California,* vol. 6, 330.

23. Sacramento *Placer Times,* May 23, 1850.

24. Lord, *A Doctor's Gold Rush,* 316.

25. Sacramento City Settlers' Association, "Notice to Immigrants!" June 14, 1850, handbill in New York Public Library.

26. Reps, *The Forgotten Frontier,* 19; *Sacramento Transcript,* June 8, 1850; Sacramento *Placer Times,* June 8, 1850. See also letters and articles about the land title dispute in the *Transcript,* June 3 through June 19, 1850, and in the *Placer Times,* May 23 through June 7, 1850.

27. State of California, *Statutes,* 1850, p. 425.

28. The act is discussed in the *Sacramento Transcript,* August 22, 1850; Bancroft, *History of California,* vol. 6, 333; and Royce, "Squatter Riot," 238.

29. Bancroft, *History of California,* vol. 6, 330; McGowan and Willis, *Sacramento,* 28–29.

30. Royce, "Squatter Riot," 238.

31. Bagley, *Scoundrel's Tale,* 310.

32. Upham, *Notes of a Voyage,* 333–34.

33. Zollinger, *Sutter,* 303.

34. Morse, *First History,* 69.

35. Ibid.

36. Ibid., 69–70.

37. Ibid., 69.

38. Alonzo Hill, letter to his parents, June 12, 1850, Beinecke Library.

39. Ibid.

40. See Pisani, "Squatter Law." Pisani astutely notes that the squatters were not merely lawless frontier ruffians, but settlers whose views were rooted in early nineteenth-century

experience and legal traditions, caught between a "vision based on equal access to property and widespread ownership" and "a competing vision that emphasized the most rapid development of wealth."

41. Upham, *Notes of a Voyage,* 335–37.

42. Ibid., 338–41.

43. Ibid., 338–40.

44. Ibid., 339.

45. Blackmar, *Life of Charles Robinson,* 60–61.

46. Upham, *Notes of a Voyage,* 335.

47. Royce, "Squatter Riot," 239.

48. Ibid., 239.

49. Upham, *Notes of a Voyage,* 335–36.

50. Ibid., 341.

51. Royce, "Squatter Riot," 239.

52. Ibid.

53. *Sacramento Transcript,* August 3 and 5, 1850.

54. Ibid., August 3, 5, and 6, 1850.

55. Ibid., August 12, 1850.

56. Ibid., August 5–14, 1850.

57. Ibid., August 14, 1850.

58. Derived from "1850 U.S. Census manuscript."

59. *Sacramento Transcript,* August 17, 1850.

60. Ibid., August 12, 1850.

61. Ibid.

62. Ibid.

63. Ibid.

64. Ibid.

65. Royce, "Squatter Riot," 240–41.

66. Ibid.

67. Ibid.

68. Ibid., 237.

69. Charles Robinson to Sara T. D. Lawrence, August 12, 1850. Reprinted in Blackmar, *Life of Charles Robinson,* 64–66, and the *Sacramento Transcript,* August 16, 1850.

70. Royce, "Squatter Riot," 242.

71. Robinson to Sara Lawrence, *Sacramento Transcript,* August 16, 1850.

72. Ibid.

73. Royce, "Squatter Riot," 242.

74. Benjamin Stillman, "Seeking the Golden Fleece," *The Overland Monthly* (November 1873): 418.

75. Upham, *Notes of a Voyage,* 341.

76. Bancroft, *History of California,* vol. 6, 331; *Sacramento Transcript,* August 14, 1850.

77. Royce, "Squatter Riot," 242.

78. Stillman, "Seeking the Golden Fleece," 418.

79. Blackmar, *Life of Charles Robinson,* 66–67.

80. Ibid., 67–68.

81. Ibid.

82. Ibid., 68.

83. Ibid., 68–69.

84. Upham, *Notes of a Voyage,* 342.

85. Ibid.; Bancroft, *History of California,* vol. 6, 331.

86. Upham, *Notes of a Voyage,* 342–43.

87. Ibid.; Blackmar, *Life of Charles Robinson,* 69.

88. *Sacramento Transcript,* August 19, 1850.

89. Upham, *Notes of a Voyage,* 343.

90. Blackmar, *Life of Charles Robinson,* 68–71; *Sacramento Transcript,* August 15, 1850; Upham, *Notes of a Voyage,* 342–45; Bancroft, *History of California,* vol. 6, 331–32; Hittell, *History of California,* vol. 3, 674–75; Royce, "Squatter Riot," 242–44.

91. Stillman, "Seeking the Golden Fleece," 418.

92. Upham, *Notes of a Voyage,* 345.

93. Ibid., 34, 350; *Sacramento Transcript,* November 29, 1850.

94. Blackmar, *Life of Charles Robinson,* 70.

95. Stillman, "Seeking the Golden Fleece," 419.

96. Ibid.

97. Blackmar, *Life of Charles Robinson,* 70–71.

98. Ibid., 71; *Sacramento Transcript,* August 15, 1850; Upham, *Notes of a Voyage,* 345; Bancroft, *History of California,* vol. 6, 332; Hittell, *History of California,* vol. 3, 675; Royce, "Squatter Riot," 244.

99. *Sacramento Transcript,* August 15, 1850.

100. Stillman, "Seeking the Golden Fleece," 420.

101. Ibid.

102. Augustus Moore, "Pioneer Experiences," ms., 1878, Bancroft Library.

103. *Sacramento Transcript,* August 15, 1850.

104. Stillman, "Seeking the Golden Fleece," 419.

105. Willis, *History of Sacramento County,* 55.

106. *Sacramento Transcript,* August 16, 1850.

107. Ibid. Blackmar, *Life of Charles Robinson,* 72, also places the blame for McKinney's posse on the urging of the speculators.

108. Stillman, "Seeking the Golden Fleece," 420.

109. *Sacramento Transcript,* August 16, 1850.

110. Ibid.

111. Blackmar, *Life of Charles Robinson,* 72; *Sacramento Transcript,* August 16, 1850; Upham, *Notes of a Voyage,* 345–49; Bancroft, *History of California,* vol. 6, 332–33; Hittell, *History of California,* vol. 3, 675–76; Royce, "Squatter Riot," 244–45.

112. Upham, *Notes of a Voyage,* 347–48; *Sacramento Transcript,* August 16, 1850; Royce, "Squatter Riot," 245.

113. Royce, "Squatter Riot," 245.

114. Stillman, "Seeking the Golden Fleece," 420–21.

115. Royce, "Squatter Riot," 244; Stillman, "Seeking the Golden Fleece," 418–20.

116. Royce, "Squatter Riot," 244; Blackmar, *Life of Charles Robinson,* 72–73; Bancroft, *History of California,* vol. 6, 333.

117. Blackmar, *Life of Charles Robinson,* 73.

118. Stillman, "Seeking the Golden Fleece," 420–21.

119. George Kenyon Fitch, "Journalism in San Francisco and Sacramento," mss., 1886, Bancroft Library.

120. Morse, *First History,* 70–71.

Chapter Seven

1. David Hewes, letter to his mother, August 31, 1850, Bancroft Library.
2. Ibid., June 29, 1850, Bancroft Library.
3. Haines, "Life and Experiences in California."
4. William Robert Prince to [Mrs.] Charlotte Prince, August 18, 1850, ms. from the William Robert Prince letters, Bancroft Library.
5. Malcolm J. Rohrbough, *Days of Gold: The California Gold Rush and the American Nation* (Berkeley: University of California Press, 1997), 197. Rohrbough calculated that this transformation began at the start of the 1851 season, although he notes that one of the forty-niners noticed it as early as December 1850. Certainly this shift took place at different times depending on the place. The mining region just east of Sacramento, however, was the site of the original gold discovery and the starting place of the search for gold that eventually spread to the rest of the Sierra Nevada range. Thus Sacramento's hinterland was the most intensively mined region by 1850 and would show the effects of the transformation earliest.
6. Paul, *California Gold,* 119–21, 349–52.
7. Franklin Langworthy, *Scenery of the Plains, Mountains and Mines* (Princeton, N.J.: Princeton University Press, 1885), 192.
8. Richard A. Dwyer and Richard E. Lingenfelter, eds., *Songs of the Gold Rush* (Berkeley: University of California Press, 1964), 64–65.
9. Bernard Reid, quoted in Patricia Nelson Limerick, *The Legacy of Conquest: The Unbroken Past of the American West* (New York: W. W. Norton and Company, 1987), 102.
10. Lord, *A Doctor's Gold Rush,* 311.
11. Mark Hopkins, letter to Moses Hopkins, July 10, 1850, Huntington Manuscript 26040.
12. Ibid.
13. Ralph Walter Cioffi, "Mark Hopkins, Inside Man of the Big Four" (master's thesis, University of California, Berkeley, 1938), 22–27; Edward H. Miller, "Notes regarding Mark Hopkins and related material, 1878–[ca. 1888]," Hubert Howe Bancroft Collection, Bancroft Library.
14. Mark Hopkins, letter to Moses Hopkins, July 10, 1850, Huntington Manuscript 26040.
15. Ibid., October 27, 1850, Huntington Manuscript 26045.
16. Haines, "Life and Experiences in California, 1887."
17. Ibid.
18. Edward Austin, letters, Bancroft Library.
19. Henry Rice Mann, diary, Beinecke Library.
20. George R. Underhill, diary, Beinecke Library, n.p.
21. On the willingness of overland migrants to part with their draft animals—"those who had just crossed the plains were disgusted with packing and with cattle and would trade for anything that would relieve them of the burden" (Haines, "Life and Experiences in California, 1887").
22. Underhill, diary, Beinecke Library.
23. Ibid.
24. Ibid.
25. Ibid.
26. Ibid.
27. Ibid.
28. Ibid.
29. Ibid.
30. Ibid.

31. Ibid.

32. Ibid.

33. Lord, *A Doctor's Gold Rush*, 296, 298.

34. Philo, California correspondence, November 10, 1850, Beinecke Library.

35. Fitch, "Journalism in San Francisco and Sacramento"; and James S. Barnes, letter, November 24, 1850, Bancroft Library.

36. W. B. H. Dodson, biography, ms., 1885, Bancroft Library.

37. James S. Barnes, letter, November 24, 1850, Bancroft Library.

38. Lord, *A Doctor's Gold Rush*, 330.

39. James S. Barnes, letter, November 24, 1850, Bancroft Library.

40. Fitch, "Journalism in San Francisco and Sacramento."

41. *Sacramento Transcript*, September 10, 1850; Morse, *First History*, 89–94; Bancroft, *History of California*, vol. 6, 333–34; Royce, "Squatter Riot," 245; Lord, *A Doctor's Gold Rush*, 317.

42. Morse, *First History*, 25.

43. Culver, *City Directory*, 78.

44. Ibid., 79. See also "1850 U.S. Census manuscript"—census taker William Johnson noted that the population was in too great a state of flux for any accurate counting. Even as early as the fall of 1849, Bayard Taylor estimated Sacramento's population as nearly ten thousand. Taylor's guess was probably distorted by the city's large temporary population of visitors, who stayed in the city only long enough to equip themselves for the mines before leaving. See Taylor, *Eldorado*, 163–64.

45. Reps, *The Forgotten Frontier*, 146.

46. Robinson, *Land in California*, 91–132.

47. Lord, *A Doctor's Gold Rush*, 300.

48. Ibid., 301.

49. Edward C. Kemble, *A History of California Newspapers, 1846–1858* (Los Gatos, Calif.: Talisman Press, 1962 [1858]), 142–46.

50. For discussions of health problems that plagued overland trail migrants, see Stewart, *The California Trail;* for specific examples of doctors' experiences in the gold rush, see Morse, *First History;* Stillman, "Seeking the Golden Fleece"; and Blackmar, *Life of Charles Robinson.*

51. See Morse, *First History;* Stillman, "Seeking the Golden Fleece"; and Blackmar, *Life of Charles Robinson*—each doctor noted that patients generally could not pay for services and that doctoring in early Sacramento was not profitable.

52. Henry Rice Mann, diary, September 13, 1849, Beinecke Library.

53. Alonzo Hill, letter, May 9, 1850, Beinecke Library.

54. Ibid., June 12, 1850, Beinecke Library.

55. Severson, *Sacramento*, 130.

56. See Morse, *First History;* Stillman, "Seeking the Golden Fleece"; and Blackmar, *Life of Charles Robinson;* see also Sacramento City Council Minutes, vols. A and B, 1849–50, ms. in Sacramento City Archives. Doctors' reports were made to the council continually throughout this period; see especially minutes for November 14 and 19, 1849; January 14, 1850; and March 20, 1850.

57. Fitch, "Journalism in San Francisco and Sacramento."

58. Severson, *Sacramento*, 79.

59. Dodson, biography, Bancroft Library.

60. Alonzo Hill, letter, September 27, 1850, Beinecke Library.

61. Morse, *First History*, 94–95; *Sacramento Transcript*, December 30, 1850.

62. *Sacramento Transcript*, February 22, 1851.

63. Morse, *First History*, 94–95; *Sacramento Transcript*, February 1, 1851.

64. Morse, *First History*, 94–95; see also issues of the *Sacramento Transcript*, October 1850 through April 1851, especially November 19 and 27, 1850.

65. Mark Hopkins, letter to Moses Hopkins, July 30, 1850, Huntington Manuscript 26041.

66. David Hewes, letter to his mother, December 13, 1850, Bancroft Library.

67. Thomas Van Dorn, diary, November 19, 1849, Beinecke Library.

68. Paul, *California Gold*, 118.

69. Agricultural statistics from *Statistical View of the United States . . .* by J. D. B. DeBow, Superintendent of the U.S. Census (Washington: A. O. P. Nicholson, Public Printer, 1854), 202–3; *The Seventh Census of the United States: 1850*, J. D. B. DeBow, Superintendent of the U.S. Census (Washington: Robert Armstrong, publisher, 1853, 976–77; and the 1852 California State Census, in DeBow, *The Seventh Census of the United States*, 983–84.

70. *Sacramento Union*, May 26, 1851.

71. Ibid.

72. Derived from "1850 U.S. Census manuscript"; Culver, *City Directory;* Sacramento *Placer Times*, April 1849–December 1850; and *Sacramento Transcript*, June 1850–December 1850.

73. Morse, *First History*, 29–30.

74. Carol Wenzel, "Historical Note," from Morse, *First History*, 4–7.

75. *Sacramento Union*, April 10, 1851.

76. Ibid., April 8, 1851.

77. Taylor, *Eldorado*, 70.

78. Ibid., 167.

79. Ibid., 168.

80. Buck, *A Yankee Trader*, 51.

81. Haines, "Life and Experiences in California, 1887."

82. Sacramento *Placer Times*, February 23, 1850.

83. Deed, John A. Sutter, Jr., to Sacramento City, January 2, 1849, Sacramento County Recorder's Book of Deeds A, p. 128; the deed is quoted in part and discussed in Helmich, "K Street Landing," 15.

84. See Sacramento City Council Minutes, vols. A and B, 1849–50, ms. in Sacramento City Archives; the problems of the waterfront constituted the bulk of city council business during the winter of 1849–50. A more detailed discussion of these regulations and citations of specific city council meetings in which they were passed is in chapter 5 of this book.

85. Mark Hopkins, letter to Moses Hopkins, August 29, 1850, Huntington Manuscript 26042.

86. Ibid., July 10, 1850, Huntington Manuscript 26040.

Chapter Eight

1. *Sacramento Transcript*, February 26 and 27, 1851.

2. Pisani, "Squatter Law," discusses one possible evolution for this dichotomy in gold rush California: that the vilification of "lawless squatters" was primarily the result of men like Sutter and Brannan, in league with western newspapers, attempting to strengthen their positions while weakening support for the squatters and at the same time attempting to cover their own less than saintly past.

3. Royce, "Squatter Riot," 244; Stillman, "Seeking the Golden Fleece," 418–20.

4. Kemble, *A History of California Newspapers*, 144–45.

5. Sacramento *Settlers & Miners Tribune*, October 30 to November 28, 1850, California State Library, Sacramento.

6. Kemble, *A History of California Newspapers*, 145.

7. Compare issues of the *Sacramento Transcript* and *Settlers & Miners Tribune* for the month of November 1850.

8. See Sacramento *Settlers and Miners Tribune*, complete run, October 30 to November 28, 1850.

9. John Plumbe, *John Plumbe's Narrative of the Sacramento "Squatter War" Attack on the Sutter Grant, and Defense of the Settlers* (Sacramento: n.p., 1851).

10. Derived from "U.S. Census manuscript."

11. Ibid.

12. Upham, *Notes of a Voyage*, 276.

13. Taylor, *Eldorado*, 167.

14. Morse, *First History*, 31–32.

15. Alonzo Delano, *Life on the Plains and Among the Diggings* (Auburn and Buffalo, N.Y.: Milner, Orton & Company, 1854), 289–90.

16. Ibid., 290.

17. Morse, *First History*, 33–34.

18. Cioffi, "Hopkins," 39. See also Brian Roberts, *American Alchemy* (Chapel Hill: University of North Carolina Press, 2000), a perceptive study of the role the gold rush played in the formation of middle-class attitudes toward business and capitalism.

19. Cioffi, "Hopkins," 40, based on Bancroft ms. "Collis P. Huntington Dictations," Bancroft Library, University of California at Berkeley, 38–41. For more on Huntington's early activities as a merchant, see David Lavender, *The Great Persuader* (Garden City, N.J.: Doubleday, 1970), 33–47; and Cerinda W. Evans, *Collis Potter Huntington* (Newport News, Va.: Mariner's Museum, 1954), 28–35.

20. Morse, *First History*, 94–95; *Sacramento Transcript*, February 1, 1851.

21. Stillman, "Seeking the Golden Fleece," 297–98.

22. Willis, *History of Sacramento County*, 70.

23. Helmich, "K Street Landing," 12; Sacramento *Placer Times*, October 13, 1849.

24. Van Dorn, diary, entry for November 19, 1849, Beinecke Library.

25. Van Dorn, letter to his wife, November 20, 1849, Beinecke Library.

26. William Robert Prince to [Mrs.] Charlotte Prince, February 4, 1850, ms. from the William Robert Prince letters, Bancroft Library.

27. Severson, *Sacramento*, 123.

28. Compiled from "I Came to this Country to make Money," *Sacramento Union*, March 20, 21, and 22, 1851.

29. *Sacramento Union*, March 21, 1851.

30. Ibid., April 11, 1851.

31. Ibid.

32. Ibid., March 22, 1851.

33. James S. Barnes, letter to his family, August 24, 1850, Bancroft Library.

34. Lord, *A Doctor's Gold Rush*, 175–76.

35. "An Honest Miner," in *Gold Rush Song Book*, eds. Eleanora Black and Sidney Robertson (San Francisco: Colt Press, 1940), 12–13.

36. Philip F. Castleman, journal, Beinecke Library.

37. "When I Went Off to Prospect," *Songs of the Gold Rush*, 71–72.

38. See, for example, Thomas Van Dorn, diary, Beinecke Library; Henry Rice Mann, diary, Beinecke Library; George McKinley Murrell, letter, October 15, 1849, Huntington Library, San Marino, Calif.; *Sacramento Transcript*, March 10, 1851; John Marsh Smith, *Dear*

Lizzie: The Papers of John Marsh Smith, 1849–1857 (Portland: The Society, 1987), 34; White, *A Yankee Trader,* 57; see also Holliday, *The World Rushed In;* and J. V. Frederick, *Ben Holladay, the Stagecoach King* (Lincoln: University of Nebraska Press, 1940).

39. H. C. St. Clair, journal, Beinecke Library.
40. "Crossing the Plains," *Gold Rush Song Book,* 47–49.
41. "Hunting After Gold," *Songs of the Gold Rush,* 60–61.
42. "Seeing the Elephant," *Gold Rush Song Book,* 50–52.
43. "Arrival of the Greenhorn," *Gold Rush Song Book,* 46.
44. Upham, *Notes of a Voyage,* 345.
45. See *Sacramento Transcript,* December 1850 through February 1851.
46. *Sacramento Transcript,* February 18, 1851.
47. Ibid., February 26, 1851.
48. Ibid.
49. Ibid.
50. Ibid.
51. Ibid.
52. Ibid., February 27, 1851.
53. Derived from *Sacramento Transcript,* February 27, 1851, and Culver, *City Directory.*
54. Derived from *Sacramento Transcript,* February 27, 1851, and "1850 U.S. Census manuscript."
55. *Sacramento Transcript,* February 27, 1851.
56. Ibid.
57. Ibid., February 26, 1851.
58. Ibid.
59. Ibid.
60. Ibid., February 26 and 27, 1851.
61. Ibid., February 27, 1851.
62. Ibid.
63. Ibid.
64. Ibid., August 16, 1850.
65. Ibid.
66. Ibid., February 27, 1851.
67. Ibid.
68. Ibid.

Chapter Nine

1. William Oscar Carpenter, letter to Lucretta Spencer, July 9, 1850, Huntington Manuscript 16777.

2. See Thomas Bender, *Community and Social Change in America* (Baltimore: Johns Hopkins University Press, 1982).

3. Roberts, *American Alchemy,* examines the formation of middle-class attitudes toward work, family, and gender roles during the gold rush through the experiences of over 150 argonauts, primarily from the northeastern United States. Though Roberts's focus is primarily on those who left California and returned home to transform middle-class values in the East, much of his discussion is helpful in understanding the concerns of former forty-niners who chose instead to relocate their families in Sacramento.

4. Charles Sellers, *The Market Revolution: Jacksonian America, 1815–1846* (New York: Oxford University Press, 1991), 9–11.

5. Ibid., 239–40.

6. Ibid., 241–46.

7. Enos Christman, *One Man's Gold* (New York: Whittlesey House, 1930), 135.

8. Lorenzo Sawyer, *Way Sketches* (New York: E. Eberstadt, 1926), 123–24.

9. Dwyer and Lingenfelter, *Songs of the Gold Rush,* 17–18.

10. Ibid., 6.

11. Ibid., 19.

12. Ibid., 15–16.

13. Ibid., 43–44.

14. Anna Lee Marston, ed., *Records of a California Family: Journals and Letters of Lewis C. Gunn and Elizabeth Le Breton Gunn* (San Diego: A. L. Marston, 1928), 66–67.

15. Alonzo Delano, *The Miner's Progress; or, Scenes in the Life of a California Miner* (Sacramento: Daily Union Office, 1853).

16. Dwyer and Lingenfelter, *Songs of the Gold Rush,* 49–50.

17. Ibid., 41–42.

18. Ibid., 10.

19. Ibid., 56–57.

20. See, for example, Reid, *Law for the Elephant.*

21. *Sacramento Transcript,* July 6, 1850.

22. Ibid.

23. Jo Ann Levy, *They Saw the Elephant: Women in the California Gold Rush* (Norman, Okla.: University of Oklahoma Press, 1990), 168–69.

24. Sellers, *Market Revolution,* 28.

25. Dwyer and Lingenfelter, *Songs of the Gold Rush,* 129.

26. R. W. G. Vail, ed., *California Letters of the Gold Rush Period: The Correspondence on John Ingalls, 1849–1851* (Worster, Mass.: American Antiquarian Society, 1938), 26.

27. Ibid., 30.

28. White, *A Yankee Trader,* 64.

29. Ibid., 69.

30. Vail, *California Letters,* 28.

31. White, *A Yankee Trader,* 63.

32. Ibid.

33. Vail, *California Letters,* 35.

34. Ibid., 37.

35. Henry Rice Mann, diary, Beinecke Library.

36. William Carpenter, letter to Lucretta Spencer, September 1, 1850, Huntington Manuscript 16777.

37. Ibid.

38. Carpenter, letter to Lucretta Spencer, late 1850, n.d., Huntington Manuscript 16777.

39. Ibid.

40. Carpenter, letter to Lucretta Spencer, September 22, 1850, Huntington Manuscript 16777.

41. Ibid.

42. Ibid., April 27, 1851, Huntington Manuscript 16777.

43. Ibid., August 10, 1851, Huntington Manuscript 16777.

44. Ibid.

45. Ibid.

46. Ibid., November 15, 1851, Huntington Manuscript 16777.

47. Ibid., December 21, 1851, Huntington Manuscript 16777.

48. Ibid., July 13, 1851, Huntington Manuscript 16777.

49. Carpenter, letter to Lucretta Carpenter, May 25, 1853, Huntington Manuscript 16777.

50. Ibid., May 28, 1854, Huntington Manuscript 16777.

51. Ibid., February 3, 1855, Huntington Manuscript 16777.

52. Ibid., February 25, 1855, Huntington Manuscript 16777.

53. See William Carpenter file, Huntington Manuscript 16777.

54. *Sacramento Union,* May 26, 1851.

55. Ibid.

56. Ibid.

57. Ibid., April 21, 1851.

58. Ibid., March 22, 1851.

59. White, *A Yankee Trader,* 94.

60. Ibid.

61. Vail, *California Letters,* 39–40.

62. Leander V. Loomis, *A Journal of the Birmingham Emigrating Company: The Record of a Trip from Birmingham, Iowa, to Sacramento, California, in 1850, by Leander V. Loomis . . . ,* ed. Edgar M. Ledyard (Salt Lake City: Legal printing company, 1928), 136.

63. Delano, *Life on the Plains,* 288–89.

64. Margaret A. Frink, "The Journal of Margaret A. Frink," in *Covered Wagon Women: Diaries and Letters from the Western Trails, 1850,* vol. 2, ed. Kenneth L. Holmes (Lincoln: University of Nebraska Press, 1983), 165–66.

65. Frink, in Holmes, *Covered Wagon Women,* 166–67.

Epilogue

1. *Sacramento Transcript,* March 8, 1851.

2. Ibid., March 8, 1851.

3. Morse, *First History,* 95.

4. See, for example, Carey McWilliams, *California: The Great Exception* (Santa Barbara, Calif. and Salt Lake City: Peregrine Smith, 1979).

5. See William Cronon, *Nature's Metropolis: Chicago and the Great West* (New York and London: W. W. Norton and Company, 1991), for the concept of the geography of capitalism.

6. The urban disorder of the mid-nineteenth century in the United States is covered in Mary P. Ryan, *Civic Wars: Democracy and Public Life in the American City during the Nineteenth Century* (Berkeley: University of California Press, 1997).

7. *Sacramento Transcript,* August 16, 1850.

Bibliography

Primary Sources

Manuscripts and Manuscript Collections

Austin, Edward. Edward Austin letters: ALS, 1849–51. Robert B. Honeyman Collection. Bancroft Library, University of California at Berkeley.

Bancroft Manuscript. "C. P. Huntington's Dictation to D. R. Sessions." Bancroft Library, University of California at Berkeley.

Bancroft Manuscript. "Moses Hopkins Dictation, April 18, 1891." Bancroft Library, University of California at Berkeley.

Barnes, James S. James S. Barnes letters to his family, October 1849 to September 1857. Robert B. Honeyman Collection. Bancroft Library, University of California at Berkeley.

Carpenter, William Oscar. Letters. Huntington Manuscript 16777, Huntington Library, San Marino, Calif.

Castleman, Philip F. "Overland journey to California." Western Americana Collection, Beinecke Rare Book and Manuscript Library, Yale University.

Cioffi, Ralph Walter. "Mark Hopkins, Inside Man of the Big Four." Masters thesis, University of California, Berkeley, 1938.

Dodson, W. B. H. W. B. H. Dodson biography: ms., 1885. Bancroft Library, University of California at Berkeley.

Dunlap, Florence McClure. "Samuel Brannan." Master's thesis, University of California, Berkeley, 1928.

Fitch, George Kenyon. "Journalism in San Francisco and Sacramento": ms., 1886. Hubert Howe Bancroft Collection. Bancroft Library, University of California at Berkeley.

Haines, James W. "Life and Experiences in California": ms., 1887. Hubert Howe Bancroft Collection. Bancroft Library, University of California at Berkeley.

Hastings, Lansford, to John Bidwell, October 11, 1853. California State Library, California Room, Sacramento.

Hewes, David. David Hewes letters to his mother, 1847–50. Robert Hanson Collection. Bancroft Library, University of California at Berkeley.

Hill, Alonzo A. Alonzo A. Hill Papers. Western Americana Collection, Beinecke Rare Book and Manuscript Library, Yale University.

Hopkins, Mark. Letters to Moses Hopkins, 1850. Huntington Manuscript 26040–26046, Huntington Library, San Marino, Calif.

Mann, Henry Rice. "The Diary of Henry Rice Mann." Western Americana Collection, Beinecke Rare Book and Manuscript Library, Yale University.

McFarlin, William H. Letter to his wife, Margaret. Western Americana Collection, Beinecke Rare Book and Manuscript Library, Yale University.

Miller, Edward H. "Notes regarding Mark Hopkins and related material, 1878-[ca. 1888]." Hubert Howe Bancroft Collection. Bancroft Library, University of California at Berkeley.

Moore, Augustus. "Pioneer Experiences": ms., 1878. Hubert Howe Bancroft Collection. Bancroft Library, University of California at Berkeley.

Moxley, Charles G. Letters to his sister Emily Moxley. Western Americana Collection, Beinecke Rare Book and Manuscript Library, Yale University.

Murrell, George McKinley. Papers. Huntington Manuscript 36350. Huntington Library, San Marino, Calif.

Philo California Correspondence. Western Americana Collection, Beinecke Rare Book and Manuscript Library, Yale University.

Prince, William Robert. William Robert Prince Papers, 1849–51. Bancroft Library, University of California at Berkeley.

Souther, Henry. "Journal of Henry Souther Begun October 30th 1849." Western Americana Collection, Beinecke Rare Book and Manuscript Library, Yale University.

St. Clair, H. C. "Journal of a Tour to California." Western Americana Collection, Beinecke Rare Book and Manuscript Library, Yale University.

Underhill, George R. "Diary of George R. Underhill from March 8th 1849 to April 17th 1852." Western Americana Collection, Beinecke Rare Book and Manuscript Library, Yale University.

Van Dorn, Thomas J. Thomas J. Van Dorn Papers. Western Americana Collection, Beinecke Rare Book and Manuscript Library, Yale University.

Winans, Joseph Webb. "Statement of Recollections on the Days of 1849–52 in California": ms., 1878. Bancroft Library, University of California at Berkeley.

Government Documents

Sacramento City. City Council Minutes. Volumes A and B, 1849–50. Sacramento City Archives.

Sacramento County. Recorder's Book of Deeds. Books A, B, C, and D. Sacramento County Recorder's Office.

State of California. *Statutes.* 1850.

U.S. Bureau of the Census. "Free Inhabitants in Sacramento City in the County of Sacramento, State of California, enumerated by me, on the day[s] of October 1 through November 19, 1850. William W. Johnson, Assistant Agent." Original Schedule of the Seventh Census of Population, for California, Microfilm Number 432, National Archives Microfilm Publications, Washington, D.C.

———. *Historical Statistics of the United States: Colonial Times to 1957.* Washington, D.C., 1960.

Broadsides and Handbills

Sacramento City Council. "Proclamation by Order of the People of Sacramento City." October 1849. Sacramento City Archives.

———. "Proclamation to the People of Sacramento City, By Order of the President and City Council." October 1, 1849. California State Library, Sacramento.

Sacramento Settlers' Association. "The Sacramento City Settlers' Association, believing the ground in and around Sacramento City …" December 15, 1849. Bancroft Library, University of California, Berkeley.

———. "Notice to Immigrants!" June 14, 1850. New York Public Library.

Diaries, Reminiscences, Collections of Letters, and Songsters

Bagley, Will, ed. *Scoundrel's Tale: The Samuel Brannan Papers.* Spokane, Wash.: Arthur H. Clark, 1999.

Black, Eleanora, and Sidney Robertson, eds. *The Gold Rush Song Book.* San Francisco: Colt Press, 1940.

Burnett, Peter H. *Recollections and Opinions of an Old Pioneer.* New York: D. Appleton & Company, 1880.

Christman, Enos. *One Man's Gold.* New York: Whittlesey House, 1930.

Delano, Alonzo. *Life on the Plains and Among the Diggings.* Auburn and Buffalo, N.Y.: Milner, Orton & Company, 1854.

———. *The Miner's Progress; or Scenes in the Life of a California Miner.* Sacramento: Daily Union Office, 1853.

Dwyer, Richard A., and Richard E. Lingenfelter, eds. *The Songs of the Gold Rush.* Berkeley: University of California Press, 1964.

Eaton, James. "From the Memoirs of James Eaton." *Golden Notes* 32 (Sacramento County Historical Society, summer 1986): 1–14.

Gray, Charles Glass. *Off at Sunrise: The Overland Journal of Charles Glass Gray.* San Marino, Calif.: Huntington Library, 1976.

Gudde, Erwin G., ed. *Sutter's Own Story: The Life of General John Augustus Sutter and the History of New Helvetia in the Sacramento Valley.* New York: G. P. Putnam's Sons, 1936.

Hannum, Anna Paschall, ed. *A Quaker Forty-Niner: The Adventures of Charles Edward Pancoast on the American Frontier.* Philadelphia: University of Pennsylvania Press, 1930.

Holmes, Kenneth L. *Covered Wagon Women: Diaries and Letters from the Western Trails, 1850.* Vol. 2. Lincoln: University of Nebraska Press, 1983.

Kemble, Edward C. *A History of California Newspapers, 1846–1858.* Los Gatos, Calif.: Talisman Press, 1962; reprinted from the supplement to the *Sacramento Union* of December 25, 1858.

Langworthy, Franklin. *Scenery of the Plains, Mountains and Mines,* ed. Paul C. Phillips, from the 1885 ed. Princeton, N.J.: Princeton University Press, 1932.

Letts, John M. *California Illustrated: Including a Description of the Panama and Nicaragua Routes. By a Returned Californian.* New York: William Holdredge, 1852.

Loomis, Leander V. *A Journal of the Birmingham Emigrating Company: The Record of a Trip from Birmingham, Iowa, to Sacramento, California, in 1850, by Leander V. Loomis . . . ,* ed. Edgar M. Ledyard. Salt Lake City: Legal printing company, 1928.

Lord, Israel Shipman Pelton. *A Doctor's Gold Rush Journey to California,* ed. Necia Dixon Liles. Lincoln: University of Nebraska Press, 1995.

Marston, Anna Lee, ed. *Records of a California Family: Journal and Letters of Lewis C. Gunn and Elizabeth Le Breton Gunn.* San Diego: A. L. Marston, 1928.

Morse, John F. *The First History of Sacramento City.* Sacramento: Sacramento Book Collector's Club, publication no. 3, 1945. Written in 1853.

Plumbe, John. *John Plumbe's Narrative of the Sacramento "Squatter War" Attack on the Sutter Grant, and Defense of the Settlers.* Sacramento: n.p., 1851.

Robinson, Charles. *Kansas Conflict.* Lawrence, Kans.: Journal publishing company, 1898.

Rogers, Fred Blackburn, ed. *A Kemble Reader.* San Francisco: California Historical Society, publication no. 37, 1963.

Sawyer, Lorenzo. *Way Sketches.* New York: E. Eberstadt, 1926.

Schafer, Joseph, ed. "The California Letters of Lucius Fairchild." *Wisconsin Historical Publications Collection.* Vol. 31. Madison, Wis., 1931.

Smith, John Marsh. *Dear Lizzie: The Papers of John Marsh Smith, 1849–1857.* Transcribed and annotated by the Historical Activities Committee of the National Society of the Colonial Dames of America in the State of Oregon. Portland, Ore.: The Society, 1938.

Stillman, Benjamin. "Seeking the Golden Fleece." *The Overland Monthly* II (San Francisco) (September, October, November, and December 1873), 226–33, 297–305, 417–21, 539–47.

Sutter, Jr., John A. *Statement Regarding Early California Experiences*. Sacramento: Sacramento Book Collector's Club, publication no. 2, 1943.

Taylor, Bayard. *Eldorado, or Adventures in the Path of Empire*. Lincoln: University of Nebraska Press, 1949. First published in 1850.

Upham, Samuel C. *Notes of a Voyage to California via Cape Horn, Together with Scenes in El Dorado, in the Years 1849–'50*. Philadelphia: S. C. Upham, 1878.

Vail, R. W. G., ed. *California Letters of the Gold Rush Period: The Correspondence on John Ingalls, 1849–1851*. Worster, Mass.: American Antiquarian Society, 1938.

White, Katherine, A., compiler. *A Yankee Trader in the Gold Rush: The Letters of Franklin A. Buck*. Boston: Houghton Mifflin Company, 1930.

Newspapers
New York *Daily Tribune*, 1848.
Sacramento *Placer Times*, 1849–50.
Sacramento *Settlers and Miners Tribune*, 1850.
Sacramento Transcript, 1850–51.
Sacramento Daily Union, 1851.
San Francisco *California Star*, 1848.

Contemporary Periodicals
Culver, J. Horace. *1851 Sacramento City Directory*. Sacramento: Transcript Press, 1851.
Niles National Register. Philadelphia, October 18, 1848.

Secondary Materials
Biographies
Blackmar, Frank W. *The Life of Charles Robinson, The First State Governor of Kansas*. Topeka, Kans.: Crane & Company, Printers, 1902.

Cornwall, Bruce. *Life Sketch of Pierre Barlow Cornwall*. San Francisco: A. M. Robertson, 1906.

Dillon, Richard. *Fool's Gold*. Santa Cruz, Calif.: Western Tanager, 1967.

Evans, Cerinda W. *Collis Potter Huntington*. Newport News, Va.: Mariner's Museum, 1954.

Lavender, David. *The Great Persuader*. Garden City, N.Y.: Doubleday, 1970.

Wilson, Don W. *Governor Charles Robinson of Kansas*. Lawrence, Manhattan, and Wichita, Kans.: University of Kansas Press, 1975.

Zollinger, J. Peter. *Sutter: The Man and His Empire*. Gloucester, Mass.: P. Smith, 1967.

Periodical Articles
Helmich, Stephen G. "K Street Landing, Old Sacramento, and the Embarcadero." *Golden Notes* 26 (Sacramento County Historical Society, fall 1980): 1–17.

Livingston, Robert D. "Sacramento's First Bankers." *Golden Notes* 30 (Sacramento County Historical Society, winter 1984): 1–6.

Pisani, Donald J. "Squatter Law in California, 1850–1856." *Western Historical Quarterly* 25 (Logan, Utah: Utah State University, autumn 1994): 277–310.

Royce, Josiah. "The Squatter Riot of '50 in Sacramento: Its Causes and Significance." *The Overland Monthly* 6 (San Francisco: California Publishing Company, September 1885): 225–46.

Monographs

Barth, Gunther. *Instant Cities: Urbanization and the Rise of San Francisco and Denver.* Albuquerque: University of New Mexico Press, 1975.

Bender, Thomas. *Community and Social Change in America.* Baltimore: Johns Hopkins Press, 1982.

Cronon, William. *Nature's Metropolis: Chicago and the Great West.* New York: W. W. Norton and Company, 1991.

Faragher, John Mack. *Women and Men on the Overland Trail.* New Haven, Conn.: Yale University Press, 1979.

Frederick, J. V. *Ben Holladay, the Stagecoach King.* Lincoln: University of Nebraska Press, 1940.

Hahn, Steven, and Jonathan Prud, eds. *The Countryside in the Age of Capitalist Transformation: Essays in the Social History of Rural America.* Chapel Hill: University of North Carolina Press, 1987.

Hibbard, Benjamin Horace. *A History of the Public Land Policies.* Madison, Wis.: University of Wisconsin Press, 1965.

Hill, Robert Tudor. *The Public Domain and Democracy: A Study of Social, Economic and Political Problems in the United States in Relation to Western Development.* New York: Columbia University, 1910.

Holden, William. *Sacramento.* Fair Oaks, Calif.: Two Rivers Publishing Company, 1987.

Holliday, J. S. *The World Rushed In: The California Gold Rush Experience.* New York: Simon & Schuster, 1981.

Hurtado, Albert L. *Indian Survival on the California Frontier.* New Haven, Conn.: Yale University Press, 1988.

Larkin, Jack. *The Reshaping of Everyday Life, 1790–1840.* New York: Harper & Row, 1988.

Levy, Jo Ann. *They Saw the Elephant: Women in the California Gold Rush.* Norman, Okla.: University of Oklahoma Press, 1990.

Lewis, Oscar. *Sutter's Fort.* Englewood Cliffs, N.J.: Prentice-Hall, 1966.

Limerick, Patricia Nelson. *The Legacy of Conquest: The Unbroken Past of the American West.* New York: W. W. Norton and Company, 1987.

Lord, Myrtle Shaw. *A Sacramento Saga.* Sacramento: Sacramento Chamber of Commerce, 1946.

Lotchin, Roger. *San Francisco, 1846–1856: From Hamlet to City.* New York: Oxford University Press, 1974.

McWilliams, Carey. *California: The Great Exception.* Santa Barbara, Calif.: Peregrine Smith, 1979.

Owens, Kenneth N. *John Sutter and a Wider West.* Lincoln: University of Nebraska Press, 1994.

Paul, Rodman W. *California Gold.* Lincoln: University of Nebraska Press, 1947.

Reid, John Phillip. *Law for the Elephant: Property and Social Behavior on the Overland Trail.* San Marino, Calif.: Huntington Library, 1980.

Reps, John W. *The Forgotten Frontier: Urban Planning in the American West Before 1890.* Columbia and London: University of Missouri Press, 1981.

Robbins, Roy M. *Our Landed Heritage: The Public Domain, 1776–1936.* Princeton, N.J.: Princeton University Press, 1942.

Roberts, Brian. *American Alchemy.* Chapel Hill: University of North Carolina Press, 2000.

Robinson, W. W. *Land in California, the Story of Mission Lands, Ranchos, Squatters, Mining Claims, Railroad Grants, Land Scrip [and] Homesteads.* Berkeley: University of California Press, 1948.

Rohrbough, Malcolm. *Days of Gold: The California Gold Rush and the American Nation.* Berkeley: University of California Press, 1997.

Ryan, Mary P. *Civic Wars: Democracy and Public Life in the American City during the Nineteenth Century.* Berkeley: University of California Press, 1997.

Scott, Mel. *The San Francisco Bay Area: A Metropolis in Perspective.* 2d ed. Berkeley: University of California Press, 1985.

Sellers, Charles. *The Market Revolution: Jacksonian America, 1815–1846.* New York: Oxford University Press, 1991.

State of California, Department of Parks and Recreation. *Sutter's Fort State Historical Monument,* n.p., n.d.

Stewart, George R. *The California Trail.* Lincoln: University of Nebraska Press, 1962.

Taylor, P. A. M. *Expectations Westward: The Mormons and the Emigration of their British Converts in the Nineteenth Century.* Edinburgh and London: Oliver and Boyd, 1965.

Unruh, John D. *The Plains Across: The Overland Emigrants and the Trans-Mississippi West, 1840–60.* Urbana, Ill.: University of Illinois Press, 1979.

Weber, David J. *The Mexican Frontier, 1821–1846: The American Southwest Under Mexico.* Albuquerque: University of New Mexico Press, 1982.

General Histories and Dictionaries

Bancroft, Hubert Howe. *History of California.* 7 vols. San Francisco: History Company, 1888.

Hittell, Theodore H. *History of California.* 4 vols. San Francisco: N. J. Stone, 1898.

Johnson, Allen and Dumas Malone, eds. *Dictionary of American Biography.* 20 vols. New York: Charles Scribner's Sons, 1928–37.

McGowan, Joseph A., and Terry R. Willis. *Sacramento: Heart of the Golden State.* Woodland Hills, Calif.: Windsor Publications, 1983.

Severson, Thor. *Sacramento: An Illustrated History, 1839–1874.* San Francisco: California Historical Society, 1973.

Willis, William Ladd. *The History of Sacramento County.* Los Angeles: Historic Record Company, 1913.

Index

Page numbers in parentheses refer to plates: (79+1) denotes the first plate following p. 79; (161+1) denotes the first plate following p. 161, and so on.